PRELUDE TO THE PARTITION
OF WEST AFRICA

THE AUTHOR

John D. Hargreaves developed his interest in African history as Senior Lecturer at Fourah Bay College, Sierra Leone, in 1952–4. Since then he has been in the History Department of the University of Aberdeen where, in October 1962, he was appointed to the Burnett-Fletcher Chair. He has written many articles on European and African history, and *A Life of Sir Samuel Lewis,* an eminent Sierra Leonean of the nineteenth century. His anthology of historical documents, *France and West Africa,* appeared in 1969. In the same year he co-edited *Nations and Empires.*

PRELUDE TO
THE PARTITION OF
WEST AFRICA

BY

JOHN D. HARGREAVES

BURNETT-FLETCHER PROFESSOR OF HISTORY IN THE UNIVERSITY OF ABERDEEN

MACMILLAN

ST MARTIN'S PRESS

Copyright © John D. Hargreaves 1963

First edition 1963
Reprinted 1966, 1970

Published by
MACMILLAN AND CO LTD
Little Essex Street London W C 2
and also at Bombay Calcutta and Madras
Macmillan South Africa (Publishers) Pty Ltd Johannesburg
The Macmillan Company of Australia Pty Ltd Melbourne
The Macmillan Company of Canada Ltd Toronto
St Martin's Press Inc New York
Gill and Macmillan Ltd Dublin

Printed in Great Britain by
LOWE AND BRYDONE (PRINTERS) LTD
London

CONTENTS

LIST OF MAPS

LIST OF ABBREVIATIONS
USED TO REFER TO SOURCES

MAE   Archives of Ministère des Affaires Etrangères, Paris

MMC   Archives of Ministère de la Marine et des Colonies, in custody of Ministère de la France d'Outre-mer, Paris

WMS   Archives of the Wesleyan Missionary Society

SP   Salisbury Papers

DP   Disraeli Papers

P.P.   British Parliamentary Papers

D.D.F.   Documents Diplomatiques Français, 1st series, 1871–1900

G.P.   Die Grosse Politik der Europäischen Kabinette

W.B.   German *Weiss Buch*

PREFACE

THIS IS a historical study with a modest aim. At a time when there is a good deal of discussion about Imperialism in general, and about the partition of Africa in particular, it seemed there was room for a straightforward account of the establishment of European rule in that part of tropical Africa where there is the longest record of commercial and cultural contact. I began work in 1954, with some hope of covering the whole period in a single volume; as my research proceeded I learned what a formidable undertaking that would be. I hope, however, that readers will observe that there are other reasons than indolence for my decision to close the main part of the present narrative in 1885. By that year, claims had been established in the coastal regions which to a considerable degree determined the pattern of interior penetration and conquest; and in the following years the spirit of European relations with Africa undergoes gradual but decided change.

In writing substantial sections of this book I have stood upon the shoulders of those who have studied special regions of West Africa; Adu Boahen, Kenneth Diké, John Flint, and Freda Wolfson are among those whose work I have exploited. I have tried to summarize — or in certain cases to re-state or qualify — their conclusions wherever these impinge upon my theme; I have done so as briefly as seemed compatible with clarity, rather than at the length which the intrinsic importance of some of the areas in question might seem to demand. My aim has been to relate the problems of the various French and British settlements to the relations of Europe with West Africa as a whole; but I cannot hope to have escaped completely the restrictions of view retrospectively imposed by colonial frontiers.

I am even more aware of my shortcomings in relation to a second objective: that of discussing European-African relations with reference to the motivation of both sides, rather than writing as if European aims were invariably unilaterally determined, and imposed by superior technology upon more or less passive Africans. I have become increasingly convinced that the course

of the partition can rarely be understood without reference to
the objectives and methods of African rulers. Though sometimes they might be used as tools by traders or colonial officials,
more often they had clear aims in view — the elimination of
commercial rivals, the maintenance of personal power, above
all the preservation of independence — and some were quite
successful in harnessing the support of foreigners in their pursuit
of these aims. In many cases it does not seem too difficult to
interpret their motives from the evidence preserved by the
Europeans themselves; but ideally the interpreter should possess
some knowledge of the traditional institutions and history of each
of the many African states and peoples involved. In many cases
I cannot pretend to any such knowledge, and in none to very
much. Nevertheless I hope my general narrative may provide a
framework which will help other scholars to develop further
the study of African statecraft in the period of foreign invasion.

Some readers may regret that I do not propose any general
interpretation or model of Imperialism. This is not because the
subject does not interest me; but such opinions as I hold upon it
have been derived from many sources, including the study of
materials different in nature from those upon which I am
reporting here. It therefore seems better to reserve theoretical
discussion for other occasions.

★   ★   ★   ★   ★

I must record my deep gratitude to the Carnegie Trust for the
Universities of Scotland, from whom I have received generous
financial assistance during my research, both directly and
through the kindness of the University of Aberdeen. I would
also like to thank the staffs of the many libraries and repositories
I have used in Great Britain, France, and the United States,
especially the staff of the Library of the University of Aberdeen.
For permission to use the Salisbury and Disraeli Papers,
respectively, I am grateful to Lord Salisbury and to the National
Trust. Miss I. Blake has given invaluable assistance with the
typing of the manuscript. Among the many friends and colleagues with whom I have discussed my work, there is none
from whom I have derived so much profit and so much pleasure

as from Christopher Fyfe. The help which I have received from
my wife has been given in too many forms to be concisely
recorded.

King's College, Aberdeen   JOHN D. HARGREAVES

PREFACE TO THE 1966 REPRINT

I HAVE taken advantage of this reprint to correct about a
dozen minor inaccuracies in text, notes or index. I am grateful
to friends and reviewers who have helped me to detect these,
and especially to Yves Person. The method of reprinting has
not permitted me to attempt any wider revision. Research work
that has been published during the last three years would have
allowed me to expand and clarify many points; in particular,
to improve the background survey in the first chapter. On
p. 368 I list some of the more important recent publications
which bear directly on my theme. The publication of Ajayi's
work has illuminated an aspect of British influence in Nigeria
to which I am conscious of having given inadequate attention.
Brunschwig, Atger and Coquery have further clarified French
policy on the coasts. Articles by Person and Legrassick have
advanced the re-assessment of Samori. Kanya-Forstner and
Saint-Martin have made major contributions to the study of the
French advance from Senegal, and Mr. Olatunji Oleruntime-
hin of the University of Ibadan is studying the empire of El Haj
Omar. I have somewhat extended my own treatment of
France-Tokolor relations in an article in *Boston University Papers
in African History*, Volume II. But in general I am content to let
this book re-appear unchanged.

Aberdeen, June 1966   JOHN D. HARGREAVES

CHAPTER ONE

Introduction: West Africa in the 1860's

THE TERM 'West Africa' has come by convention to be applied to a relatively restricted region in the north-west of the continent, and it is that region which forms the subject of this book. To the west and south its boundaries are clearly defined by the ocean, to the north by the edges of the Sahara desert. Its eastern boundary is less obvious, but is usually taken as following the frontier line drawn in 1919 between the French and British Cameroons from Lake Chad to the coast opposite Fernando Po. The usage which thus restricts the boundaries of 'West Africa' is, in the opinion of an eminent geographer, 'based upon a real physical separation.'[1]

But in the nineteenth century, before the modern frontiers were drawn on the map, this 'separateness' was by no means self-evident. As far as the coast was concerned, this was recognized by the administrative practice of European powers. For the British Government the 'West Coast of Africa' stretched from the borders of Morocco to those of the Cape; French interests south of the Senegal were supervised from a headquarters at Gabon. Inland the Sahara desert was traversed by well-marked caravan routes, along which Arab traders forged economic and cultural links between the northern Negro peoples and the Mediterranean. Lake Chad itself was historically an important route-junction rather than a boundary; the stream of pilgrims to Mecca kept West and East Africa in continual contact. In 1897 Sir George Goldie found Muslim Africans on the Niger responding to appeals from the Khalifa, threatened by Kitchener's advance towards Omdurman, and wrote, with historical accuracy, 'the Nile and Niger questions are not disconnected, but are two sides of a single question — that of

[1] R. J. H. Church, *West Africa* (London, 1957) p. xxiii.

the Sudan.'[1] And linguistic evidence also suggests strong historical affiliation between the peoples of the Niger and Congo basins.[2]

These trans-continental contacts and affiliations must have meant little to most of the millions of Africans — possibly something like thirty millions in all — who lived there. Some of them would be conscious of membership in a sizeable, organized state, which they might be able to identify with their own tribal name; in the north, millions of Africans adhered to the world-religion of Islam; and on the coast individuals and peoples had come into more or less intimate contact with certain aspects of Western society. But the horizons of most Africans were contracted to a relatively isolated local community, and social, religious or artistic experience was deepened only within its limits. Generalization is difficult, for West Africa was a region of much ethnic, linguistic and cultural diversity; but often the only social and political units which had real meaning for the individual were small and intimate — the family, kindred or sib, and the village.

Some physical unity was indeed given to the region by two great river-systems. The Niger, 2,600 miles long, with its tributary the Benué, drains much of the area, while the Senegal and Gambia dominate the lands to the north-west. But physical and political obstacles have prevented any of these rivers from uniting the peoples of its basin, or facilitating the penetration of foreign influences. The Niger is navigable only in three separated reaches; and its mouth was unidentified by Europeans until 1830. The Senegal has a difficult bar; its waters fall rapidly and unpredictably after the rainy season; and rapids are frequent above Kayes. The smaller rivers which drain the high land to the south of the Niger bend are similarly affected by shallows and rapids, and are mostly rendered inaccessible to sea-going ships by dangerous sandbars at the mouth. And

---

[1] Preface to S. Vandeleur, *Campaigning on the Upper Nile and Niger* (1898) reproduced by D. Wellesley, *Sir George Goldie* (London, 1934) p. 178.

[2] This evidence is summarized in J. H. Greenberg's 'Africa as a Linguistic Area' in W. R. Bascom and M. J. Herskovits, *Continuity and Change in African Cultures* (Chicago, 1959).

equally grave impediments to communications and commerce were often imposed by political frontiers — before as well as after the European conquest.

* * * * *

Though many geographical zones may be distinguished within West Africa according to vegetation, climate and other features, one distinction is of especial importance: that between 'forest' and 'savanna'. The 'forest belt' mostly lies south of $7\frac{1}{2}°$ N, though along the coast it extends as far north as the Gambia; it is characterized by heavy annual rainfall, which leaches the soil, and by large areas of thick forest where communications are difficult. But long before 1860, Africans clearing land for cultivation or cutting timber for export, had begun to reduce the area of natural forest vegetation. Mosquitoes and tsetse flies flourished in swamps and stagnant pools. The former carried malaria and yellow fever which, in conjunction with other diseases and deficiencies, and with sociological factors, lowered human vitality and expectation of life, and produced a high, occasionally devastating, death-rate among Europeans.[1] The latter made it virtually impossible to raise good breeds of cattle, and so precluded mixed farming. They also killed horses, which hindered communications and prevented the use of cavalry by invaders from the north.

North of the forest belt the annual rainfall decreases progressively up to the Sahara desert. The soils are less leached, and greater diversity in cultivation is possible; there is much open grassland, which gives the whole region its general name of 'savanna belt'.[2] Cattle were kept in large numbers, and bigger varieties of sheep and goats; mixed farming was possible, and sometimes systematic application of manure.[3] Horses, and in the

[1] Factors affecting mortality in British West Africa are discussed by R. R. Kuckzynski, *Demographic Survey of the British Colonial Empire*, Vol. I (London, 1948) pp. 8–18.

[2] It must again be emphasized that there are great physical differences within this region, and that large areas, especially near the borders with the desert and the forest, have much less favourable conditions than are here described.

[3] H. Barth, *Travels and Discoveries in North and Central Africa* (London, 5 Vols. 1857–8) Vol. III, p. 208.

north camels, could be used for transport and in war. These physical conditions aided the peoples of the region, with their long commercial and cultural relationships with the north and east, to develop a more diversified economy and well-ordered states. Their cultural affinities with the country of the middle Nile were recognized in the name which Europeans (narrowing the sense of an Arab term for 'land of the Negroes') applied to the savanna belt of West Africa; they called it the western Sudan.

*   *   *   *   *

Europeans, long interested in the coasts of Africa, showed increasing interest in the interior from the later eighteenth century. Between 1788 and 1830 Park, Clapperton, Lander and other travellers recorded much geographical and political information about parts of the western Sudan. In the 1850's a great new contribution to knowledge was made by Heinrich Barth of Hamburg and Berlin. He arrived in Tunis in December 1849 on an official British expedition under James Richardson, whose principal aim was to explore the possibilities of developing trade across the Sahara on a scale sufficient to destroy the traffic in slaves, which was continuing at a rate approaching 10,000 persons a year.[1] Midway across the Sahara the party separated, and Barth travelled by Kano and Katsina into the large Kanuri state of Bornu, whence he made expeditions north and south of Lake Chad into Kanem and Baguirmi. When Richardson died in March 1851, Palmerston authorized Barth to continue his explorations, and he remained south of the Sahara until 1855, observing and recording on a heroic scale. Deterred by physical and political obstacles from realizing his early hopes of exploring the Sudan between Lake Chad and the Nile, and even of pushing on to Mombasa, Barth turned westwards instead, and succeeded in reaching Timbuktu. Even though much of this country had been visited by Europeans before, the five volumes which Barth published in 1857–8 gave the world an account of the western Sudan unrivalled in scale or scholarship.

[1] For the origins of this mission, see A. A. Boahen, *British Penetration of the Sahara and Western Sudan, 1788–1861*, Ph.D. thesis (London, 1959).

Though much of this region had been Muslim since the sixteenth century, the strength of Islam was always uneven. Some peoples never accepted the new religion; others assimilated Koranic usages more or less imperfectly into their traditional laws and institutions, but subsequently lapsed from strict observance. But the eighteenth century saw a Muslim revival in the extreme west; new theocratic states were formed by revolution in two districts near the Atlantic coast and became important sources of peaceful proselytization. After 1725 Futa Jalon passed under the rule of recently-converted Fulas; in 1776 Tokolors, a people much intermarried with Fulas, and speaking their language, took power in Futa Toro on the Senegal.[1]

The Fulas, moving spirits in this advance, were a pastoral people who over the centuries had become dispersed across the Sudan as far as Darfur; they were numerous in Hausa country, where some had settled in towns, often becoming eminent as Islamic scholars and teachers.[2] This urban minority in the Hausa states was influenced by the revolutions led by their kinsmen in the west; in 1804 the Habe rulers of Gobir became alarmed by the preaching of Othman dan Fodio (a Fula of Tokolor descent), and tried unsuccessfully to arrest him. Their failure moved Othman and his followers to launch a *jihad* or holy war, which soon won massive support throughout Hausaland and beyond. Though some accounts emphasize his appeal to Fulani national feeling, it is clear that Othman's call to a stricter Koranic observance appealed equally to many Habe. By 1810 his followers had supplanted the ruling dynasties of most Hausa states (though some were never completely subdued), and Othman, as Commander of the Faithful, had founded a new state capital at Sokoto. In the east, the Fulani advanced into Bornu, but were later repelled by another great Muslim ruler, El Kanemi; southwards, they began to achieve

[1] A. Gouilly, *L'Islam dans l'Afrique Occidentale Française* (Paris, 1952) Part 1, 'Histoire de l'Islamisation', Ch. VI, 'La Phase Peule'.

[2] English writers commonly refer to *these* Fulas by their Hausa name of Fulani; this confusing practice is so well established that I regretfully follow it here.

B

positions of power in Nupe, and among the Yoruba of Ilorin.[1]

Before he died in 1817 Othman dan Fodio divided his political authority between his brother Abdullahi and his son Bello. The former, established as Sultan of Gwandu, acknowledged the superiority of his nephew at Sokoto, while in practice enjoying effective independence; by Barth's time relations between these two Sultanates appear to have been those of sovereign and rather hostile powers. In eastern Hausaland at least the authority of Sokoto — though it declined during the nineteenth century — was never a mere theocratic sovereignty, but rested on a genuine governmental machinery, controllable by written instructions from a central administration, and inspired by Koranic law. Emirs and rulers of subordinate states were appointed by the Sultan from new Fulani dynasties, locally based; he received taxes and military contingents, including cavalry, from these vassals, who in turn had subordinate chiefs standing in similar quasi-feudal relationships to them.[2] Administrative machinery of the Hausa states, already well articulated, was incorporated into the new Fulani political order. Even in remote Adamawa in 1851, the local Sultan told Barth that 'he was nothing but a slave of the Sultan of Sokoto', incompetent to negotiate with foreigners without explicit authority.[3]

In Barth's time a good deal of disorder and insecurity persisted even within the Sokoto empire. Many enclaves of Habe, and of weaker pagan peoples, were still successfully resisting Fulani rule; marauding bands frequently attacked peaceful

[1] The commonly accepted account of the *jihad* is summarized by E. W. Bovill, *The Golden Trade of the Moors* (London, 1958) pp. 225–32. For Nupe, see S. F. Nadel, *A Black Byzantium* (London, 1948) pp. 76–82. There is new material on the *jihad*, indicating possible points of revision, in M. Hiskett, 'The State of Learning among the Fulani before their Jihad', *Bulletin*, School of Oriental and African Studies, xix (1957). For a brief discussion, with documentation, see T. L. Hodgkin, *Nigerian Perspectives* (London, 1960) pp. 34–45, 188–205.

[2] M. G. Smith, *Government in Zazzau* (London, 1960) pp. 73–7; cf. M. F. Smith, *Baba of Karo* (London, 1954) pp. 29–30; F. Shaw [Lady Lugard], *A Tropical Dependency* (London, 1905) Ch. 43.

[3] Barth, *op. cit.*, II, pp. 496–7.

settlements in search of booty, or of slaves for export. Hostilities continued between Sokoto and Bornu, and in 1853 Bornu itself was weakened by a dynastic civil war. Barth even described Gwandu as 'plunged into an abyss of anarchy'.[1] Yet the region as a whole was very far removed from the 'state of nature'. Trade-routes, though narrow and dangerous, were still trodden over long distances. Arabs travelling from the Mediterranean coast, Touareg merchants based in Sudanese market-towns, Africans from as far south as Nupe and Dagomba, were not deterred by lack of security. Over the Sudan as a whole Barth found facilities (though of varying efficiency) for the delivery of letters, the obtaining of credit, the collection of debts.

There was already a certain amount of diversity in the economy of Hausaland, and apparently good prospects of further development. A fair range of food-crops, supplemented by the pastoral produce of Fulani herdsmen, provided variety in many local markets; cash-crops of possible interest to Europeans included timber, groundnuts, sugar-cane, indigo, and cotton.[2] Urban craftsmen included weavers, leather-workers, carpenters, blacksmiths, and silver-smiths: 'commerce and manufactures go hand in hand', Barth wrote of Kano, with its 30,000 inhabitants; 'almost every family has its share of them.' Sandals, hides, and a range of African cloths of pleasing and distinctive design were exported northwards to Murzuk and Tripoli, westwards to Timbuktu and to Arguin on the Atlantic, southwards into Nupe and Adamawa.[3] From other African territories, Hausaland imported salt and kola-nuts; from across the Sahara, luxury textiles and articles of adornment, paper, Solingen swords and scissors. This trans-Saharan trade was not large in quantity; its total value, by all routes and in both directions, was of the order of £250,000.[4] Yet over the centuries its profits had assisted the

[1] ibid., IV, p. 203.

[2] ibid., I, p. xx.

[3] ibid., II, pp. 124–6. For a comment on the wide extent of Hausa trade in 1885, cf. J. B. Thomson, Joseph Thomson, African Explorer (London, 1896) p. 155.

[4] Boahen, op. cit., p. 385. See also his paper 'The Caravan Trade in the Nineteenth Century', presented to the third African History Conference, School of Oriental and African Studies, London, 1961.

evolution of a distinctively African urban culture, linked with
the wider Muslim world by the continuing stream of pilgrimage, as well as by visiting Arab and Berber merchants. Early
European visitors met Africans and Arabs with an informed
interest or skill in theological disputation; in distant Baguirmi
Barth met a learned Fula who possessed Arabic translations
from Plato and Aristotle.[1] Ethnocentric Victorians might not
recognize all this as what they meant by the term 'civilization',
and there was much in Barth's record about slave raiding and
cruel punishments which they could only deplore. But in
Hausaland, more than in any other part of Africa, they acknowledged the presence of societies which seemed ripe for
civilization.

★   ★   ★   ★   ★

Westwards of the Hausa country, along the middle Niger,
Barth found the framework of political order was gravely
weakened by internal dissension and external attack, though
unifying commercial and cultural forces were evidently still at
work. The medieval Songhai empire of Gao had left no successor; after the Moroccan invasion of the later sixteenth century it seems that much of the Sahara trade on which its power
had rested was diverted to more easterly routes, to the benefit
of Hausaland.[2] Much of the middle Niger and the country to the
south of its great bend was dominated by raiding Touareg and
other desert tribes, and was less frequented than other parts of
the Sudan, but regular trade continued nevertheless. In Libtako
Barth found markets frequented, not only by Arabs from
north of Timbuktu, but by Mandinkas from Wassulu on the
upper Niger, bringing kola-nuts and cowries imported from the
west coast, and by people from the Mossi-Dagomba states near
the upper Volta.[3] At Timbuktu itself, with its estimated
population of 13,000 and its three large and three small
mosques, Barth again found much scope for theological debate.
And, despite acute political uncertainties, the city retained

[1] e.g. Barth, *op. cit.*, II, 62–3, 318, III, 373–5; V, 43, 63, 103–4. Earlier
examples may be found in Clapperton's *Travels*.
[2] Boahen, *op. cit.*   [3] Barth, *op. cit.*, IV, 287–9.

importance as an entrepôt for trade in gold and salt, kola-nuts and Kano cloth.

Much of this political uncertainty was caused by the western repercussions of the Fulani *jihad*. About 1810 the Bari dynasty of Fulas seized power in the state of Macina, previously tributary to the pagan Bambaras of Ségou; its leader, Amadu Lobbo, was a disciple of Othman dan Fodio, and soon surpassed his master's successors in the rigour of his religious demands.[1] Not only was Bambara suzerainty shaken off, but the boundaries of the new state were greatly extended; Timbuktu, after long struggles injurious to its trade, could secure nothing more than an uncomfortable and limited autonomy. Ségou and Kaarta to the east felt their independence threatened; as in many pagan states of the Sudan, Islamic influences were already evident in many of their customs. In 1859 Ali-Diara of Ségou agreed to embrace Islam in order to secure the alliance of Macina against a new threat from the west.[2] This came from a new religious leader, El Haj Omar; a man who, though immediately he brought war and insecurity, seemed to have the capacity to create a new and still more powerful state in the extreme west of the Sudan.

Omar was born about 1797, a Tokolor from Futa Toro on the lower Senegal. His father was a *mallam*, and Omar was initiated young into the Tijaniyya, a reforming fraternity which reached his homeland from Morocco in the later eighteenth century.[3] To an uninstructed outsider, this seems not unlike a Muslim equivalent of Calvinism. By virtue of verbal communications from Muhammad to the founder, members of the Tijaniyya claimed to have been chosen for a special dispensation of Divine grace; yet they fought to make this spiritual privilege available to all men. Teaching the faithful a few simple texts and formulae as the essentials of belief, the Tijaniyya had a more egalitarian

[1] Barth, *op. cit.*, IV, 256–7.

[2] M. Delafosse, *Haut-Senegal—Niger*, Vol. II (Paris, 1912) Chs. 8, 10.

[3] For an account of his career given to a French officer by his followers, see E. Mage, *Voyage dans le Soudan Occidental* (Paris, 1868) pp. 231–82. A version in Fula is M. A. Tyam, *La Vie d'el Hadj Omar*, trans. H. Gaden (Paris, 1935). European interpretations include Gouilly, *op. cit.*, pp. 72–6; J. Suret-Canale, *Afrique Noire* (Paris, 1958) pp. 174–8; M. Delafosse, *op. cit.*, Ch. 12.

flavour than the traditional forms of Islam favoured by chiefly families, in which only an *élite* achieved the most worthy forms of religious life.[1]

Omar's career well illustrates the underlying unity of West African Islam. About 1820 he made the pilgrimage to Mecca, where he was named *Khalifa* of the Tijaniyya for the Sudan. He spent many years on his return journey, staying in Mecca, Jedda, and Cairo, and with the two great Muslim rulers of West Africa, El Kanemi of Bornu and Bello of Sokoto. He married wives from the families of both these rulers. About 1838 he passed more rapidly and less amicably through Macina and Ségou, and settled in Futa Jalon, the noted centre of Muslim scholarship in the hills where both the Senegal and Gambia rivers rise. The prestige which he gained through his travels and studies attracted many followers, and his influence began to cause concern in neighbouring Muslim states.

In 1846–7 Omar visited his homeland on the lower Senegal, where his preaching — summarized by hostile observers in the words, 'You are like the unfaithful, eating and drinking injustice, and your chiefs violate God's law by oppressing the weak'[2] — attracted new disciples, or *talibés*. A new *jihad* now seemed imminent. About 1848 Omar moved to Dinguiray, east of Futa Jalon, where his followers were organized into a military force. Devout Muslims, and less devout individuals on the make, came to join him; the gifts they brought were used to buy weapons on the coast. Gradually Omar became the head of a formidable theocratic state, sometimes through the conversion and submission of ruling chiefs, or by exploitation of existing tensions in their states, sometimes as a result of conquest and the installation of his own nominees. By 1854 he controlled many of the Bambara and Mandinka states of Bouré, Bambouk and Fuladugu, in the upper basins of the Niger and the Senegal, and was opening a campaign against Kaarta. Koranic usages were

---

[1] J. S. Trimingham, *Islam in West Africa* (Oxford, 1959) pp. 97–8; Gouilly, *op. cit.*, pp. 108 ff; Jamil Abun-Nasr, 'Some Aspects of the Umari branch of the Tijaniyya' (a paper presented to the third African history conference, School of Oriental and African Studies, London, 1961).

F. Carrère and P. Holle, *De la Sénégambie française* (Paris, 1855) p. 194.

strictly enforced: women were segregated, men were rationed to four wives, heads were shaved, and fermented liquors were prohibited. Some of these measures were not popular with Omar's new subjects.[1]

Talking to Lieutenant Mage in 1864, Omar's followers declared that their leader had not intended to fight the French, but only 'black Kaffirs'.[2] Though testimony given in these circumstances must be examined sceptically, some confirmation can be found in the record of Omar's actions. In 1847 he proposed collaboration to the government of Senegal; they were to supply arms and help him to become ruler of Futa, and he in turn would guarantee order and allow Christians to trade on payment of customs. This request for arms was unsuccessfully repeated in 1854.[3] The prospect of unified control of the Senegal might have tempted the French; but devout Catholics hesitated to assist the spread of militant Islam, and others feared that the creation of a powerful African state with egalitarian principles might increase racial dissension within St. Louis itself. So the French were already somewhat hostile when, about 1854, Omar turned against Senegalese traders on the river, capturing trade goods sent up on credit by St. Louis merchants, and in some cases receiving them voluntarily from Muslim trading agents attracted by his preaching. The reason for this move is not clear. Omar may have suspected the traders of supplying arms to his enemies, or simply have needed some himself; another explanation is that the Tokolors, who formed the dominant group among his disciples, wanted to avenge Governor Protet's attack on Podor in their homeland.[4] But even now, Omar did not move his army against the French, though they were very fully engaged lower down the river, but continued his operations in Kaarta. An appeal in 1855 to the Muslims of St. Louis to join his holy war against the unbelievers brought him many recruits among traders and artisans, some of whom served his army by

[1] Mage, *op. cit.*, pp. 119, 132, 137, 141, 155, 262; Delafosse, *op. cit.*, p. 310; cf. within pp. 99–103.

[2] Mage, *op. cit.*, pp. 240, 248, 251.

[3] Carrère and Holle, *op. cit.*, pp. 165–6, 202, and cf. p. 135.

[4] *MMC*, Sénégal 1/45, memo. by Faidherbe, 14 Oct. 1858; Mage, *op. cit.*, p. 241.

building forts and maintaining his guns.[1] But until 1857 at least he showed no eagerness to fight the French; there is evidence that he was already planning rather to reunify the middle Niger by conquering Ségou and Macina.

★   ★   ★   ★   ★

It was not only Christians and pagans who felt menaced by Omar's growing prestige and power; he also challenged the authority of ruling groups in older Muslim states. His own homeland, Futa Toro, had been Muslim since the Tokolor revolution of 1776; though he did not, it seems, deliberately set out to subvert its ruling class, his prestige as a religious leader soon overshadowed that of the Alimami, elected sovereign and religious head of this federation of eight small states.[2] It was from the Tokolors that Omar, once he had opened military operations, drew his most ardent and intelligent disciples; they provided staff-officers and technicians at his headquarters, as well as much of the feudalistic ruling class through which he controlled his empire. The three corps of his army were designated by the names of three of the provinces of Futa.[3] While many of the people of Futa who remained at home felt proud solidarity with the new Tokolor empire, the ruling groups were jealous. Tensions were set up which the French in Senegal tried to exploit; between 1856 and 1860 they succeeded in establishing close relations with the three states of western Futa. But such intervention in turn provoked anti-French reactions, surreptitiously from Abdul Boubakar, ruler of one of these states, whom Omar nominated as Alimami of Futa in 1861, more openly in the early 1870's from Amadu Cheikou. The French had not the strength to conquer Futa Toro until the 1880's; until they did so it remained the principal bridge by which political and religious ferments among the Muslims of the western Sudan passed down towards the coast of Senegambia.

During the second half of the nineteenth century, the history of Cayor, Joloff and the other states between the Senegal and the lower Gambia valley is one of intermittent wars in which

[1] Carrère and Holle, op. cit., pp. 204–7; Mage, op. cit., pp. 221, 241.
[2] P. Marty, Etudes sur l'Islam au Sénégal, I (Paris, 1917) pp. 81–90.
[3] Delafosse, op. cit., p. 320.

the French frequently, and not always successfully, intervened. In the Gambia valley itself, British officials repeatedly had to record fighting, which it became customary to analyse within a pattern of 'Soninke-Marabout wars'.[1] These still await a comprehensive study; no doubt hostilities were often caused by trade disputes or parochial dynastic quarrels. But the general pattern is clearly of the advance (though not unchecked) of stricter versions of the Muslim discipline, and of their wider acceptance by chiefs and peoples. How this movement reflects the influence of El Haj Omar can be seen in the career of the *marabout* known as Maba. Born about 1809 in the state of Badibu, or Rip, he studied the Koran in Cayor, and opened a school in Joloff. In 1850 he met Omar, and there was talk of a future *jihad*. In 1862 Maba declared himself Alimami, and launched a religious war against the rulers of Badibu;[2] until he was killed in 1867 he engaged with much success in campaigns between the Gambia and the Senegal in alliance with the deposed *Damel* of Cayor. His aim seems to have been the establishment of strict Muslim rule throughout the area, rather than the acquisition of personal power, and after his death his tomb became a place of Muslim pilgrimage.[3]

Further south the Muslim Fulas who had ruled the upland state of Futa Jalon since 1725 also viewed Omar's rise with some distaste.[4] Like Senegalese Futa, this was a theocratic state with a federal type of constitution; it was ruled alternately by two Alimamies, descendants of leaders in the eighteenth-century *jihad*, who alternated in power for two years at a time. Militarily, Futa Jalon was not strong, incapable of suppressing a group of rebellious subjects known as Houbous; but its religious prestige remained considerable, and a modern scholar regards it as 'the primary factor leading to a diffusion of Islam throughout Western Guinea'.[5] The Alimamies claimed a form of suzerainty,

[1] J. M. Gray, *A History of the Gambia* (Cambridge, 1940) Chs. 26, 28, 30.
[2] CO 87/73, D'Arcy to Newcastle, 102, 22 May 1862.
[3] Ba, Tamsir Dusmane, 'Essai Historique sur le Rip', *Bulletin de l'IFAN*, xix, 1957; cf. Gray, *op. cit.*, pp. 418 ff.
[4] P. Marty, *L'Islam en Guinée* (Paris, 1921) pp. 1–7; J. Bayol, 'La France au Fouta-Djalon', *Revue des Deux Mondes*, 15 Dec. 1882.
[5] Trimingham, *op. cit.*, p. 18.

B*

carrying the right to confirm the election of chiefs, over Susu chiefdoms on the sea-board, and their influence seems to have been leading gradually to a wider, though sometimes reluctant, acceptance of Islam among pagan peoples to the south.[1]

*   *   *   *   *

To what extent the peoples of the forest-belt and the coastal regions as a whole felt the impact of events in the nineteenth-century Sudan remains uncertain. It would certainly be misleading to imply any cultural iron curtain between the two regions. 'Caravans' from the western Sudan visited Freetown to trade throughout the century — more than 10,000 individuals in a good year; *marabouts* peddling Koranic texts as powerful medicine, and thereby spreading at least some knowledge of their religion, were known from Futa Jalon to Porto Novo; northern Yoruba felt the direct military pressure of the Fulani *jihad*. But in social and political organization the two regions conveyed radically different impressions. Between Futa Jalon and Ashanti the forest-belt was in political fragmentation. A population which can hardly have approached five million was divided into twenty or thirty distinct tribal groups, each with its own language; most of these were in turn split into small independent chiefdoms, whose subjects might be linked with their neighbours by language, history, or common membership in a country society, but might equally be divided from them by disputes over land, slaves or trade. The *völkerwanderungen* of centuries had here produced a baffling mosaic of peoples, a historical palimpsest still to be deciphered.[2] Europeans, seeking security for commerce, tended to equate this shortage of strong political authorities with an absence of 'civilization'.

Yet, even within this south-west area, trade could in fact be effectively protected without centralized political institutions of any conventional type. The classic demonstration of this was provided by the peoples of the rich and populous oil-palm producing area to the east of the Niger delta. The Ibo, and many of

[1] J. S. Trimingham and C. H. Fyfe, 'The Early Expansion of Islam in Sierra Leone', *Sierra Leone Bulletin of Religion*, II, 1960.

[2] For a contribution towards the deciphering of one section, see the Introduction to C. H. Fyfe, *A History of Sierra Leone* (London, 1962).

their neighbours, had rarely formed states in which supreme authority was represented by the person of a political chief; the extended family and the group of contiguous villages remained the basic social and political institutions. Nevertheless, as Diké has cogently argued, 'Beneath the apparent fragmentation of authority lay deep fundamental unities not only in the religious and cultural spheres, but also . . . in matters of politics and economics.'[1] In the trading states of the coast effective power was exercised in various forms by the African trading class; inland, the quasi-religious sanctions of the Aro Chuku oracle provided means for settling disputes and regulating the very profitable trade.[2] In common European judgment the Ibo might be further removed from 'civilization' than the Sudanese peoples; yet they — and other supposedly 'backward peoples' on this coast — displayed a highly sophisticated intelligence in adapting their traditional economic and political institutions to the successive demands made upon them by oceanic commerce.

★   ★   ★   ★   ★

Political fragmentation was not found everywhere in the forest-belt. Between the Niger and the Tano river four sizeable states had flourished during the eighteenth century. Culturally, they had much in common, notably a high level of technical and imaginative achievement in the plastic arts; and each faced the same general problems of adapting traditional economic and political institutions to the demands of commercial contact with Europe, first in the period of unrestricted slave trade, then in the changed conditions of the nineteenth century. Their success in solving these problems varied. In the latter period Benin was least successful and fell into decline. Though it still claimed nominal suzerainty over a wide area its rulers had few important dealings with Europe before the sordid and bloody campaign of 1897. The other three responded to change with varying success.

[1] K. O. Diké, *Trade and Politics in the Niger Delta* (Oxford, 1956) p. 44.
[2] Diké, *op. cit.*, pp. 33–46; cf. C. K. Meek, *Law and Authority in a Nigerian Tribe* (London, 1937). For a lively contemporary account, see the appendices by C. de Cardi to M. H. Kingsley, *West African Studies* (London, 1899).

Ashanti was a militarily formidable state, formed by the union of the more northerly groups of Akan peoples under the leadership of Kumasi during the late seventeenth and early eighteenth century. By the beginning of the nineteenth century, Ashanti was pressing hard on its Fanti kinsmen on the Gold Coast, with the aim of participating more directly in the Atlantic trade and obtaining foreign goods, especially firearms, on advantageous terms. Far from being anti-European, the Ashantis desired chiefly to enter into more direct intercourse with Europe — originally in order to sell slaves, though they later showed some willingness to adapt their economy to suit the changing moral climate on this subject. But, since they could only satisfy this ambition at the expense of the coastal peoples with whom Britain, in particular, had already established close relations, they did in fact repeatedly tend to come into armed conflict with them throughout the nineteenth century.

While Ashanti maintained its independence until the 1890's at the cost of repeated wars against the British, its neighbour Dahomey survived almost as long without fighting Europeans at all. In this state, whose population was probably about 200,000, authority was highly centralized, and the power of the King was virtually absolute.[1] The system was originally based on success in the slave trade. The heavy costs of the army, the administration, the court and the royal wives, had been met by the capture or conviction and export of slaves; the firearms and powder imported in return served to consolidate the power of the King. Even more obviously than in mercantilist Europe, power depended upon trade, and eighteenth-century kings saw the importance of controlling it themselves. More successful than Ashanti, Dahomey secured direct access to the coast by conquering Whydah in 1727.

The slave trade continued to be a major support of the kingdom well into the nineteenth century. Consul Burton reported the despatch of a maritime cargo as late as

---

[1] M. J. Herskovits, *Dahomey; an Ancient West African Kingdom* (New York; 2 Vols. 1938), gives the best and fullest account of the political system. Population estimates are discussed in Vol. II, pp. 71–2.

1863,[1] and slaves were captured in battle, for sale inside Africa or for employment or sacrifice within Dahomey, until the French conquest of 1894. But under two able rulers, Gezo (1818–58) and Gelele (1858–89), Dahomey began to adapt its institutions to the changing demands of the European economy. After a Marseille firm opened at Whydah in 1841 trade in palm-oil increased rapidly. Gezo supplemented the yield of forest trees by establishing royal plantations, tended by the slaves who were no longer needed for export; by the 1870's exports of palm produce were valued at nearly £500,000 a year.[2] Taxation of this trade bolstered the royal revenues; in particular a levy in kind on producers of palm-oil was used 'to bring back guns and powder to Dahomey'.[3]

Regulation of foreign commerce remained essential to the Dahomean monarchy; hence the care with which royal functionaries maintained the kingdom's claims to the port of Cotonou. But it was the independence of the state, rather than the personal income of the monarch, which was put first. When the British blockaded Dahomey in 1876 to secure redress for the ill-treatment of a mercantile agent, Gelele showed no readiness to compromise his political rights for the sake of re-opening trade, justly reasoning that the European traders in his kingdom were losing more by the blockade than he was.[4]

To maintain their independence, and discourage European intervention, the nineteenth-century kings of Dahomey may even have encouraged the European tendency to regard them as blood-stained savages. There was an old tradition that kings of Dahomey must never look upon the sea; this provided a most convenient justification for the court remaining at Abomey,

[1] R. F. Burton, *A Mission to Gelele, King of Dahomey* (London, 1893) Vol. 1, p. 74.

[2] *MAE*, Afrique 77, d'Elteil to Freycinet, Oct. 1880 gives figures estimating the average annual exports of palm produce from the ports of Whydah, Godomey and Abomey Calavi, by two French firms alone, in the years 1874–9, at over ten million francs. But these figures are probably too high. On Dahomean trade, see also P. Masson, *Marseille et la Colonisation française* (Marseille, 1906) pp. 369 ff; Church, *op. cit.*, pp. 103–5.

[3] Herskovits, *op. cit.*, I, pp. 116, 128–31, Ch. 7.

[4] See below pp. 202–7.

ninety miles inland, far out of range of naval artillery or landing parties. On the coast, political relations with Europeans were conducted primarily by the *yavogan*, a royal functionary who made full use of the well-known diplomatic expedient of referring inconvenient demands to his master;[1] his authority was also checked by that of the *chacha*, a member of the Portuguese family of da Souza. Francisco da Souza had helped Gezo to secure the throne in 1818, and in return was appointed royal broker at Whydah, with commercial privileges for himself; under Gelele these were enjoyed, more intermittently, by his descendants.[2] If necessary, the *yavogan* might go far to meet the demands of the European traders, for the essential thing was to prevent their governments from mobilizing their strength against Dahomey; 'he who makes the powder must win the battle,' as Gelele shrewdly commented.[3] European governments, particularly Britain, with her repeatedly unhappy experiences in Ashanti, would hesitate to launch military operations against formidable inland kingdoms; hence it suited Dahomey that her army and her king should have the reputation of formidable warriors — and notably cruel and barbaric ones at that. Thus even the practice of detaining European visitors to Abomey and compelling them to witness the annual human sacrifices to the national gods may have had a practical purpose to fulfil, by discouraging visitors and enhancing the national reputation for 'savagery'. Only a few observers, like Burton, appreciated that nineteenth-century Dahomey was a declining power which might 'crumble to pieces with the first heavy shock'; and that stories of her military prowess might be deliberately encouraged with the aim of postponing that shock.[4] There seems to have been much subtlety and statecraft about the methods by which Dahomey deferred any European invasion until the 1890's.

This model of Dahomean policy is of course greatly over-

[1] Herskovits, *op. cit.*, II, pp. 26–9.

[2] N. F. da Souza, 'Contribution Historique à la Famille de Souza', *Etudes Dahoméennes*, XIII, 1955; cf. Foà, *op. cit.*, pp. 19–36.

[3] Herskovits, *op. cit.*, I, p. 24.

[4] Burton, *op. cit.*, II, pp. 57, 87, 155–6; cf. his *Abeokuta* (London, 1863) I, p. 125; P. Bouche, *La Côte des Esclaves et le Dahomey* (Paris, 1885) pp. 398–400.

simplified. The customs and institutions of the country were formed long before the nineteenth century, and were rooted in a traditional cosmology. It would be rash to explain the actions of Dahomey's kings exclusively in terms of *realpolitik*. In the 1890's Behanzin, styling himself 'the shark that troubled the bar', probably did mystically identify himself with the real sharks which actually impeded French landings at Cotonou; at the same time he also opposed the French by more conventional methods. But traditional institutions were often adapted with some success to serve the threatened cause of national independence.

★ ★ ★ ★ ★

Until the late eighteenth century the kingdom of the Yoruba was unquestionably the greatest of the forest states. Believed to be immigrants from the east many centuries earlier, they had long established a religious capital at Ile-Ife, centre of much great artistic achievement, whence later groups of emigrants went out to exercise power and influence in varying degrees in Nupe and Benin, Porto Novo and Little Popo. In 1726 a Yoruba army defeated Abomey, and for about a century thereafter Dahomey paid tribute to the Alafin of Oyo, political sovereign of the Yoruba. The central area of Yoruba settlement was characterized by the presence of unusually large towns, inhabited by agriculturalists, craftsmen and traders; the subjects of the Alafin must have outnumbered many times those of any other ruler south of the Niger. But before the end of the eighteenth century the loyalty of provincial rulers and their subjects began to crack; provincial particularism, resentment of central taxation, and perhaps the desire for a larger share in the profits of the slave trade, may all have encouraged centrifugal tendencies. Towards 1780 the Egba, led by Lishabi, massacred the officials of Oyo and asserted their independence. About 1817 the governor of Ilorin invoked Fulani assistance against the Alafin; the undesired result was the imposition of a Fulani dynasty upon his province, the conversion of many of its people to Islam, and a series of wars which led to the sacking and abandonment of the original site of Oyo. In 1821 a period of confusion and civil war began in Yorubaland; the effective power of Oyo seemed broken, and many European observers concluded that there was no longer any barrier to the advance of Islam up to the Atlantic coast.

These apprehensions proved exaggerated, for many of the component parts of the Yoruba empire still retained much strength. The Alafin, after his flight southward, founded a new Oyo, nearer to the ancient cultural capital of Ife; forces loyal to him established a new city and communication centre at Ibadan, soon the centre of a formidable military force. The Egba, allied with other groups of Yoruba fugitives, founded in 1830 a new capital city at Abeokuta, which became the centre of a substantial federal republic. South of Ibadan were various sections of the Ijebu; fronting on the long coastal lagoon, they were favourably placed for engaging in foreign trade and importing foreign weapons. The desire of these various groups of Yorubas to assert their independence and their rights, to defend themselves against the Fulani in the north and the slave-raids of Dahomey in the west — especially, perhaps, their drive to occupy localities favourable to the development of maritime trade — led to a confused series of wars in the nineteenth century, which in some respects may have favoured, but in others certainly retarded the penetration of the country by Europeans.[1]

*   *   *   *   *

Dahomey, Ashanti, and the Yoruba succession states, like the smaller states and peoples to eastwards and westwards, were becoming increasingly oriented towards the ocean. All had formerly learned methods of supplying slaves to Europeans,

[1] For this bald summary I have relied largely on the early chapters of S. O. Biobaku, *The Egba and their Neighbours 1842–72* (Oxford, 1957). Many opinions may be modified as a result of the Yoruba Historical Research Scheme, now proceeding under Dr. Biobaku's direction. Meanwhile, see also S. Johnson, *History of the Yoruba* (Lagos, 1921). Yoruba politics after 1863 are studied by A. Aderibigbe, *Expansion of the Lagos Protectorate, 1863–1900* (Ph.D. Thesis, London, 1959). Ethnographic materials, with some historical evidence, are discussed in D. Forde, *The Yoruba-Speaking Peoples of South-Western Nigeria* (London, 1951).

and were learning with some success how to sell produce instead; all had come to desire the luxury consumption goods, and
especially the firearms, which they received in exchange. Many
Europeans, observing their aptitude for trade, and seeing states
further inland, such as Nupe, equally anxious for European
goods, thought hopefully of developing commerce from the
coast towards the great interior markets of the Sudan. But it
would not be as simple as that. Free trade with their neighbours was not, as some Cobdenites believed, the instinctive
preference of wise rulers everywhere. Some African rulers
aimed to monopolize the profits of brokerage; others put
political or territorial claims before commercial expansion; all
were reluctant to extend the supply of firearms — one of the
staples of European commerce — to potentially hostile neighbours. The extension of overseas trade was not merely a matter
to be settled between Africans and Europeans; it raised serious
problems between different African states — and among
Europeans too.

Slavery also continued to present grave barriers to economic
development. By 1860 the sea-borne export of slaves from West
Africa was greatly reduced, and five years later it seems to have
ceased completely. The attempts led by the British government
to suppress the trade by agreement among the maritime powers,
backed by naval operations and consular diplomacy, had not
proved effective alone; the trade only died when the markets in
the United States, Brazil and Cuba disappeared. Before this
happened, some regions of Africa had already largely adapted
their economies to serve new export trades in degrees which
varied according to the proximity of European settlements, and
the facilities available for profitable trade in produce. But even
the complete cessation of slave exports eliminated neither
slavery itself nor trading in slaves within Africa.

It is difficult to generalize about the forms of African slavery.
Sometimes it seems to have been a relatively mild and unob-
jectionable institution where slaves were virtually members of
the household; the rights of masters over their slaves and their
obligations towards them were usually controlled by custom or
by Koranic law and slavery seemed an integral and necessary

feature of society.[1] But it was not always simply a question of personal freedom perpetually surrendered in return for protection and patronage — the rudimentary social security scheme which some apologists seem to suggest. Often slaves were sought as an index of personal power or as currency for the payment of tribute; in Dahomey, some were regularly killed as religious sacrifices; and in many areas their labour was of increasing economic importance in the development of a more commercial agriculture. (Ironically, it may have been just where Europeans had successfully established a demand for export crops instead of slaves that the conditions of African slavery approached most closely to those of the American plantations.) There were thus internal demands for slaves which, added to those of the trans-Sahara traffic, ensured the continuance of important slave markets through most of West Africa until the very end of the nineteenth century. Often — just how often it is impossible to say — slaves were obtained by the lawless use of force, ranging from minor raids by predatory brigands on the make to regular military campaigns organized by states like Dahomey and many of the Fulani emirates. Such conditions added to the difficulties of extending 'legitimate' trade. European merchants might join the philanthropists in regretting them; but very few anti-slavery zealots in mid-Victorian Europe took their cause seriously enough to propose that their governments should undertake the pacification of the African interior.

Instead they continued to look, though with somewhat diminished confidence, to the civilizing effects of commerce. And indeed the European settlements studded along the coast, and the merchants who traded outside them, were still having profound influences upon the economic and cultural life of West Africa. Increasingly, too, their influence was being reinforced by Africans whose thought and behaviour had become partly assimilated to European patterns by long residence in the coastal settlements or by visits to Europe. The Sierra Leone

[1] For a discussion of the institution, with especial reference to Zaria, see M. G. Smith, 'Slavery and Emancipation in Two Societies', *Social and Economic Studies* (Jamaica) Vol. III, 1954. For chattel slavery in the Oil Rivers, see de Cardi, *loc. cit.*, pp. 534 ff.

Creoles, the 'educated Africans' of the Gold Coast, the *habitants* of St. Louis and Bissao, were moving further from their homes, along the coast and up the river, as traders, clerks or missionary agents. Winwood Reade, an erratic but occasionally prophetic observer, came to look to 'educated Negroes' for the future development of the interior of tropical Africa; in a striking passage he saw these eventually sharing the work of 'civilizing' the whole continent with Muslim Negroes from the Niger and with white settlers and miners from the south. But he admitted that such prospects, in 1872, seemed 'uncertain, and . . . exceedingly remote'.[1] Any wholesale and organized attempt to impose European power more widely within the tropics — any partition of tropical Africa — seemed, in view of prevailing European attitudes, even more improbable.

★   ★   ★   ★   ★

European settlements on the West African coast in 1860 were small and scattered; though their commercial or cultural influence might be quite extensive, in military power all were more or less weak. Where Europeans were feared this was on account of their power to call up warships rather than their visible strength on land. The special problems and characteristics of individual settlements will be discussed in later chapters; here it may be convenient simply to list them in the order in which they were approached by ships from the north.

On the Senegal river the French held a somewhat precarious chain of trading stations. St. Louis, on an island near the mouth, was a more substantial colonial town, founded in the seventeenth century. A hundred miles or so to the south another old French fort on the off-shore island of Gorée served as headquarters for a number of trading-posts on the mainland. In 1857 French control was extended to the Cape Verde peninsula, opposite Gorée, where they gradually developed the port of Dakar.

Next came the British settlements on the Gambia river. The capital, Bathurst, was founded in 1816 on St. Mary's island, an

[1] W. Winwood Reade, *The Martyrdom of Man* (London, 1872: rep. 1924) pp. 317–18.

insalubrious site in the estuary; the older centre of British trade was up-stream at Fort James. The British colony also included part of the Combo chiefdom, on the south bank of the estuary; a 'ceded mile' of coastline on the opposite shore, subject to the colonial tariff though actually occupied at few points; and MacCarthy's island, a trading depot 160 miles up-river. In 1857 Albreda, previously a French enclave in the river, was also transferred to the British flag.

In the Bissagos islands and the neighbouring mainland, Portugal retained vestiges of her once extensive influence on this coast. Over quite a wide area individual Portuguese had settled and married and professed the Catholic faith; but outside the unimpressive capital town of Bissao there was only sparse evidence of effective Portuguese sovereignty. The small island of Bulama was being disputed with the British; and in the Casamance river a tiny Portuguese garrison faced developing French claims.

The next two hundred miles of coastline, heavily indented with estuaries and frequented by European traders, contained no foreign sovereignties until 1865. The dominant influence was that of the British colony of Sierra Leone, and its active population of Liberated Africans. By 1860 this colony was showing strong tendencies to expand from the mountainous peninsula where it was founded in 1791; but as yet its only significant dependency was the Isles de Los.

South of the Gallinas river there began the Liberian settlements, colonies of American Negroes built up since 1821 under the auspices of the (white) American Colonization Society. The largest numbers were at Monrovia and on the lower St. Paul's river, but there were small trading settlements at several points on the coast; that at Cape Palmas had maintained separate identity until 1857 under the Maryland Colonization Society. Although the total Americo-Liberian population at this time, even allowing for intermarriage and assimilation of local people, cannot have been greatly over 10,000, Liberia had since 1847 achieved international recognition as an independent republic; its government claimed that it had acquired sovereign rights, by treaty, along more than three hundred miles of coast.

On the Ivory Coast the French flag had been raised in 1843 at Grand Bassam and Assinie, and there was a small military fort at Dabou. There were very few European civilians resident, and the condition of these posts was particularly unimpressive.

In earlier centuries European competition had covered the Gold Coast with a remarkable concentration of forts. Seven nations were represented at some period, but only three remained into the nineteenth century. In 1850 the Danes handed over their possessions (which lay in the east, between Accra and Keta) to the British, whose own forts already included Cape Coast, Accra, Dixcove, Annamabo, Sekondi, and Kommenda. The Dutch, the only other European survivors, also had a fort at Accra, and others at Axim, Elmina, and Kormantine.[1] This interspersing of possessions created many difficulties for local administrators.

Although countries east of the Gold Coast provided by far the most important sources of palm-oil in Africa, in 1860 they were still largely free from European territorial claims. At Whydah, principal port of Dahomey, three buildings still bore respectively the names of French, British, and Portuguese forts; but none of these governments exercised jurisdiction there. At Lagos the British had established a veiled protectorate in 1851, shortly to be turned into a colonial possession. France held a naval station at Gabon, with a tiny settlement of Liberated Africans at Libreville. The Spanish island of Fernando Po provided British traders on the mainland with invaluable services. But this major area of British trade remained largely free of European flags: a fact from which many mid-Victorian politicians drew their own conclusions.

[1] For full lists, see W. E. F. Ward, *A History of Ghana* (London, 1958) App. I.

CHAPTER TWO

British Policy and Opinion in the 1860's

[1]

Attitudes to West Africa in the 1860's

THE END of the maritime slave trade from West Africa marked the success of a policy which British governments had pursued through nearly sixty years, at the cost of serious diplomatic effort and many sailors' lives. It may be conceded that some supporters of this policy were actuated by mixed motives; that the methods used had sometimes been wasteful and inefficient, causing temporary increases in the sufferings of captive Africans; that in the end changing conditions in the importing territories proved more decisive than the maritime blockade. But when all this is said, Great Britain's persistence in this policy — to state it crudely in financial terms, her expenditure of annual sums variously estimated at between £150,000 and £1,000,000 out of an annual budget jealously pegged at about £40,000,000 — represents an acceptance of altruistic responsibility rare in the history of nation-states.[1] The rulers of mid-Victorian Britain have often been accused of moral complacency; in their discussions of West African policy one might expect to detect a mood of self-congratulation, and perhaps a sense of continuing mission. But this was not the case.

The campaign against the slave trade had been promoted by the Evangelical group at Westminster in full confidence that commerce and civilization would advance together. While British warships, atoning for the sins of past generations, kept watch for the slavers, British traders, opening new frontiers in

[1] For discussion of casualties and cost, see C. Lloyd, *The Navy and the Slave Trade* (London, 1949) pp. 129–38, 183, 288–9. By any realistic calculation the lower of the figures cited is more accurate, but the higher one was kept before the public by opponents of the anti-slavery policies.

their search for African produce, would stimulate Africans to free, healthy and productive labour within their own continent. By mid-century this simple faith was being shaken; the Evangelicals were fighting rearguard actions at Westminster and 'Exeter Hall' was becoming a target for satire. The disastrous failure of the attempt to further trade by philanthropic colonization on the Niger, wished upon the Whigs by their evangelical allies in 1841, proved something of a turning-point in British attitudes towards tropical Africa.[1] Thereafter Parliament grew more wary of great schemes for African advancement; responsibilities originally assumed in a mood of dedicated endeavour became burdensome. Philanthropic motives remained strong enough to prevent the sudden withdrawal of the naval squadron, but they could generate little enthusiasm either for new departures or for existing British colonies on the African coast.

Commerce with Africa, of course, was still desired; but many mid-Victorians were becoming disenchanted about the prospects of exporting their civilizati n. Ancient cultures in Asia were offering distressingly strong resistance to progressive western influences — most recently and most alarmingly in the Indian mutiny of 1857.[2] And the outlook in Africa seemed hardly better. The problem here was not so much in the conservatism of old societies; except to a limited extent in Ashanti, Europeans had not yet established sufficiently regular relations with the larger states of the interior to encourage them to expect much response in any case. But near the coast — most notably at Sierra Leone, but also in the Gambian and Gold Coast settlements — communities of Africans whose bonds with traditional society had been interrupted had, according to one widely-held opinion, proved only too malleable under certain western influences.

Sierra Leone, and schemes of 'sentimental colonization' in general, had enemies throughout the nineteenth century, many

---

[1] J. Gallagher, 'Fowell Buxton and the New African Policy', *Cambridge Historical Journal*, X, 1950.

[2] See R. Robinson and J. Gallagher, with Alice Denny, *Africa and the Victorians* (London, 1961) Ch. 1, 'The Spirit of Victorian Expansion', esp. pp. 10–11.

of them with personal axes to grind. But to explain all the contemptuous hostility which Victorians, and their successors,
directed towards those African communities which had begun
to assimilate some of the cultural attributes of their own society,
it would seem necessary to appeal to a social psychologist. Such
honoured virtues as respect for the law, desire for representative
institutions, commercial acumen, when imitated by Africans
became litigiousness, insubordination, devotion to 'huckstering'.
Britons who had set out to mould Africans to the image of their
own society scornfully disavowed the communities they had
helped to create. Captain Richard Burton, a pioneer in applying
anthropological analysis to traditional African societies, spent
three days at Freetown while travelling along the coast by mail-
steamer, and wrote a blistering ethnocentric account which
exerted an influence quite disproportionate to its merits.[1] Lord
Stanley, on most questions both thoughtful and benevolent,
asserted that philanthropic endeavour at Sierra Leone — which
he had never visited — 'had produced a race the most worthless
of any in the world'. With such opinions, Stanley naturally
challenged the view 'that in some way or other we are responsible for the fortunes and destiny of the African race'; and many
followed him in rejecting all idea of 'civilizing' policies.[2]

As for commerce, there was room for discussion about the
means by which governmental power could best promote it.
The first half of the nineteenth century had seen some growth in
the 'just and equitable traffic' with Africa foreseen by the
abolitionists, but it had been rather slow.[3] The traditional
tropical plantation crops, from which much had formerly been
hoped, developed hardly at all (though the American Civil War
brought renewed interest in the commercial possibilities of
African cotton); no new mineral resources were found, and gold
exports did not exceed their general level of the eighteenth

[1] R. F. Burton, *Wanderings in West Africa* (London, 2 Vols., 1863) Vol. I,
Ch. V.

[2] *Hansard*, 3rd series, CLXXVII, 550–3, speech of 21 Feb. 1865.

[3] On this general subject, see W. K. Hancock, *Survey of British Common-
wealth Affairs*, Vol. II, Part II (London, 1942) pp. 154–72; Robinson,
Gallagher and Denny, *op. cit.*, Ch. II; J. Gallagher and R. Robinson, 'The
Imperialism of Free Trade', *Economic History Review*, 2nd series, VI (1953).

century. The one European need which West Africa was successfully meeting was that for vegetable oils, increasingly needed for
lubrication, for candles, and for soap. France, from the 1840's,
imported growing quantities of groundnuts, cultivated by
African peasants in districts north of Sierra Leone; further down
the coast, Britain had already built up a very sizeable trade in the
produce of the great natural palm forests. But it was not clear
how far this trade required any direct exercise of British
authority. In the richest palm regions the traders were protected
only by a sort of 'informal empire'; British power, in the shape
of the anti-slavery squadron, remained discreetly in the background, sailing inshore only when called upon to rescue traders,
coerce African rulers, or compel the signature of commercial
treaties. The available evidence invited the general inference
that Britain's African commerce could be more effectively and
economically promoted by such methods than by the establishment of formal colonies.[1]

This view many, though not all, of the merchants were prepared to support. Individual attitudes varied according to local
conditions; the one demand common to all traders was for
security of trade — for a *pax*. Their stores and factories needed
protection against thieves and brigands, and against arbitrary
exactions by petty tyrants; the areas from which they drew their
produce needed sufficient tranquillity to allow harvesting, and
where necessary cultivation, to go on. Merchants accustomed to
letting out goods on credit to local middlemen needed access to
procedures for bringing defaulters to account. Where, as in the
great trading area around the Niger delta, all these conditions

[1] Robinson, Gallagher and Denny, *op. cit.*, p. 32n, quote figures of imports
into the U.K. from the four British West African colonies totalling £593,000
in 1870, and averaging £700,000 for the years 1880–4. These may be compared with their figures for imports into the U.K. of palm-oil *alone* from non-
colonial West Africa (p. 38n), which give £1,721,632 in 1870 and an average
of £1,683,474 for 1880–4. Different figures, but of similar magnitude, are in
CP. 5033, No. 17. Though these figures illustrate the quantities involved,
nineteenth-century trade statistics are tricky things. They are usually based
on declared values, and customs declarations are notoriously liable to be
affected by prevailing rates of duty. The above figures are in conflict with
those quoted by Robinson, Gallagher and Denny in a note, important for
their argument, on p. 6.

were satisfactorily provided under African rule, British traders were well satisfied by the system which withdrew their own activities from direct Imperial supervision, yet allowed them to call up Imperial power in emergencies. The presence in the region of British warships and, after 1849, a British Consul, provided all the Imperial support which the traders could yet desire.[1]

For some merchants, however, trade within the British settlements could have distinct advantages. Freetown and Bathurst, if not the best governed of towns, were places where modified forms of English mercantile and criminal law were fairly effectively enforced; to the honest merchant carrying valuable stocks this could be very beneficial. On the other hand, to pay for the somewhat elaborate administrative structure judged necessary in even the smallest British colony, customs tariffs were imposed which cut into profit margins, sometimes substantially. To strike a balance of advantages, some houses spread their operations; thus merchants whose stores in Freetown catered for local residents and visiting traders from the interior might also maintain trading factories in neighbouring rivers like the Mellacourie, where the political hazards were greater but no customs duties were payable. When, as was to happen in 1865, the security of these outstations was menaced, they would hope for naval support; if the worst came to the worst, and permanent European control seemed inevitable, they might even calculate that French customs duties would be lower than British, French mercantile law less exacting, and French rule more effective.

In general, then, those merchants already operating inside British territory were reluctant to contemplate losing the protection of the flag, but those who traded elsewhere would press for its extension only in especial need. This division of outlook was well illustrated among the seven merchants who testified before the Parliamentary Committee in 1865. William McCoskry, who as acting Consul was largely responsible for the British occupation of Lagos in 1861, and thereafter usually found the governors sympathetic towards his commercial interests, testified that British settlements assisted trade; his less

---

[1] For the system in operation, see K. O. Diké, *op. cit.*

favoured competitor David Chinery disagreed. J. A. Tobin and J. Croft, who were interested in developing trade up the Niger, and J. M. Harris, who had established a lucrative trade in the territory of Prince Manna, all opposed any extension of formal British rule. Henry Barnes, an African, and Andrew Swanzy, of a long-established London house, both traded on the Gold Coast, and both supported the maintenance of British authority there; Swanzy went further, and suggested the re-occupation of Keta, a port in the east which Krobo traders had used in 1861–2 to break his attempted monopoly of the palm-oil trade.[1] But Swanzy rejected the idea of any other extensions, and in 1875 was to be active in opposing British annexation of points on the Ivory Coast, where he was conducting a duty-free trade with Ashanti.[2] From these testimonies it was clear that merchants took a pragmatic view of the problem of how British power should be exercised in West Africa; they certainly would not support territorial expansion for its own sake.[3]

[2]

Official Policies

If mercantile opinion did not in general support territorial expansion, government officials were even less inclined to do so.

---

[1] F. Wolfson, 'The Krobo Oil Boycott, 1858–66', *Economic History Review*, 2nd series, VI (1953).

[2] Cf. below, pp. 183, 188. Swanzy's career is discussed by H. Swanzy in *Transactions*, Gold Coast and Togoland Historical Society, Vol. II (Accra, 1956). The testimony of all the merchants discussed here may be found in P.P., 1865, V.

[3] In general commentary upon these discussions of the relation between power and trade, it may be suggested that many participants exaggerated the assistance which commerce could expect from political authorities. Access to export markets and favourable terms of trade were more basic requirements than peace and tranquillity. (In fact, African wars sometimes stimulated trade.) In those relatively rare cases where profitable markets for African produce opened up — for Niger palm-oil in the 1830's, or Congo rubber in the 1880's — commercial expansion took place regardless of political conditions in the producing areas. No doubt many merchants understood this; but it did not always affect the expression of their opinions on government policy.

Some of the great departments of state consistently used their influence to prevent it. This was most clearly so with the Treasury, which, as all students of the later Victorian period know, was now systematically perfecting and extending its procedures for controlling all aspects of policy involving public expenditure. After Gladstone returned to the Treasury in 1859 officials in the Colonial Office — themselves men far from spendthrift in their administrative practice — noted a new and unreasonable rigour in the scrutiny which that department gave to even the most modest proposed additions to colonial estimates.[1] Its increasingly successful claim that financial considerations should be decisive in the formation of policy was to move many statesmen — even Prime Ministers — to impotent fury. And yet, as Lord Salisbury was to note, Treasury control was singularly undiscriminating. Large and costly enterprises with strong political support — such as the anti-slavery squadron — might well escape their axe; it was often modest proposals for new appointments or for some small investment of public money which were forbidden, on grounds of principle irrelevant to the long-term merits of the case. The Treasury would never propose any policy so definite as withdrawal from the settlements; but increasingly its attitude made their efficient maintenance more difficult.

The Service departments too regarded African settlements with small affection. The War Office, anxious to make the army cheaper yet more efficient by reducing the small colonial garrisons distributed throughout the world, objected strongly when colonial governors sent small detachments to occupy makeshift and insanitary quarters in such outposts as MacCarthy's Island, Bulama, Sherbro, and Addah.[2] The Admiralty, which had campaigned so long against the slave trade at sea, took a more positive view of its responsibilities in Africa; indeed, naval officers probably retained the old evangelical spirit of high endeavour longer than any other group of men. But this did not

[1] For one sample comment among many, see C.O. 87/75, minute by Elliot on Treasury to C.O., 2 April 1862.
[2] C.O. 267/285, W.O. to C.O., 24 March 1865; C.O. 267/292, W.O. to C.O., 21 June, 17 July 1867; Blackall to Rogers, 12 Oct. 1867.

mean that they liked using their ships to support colonial traders operating beyond the frontiers, or to help colonial governors out of trouble, since this usually meant sailing into pestilential estuaries and incurring casualties without glory. When it was a question of assuring supplies of hardwood timber for British dockyards they would reluctantly co-operate;[1] but when Governor Hill committed sailors to land fighting in Koya,[2] or sent a boat's crew fifty miles up the Bramaya river to seek redress for the dubious interests of a Sierra Leonean trader,[3] when Governor D'Arcy asked the navy to protect commercial agents high up the river Gambia,[4] the naval authorities protested vigorously. The Colonial Office responded by trying to define the circumstances in which governors might seek naval support for colonial interests. While it was in general desirable to support trade, traders' complaints should be treated with discrimination.

'The traffic with half-civilised peoples has risks of its own, which are generally compensated by more than ordinary profits. . . . [However, if] a chief habitually violates his engagements with large numbers of British traders, this may constitute a proper object for interference; and any acts of violence towards British subjects will always call for punishment and repression.'[5]

But in the last resort all depended on the Governor's discretion; and naval officers did not always judge governors to be discreet. Their reluctance to use their ships to protect traders in remote rivers reduced the effectiveness of the settlements in protecting trade beyond their own restricted borders.

[1] C.O. 267/265, Admty to C.O., 3 Dec. 1859; C.O. 267/269, Admty to C.O., 2 March, 19 May, 29 June, 5 July 1860.

[2] C.O. 267/273, Hill to Newcastle, 76, 2 April 1862; C.O. 267/275, Admty to C.O., 11 Feb. 1862.

[3] C.O. 267/270, Hill to Newcastle, 17, 28 Jan. 1861; C.O. 267/275, Admty to C.O., 13 May 1862; Newcastle to Hill, 27 May; C.O. 267/274, W. Hill to Newcastle, 158, 16 Aug. 1862.

[4] C.O. 87/73, D'Arcy to Newcastle, 92, 14 March 1862; C.O. 87/75, Admty to C.O., 4 Dec. 1862.

[5] C.O. 267/274, Newcastle to Blackall, 343, 23 Oct. 1862; cf. C.O. 87/75, minutes on Admty to C.O., 4 Dec. 1862.

Foreign Office policy and the Niger

While Palmerston and Russell lived it was usually the Foreign Office that was most active in supporting the use of British power in West Africa. These robust elder statesmen retained enough Whig idealism to regard the final extinction of the slave trade as a solemn duty, 'a noble task'.[1] They went beyond the point of merely

> 'wishing most earnestly that civilization may be extended in Africa, being convinced that commerce is the best pioneer for civilization. . . .'[2]

and understood that commercial development in the tropics might occasionally require unfashionable demonstrations of British power. The most successful example of their 'Foreign Office system' was in the Oil Rivers, as the region between the Niger delta and the Cameroons was commonly called; but elsewhere too Palmerston applauded zealous officials who displayed 'a little real vigour' by such methods as heavily bombarding the town of Porto Novo.[3] There were limits to what could be achieved by warships, consuls, and treaties, as was shown when Palmerston and Russell came round to supporting the formal occupation of Lagos in 1861; but so long as these methods worked the Foreign Office could command general support for them, in other government departments as well as in Parliament. Only in the important area of the Niger valley did their system become seriously controversial.

After the Lander brothers finally traced the lower course of the Niger in 1830, hopes of using the river to develop trade with Hausaland had inspired a number of pioneering voyages. The first of these were sponsored by Macgregor Laird, a shipbuilder and merchant on Merseyside, whose faith in the ultimate triumph of commerce allied with Christianity was not destroyed when his ventures failed, largely because of formidable

[1] C.O. 147/5, Russell to Grey, Sept. 1865.
[2] Palmerston, 20 Dec. 1850, quoted Robinson, Gallagher and Denny, *op. cit.*, p. 35.
[3] cf. W. H. Scotter, *International Rivalry in the Bights of Benin & Biafra*, Ph.D. Thesis, University of London (1933) pp. 92–3.

sickness and mortality rates. The last voyage of the series, sponsored by Russell in 1841, was similarly disastrous, and for a time it killed official interest in the navigation of the Niger. The Richardson-Barth expedition of 1849–55 was a discreet attempt to establish commercial contact with Hausaland from the north rather than the south. But Barth's reports, invaluable as they were, hardly suggested that such a plan could succeed; instead, he repeatedly insisted that the Niger, and particularly its Benué tributary, offered the most promising approach.[1] So, in 1854, the British government agreed to promote another exploration of the river route. Surgeon Commander W. B. Baikie, who assumed command of this expedition, succeeded in taking the steamer *Pleiad* three hundred miles up the Benué beyond its confluence with the Niger; still more important, by compelling his crew to take regular prophylactic doses of quinine he managed to bring all sixty-six of them safely home.[2] Up-river trade seemed feasible once more.

Macgregor Laird, supported by such influential bodies as the Church Missionary Society, the British Association, and the Royal Geographical Society, quickly came forward to try to take advantage of it. But even with the malarial barrier broken, the remaining problems, economic and political, still seemed too formidable for any merchant to solve unaided. To provide ships and a trading organization capable of operating far up-river would require considerable capital investment; hence in 1857 Palmerston's government agreed to provide subsidies of £6,000–£8,000 for the next five years on condition that Laird made at least one voyage above the confluence each year. Baikie led the first of these voyages in the *Dayspring* in 1857, and remained in the Niger until 1864, founding Lokoja, a small settlement at the confluence of Niger and Benué, as a base for developing commerce with Kano, Zaria and Lagos. Baikie was recognized by the Foreign Office

---

[1] Barth, *op. cit.*, Vol. II, pp. 348n, 467–8, 507–8, Vol. III, pp. 131–5, 365–6. For the connection between the Barth and Baikie missions, cf. A. Boahen, *op. cit.*

[2] W. B. Baikie, *Narrative of an Exploring Voyage up the Rivers Kwora and Binue* (London, 1856) *passim*.

as holding some rather ill-defined official status, and sent reports to them; in 1866 Lokoja was temporarily made a consulate.

Potentially, the up-river trade was highly profitable; but immediately Nupe, the only state beyond the palm-belt so far reached, had little commercial produce to offer — some ivory, and a vegetable oil called shea-butter. Even with subsidy, Laird's enterprise could only pay if his ships also traded downstream for palm-oil. Here good profits could be made by cutting out the delta middlemen, and by providing cheaper transport than they could between the palm-forests and the sea; according to one calculation, a puncheon of oil for which Liverpool traders in the delta would pay four and a half tons of salt could be bought near Lokoja for three-quarters of a ton.[1] So, in 1857 Baikie stationed hulks at Abo and Onitsha, and the oil they bought helped to finance the pioneering venture higher up. Brass and other delta middleman states, encouraged by Liverpool traders whose livelihood was likewise threatened, reacted violently — as they had previously done when Laird tried to open the Niger in the 1830's. Their violent attacks on some of Laird's vessels, quite apart from losses directly inflicted, sent up his insurance premiums and made it difficult to recruit sailors. Hence, in 1860 Laird had to ask the government, not only to renew his subsidy, but to provide him with naval protection in the Niger.[2]

After some hesitation, the Foreign Office responded favourably. Palmerston at least was clear that here was a proper case for using British power:

'The extension of our trade on the W[est] C[oast of] A[frica] generally, and upon the Niger in particular, is an object which ought to be actively and perseveringly pursued, but it cannot be accomplished without physical effort for the protection of that trade. It may be true in one sense that trade ought not to be enforced by cannon balls, but on the other hand trade cannot

[1] A. F. Mockler-Ferryman, *British Nigeria* (London, 1902) p. 61. Robinson, Gallagher and Denny, *op. cit.*, p. 37, quote another, less striking, figure.

[2] F.O. 2/34, Proposals of Laird, 10 March 1860.

flourish without security, and that security may often be unattainable without the exhibition of physical force. . . .'[1]

So not only was the subsidy renewed, but punitive naval action against Brass, which the local commander had refused to take in 1860, was carried out in 1861.

When Laird died in 1861, much of the impetus went out of the Niger projects. The Foreign Office for a time remained favourable. Russell agreed in 1864 to continue the subsidy to a new 'Company of African Merchants', formed by Laird's executor, Archibald Hamilton, to continue his work on the Niger: this despite intensified opposition from the Liverpool delta merchants, and although a rival Niger scheme, the West Africa Company of Manchester, was now in the field. Russell still believed, as he wrote in another context, that,

> '. . . it is the true policy of this country to assist by all legitimate means the development of lawful trade on the African coast and rivers . . . instead of protection being withdrawn from British traders, they should be encouraged to pursue, and if possible increase, their trading transactions with the natives, for it is only by the establishment of legitimate trade that we may hope totally to eradicate the slave-trade.'[2]

But by 1865 Palmerston and Russell were ending their careers, and other opinions about the duty of government to support African trade were prevailing. The Atlantic slave trade being virtually at an end, no new arguments for active African policies were strong enough to overcome the newly militant opposition of the Gladstonian Treasury, supported as it was by much public indifference. In the end the Niger subsidy was not after all renewed; the Lokoja consulate lasted only until 1869;

---

[1] F.O. 2/34, minute by Palmerston, 22 April on report by Washington, 12 April 1860. For further discussion of Palmerston's attitude, see R. J. Gavin 'Nigeria and Lord Palmerston' *Ibadan*, June 1961.

[2] C.O. 267/285, F.O. to C.O., 9 Oct. 1865; cf. C.O. 267/275, F.O. to Admty, 19 Feb. 1862; F.O. 97/435, memo. by Russell, 13 Dec. 1865, cited by Cherry Gertzel, *Imperial Policy towards the British Settlements in West Africa, 1860–75* (B.Litt. thesis, Oxford, 1953) p. 23.

and the Foreign Office temporarily ceased to advocate strong or progressive policies in Africa.[1]

The Colonial Office approach

In the Colonial Office at least, it might be expected, a coherent and constructive view of British policy in West Africa would be taken. In fact the mid-Victorian Colonial Office was generally much influenced by 'separatist' thought, and even less inclined than the Foreign Office to support formal territorial expansion in Africa. 'If we could acquire the Dominion of the whole of that Continent it would be but a worthless possession,' wrote James Stephen, its dominant figure in 1840.[2] Anti-slavery zeal had certainly been strong in the office; and in public Edward Cardwell, the able Peelite administrator who became Secretary of State in 1864, claimed that existing settlements aided the suppression of the slave trade. 'Our policy', he told the Commons,

> 'is solely and entirely a disinterested one — namely at great inconvenience and no inconsiderable sacrifices to ourselves, to abolish a trade disgraceful to human nature, and extend the advantages of religion, civilisation and commerce to the miserable inhabitants of Africa.'[3]

Yet in the actual conduct of business Cardwell, and more particularly his official advisers, were becoming inhibited by their increasing appreciation that the instruments at their disposal were very imperfectly suited to this proclaimed objective of regenerating Africa.

The two senior officials of the Colonial Office during the

[1] This account of British Niger policy is based generally upon Diké, *op. cit.*, pp. 168–80; W. H. Scotter, *op. cit.*; J. E. Flint, *Sir George Goldie and the Making of Nigeria* (London, 1960) Ch. 2; cf. A. C. G. Hastings (ed.) *The Voyage of the 'Dayspring'* (London, 1926); Mockler-Ferryman, *op. cit.*, Ch. 5; P.P. 1865, V, evidence of Wylde, Tobin, McLeod, Croft; P.P. 1864, XLI, *Papers relating to the grant of a subsidy to the Company of African Merchants*. Some additional material on Lokoja may be found in H. J. Pedraza, *Borrioboola-Gha* (London, 1960), Chs. 4 and 5.

[2] Minute by Stephen, 21 Dec. 1840, quoted Robinson, Gallagher and Denny, *op. cit.*, p. 16.

[3] *Hansard*, 3rd series, CLXXVI, 1667–70, 18 July 1864.

1860's were both men of considerable ability; but their comments on West African business are dominated by modesty, introspection, and reserve to an extent which contrasts sharply with the self-assurance of the Palmerstonian Foreign Office. Sir Frederic Rogers, Permanent Under-Secretary from 1860 until 1871, was a Liberal lawyer and High Churchman, thoughtful, clear-headed, humane — and sympathetic with the colonial 'separatists'. T. F. Elliot, who as Assistant Under-Secretary had primary oversight of West African problems, was an experienced public servant, whose family had a varied and distinguished record overseas.[1] Both men were naturally sceptical about the possibilities of drastically improving the condition of humanity through governmental action; and particularly so in Africa, where 'the disparity between our power and our knowledge'[2] seemed terribly obvious. As Elliot put it,

'the government has almost boundless power on the Coast, very imperfect information, and no control of any effective public opinion in this country, so that everything depends on our own consciences.'[3]

Rogers and Elliot both had consciences too sensitive to make it easy for them to carry the responsibilities of Empire; fear of abusing their power often drove them into conclusions whose caution came near to feebleness.

Uncharitable critics might conclude that they simply found African colonies a nuisance — 'expensive and troublesome', as Rogers called them.[4] This would be unjust. These high-minded gentlemen would gladly accept burdensome duties, and would even propose higher government expenditure, if they could thereby secure the extension of civilization and the extirpation of the worst evils of slavery. But though officials, missionaries

[1] On them, cf. J. D. Hargreaves, 'Colonial Office Opinions on the Constitution of 1863', *Sierra Leone Studies*, n.s. 5 (1955). For Rogers, see G. E. Marindin (ed.), *Letters of Frederic Lord Blachford* (London, 1896).

[2] Minute by Elliot, 12 July 1862, quoted in J. Simmons, *From Empire to Commonwealth* (London, 1949) pp. 158–9.

[3] C.O. 267/282, minute by Elliot, 14 May 1864, on F.O. to C.O., 10 May.

[4] C.O. 87/71, minute by Rogers, 5 Aug. 1861, on D'Arcy to Newcastle, 24 July.

and traders might land in Africa, though they might even succeed in finally suppressing the export of slaves, it was not clear that this would cause the natives of that continent suddenly to cease exploiting and ill-treating one another. It might conceivably be that the greatest service which Europe could render to Africa would be simply to leave it alone. Rogers' doubts led him to conclusions only too similar to the position occupied by less disinterested critics of traditional anti-slavery policies. He feared

> 'that the extinction of the foreign slave-trade, coupled with the progress of "legitimate trade" in Africa and unaccompanied by the extinction of internal slavery in Africa, would have this result: that chiefs and masters of slaves would become alive to the commercial value of labour — that they wd. therefore be rigid in exacting it — that an easy serfdom would thus be changed into a punishing slavery. [This would be] more grinding than that of Cuba because, being carried on under the inspiration of a white trader, it would be as complete . . . being carried into effect through the instrumentality of a Dukeman or Ashanti chief it wd. be more brutal — and . . . being carried on in the centre of populous country it wd. not be checked by the expensiveness of replacing the human beings as they are used up. . . . My moral is that if we cannot stop this we are doing no good in trying to stop the export of slaves to places where, after all, they are likely to be better treated than, under the pressure of legitimate trade, they are likely to be at home.'[1]

About 1863 Elliot and Rogers came to the disturbing conclusion that the British settlements in West Africa were always likely to display an irresistible tendency to expand. Since each colony existed largely to promote legitimate trade, its Governor was bound to interest himself in promoting propitious conditions in the neighbouring territories; he would therefore seek authority to conduct punitive expeditions or annex border districts. If permission were granted — and the Colonial Office in its ignorance might find it hard to refuse — new requests would follow, for the new territories would need

[1] C.O. 267/282, minute by Rogers, 3 March 1864, on Admty to C.O., 18 Feb. In the interests of clarity I have amended the punctuation of this hastily-penned minute.

' . . . Managers with strong moral and physical constitutions, and no mean legal requirements; Barracks; Troops; Police; Customs Officers, Surveyors, and the means of constant steam communication with the capital.'

Under pressure from governors, traders, missionaries, Elliot feared,

'. . . we are insensibly sliding into a new policy (or rather a new practice, for it never seems to have received deliberation enough to deserve the name of a policy) of trying to stop the slave trade by means of soldiers instead of sailors.'

This move towards a more formal exercise of Imperial authority the Colonial Office now sought, rather tardily, to check; for no local interest could justify the extension of responsibility beyond the colonial government's power to fulfil it. Though the passages quoted were written with direct reference to Sierra Leone, they could be applied with little change to events of the years 1860–5 in any of the four West African colonies. It was time to call a halt: or, 'are we for ever to extend our boundaries?'[1]

[3]
Problems of the Existing Settlements

Sierra Leone, Sherbro and Bulama

Although the name of Sierra Leone could still provoke strong hostility in many Englishmen, it was clear long before 1860 that this colony of liberated captives and their descendants would survive, and might even modestly prosper. Early hopes of agricultural or industrial development directed beyond local demand had been disappointed, for the geographical environment was hardly favourable; but many Sierra Leoneans had shown great enterprise in trading, both on the adjacent coast and rivers and in more distant countries. A small African

---

[1] Minutes by Elliot, 16 March 1863, on Blackall to Newcastle, 25, 21 Feb. (C.O. 267/280); 29 Aug. 1863, on F.O. to C.O., 10 Aug. (C.O. 267/279); 4 April 1864, on Churchill to C.O., 31 March (C.O. 267/282); 14 May 1864, on Blackall to Cardwell 48, 19 April (C.O. 267/280).

middle-class, which grew and prospered during the 'sixties, was building substantial shops and houses, publishing newspapers, and generally turning Freetown into a genuine urban community, with that distinctive flavour which many Europeans found so unattractive.[1] But since the wealth which supported the town, and provided the taxable capacity to maintain a rather elaborate colonial administration, was drawn from trade beyond the colonial borders, merchants and governors alike were obliged to watch carefully over events in the neighbouring African territories.

Freetown's commercial hinterland was inhabited by many different African peoples living in small political units. In the absence of any African authority strong enough to establish control over a wide area, skirmishings, boundary disputes, and petty wars were frequent; sometimes they originated in traditional feuds or dynastic quarrels, sometimes in a struggle to control the export trade. Often — as in August 1860, when fighting in the Rokelle and Bumpe valleys led to the death of a British subject, destruction of British property, and delays in the export of timber — Freetown merchants or interested chiefs might call on the colonial government to impose the authority which was lacking.[2] During 1861 demands of this nature led S. J. Hill, a combative officer of the West India Regiment who had been Governor since 1854, to initiate two territorial extensions.

The smaller of these lay within the small chiefdom of Koya which, situated between the Rokelle and Ribbi rivers, commanded Freetown's overland routes to the interior. In 1860 Hill had suggested leasing part of its territory for agricultural settlement; but before the Colonial Office could reply he used the robbery of a British subject by men from Koya as the occasion for sending troops and securing a treaty ceding sovereignty over about 150 square miles.[3] This encroachment only encouraged

---

[1] For development of these points, see J. D. Hargreaves, *A Life of Sir Samuel Lewis* (London, 1958) Chs. 1 and 2. More generally, see C. H. Fyfe, *A History of Sierra Leone* (London, 1962).

[2] C.O. 267/267, Fitzjames to Newcastle, 119, 20 Aug. 1860.

[3] C.O. 267/268, Hill to Newcastle, 192, 19 Dec. 1860; C.O. 267/270, Hill to Newcastle, 46, 19 March; 61, 16 April 1861.

disorder among the inhabitants of Koya; before the end of the year new complaints by British subjects led Hill to launch a fierce little military campaign and to exact a second treaty, asserting closer British control over a wider area.[1] Hill hoped that in this new territory, 'village after village must arise and convert that highway of slave dealers and haunt of cruel superstition into a land of peaceful liberty and enlightened morality';[2] but his lyrical enthusiasm was not shared by the Colonial Office. Koya had produced 'nothing but inconvenience and insecurity', Elliot wrote after a year of British rule; 'perhaps the reason may be that, besides convenience, there is also some inconvenience attendant on appropriating to oneself what belongs to others.'[3]

Hill's second acquisition was more important. The shores of the Sherbro estuary, nearly a hundred miles south of Freetown, were first ceded to the Colony in 1825 during Governor Turner's campaign against slave-traders; although Turner's treaties were disallowed, close links with Freetown had persisted. American missionaries arrived, and also Creole and British traders, who stimulated production for export on the many tributaries of the Sherbro. Rice was grown for consumption in Freetown, palm products were exported to Europe, and during the 1850's hardwoods from the forests supplied European dockyards. About 1856 a French trader called Geislinger arrived from the Senegal; by 1861 there were four or five French houses, who claimed that their annual trade, valued at 450,000 francs, was already half the size of Britain's.[4] Their rapid development provided Sierra Leonean traders with unwelcome competition; it also suggested political dangers to Hill's patriotic mind.

In February 1861 Hill reported that at the request of T. S. Caulker of the Plantain Islands he had revived Turner's treaty and accepted the sovereignty of Bendu, a trading-centre on the

[1] Fyfe, *op. cit.*, pp. 310–12, 316.

[2] C.O. 267/274, Hill to Newcastle, 139, 20 July 1862.

[3] C.O. 267/274, W. Hill to Newcastle, 190, 7 Oct. 1862 and minute by Elliot, 17 Nov.

[4] *MAE*, Afrique 55, Lefebvre to Bosse, 6 Dec. 1861; M.A.E. to M.M.C., 15 Jan. 1862; *MMC*, Sénégal III/9/b, Geislinger to Poisson, 11 April 1863; Afrique IV/19/b. Note on the Sherbro *c.* 1863.

eastern shore of the Shebar Channel. Caulker's title to dispose of this territory was not unquestioned; he came from a ruling family that had long been in relationship with Europeans, and his vigorous assertion of his claims had frequently led him into trouble. As recently as 1859 Hill himself had deported him to Freetown. Caulker had several times quarrelled with the French traders, who in 1857 and 1859 called in the warship *Grondeur* to force him to redress their grievances.[1] It appears that these experiences had convinced Caulker that France might threaten his independence, and to obtain protection he appealed to Hill's empire-building instincts. This apparently spontaneous change of policy by an African ruler provided the Governor with an opportunity to invoke the danger that the French might establish themselves at Bendu, and subsequently 'extend their authority, and eventually deprive us of the best teak timber in this part of Africa'. The Colonial Office, trusting in Hill's good judgment, approved what they assumed to be a merely nominal extension of title, and asked that it should be regularized by a new treaty.[2]

But when Hill went to the Sherbro to secure this in November, it proved that more was involved than the Colonial Office had expected. Besides Bendu, Hill obtained from other chiefs the cession of Sherbro and York islands and of the timber-producing Bagru river, together with an inexactly determined tract of territory extending 'about thirty miles inland'. This new action was approved, though with raised eyebrows; the Secretary of State noted that 'the "suppression of the Slave Trade" is leading us into serious territorial complications on the whole W. Coast of Africa', and Hill was warned to accept no more territory without explicit authority.[3] Soon protests began to arrive. The French traders, resentful and fearful of the effects if the heavy Sierra Leone tariff on spirits should be applied to their trade, alleged that Hill had got his treaties only by lavish

[1] C.O. 267/263, Hill to Lytton, 27, 16 Feb. 1859; C.O. 267/264, Fitzjames to Newcastle, 135, 11 Aug. 1859; *MMC*, Afrique IV/19/b. Note on the Sherbro.

[2] C.O. 267/270, Hill to Newcastle, 23, 2 Feb. 1861; C.O. to F.O., 20 March. Cf. Fyfe, *op. cit.*, pp. 248–50, 284–6, 308–10.

[3] C.O. 267/271, Hill to Newcastle, 184, 187, 188, 14–15 Nov. 1861. Texts of the treaties may be found in C.O. 806/346.

presents of liquor, and that trouble would recur as soon as these were consumed.[1] Some British traders also were apprehensive about the effects of colonial control, preferring the prospect of lower liquor duties under French rule. Hanson, a timber merchant of doubtful reputation and former British Consular Agent, submitted protests in the name of 'the chiefs and principal men of Sherbro'; Caulker retorted that those whom Hanson represented as rulers of the country were simply his own rather numerous fathers-in-law.[2] The Colonial Office, unable to follow the intricacies of Sherbro politics, could only support its Governor, though with growing misgiving.

* * * * *

The acquisition of the Sherbro also involved difficulties with Liberia. Hitherto most Britons had looked favourably on the little republic, on account of its achievements in combatting the slave trade; in 1850 Lord Shaftesbury and other British philanthropists had provided money for Liberia to purchase territorial sovereignty between Cape Mount and the Sherbro estuary.[3] Treaties purporting to complete these transactions were duly signed, but not immediately acted upon; as so often in Africa, it is likely that the contracting parties interpreted these documents in different ways. The question of Liberian rights on this coast ceased to be academic in 1860, when an Anglo-Jewish merchant called J. M. Harris transferred his main business from the Sherbro to Sulima, on the Gallinas (or Moa) river, and came into conflict with the Liberian authorities by trying to land his imports near Cape Mount without paying duty. Harris's protests were supported by Prince Manna of the Gallinas chiefdom, a leading member of the Poro society, whose authority was very widely respected on this coast: a ruler quite strong enough to resist the imposition of Liberian control.[4]

[1] *MMC*, Afrique IV/19/b, Caillet to Didelot, 17 Dec. 1861.
[2] C.O. 267/273, Hill to Newcastle, 18, 19 Jan.; 63, 20 March 1862.
[3] H. H. Johnston, *Liberia* (London, 1906) Vol. 1, pp. 226–7.
[4] Harris' version of the initial conflict is in C.O. 267/268, Hill to Newcastle, 190, 19 Dec. 1860; C.O. 267/270, Hill to Newcastle, 7, 17, Jan. 1961. For a Liberian view, see E. J. Yancy, *The Republic of Liberia* (London, 1959) pp. 55–8.

c*

In 1862 President Benson travelled to London to seek recognition of Liberian claims. At first he was sympathetically received; both Admiralty and Colonial Office seriously considered passing on Bendu to Liberia, together with the responsibility for combating the slave trade.[1] But reports from British representatives on the coast, both naval and colonial, advised strongly that Liberian claims should not be recognized north of the Gallinas river; questioning both the validity of her treaties and the efficacy of her rule, they prophesied strong resistance from chiefs and people, injurious alike to good order and to commerce.[2]

Stiffening their attitude, the Colonial Office therefore decided to submit Liberia's claims to a locally-constituted Commission. British members were to be in a majority, with instructions to try to restrict Liberian claims to the line of the Gallinas river. But even if the evidence made it necessary to admit Liberia's rights further north, the government declared that it would not abandon Bendu, nor help to force Liberian rule upon unwilling peoples, nor even advise British subjects to obey Liberian authority until they received effective protection for their trade.[3] On this basis the Commission had little hope of unanimity. The Liberians refused to restrict their boundary either to the Mano or the Gallinas river; neither the British Commissioners nor the Colonial Office would admit their claims further north. Harris could have asked for no better result; his government would support the exclusion of Liberia from the Gallinas, but would not move their own police and customs-officers south of the Sherbro.[4]

In the territories actually ceded to Hill the consolidation of British authority was already taking place. In 1862 a garrison of forty was sent from Sierra Leone to protect the Sherbro traders.

[1] C.O. 267/272, F.O. to C.O., 3 Aug., 28 Dec. 1861; C.O. to F.O., 1 March 1862; C.O. 267/275, F.O. to C.O., 5 July 1862 and minutes.

[2] C.O. 267/274, W. Hill to Newcastle, 182–3, 21 Sept.; 195, 21 Oct. 1862; Blackall to Newcastle, 208, 19 Nov.; C.O. 267/275, F.O. to C.O., 6 Nov., 1 Dec. 1862; cf. C.O. 267/277, Blackall to Newcastle, 7, 15 Jan. 1863.

[3] C.O. 267/275, Admty to C.O., 19 Dec. 1862; minutes; C.O. to Admty, 22 Dec. 1862.

[4] C.O. 267/277, Blackall to Newcastle, 64, 10 June 1863; C.O. 267/282, F.O. to C.O., 10 May 1864 and minute by Elliot, 14 May.

Next year Blackall, Hill's successor, asked authority to impose customs duties, and set up a rudimentary administration to enforce their collection; otherwise, the Sherbro would remain a liability to Sierra Leone. The Colonial Office, who had originally envisaged only a nominal overlordship, now feared a progressive extension of their commitments. Blackall's proposals were accepted, for, as Elliot wrote, 'unless we exercise power and do good, must not such extensions be rather a mockery and a discredit?'[1] But for politicians no longer strongly impelled to do good in Africa, the case of the Sherbro suggested a need for caution in accepting further responsibilities.

*   *   *   *   *

Another target for zealous officials was Portuguese Guinea. The commerce of this area was largely undeveloped — in 1863 a French officer estimated its total annual value at £60,000 — and foreigners complained of maladministration and insecurity.[2] And British observers were usually convinced, though sometimes on the inadequate basis of prejudice or past experience, that all Portuguese, whether traders or officials, were implicated in the slave trade.

For this reason the British government had maintained a claim to the sovereignty of the small island of Bulama, on the basis of treaties first made in 1792 during a tragically unsuccessful attempt to colonize the island. Although this attempt had not been renewed, except briefly in 1814, concern lest Bulama become a slaving base had prevented the government from recognizing Portugal's counter-claim, which she based on priority of discovery and on an alleged proclamation of sovereignty in 1752. After Palmerston decided to take stronger measures against Portuguese slavers in 1839, it became the Navy's custom to visit the island occasionally and remove any Portuguese residents.[3]

[1] C.O. 267/274, W. Hill to Newcastle, 179, 18 Sept. 1862; C.O. 267/277, Blackall to Newcastle, 18, 6 Feb.; 25, 21 Feb. 1863, minute by Elliot, 16 March.

[2] *MMC*, Sénégal III/9/b. Report by Poisson, 1863.

[3] See the retrospective minutes in C.O. 267/285, F.O. to C.O., 4 Jan. 1865.

In August 1858 and January 1859 such visits were made by an especially energetic naval officer, Commander Close. He declared the island to be British territory, liberated many domestic slaves, and on his second visit hoisted the Union Jack. A Eurafrican trader from the mainland, D. J. Lawrence, was given a grant of land on the island, and left in charge of the flagpole; next April he was naturalized as a British subject by local Sierra Leone Ordinance.[1] It seems clear that Close and Hill worked with Lawrence to promote stronger British control. Petitions from 'chiefs' of Bulama, and from the neighbouring mainland, began to reach Freetown; some two hundred domestic slaves from the mainland crossed to the island, where they were emancipated by Lawrence (and sometimes enrolled in his service). From these developments Hill and Close concluded that Bulama should be annexed to Sierra Leone 'for the sake of humanity, civilization, and a check to the slave-trade'.[2]

Although Carnarvon, the Conservative Under-Secretary, did not find these arguments very convincing, the Colonial Office of 1859 had not yet learned to distrust such proposals for cheap and effortless expansion. Bulama was annexed by Order-in-Council, and the costs of administration placed, rather meanly, upon Sierra Leone. But matters did not rest there. In December 1860 Hill answered Portuguese attempts to tax Bulama's local trade by proclaiming the annexation of substantial mainland areas; Lisbon rejected the British government's suggestion of a compromise or *modus vivendi*, angrily demanding that the rights of the question should be sent to arbitration. Then, in 1863, Blackall, having posted a small garrison on the island, renewed the suggestion of occupying points on the mainland. Holding these, he claimed, Bulama could become fiscally self-supporting, or better; but if British authority were restricted to the island it would be impossible to suppress either smuggling or coastwise slave-dealing, and 'the heavy expenditure already incurred will be entirely wasted'.[1]

These proposals, although they followed logically enough from the original decision to occupy the island, seemed to the Colonial Office, 'wonderfully like the story of what is going on at Lagos.' Elliot prophesied an indefinite series of irrefutable arguments, from Governors and merchants, in favour of new frontier extensions; Newcastle saw Lawrence's hand behind Blackall's proposal. As a good Peelite he hesitated to treat Portugal's claims in the Palmerstonian manner, especially in view of signs that France was undertaking an advance in the Senegal: 'it certainly cannot be for our interests to justify her increase of territory, or to throw her and Portugal into league against us on the Coast of Africa.' Blackall was therefore refused permission to occupy mainland territory, and warned that 'some limit must be put to the growing extensions of British territory on the Western Coast of Africa, both on account of the additional responsibility which they occasion, and also of the discussions in which they involve us with Foreign Powers'.[2] But this tardy application of the brake did not settle the existing problem of Bulama island, which remained a financial liability to Sierra Leone and a source of friction with Portugal: a further monument to the embarrassing energy of Governor Hill.

The Gambia

Hill left Sierra Leone in 1862, and Blackall, a former Liberal M.P. for Longford, showed greater caution in office. But between 1859 and 1867 the government of the Gambia remained in less predictable hands. Its Governor, George Abbas

[1] C.O. 267/265, C.O. to F.O., 5 May 1859; F.O. to C.O., 22 Aug. and minutes; Newcastle to Fitzjames, 16 Sept. and minutes; C.O. 267/268, Hill to Newcastle, 178, 11 Dec. 1860; C.O. 267/272, F.O. to C.O., 5 April 1861; C.O. 267/277, Blackall to Newcastle, 72, 17 June 1863.

[2] C.O. 267/279, F.O. to C.O., 10 Aug. 1863, minutes by Elliot, 29 Aug.; Newcastle, 31 Aug., Newcastle to Blackall, 416, 4 Sept. 1863; C.O. 267/296, C.O. to F.O., 26 Oct. 1868. For the French considering, briefly, the idea of collaboration with Portugal; MAE, Afrique 55, M.M.C. to M.A.E., 16 Feb. 1864.

Koolie D'Arcy, was an old soldier who had served in India with Outram, and later commanded the 3rd West India Regiment. He had the temperament of an evangelical; deeply devoted to the welfare of Africa and the eradication of the slave trade, he longed to lead a crusading expedition against Dahomey.[1] His many prejudices and eccentricities, his tendency to quarrel with European subordinates, and his extraordinary literary style — lurid, rhetorical, but rarely precise — caused the Colonial Office, in terror lest he rashly plunge them into new responsibilities, to do less than justice to his loyalty, courage, and tenacious devotion to his thankless duty.[2]

Britain's interest in the Gambia had always been to use the waterway for trade, not to hold territory. Bathurst's European merchants and its four thousand African residents — who included Liberated Africans, descendants of men who moved from Senegal after the Napoleonic war, and immigrants from the interior — were all, directly or indirectly, dependent upon commerce. Since the later 1840's this consisted almost exclusively of the export of groundnuts, cultivated by African labour in countries adjacent to the river, and destined principally for French markets. The prosperity of the town and the solvency of the government depended on a good harvest; and this could be jeopardized either by bad weather or by political disorder in the small African states along the river.

Among these states, old rivalries were often reinforced by differing responses to El Haj Omar and his followers, or alternatively by commercial competition; when such tensions resulted in armed conflict, groundnuts would not be harvested, and trading factories might be robbed. Then the merchants would look to the colonial government for protection. To provide this might involve serious risks; there were many cautionary cases when the Colony had been drawn into African wars beyond its capacity to control. But since 1857 Britain claimed to

---

[1] C.O. 87/71, D'Arcy to Newcastle, Conf., 24 May 1861.
[2] e.g. C.O. 87/73, minute by Elliot, 18 Sept. 1862. '. . . one cannot help feeling one's confidence impaired in a Governor who seeks to fortify his judgement on the course to be pursued in the village of Bathurst by precedents drawn from Mithridates the Great.'

be suzerain power of the whole river, to the exclusion of foreign powers; this claim implied a responsibility for protecting foreign citizens against theft and violence. In 1859 a complaint lodged by a Bordeaux firm obliged the British government to admit that foreign merchants domiciled in the Colony might properly claim the same protection as British subjects when trading outside the colonial borders. The Queen's Advocate added the ominous opinion that, if such protection should prove unsatisfactory, the French government would be entitled to send their own forces into the river.[1] The Gambia government had few armed men at its disposal, and nobody in London wished to supply more; yet the price of failing to do so might be, not merely the humiliation of witnessing French intervention, but the decay of trade, and a financial crisis from which the colony would be rescued only by perpetuating the universally-deplored Parliamentary subsidy. D'Arcy's lurid language sometimes obscured his immediate intentions, but he well understood the crucial necessity of providing some sort of security in the river, at least as far as MacCarthy's Island. While the Colonial Office preferred to ignore this problem as long as possible, D'Arcy bravely tried to solve it with the inadequate resources available to him.

During 1860 the British merchants, strongly represented in the Legislative Council, complained persistently of arbitrary treatment by the chiefs of the north bank state of Badibu. In October D'Arcy agreed to declare a blockade, thus cutting off the market for the local groundnut crop; but, just when the chief seemed about to give way and pay the compensation demanded, some African traders went in in search of cheap groundnuts, and the blockade became ineffective. Under new mercantile pressure, D'Arcy applied to Sierra Leone for reinforcements; in February 1861 he attacked Badibu with two or three warships, four companies of soldiers, and the personal assistance of Governor Hill. The chiefs made peace, promising to pay up; it seemed to the Colonial Office that British power

[1] C.O. 87/67, Robertson to Lytton, 9, 20 June 1859; Newcastle to D'Arcy, 8, 12 Dec. 1859; C.O. 87/68, F.O. to C.O., 19 May, 11 Nov. 1859, with minutes; Q.A. to C.O., 27 July, with minutes.

had been convincingly demonstrated.[1] But soon the troops and
warships departed — even the Gambia's own steamer was sent
to Sierra Leone for the Koya campaign — and the peace-terms
became impossible to enforce. In August D'Arcy had to
negotiate a new treaty, remitting three-quarters of the indem-
nity in return for a vague assurance about freedom of trade.
Little remained of the fruits of this display of force except the
bills, which D'Arcy struggled uncomplainingly to meet by
severe economies in colonial expenditure.[2] His intervention had
done the colony more harm than good; but similar incidents
were always liable to recur, so long as traders in the Gambia
could demand support in business carried on beyond the range
of effective British power.

Even more serious was the impact in the Gambia valley of the
Muslim revival initiated by El Haj Omar. While knowing little
of the wider background, the British at Bathurst became aware
of new conflicts in the river, which they interpreted as caused by
pressure by 'Marabouts', puritanical and reforming Muslims,
upon the nominal or degenerate Islam of the 'Soninkes'. When
Maba in 1862 launched his attack upon the chiefs of Badibu,
reactions in Bathurst were based upon imperfect intelligence
and conflicting principles. Some Europeans, observing that
Maba professed friendship and respected British property,
began to hope that the Colony might find means to pacify the
river by recognizing and co-operating with the advancing
'Marabout' power. But the smaller African traders, especially
the Christians, doubted the wisdom and the efficacy of such a
policy; they were supported by D'Arcy, who retained anti-
Muslim prejudices from the days of the Indian Mutiny, which
his contacts with St. Louis may have encouraged. To him the
'Soninkes' represented 'legitimacy'; they were peaceful culti-
vators of the soil, and better customers for imported liquor than
strict Muslims could ever be. He suggested establishing a British

[1] C.O. 87/69, D'Arcy to Newcastle, 40, 23 Aug.; 54, 23 Nov. 1860; C.O.
87/71, Pine to Newcastle, 2, 22 Jan. 1861; D'Arcy to Newcastle, 7, 26 Feb.
1861; C.O. 87/72, W.O. to C.O., 1 Feb. 1861 and minutes.

[2] C.O. 87/71, D'Arcy to Newcastle, 54, 21 Aug. 1861; C.O. 87/72,
Treasury to C.O., 20 Nov. 1861; C.O. 87/73, D'Arcy to Newcastle, 90, 14
March; 92, 16 March 1862.

protectorate over the river banks below MacCarthy's Island, to be settled with refugees and planted with cotton. This would have amounted to an attempt to create a barrier against militant Islam under British protection: a formidable responsibility which the Colonial Office quickly vetoed.[1]

Restricted to policies based upon military non-intervention, D'Arcy did what he could to settle local conflicts; but Maba's influence continued to spread. The social egalitarianism which underlay his teaching was destroying much of the respect felt for the hereditary chiefs of the lower Gambia; yet the self-imposed limitations of British policy precluded any hope that the colonial government might exercise sufficient authority to fill the vacuum. So the situation deteriorated. In 1864 D'Arcy resorted, without permission, to minor military operations at Albreda, and also near MacCarthy's Island; and again he suggested military co-operation with the French. These alarming incidents warned the Colonial Office of their endemic risk of becoming involved in expensive annexations or 'little wars' in the Gambia.[2]

Lagos and its Neighbours

Further down the coast, near the large African states of the forest belt, there was danger that the wars would not remain very small. But here too British power was becoming more deeply committed; the commercial stakes were higher, and at Lagos Foreign Office policies of 'informal empire' were gradually modified in the direction of colonial control. This port, which commands the only easily navigable entrance to the long coastal lagoon which flanks the Bight of Benin, was a centre of clandestine slave trade in the 1840's, exporting prisoners captured during the wars of the Yoruba succession states. But Yoruba country was believed to be highly productive, and once

[1] C.O. 87/73, D'Arcy to Newcastle, 102, 22 May; 108, 16 June 1862; C.O. 87/74, D'Arcy to Newcastle, 123, 8 Aug.; 147, 24 Oct. 1862 and minutes, C.O. 87/76, D'Arcy to Newcastle, 172, 21 Feb.; 179, 24 March; Sep. 23 April; 184, 24 April 1863.
[2] C.O. 87/79, D'Arcy to Newcastle, Mil. 4, 22 Feb. 1864; D'Arcy to Cardwell, 43, 18 June; 44, 20 June; 46, 22 June 1864; C.O. 87/80, D'Arcy to Cardwell, 60, 22 Aug., Mil. 5, 16 Sept.; 74, 21 Nov. 1864.

pacified it might provide a strong political framework for the development of British commerce; control of Lagos might be the key which would admit British merchants to successful competition with the slave-traders through a rich and populous region. In 1851 traders and missionaries interested in the region induced Palmerston to authorize consular intervention in a succession dispute within the Lagos royal family. Kosoko, the ruling chief, was deposed in favour of the rival claimant Akitoye, who promised to suppress slaving and promote missionary work and trade in produce. For the next ten years the British attempted to maintain a dominant influence through a resident consul, with the Royal Navy in the background; but with imperfect success. Akitoye and his successor Dosumu proved weak and unpopular rulers; the merchants they were supposed to encourage complained that their property was unsafe, and that they could not recover debts; there were persistent rumours of slave exports. To remedy these conditions more direct British intervention seemed necessary, possibly extending beyond Lagos itself.

Many observers doubted whether slaving could be eradicated at Lagos without direct action against Dahomey, generally believed to be the main centre of that trade. Though figures of its extent are hard to come by, it is clear that slaves as well as palm-oil were shipped from Whydah even in the 1860's. Others passed through the small state of Porto Novo, whose capital lay sixty miles west of Lagos along the lagoon; it had been conquered by Dahomey during the eighteenth century, but the native dynasty had reasserted a rather precarious independence. To counter Dahomey's power many Britons, including Consul Beecroft and senior naval officers, favoured close collaboration with the Egba, who appeared so progressive and receptive to western culture. By 1851 the influence of Protestant missionaries and recaptives returning from Sierra Leone had assisted an anti-slavery party to gain ascendency in Abeokuta, reconstitute the government, and win a striking military victory over Dahomey. Hopes of working with the Egba supplied one major incentive for Britain's original intervention against Kosoko. In November 1860 the naval commander on the

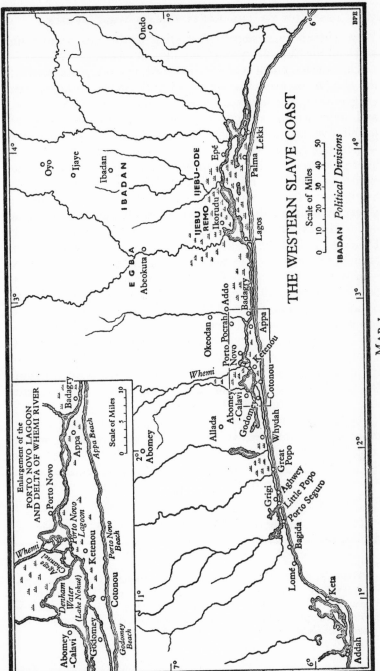

THE WESTERN SLAVE COAST

Scale of Miles

0   10   20   30   40   50

IBADAN *Political Divisions*

Enlargement of the
PORTO NOVO LAGOON
AND DELTA OF WHEMI RIVER

Scale of Miles

0   5   10

MAP I

West African coast suggested sending British officers to train and lead the Egba army in a full-scale campaign.[1]

This was too much even for an anti-slavery zealot like Russell; the Dahomean army was estimated to be 40,000 strong (a vast exaggeration, possibly attributable to the slavers of Whydah), and under-writing an Egba campaign seemed likely to involve prohibitive risks and expense. Yet unsupported naval pressure was ineffective. Blockading Dahomey in 1851–2 had led to international complications, without permanently checking the export of slaves or restraining the King from attacking his neighbours. Palmerston therefore proposed to assert British power by bringing the 'anomalous quasi-protectorate' of Lagos under direct British sovereignty. He hoped thus to check Dahomey's influence, sustain the Egba, assure the Lagos traders of more stable protection, and encourage neighbouring peoples to grow cotton for export: all for the cost of formalizing Britain's position on a small island where she already held ultimate responsibility. The Duke of Newcastle, foreseeing that difficult administrative problems would fall to the Colonial Office to solve, demurred for a time; but the Foreign Office, hoping that Lagos might provide a base for developing overland trade-routes towards the Niger, pressed their case.[2] On 6 August 1861 Dosumu was compelled to accept a pension and to cede sovereignty over Lagos to Great Britain.[3]

It soon became evident that this intervention created more problems than it solved. It had little effect on Dahomey, which continued to export slaves through Whydah. In November 1862 the new Commodore, Wilmot, went to Abomey to press Gelele to fulfil his promises to renounce the slave trade; but his mission proved fruitless and, in the opinion of Governor Freeman of

[1] C.O. 96/56, Edmonstone to Admty, 15 Nov. 1860; S.O. Biobaku, *op. cit.*, Chs. 3, 4, 5.

[2] C.O. 96/56, F.O. to C.O., 7 Feb.; 21 March; 10 June 1861, with minutes.

[3] Treaty printed in A. C. Burns, *History of Nigeria* (London, 1948) pp. 289 ff; cf. J. F. Ade Ajayi, 'The British Occupation of Lagos, 1851–61', *Nigeria*, No. 69, Aug. 1961; Gertzel, *op. cit.*, pp. 72–5. An important contribution which appeared after this book was completed is C. W. Newbury, *The Western Slave Coast and its Rulers* (Oxford, 1961).

Lagos, positively harmful to British prestige.[1] On 1 July 1862 Freeman proposed to coerce Dahomey by occupying a strip of coastline as far westwards as the Gold Coast border.[2] This was of course immediately vetoed; the British government had hoped that the occupation of Lagos would make such direct action unnecessary by encouraging a policy of collaboration with the Egba.

Although such a policy was favoured by many missionaries and naval officers it was unacceptable to certain Lagos merchants, notably William McCoskry, who did not wish to become exclusively dependent on the Egba for the expansion of either civilization or commerce. Their doubts were shared by Freeman, by his successor as Governor, J. H. Glover, and by Richard Burton, the noted traveller and pundit, who was British Consul at Fernando Po from 1861 to 1865. These men, rejecting any suggestion that evangelized states were the natural allies of Britain, maintained that in Yorubaland, 'all should have equal favour'. To avoid dependence on the Egba trade-routes they wished to encourage commerce with Ibadan through Ijebu-Ode. With a similar purpose in mind Benjamin Campbell, a former Consul at Lagos, had in 1854 affronted missionary opinion by turning to the former slave-trading ruler Kosoko, and recognizing him as ruler of Palma and Lekkie, trading-towns in the eastern lagoon, in return for promises to develop legitimate commerce.[3]

But after 1860 new wars among the Yoruba states restricted the commercial growth of Lagos, and made it increasingly difficult to operate any policy of 'equal favour'. Armies from Ibadan moved to restore the authority of a new Alafin of Oyo over the state of Ijaye; they were resisted by the Egba, jealous of Ibadan's growing power, and by Ijebu-Ode, the state which controlled the direct route from Ibadan to the coast. As it proved necessary to choose between the combatants, Burton,

---

[1] C.O. 147/2, draft instructions to Wilmot, 14 Nov. 1861; C.O. 147/1, Freeman to Newcastle, 70, 9 Dec. 1862.

[2] C.O. 147/1, Freeman to Russell, S.T. 12, 1 July 1862, encl. in Freeman to Newcastle, 27, 3 July.

[3] Biobaku, op. cit., pp. 49–51.

Freeman and Glover tended to the side of Ibadan. Burton in particular, a leader of the growing fashion for idealizing Muslim states, was contemptuous of the more superficial results of Christian missionary work among the Egba; in face of the progress of Islam among the northern Yoruba, he argued, 'those who support Abeokuta are but shoring up a falling wall.'[1] Moreover, Burton argued from his experience in the Niger delta that the Egba were aiming at a middleman's monopoly; mistaking the strength and purpose of the influence wielded by African traders in political decisions at Abeokuta, he argued that, 'puffed up by the attentions of England,' they aspired to control all transit trade, and so 'to change honest labour for the lazy life of brokers or middlemen'.[2] The Lagos authorities, debarred from direct action against Abeokuta, therefore prohibited all imports of firearms. Apparently an impartial measure, this actually worked to the disadvantage of the Egba and their allies, who would otherwise have had sole access to foreign armaments. When their missionary friends complained, Lagos replied with denunciations of Egba character and aims — to the astonishment of the Colonial Office, who had understood that one purpose of occupying Lagos had been to assist this Christian people. Henceforth, bewildered by these complexities of Yoruba politics, they automatically applied the brake to almost every proposal by Freeman or Glover for intervention inland.[3]

But along the coastal lagoon, practical arguments, less easily discounted, were leading to extensions of colonial control. Since Lagos could only pay for its administration by imposing customs duties, its governors were anxious to control all imports of goods intended for its commercial hinterland, wherever they might be landed. The Colonial Office was bound by its own

[1] R. F. Burton, *Abeokuta and the Camaroons Mountain* (London, 1863) Vol. 1, pp. 171, 224 ff.

[2] C.O. 147/2, Burton to Newcastle, 20 Nov. 1861. The best criticism of Burton's analysis is in A. A. B. Aderibigbe, *Expansion of the Lagos Protectorate, 1863–1900* (Ph.D. Thesis, London, 1959). Biobaku, *op. cit.*, p. 72, suggests that Burton failed to recognize that many Egba were agriculturists; in fact he calls them 'a race of farmers bred to moderate work'.

[3] C.O. 147/2, F.O. to C.O., 19 Nov. 1861; C.O. 147/1, Freeman to Newcastle, 20, 4 June 1862 and minute by Elliot.

financial principles to sympathize with this aim; yet the consequent extensions of boundary inevitably involved them more
deeply in Yoruba politics.

In June 1862 Freeman went to Badagry, a port much used by
the Egba; proclaimed that, historically, it formed part of the
territory of Lagos; and imposed the colonial tariff.[1] In February 1863 he turned eastwards and obtained from Kosoko the
cession of Palma and Lekkie. Again there was a dual purpose:
to supervise the route from the interior which terminated in
Ijebu-Ode as well as to obtain revenue. Freeman had just
revised the colonial tariff, raising the general rate of import duty
from 2% to 3% but imposing much higher specific rates on
wines, spirits, tobacco, guns and powder; this was resented by
foreign merchants, whose trade was largely in the goods named.[2]
The Marseille house of Régis had since 1855 cultivated close
relations with Kosoko, giving him generous trading credits in
the hope that he would offer them a port of entry beyond
British control; they were thus doubly struck by the application
of the new duties to their Palma trade. At their instigation the
military chief resident at Epe resisted British control; Freeman,
fearing French political intrusion, reduced his power by two
naval bombardments, and so secured the eastern section of the
lagoon under British control.[3]

But one key port on the lagoon still escaped British control.
Porto Novo also offered a route to Abeokuta and, many believed, to the Niger; oil- and slave-traders anxious to prevent a
Lagos monopoly were working to develop its independent outlets to the sea. Early in 1861 Consul Foote twice had the
town bombarded, claiming that this procedure would destroy
the slave traffic, re-open the palm-oil trade with Lagos, and
encourage Abeokuta in its struggle against Dahomey.[4] But, even
by Foote's own account, casualties in Porto Novo were heavy;

---

[1] C.O. 147/1, Freeman to Newcastle, 31, 9 July; 56, 9 October 1862.

[2] C.O. 147/3, Freeman to Newcastle, 7, 8 Jan.; 12, 10 Feb. 1863.

[3] P.P., 1863, XXXVIII, *Papers Relating to the Destruction of Epe*; C.O.
147/4, memo. by Freeman, 10 March 1863 (encl. in Conf. despatch of 10
Dec.); *MMC*, Gabon 1/2/b, Didelot to M.M.C., 54, 6 March; 56, 7 March
1863.

[4] P.P. 1861, LXV. *Papers relating to . . . Porto Novo*; Scotter, *op. cit.*, p. 92.

the chief result of this aggression was to strengthen the influence
of the anti-British party (led by Negro and mulatto traders from
Brazil) against those (Sierra Leoneans and itinerant Muslims)
who favoured closer connections with Lagos. King Soji, hoping
to resist further British pressure and also to obtain protection
against Dahomey, was therefore persuaded to place his country
under French protection by a treaty of 25 February 1863. The
French Admiral claimed that this action narrowly forestalled a
new attempt, inspired by McCoskry, to bring Porto Novo under
British control.[1]

Although this report cannot be confirmed from the Colonial
Office records, the loss of Porto Novo certainly jeopardized the
interests of Lagos. The town represented a channel through
which goods might be imported into Yorubaland without
paying duty at Lagos, and by which the blockade of Abeokuta
(extended in March 1863 to exclude all imports, not merely
firearms) might be evaded. Freeman only acquiesced in the
French protectorate after securing a promise of co-operation in
the maintenance of this blockade, and he watched developments
at Porto Novo with suspicion.[2] In June 1863 the local French
authorities extended their control eastwards to Appa and its
beach, thus securing direct, though difficult, access to the sea.
Glover, as acting Governor, feared their next step might be to
claim Badagry; Freeman had judged a treaty unnecessary, but
now an anti-British party was making headway. Glover therefore secured a formal treaty of cession there, and proceeded to
encircle the French position by further treaties with Pocrah,
which straddled the lagoon between Appa and Porto Novo
town, and with Addo and Oke-odan, which controlled the only
known route from Porto Novo to Abeokuta.[3] Colonial Office
anger at these new extensions was equalled only by that of the
French commandant at Porto Novo; there was a good deal of
tension locally until 1 August, when Glover reached an amicable *modus vivendi* with Didelot, the French naval commander on
the coast. A joint Commission was to mark out an Anglo-French

---

[1] *MMC*, Gabon 1/2/b, Didelot to M.M.C., 25 Feb. 1863. Below, pp. 110–15.
[2] C.O. 147/3, Freeman to Newcastle, 18, 2 March; 23, 8 March 1863.
[3] C.O. 147/3, Glover to Newcastle, 58, 9 July; 62, 10 July 1862.

boundary; meanwhile the British withdrew provisionally from Pocrah, leaving their claim in abeyance, while France definitely recognized British control of Addo, and so of the road to Abeokuta.[1] A tacit condition was that France would continue to co-operate in the blockade.[2]

So, within two years of occupying Lagos, the British government had been led to extend its control along most of the adjacent lagoons; to intervene indirectly in the Ijaye war, in a sense objectionable to the missionaries and their influential friends at Westminster; and to engage in sharp controversy with the French. These episodes may now appear minor incidents in a great and fruitful development of British influence in Yorubaland; but to most politicians and officials they merely illustrated the embarrassments consequent upon over-ready acceptance of advice from African governors. In September 1863, before any Parliamentary enquiry had been suggested, Rogers posed the question whether Lagos was to be

'a mere entrepot for trade and base and rendezvous for officers and vessels employed in the suppression of the Slave Trade, or whether it is to be a centre of more or less acknowledged empire, occupied by a force capable of protecting native tribes and interfering with effect in native quarrels.'

Between these alternatives, the Colonial Office would certainly choose the more restricted role. But while Fortescue, the Parliamentary Under-Secretary, hoped that 'it may . . . become a centre of British influence, without being the nucleus of an increasing dominion or protectorate',[3] Freeman believed that eventually the choice must lie between total evacuation and the gradual absorption of all surrounding countries.[4] He and Glover continued to intervene in the politics of Yorubaland, and especially in the foreign relations of the Egba, as actively as the tightening reins of Colonial Office control would allow.

[1] Text in *Etudes Dahoméennes*, IX (1953) pp. 13–15; C.O. 147/4, Glover to Newcastle, 68, 8 Aug. 1863; *MMC*, Gabon 1/2/b, Didelot to M.M.C., 7 Aug. 1863. (The enclosures are in Gabon IV/3/b.)

[2] *MMC*, Gabon IV/3/b, memo. by Zveppfel, 10 Feb. 1864.

[3] C.O. 147/5, F.O. to C.O., 5 Sept. 1863, minutes by Rogers, Fortescue.

[4] C.O. 147/6, Freeman to Newcastle, 1, 9 Jan. 1864.

The Gold Coast and the Ashanti War of 1863–4

The stimulus which ultimately compelled the British government to review their West African policy came from the Gold
Coast, a region where their responsibilities had been assumed
only gradually and unwillingly. The Crown first assumed direct
control of the British forts and factories on this coast in 1821,
relaxed it in 1828, resumed it in 1843, and even extended
it in 1850 by purchasing the Danish forts; but through all
these changes the aim of the Colonial Office was generally
to restrict its political responsibilities, withdrawing the tiny
garrisons from as many forts as possible and keeping small civil
establishments only at Cape Coast and Accra. In practice, however, it proved impossible to restrict the exercise of British
authority so narrowly. Since the forts existed primarily to
promote trade, strong ties of mutual interest were inevitably
created between their inhabitants and their immediate African
neighbours. Their Governors, recognizing that the value of the
forts depended on their success in encouraging commerce and
civilization through a much wider area, worked gradually to
promote order and security within the coastal region. A series of
treaties or 'Bonds', negotiated by George Maclean in 1844,
empowered the British government to supervise the administration of justice in many of the Fanti states near the coast. 'The
protection of individuals and property' and the abolition of 'barbarous customs' were acknowledged as goals, and British judicial
officers, sitting with the chiefs, assumed the responsibility of
'moulding the customs of the country to the general principles of
British law'. Similar arrangements were made with other states
in the following years, and after the transfer of the Danish forts in
1850 many Ga-speaking principalities in the east were included.
Though none of these treaties conferred political sovereignty the
British came to refer to the area they covered as 'the Protectorate'; soon it embraced most of the country south of Ashanti.[1]

[1] For details see W. E. F. Ward, *A History of Ghana* (London, 1958) pp.
189–200; cf. J. D. Fage, *Ghana: A Historical Interpretation* (Madison, 1959).
This summary of events on the Gold Coast relies heavily on these two
standard works and on Freda Wolfson, *British Relations with the Gold Coast,
1843–80* (Ph.D. Thesis, London, 1950).

But the economic basis for British suzerainty still remained defective. Though the area was by no means unproductive, no satisfactory export staple had yet been found to replace the slave trade. Gold production continued to disappoint the optimists; the developing palm-oil trade was centred in the east, and provided only about 4% of British needs. Some believed that government investment in roads and schools could greatly develop the wealth of the country, but this was not practicable within the framework of Treasury finance. In the other settlements, some revenue at least could be raised from customs duties; but so long as the Dutch, with their settlements interspersed among the British, refused to impose comparable duties, the imposition of a British tariff on the Gold Coast would simply have driven all imports destined for the interior into their hands. In 1852 an attempt was made to collect a poll-tax with the co-operation of the 'Protectorate' chiefs; but the British handled this delicate operation unskilfully, and it had to be abandoned nine years later. In 1860 the revenue collected in the settlements was £3947; Parliament, complaining bitterly, supplied an annual subsidy of £4000; the cost of the unimpressive administration was £9558.

In the long run, the crucial problem for the British on the Gold Coast, both politically and economically, was that of relations with Ashanti. British attitudes towards this state were divided. It was still imperfectly known, despite a series of European visits to Kumasi and the beginning of missionary work after 1839; its political organization seemed impressive, its customs and morality frighteningly unfamiliar and violent, and its military power quite clearly formidable. Many Europeans regarded it as a barbarous despotism, 'arbitrary, cruel, and sanguinary',[1] whose policy, if unchecked, would be to revive the slave trade (which was not extinct on the Volta river until the sixties), and to drive the British from the coast. But others thought of Ashanti as a rising power, capable of bringing order and peace to the region and of providing a great commercial market; once Ashanti had secured its legitimate object, a direct outlet to the sea, this school argued that the civilizing influences

[1] J. J. Crooks, *Records relating to the Gold Coast Settlements from 1750 to 1874* (Dublin, 1923) p. 355; R. Pine to Newcastle, 12 May 1863.

of Europe would quickly reform the less desirable social customs
of the people.

Unfortunately, the British government could not approach
this interesting problem impartially. Its commitments in the
settlements threw it into association with Fanti and other states
which had their own conflicts with Ashanti, both of interest and
tradition. Allies of Britain controlled most of the direct routes
from Ashanti to the sea (with the important exceptions of those
by Dutch Elmina, by Assinie in the west, and by the Volta
valley in the east); these states were able, not only to help
Britain check the export of slaves and regulate the supply of
firearms to Ashanti, but to profit from the role of commercial
middlemen. So when Ashanti put forward historic claims to
sovereignty over some of these states, or tried to obtain more
direct access to the coast, the British tended to become drawn
into opposition to her claims. Some governors handled such cases
with tact, and with some appreciation of the complexities of inter-
state relations on the Gold Coast; others proved less skilful.

In 1863 Governor Richard Pine, by his conscientious but
probably ill-advised refusal to return a fugitive slave and an
alleged criminal to Kumasi, provoked an Ashanti invasion of the
'protectorate'. Its early success revealed the critical military weakness of the British settlements, and led Pine to ask for reinforcements strong enough to strike 'a final blow' at Ashanti power by
marching on Kumasi. These reinforcements were sent, but the
campaign of 1864 proved a dismal fiasco. When the rains set in
early, thirteen British officers and forty-five troops died of fever,
and in May the British government called off the operations,
with little advantage gained for herself or her allies. No peace
treaty was made; Ashanti had been alienated but remained
undefeated. It had been a futile and disastrous campaign.

[4]

The Growth of Parliamentary Criticism,
and the Committee of 1865

The Ashanti campaign, and the incompetence with which it
appeared to have been conducted, stimulated the House of

Commons to show a little unwonted interest in West African affairs. On 17 June 1864 Sir John Hay, a former naval officer who sat as Conservative Member for Wakefield, and whose brother had died during the campaign, moved a resolution implying censure on the Palmerston ministry. Most speakers in this debate, understanding nothing of the African background, concentrated on criticizing the administrative and medical arrangements which had been made for the military operations; General Peel compared the muddle to that in the Crimea. Normal supporters of the ministry joined in the attack; only one private member spoke in its defence, and Hay's motion was defeated by only 233 votes to 226. And it was already notable that some Conservatives attacked, not merely the military measures, but the whole imbroglio with Ashanti as a deplorably logical consequence of 'meddling' and accepting political responsibilities in Africa. On 18 July Hay moved a reduction of vote for civil establishments in West Africa. C. B. Adderley now spoke strongly against the 'wasteful and mischievous' policy of 'sentimental colonization' in West Africa, and gave notice that at the start of the following session he would propose the appointment of a Select Committee of enquiry. There had been hostile investigations of African policy earlier in the century, but these had usually been inspired by some sectional interest; the hostility aroused by the Ashanti fiasco appeared to represent broader currents of political criticism.

It is well-known that the 1860's were a period when interest in colonial problems was low among British politicians. Many seemed indifferent to the maintenance of constitutional links even with the colonies of white settlement, and strongly hostile if there was any question of continuing to pay for their local defence out of the British Treasury. If relatively few followed Goldwin Smith in actually advocating separation between the United Kingdom and her colonies, many believed that separation was likely to come in any case, and that this would be no disaster.[1] When such views influenced British relations with Canada and the Australian colonies, it is not surprising that the

[1] On this subject, see C. A. Bodelsen, *Studies in Mid-Victorian Imperialism* (N.Y., 1925) Ch. 1.

West African settlements should come under heavy fire as soon as they involved British taxpayers in substantial sacrifice. When Adderley turned his guns upon them, his criticisms carried the weight of his reputation as an earnest and constructive (though sometimes tediously dogmatic) student of general colonial policy.

A pious and conscientious country gentleman, Adderley had been Conservative Member for North Staffordshire since 1841, and a junior minister in 1858. He scored his first Parliamentary success in 1849 by resisting a proposed penal settlement in Cape Colony; thereafter he became Secretary of the Society for Reform of Colonial Government, and formulated some rather simple principles of colonial policy. The first article was the importance of economy in Imperial expenditure, a point sufficiently popular to win support from politicians of very varied views.[1] But Adderley looked beyond the self-interest of British tax-payers, claiming that colonies which depended on Parliamentary subsidies would inevitably lack moral qualities of self-reliance. Insistence on financial self-sufficiency was linked with the assertion of the right of self-government, which Adderley regarded as 'the normal current of colonial history'. Once the principle of full colonial responsibility in politics and finance had been established, he looked to the re-establishment of imperial unity on a firmer foundation.[2]

These colonial principles seemed immediately applicable only to the territories of European settlement. Adderley was less interested in colonies whose people he judged incapable of equal citizenship; they were difficult to fit into his Procrustean bed. Some, like the West Indies, might in time recover the conditions necessary for representative government; others, of strategic importance, might properly be retained under Crown authority; but colonies wished upon the country by the

[1] cf. W. S. C. Pemberton, *Life of Lord Norton* (London, 1909) p. 89, Cobden to Adderley, 29 Nov. 1850.

[2] C. B. Adderley, *Letter to the Right Hon. Benjamin Disraeli, M.P. on the Present Relations of England with the Colonies* (London, n.d., c. 1862). In his old age — he lived until 1905 — Adderley simultaneously found himself supporting Irish Home Rule and the colonial policies of Joseph Chamberlain.

misguided philanthropists of Exeter Hall had no evident justification. Adderley did not believe that they effectively promoted commerce, civilization, or even the suppression of the slave trade. Indeed, they might actually be hindering these causes. Like other critics of British African policy Adderley believed that the government should seek to ally itself with strong native states, capable of providing foreign merchants with extensive markets and secure conditions of trade. When it came to identifying these prospective allies, ignorance of African conditions left Adderley in some difficulties; the Muslim states of the Sudan might fill the role eventually, but nearer at hand Ashanti and possibly Dahomey seemed to offer the best prospects, unsatisfactory though some of their national institutions might appear to British eyes. Yet the Colonial Office, because of its commitments to the Fanti peoples of the Gold Coast, was actually obstructing Ashanti's efforts to reach the coast, and so interfering with the process of natural selection. The fiasco of 1863–4 was thus the last straw which provoked Adderley into a general attack upon 'the mistaken policy we had adopted upon that coast'; his Parliamentary Committee was intended to prove the case for withdrawal from most of the West African settlements, but certainly from the Gold Coast.[1]

Though respected for his sincerity, Adderley was a figure of the second rank, whom many politicians found rather boring. Before his Committee was constituted he found an influential ally in Edward, Lord Stanley, later fifteenth Earl of Derby, and at this time a serious candidate for the Conservative leadership.[2] In discussing such questions as political reform, religious tests, education, and sanitary reform, Stanley had displayed considerable capacities for constructive criticism and

[1] *Hansard*, 3rd series, CLXXVI, 1670–4, CLXXVII, 535–45, for Adderley's speeches of 18 July 1864, 21 Feb. 1865. For a general statement of his views, based on a book review published in 1853, but expanded for separate publication after his experience as Under-Secretary to the Colonial Office, see his *Review of 'The Colonial Policy of Lord John Russell's Administration' by Earl Grey, and of Subsequent Colonial History* (London, 1869) esp. pp. 13, 195–218.

[2] W. D. Jones, *Lord Derby and Victorian Conservatism* (Oxford, 1956) pp. 282–3.

unconventional thought;[1] unfortunately for his future reputation his ministerial career was to be devoted entirely to external affairs. Having refused to be Palmerston's Colonial Secretary in 1855, he held that post for a short period in his father's government of 1858, before becoming the first Secretary of State for India. Though this was not yet evident, his talents were not well suited to the direction of Imperial policy; in the words of Lecky,

> 'His clear perception of the objections to any course, combined with a very deep sense of responsibility, not infrequently enfeebled his will in moments when bold and decisive action was required.'[2]

On West African affairs at least, however, Stanley's opinions seemed fairly definite. Earlier contacts with West Indian planters had made him scornful of schemes of African philanthropy; the deep aversion from war, which had coloured his attitude during the Crimean campaign, made him oppose colonial military adventures. Supporting Adderley's motion for a Committee, he referred to the waste of lives and money involved in the maintenance of the African naval squadron.

> 'I do not believe,' he said, 'there is a year or even a month that passes in which the service on that coast does not put an end to some life among our officers which, measured by any rational standard of comparison, is worth more than the merely animal existence of a whole African tribe.'

As for the settlements, he expressed fears about 'the responsibility you have undertaken, and the limit of which you do not know, and nobody knows'. It was possible, though doubtful, that the settlements were promoting trade; but this should be the subject of factual enquiry.[3]

Though both Adderley and Stanley sat as Conservatives, their aims in many matters such as this lay across the loose party lines of the period. Stanley's opposition to the Crimean war and Adderley's zeal for economy in colonial policy, among other

[1] *ibid.*, pp. 193–5, 245–8; T. H. Sanderson and E. S. Roscoe (eds.), *Speeches and Addresses of Edward Henry, XVth Earl of Derby* (2 Vols.; London, 1894).

[2] *ibid.* Prefatory memoir by W. E. H. Lecky, p. xv.

[3] *Hansard*, 3rd series, CLXXVII, 550–3.

things, had already led both men into co-operation with Manchester radicals; in mid-Victorian politics an alliance of extremes was often a serious possibility. It was natural enough that Adderley, having decided to press for a Committee, should seek the collaboration of John Bright, with whom he had worked on a Slave Trade Committee in 1853. And Bright strongly agreed that the time was ripe for a critical enquiry into West African policy:

> 'for there is evidently a more reasonable temper in the House on questions of this sort than formerly prevailed, and the evil principles so long taught by Lord Palmerston seem to be losing their influence.'

But he asked to be excused the labour of serving personally on the Committee; as substitute he proposed W. E. Baxter, an economical and pacific Dundee merchant who sat for Montrose Burghs, whom Bright regarded as 'acute and well-informed and a good man of business'.[1]

Among the other Members eventually appointed to Adderley's Committee were men disposed to support radical retrenchment in West Africa for curiously varied reasons. There was Hay, shocked by the Ashanti campaign into demanding disengagement; Arthur Mills, a Conservative with whom Adderley had worked in a Select Committee on Colonial Military Expenditure in 1861,[2] who condemned 'the indefinite expenditure involved in protecting native tribes'; Sir Francis Baring, an elderly Whig, who spoke for the Church Missionary Society in deploring the hostility shown to the Egba mission by the new colonial authorities in Lagos.[3] From the criticisms voiced by these and other Members in the debate of 18 July, it might seem that there was very general support for Adderley's objectives.

[1] Pemberton, *op. cit.*, p. 189, Bright to Adderley, 25 Aug. 1864. For the attitude of free trade radicals to naval operations against the slave trade, see Lloyd, *op. cit.*, pp. 107–13.

[2] On this, see R. L. Schuyler, *The Fall of the Old Colonial System* (N.Y., 1945) pp. 225–7.

[3] *Hansard*, 3rd series, CLXXVI, 1658–81. Speeches by Baring, Hay, Mills; also by W. Williams, J. Whiteside, 18 July 1864.

D

But this appearance was misleading. Even if it could have been conclusively demonstrated that all African colonies were costly, dangerous, and unprofitable, not all M.P.s would have agreed to abandon them like worn-out clothes. Palmerston was still Prime Minister; and the notion that national interests were served by flying the national flag had not been completely obliterated by Manchester economics. Disraeli, for example, though still tending to regard colonies as 'millstones' rather than as sources of Imperial power, was too astute a politician to identify himself openly with Adderley's campaign. When invited to do so, he replied:

> 'I agree with you very much in your general views respecting our Colonies, but I can't conceal from myself that the country is not yet ripe for them. It has been so long accustomed to the idea of what they call Colonial Empire, and the power and profit which they erroneously associate with their obsolete conceptions, that it is in the highest degree painful and perplexing for them to contemplate the altered relations which now exist between the metropolis and its settlements. I think we could count on no united party support in favour of a resolution which on such matters asserted a principle; but a Committee of Inquiry, as you contemplate, is another affair, and in my opinion it would be a favourable move. . . .'[1]

Even at the height of the anti-imperialist reaction, a hard substratum of patriotic fervour made many British politicians reluctant to contemplate the abandonment of territory. Thus on 18 July 1864 the Liberal Henry Seymour attacked Adderley's arguments in terms which illustrate the danger of dogmatizing about the attitudes of mid-Victorian Liberals to empire. Adderley, declared Seymour,

> 'was riding his hobby too hard when he designed to confine England to the limit of these islands; it seemed to him absurd to talk of restraining this nation within such narrow limits . . . the natural course of a people so powerful, vigorous and enterprising as that of England was to expand and occupy nearly every region of the

---

[1] Pemberton, *op. cit.*, p. 188, Disraeli to Adderley, 13 Sept. 1864; cf. W. F. Moneypenny and G. E. Buckle, *Life of Benjamin Disraeli* (London, 1910–20) Vol. IV, p. 329, Disraeli to Adderley, 26 Jan. 1862.

world; and if Napoleon had seen the present wealth, power and influence of this country in all parts of the world, he would have approved of the policy of the British Government for the last thirty or forty years. . . . Instead of restricting our present policy, he would extend it still further . . . he should be prepared to prove that our expenditure all over the world was returned to us a hundred-fold by the prosperity of our colonies and possessions.[1]

Such expressions of national pride and confidence were reinforced by the residual zeal of the anti-slavery zealots. Lord Alfred Churchill, a Conservative converted to the support of Palmerston, was the only private Member to defend the government in the debate of 17 June. His concern to do good in Africa even led him to advocate expansion there; as chairman of the African Aid Society (a philanthropic body with commercial connections) Churchill was continually besieging government offices with schemes for extending British rule south of the Sherbro, or to 'place Christian coloured families from Canada on the lands at the foot of the Cameroon mountain'.[2] Adderley's attack on 'sentimental colonization' would not go unopposed.

*   *   *   *   *

How far the Colonial Office itself would go in resisting it was at first not certain. Its staff, while sympathizing with many of the strictures passed upon the expansionist tendencies of African governors, did not wish the Committee to reach its conclusions without full knowledge of those purposes which the settlements did actually serve. Since the debate of Hay's motion took place too late in the session for Adderley's Committee to be constituted at once, the period until Parliament re-assembled in February 1865 could be used for preparatory study. So in October Colonel Henry Ord, an engineer officer with West African experience, currently on extended leave from the governorship of Bermuda, was hurriedly despatched on a tour of the settlements.

Despite the short time available for his investigation, Ord's

---

[1] *Hansard*, 3rd series, CLXXVI, 1674–6.
[2] e.g. C.O. 267/282, Churchill to Newcastle, 31 March 1864; C.O. 267/279, African Aid Society to Palmerston, 31 Dec. 1862 (copy).

terms of reference were broad. He was to examine all aspects of conditions in the settlements, but especially problems involving relations with their African neighbours, and the possibility of administrative economies.[1] He was also sent, presumably as some indication of officially-favoured views, a long despatch which Blackall had written from Freetown after the Parliamentary discussions. Blackall defended the settlements' achievements in checking the slave trade, and even hinted that territorial expansion along the coast (as distinct from the acquisition of ill-defined protectorates inland) might bolster colonial revenues and 'lead to increased powers of self-support'. He also suggested that by employing steamships for communications with and within West Africa it would be possible to bring the governments of the settlements, so tiresome in recent years, under more effective central control. Blackall suggested appointing a single, powerful Governor-in-Chief, resident in Freetown, but with steamers under his control which he would use to supervise personally the affairs of all four colonies. For this responsible post, it was not difficult to see, Blackall would gladly offer his own candidature.[2]

Ord's activities during his African journey do not appear to have been recorded in detail. Though his time was short, he was familiar with the coast, and appears to have directed his en quiries fairly purposefully. The report which he submitted to Cardwell on 9 March 1865 seems to have provided satisfactorily concrete support for the general approach to West Africa which was already coming into official favour.[3] He supported Blackall's scheme for the union of the colonies, and hoped that improved administration would allow them to achieve financial self-sufficiency. He refused to recommend territorial withdrawal from Koya, Sherbro, MacCarthy's Island or the Gold Coast. In general, he concluded, the settlements 'satisfactorily attain the principal objects for which they are maintained'; their abandonment would bring risks of damage to British commerce and

[1] C.O. 267/282, F.O. to C.O., 24 Oct. 1864; Cardwell to Ord, 25 Oct. 1864.
[2] C.O. 267/281, Blackall to Cardwell, 129, 21 Sept. 1864 and minutes.
[3] It is printed in *P.P.*, 1865, V.

revival of the slave trade. More than this: Ord even re-introduced a little humanitarian fervour into the discussion. By promoting:

> 'the abolition of human sacrifice, and other similar barbarous practices, the removal of that oppression and injustice which too often attend the administration of the native laws, and the intro-duction of such modifications into the laws and customs regarding domestic slaves as shall at least lead to some improvement in their condition . . . there has been spread widely abroad an appreciation of the superiority of European civilisation, and of the advantages it brings with it, the results of which, . . . will be seen hereafter.'

Though Elliot and others might doubt whether such hopes would ever be realized in places like Bulama, Ord's report was accepted by the Colonial Office and used as an official document before the Parliamentary Committee. Ord himself appeared as a depart-mental witness, and his evidence was carefully 'led' by Chichester Fortescue, the Parliamentary Under-Secretary. The office would not support adventures, or willingly extend its territories; but its existing responsibilities were not to be hastily abandoned.

Yet the Parliamentary Committee, as appointed in March 1865, was initially somewhat biased against even so reasonable an approach. Adderley, though a conspicuous partisan, was appointed chairman; he frequently began the examination of witnesses with leading questions, designed to show what en-tanglements necessarily followed from the exercise of territorial power. To support his thesis that trade and missionary work could flourish without direct European protection, Adderley sought diligently for information about any African state which might be capable of providing an extended *pax* under its own 'strong native government'. The Oil Rivers of course served him as *locus classicus*; since no representative of the Foreign Office sat on the Committee, witnesses could be encouraged to praise the informal system of supervision exercised there without fear of expert examination about its limitations and disadvantages. Elsewhere, not only Ashanti and the Muslim states to its north, but Liberia, and Manna's chiefdom in the Gallinas, were in turn cast in the role of 'strong native government'.[1] And,

[1] *P.P.*, 1865, V, Questions 3246 ff, 7396, 5927; 2771, 6916 ff; 4919–22; 4386–95; 4622–3.

though he had earlier expressed the fashionable contempt for Sierra Leoneans, Adderley was even prepared to seek the basis for his new political order in the grant of self-government to the 'educated natives' of the coast.[1]

Adderley's preparation had ensured the presence among the seventeen members of the Committee of several men sympathetic to his general views, though for oddly assorted reasons. There were the Conservatives Hay, Mills, and Fitzgerald; there was Bright's friend Baxter and the Whig Baring, a high-principled Anglican who had opposed action against Kosoko when at the Admiralty in 1851. Baring's hope was that missionary education, not colonial rule, might 'create governments in Africa which may themselves get rid of the slave trade'.[2] Adderley's most influential ally, Stanley, was often brutally forthright in his interrogation of witnesses; only he was prepared to press really hard upon David Livingstone, in order to demonstrate how little that national hero actually knew of conditions in Western Africa.[3] Profoundly sceptical about the idea of promoting African self-government,[4] Stanley was particularly scathing towards witnesses who spoke of 'moral obligations' in such places as the Gold Coast protectorate. Did these obligations include the prohibition of domestic slavery? If not, this would mean tolerating 'a principle which is repugnant to English ideas'; but if so, 'do you not entirely subvert the principles on which African society rests?'.[5]

Against such criticisms the settlements were defended by officials and philanthropists. There were three Ministers on the Committee; Hartington (who represented the War Office, and took little part in proceedings), Cardwell, and Chichester Fortescue, who assumed the main responsibility for examining witnesses on behalf of the Colonial Office. Seven years as Under-Secretary had made Fortescue sufficiently well acquainted with West African problems to demonstrate some of the practical

[1] *ibid.*, qq. 3012 ff, 3051–3, 3146, 3180–9.
[2] *ibid.*, qq. 8059–60; cf. R. J. Gavin, *loc. cit.*
[3] *ibid.*, qq. 5665 ff.
[4] *ibid.*, qq. 3081–2, 3705–16, 3778, 4473, 5002 ff.
[5] *ibid.*, qq. 986, 3093 ff.

objections to any immediate withdrawal of the settlements. He was particularly successful in suggesting that even if a policy of non-intervention did encourage the emergence of 'strong native powers', these might well prove more disposed to engage in slave-raiding than in commerce.[1]

Four unofficial members of the Committee were already on record as favouring, with varying enthusiasm, the maintenance of the settlements. Lord Alfred Churchill was most active in attendance and interrogation; his questions seemed to favour territorial extensions, as well as financial support for the Niger trade. The Liberal Charles Buxton, third son of the abolitionist leader, seems to have occupied a rather similar position, though he sustained it less actively in Committee. Henry Seymour asked some shrewd and informed questions, revealing his conviction that the settlements were promoting, not merely commercial development, but 'a social and moral revolution' in African society. Stephen Cave, Conservative chairman of the West India Committee, though critical of misapplied philanthropy, believed that withdrawal would settle nothing, and might permit a revival of slave exports to foreign sugar plantations.[2]

Three members may have entered the Committee with relatively open minds, and become converted to support of the settlements by the evidence they heard: W. H. Gregory, a Peelite supporter of Palmerston; John Cheetham, a hard-headed Liberal cotton manufacturer from Stalybridge; and, most important, W. E. Forster. A Yorkshire woollen manufacturer of Quaker descent, blunt, forthright, a tireless enemy of slavery, Forster spoke for the middle-class Victorian sense of duty. Long convinced that 'we must not abdicate the duty which our right as the strong and the wise gives us to rule the weak and the ignorant',[3] Forster nevertheless spent the early meetings of the Committee in seeking factual information. Then, on 30 March, he asked Ord a series of searching questions

[1] *ibid.*, qq. 2780–3, 3366–70, 5329–32, 5665, 8288–90.

[2] *ibid.*, qq. 4783, 5006 ff, 6051–6. For earlier speeches by these men; cf. above, pp. 69–71; *Hansard*, 3rd series, CLXI, 950–74 (Cave, Buxton, Churchill, 26 Feb. 1861); CLXXVII, 545–7 (Cave, 21 Feb. 1865).

[3] T. Wemyss Reid, *Life of W. E. Forster* (London, 1889) Vol. I, p. 287. This is a comment on the 'Kaffir war' of 1852.

about the probable effects of British withdrawal from the Gold
Coast. Ord replied that withdrawal — perhaps even a tight
restriction of British jurisdiction to the forts —

> 'would lead to the probable conquest of the country by the King
> of Ashantee, its subjection to the barbarous and bloody practices
> of the Ashantees, and probably to a large slave trade being carried
> on . . . [it would] . . . entirely destroy the influence of the British
> name on that coast.'

The general argument which was most clearly brought forward
by these questions was, according to the later opinion of a
perspicacious official, a decisive deterrent against any recommendation for general withdrawal.[1]

But disagreement within the Committee still remained. On
22 June, when all evidence had been heard, Adderley produced
a lengthy draft report which dogmatized about past policy,
summarily prohibited further expansion, and, while reluctantly
deciding against immediate withdrawal even from the Gold
Coast, proposed 'immediate reduction and consolidation' as an
earnest of future intentions.[2] On Seymour's motion this controversial document was laid aside in favour of decisions to be
taken by resolution, apparently on the ground that it was too
late in the session for full discussion.[3] Adderley then prepared
six draft resolutions, five of which were accepted unchanged by
the Committee. Among other things these recognized that total
withdrawal was nowhere possible; recommended the evacuation of troops from MacCarthy's Island; and proposed to unite
the four settlements under one Governor-in-Chief. But Adderley's third and most important resolution was on Cardwell's
motion amended in two particulars. Adderley's proposal was:

> 'that all further extension of territory or assumption of govern-
> ment, or new treaties offering any protection to native tribes,
> would be inexpedient; and that the object of our policy should be
> to transfer to the natives the administration of all the governments

[1] *P.P.* 1865, V, qq. 1063–72; cf. C.O. 806/12, memo. by Hemming,
1 April 1874.
[2] *ibid.*, pp. x–xvi.
[3] C.O. 87/85, minute by Adderley, 13 Oct. 1866 on Blackall to Carnarvon,
20 July.

with a view to our ultimate withdrawal from all except, probably, Sierra Leone.'

In the adopted version the promotion of self-government was recognized to be a long-term solution: 'the object of our policy' was now to be

> 'to encourage in the natives the exercise of those qualities which may render it possible for us more and more to transfer to the natives. . . .'

And an important qualification was added to the whole paragraph:

> 'That this policy of non-extension admits of no exception, as regards new settlements, but cannot amount to an absolute prohibition of measures which, in peculiar cases, may be necessary for the more efficient and economical administration of the settlements we already possess.'[1]

In form and in fact, the recommendations of this somewhat notorious Committee were thus a compromise. Such an assorted and imperfectly-informed group of politicians could hardly have been expected to produce precise directives for the conduct of policy; apart from directing the evacuation of MacCarthy's Island and endorsing Blackall's scheme for uniting the colonies, they agreed only in forbidding the establishment of new settlements. They failed to support withdrawal from the Gold Coast, which even Blackall and Elliot favoured;[2] and their recommendations concerning future frontier policy were so widely drawn as to remain capable of widely different applications.

Possibly the Committee's discussions had most influence on policies for the protection of British interests outside the colonial boundaries. Some changes in these would in any case have fol-

---

[1] *P.P.* 1865, V, p. xvi. Robinson, Gallagher and Denny, *op. cit.*, p. 30, regard the exemption of Sierra Leone as a genuflection towards the humanitarians. This seems unlikely; most humanitarians would have been happy to see the goal of African self-government achieved there. More probably Sierra Leone was excepted because the Navy had come to appreciate the value of Freetown harbour; and because the Colony had temporarily achieved a balanced budget and an expanding trade.

[2] C.O. 87/86, Blackall to Cardwell, 4 June 1866, minute by Elliot, 13 July.

D*

lowed Palmerston's death; the new generation of politicians was notably less willing to subsidize development or use warships in the interests of 'civilization and commerce'. But the Committee's examination of the concept of 'strong native government', inadequate and ill-informed though it was, provided a clue which Ministers seized upon for guidance through the perplexing problems of African politics. On the Gold Coast serious attempts were made to find a basis for peaceful co-existence with Ashanti; at Abeokuta, the Egba enjoyed another period of favour (though not from all British officials) in their attempt to re-organize their government with the help of agents returned from Sierra Leone.[1] On the Niger, British traders were at first left to advance the commercial frontier without subsidies, and even, after 1869, without a resident Consul; but in 1871 a special envoy, W. H. Simpson, was sent to negotiate terms for the protection of British trade with the 'strong native government' of Emir Masaba of Nupe.

But such policies suffered from one inherent weakness, more or less serious in different areas. Collaboration with any African government meant collaboration with the *de facto* authority, and implied support of that authority against minority interests and enemies, both internal and external. To work with Nupe involved opening the Niger navigation by repeated naval expeditions against the delta middlemen; it also involved accepting restrictions imposed by Masaba against deeper penetration among the states of the Fulani empire.[2] As a short-term policy, the 'strong native power' theory might work more or less conveniently; but in the long run it could entangle the British government just as seriously as the settlements did.

[5]
The Consequences of the Parliamentary Committee

So far as the Colonial Office was concerned, the final form of the Committee's resolutions represented fairly accurately the

[1] S. O. Biobaku, *op. cit.*, pp. 78 ff.
[2] J. E. Flint, *op. cit.*, pp. 24–7. Below, pp. 272–3.

prevailing views of that department itself. Since 1861 the perils
and difficulties attendant upon colonial rule in Africa had been
no less evident to officials than to colonial reformers and econo-
mizers; Cardwell's amendments had been concerned less to
refute Adderley in principle than to prevent his Committee
from issuing over-rigid directives. In the view that territory
should not be extended, that self-government should be encouraged, and that withdrawal should be envisaged as an
ultimate objective, there was nothing to trouble the convictions
of Cardwell or Fortescue, Rogers or Elliot.

This does not mean that the resolutions had no effect upon
policy. Principles hitherto tacitly accepted and empirically
applied were now endorsed by the authority of the House of
Commons. When, later in 1865, the governors of Sierra Leone
and Lagos sought authority to make small extensions in the
Mellacourie river and at Porto Novo, permission was refused
immediately and uncompromisingly. No doubt if officials had
given these proposals full and unprejudiced examination, their
decision would have been the same; the point is that they had
been absolved from the need for any such examination. The
period during which the resolutions retained their over-riding
authority had ended by 1874; but during those nine years, in
the opinion of a younger official of different views, they 'fettered
the hands of Her Majesty's Government, and hampered its action
in pursuing a firm and distinct policy towards the natives'.[1]

On those few points where the resolutions were precise, action
was quickly taken. The union of the settlements was effected by
the issue of a new Charter in February 1866; Blackall was
appointed first Governor-in-Chief, continuing to reside at
Freetown. This did not prove a very satisfactory arrangement.
The steamer assigned to enable Governors-in-Chief to visit their
three out-stations tempted them (when it was in working order)
to exercise a more direct control over the policies of their
Lieutenant-Governors (who were in some cases known also as
Administrators). But only a telegraph would have allowed the
Governor-in-Chief to maintain that control between visits; in its
absence, policy in the out-stations often vacillated.

[1] C.O. 806/12, memo. by Hemming, 1 April 1874.

Encouraging African self-government proved even more difficult. Adderley seems to have vaguely imagined new developments out of traditional African institutions;[1] officials did not look beyond the existing Legislative Councils, conventional institutions of Crown Colony government. These bodies, recently reinforced by their first African members, served to give governors independent advice on legislation and to allow grievances to be aired free from the taint of faction; but any real transfer of authority to Africans through such channels clearly lay far ahead.[2] Yet official thinking, recently perturbed by alarming events in Jamaica, would not tolerate any alternative claimant to constitutional authority within the settlements. When repeated protests from John Aggery, town chief of Cape Coast, against the Administrator's policy seemed to be amounting to such a claim, they became 'seditious and menacing proceedings'; in December 1866 Aggery was deposed and deported to Freetown. Nobody in London thought this seriously improper; no question was asked in Parliament. The Colonial Office, though Adderley was now its Under-Secretary, regarded Aggery as merely 'an insolent, ignorant and stubborn man', his supporters as 'Chartists and Fenians'.[3] Hardly anybody reflected that, if an early transfer of responsibility was seriously intended, it might even be desirable to encourage constitutional pretensions on the part of those who combined a little western education with a recognized status in African society. Nobody took early self-government seriously.

Since 'withdrawal' had been envisaged as following 'self-government', the prospects of this remained even more remote. But at least further advances by over-enterprising governors could be discouraged. A proclamation by the governor of the Gold Coast which defined British territory as extending for five

[1] Adderley, Review . . . , p. 214.

[2] cf. Hargreaves, op. cit., Sierra Leone Studies, n.s. V (1955); and more generally M. Wight, The Development of the Legislative Council (London, 1946).

[3] The best account of Aggery is F. Wolfson, British Relations with the Gold Coast, 1843–80 (Ph.D. thesis, London, 1950); cf. J. J. Crooks, Records . . . pp. 376–82; Ward, op. cit., pp. 234–5; H. L. Hall, The Colonial Office (London, 1937) pp. 206–8.

miles around the forts of Cape Coast, Accra, Annamabo and Dixcove was repudiated by Cardwell; the offender was warned not to encourage hopes of protection in traders operating beyond the forts themselves.[1] Even tighter control over expansive tendencies seemed likely when Lord Derby formed a Conservative government in July 1866. Stanley was Foreign Secretary; Disraeli at the Treasury was urging the Prime Minister to concentrate the employment of British resources at essential points — to

> 'leave the Canadians to defend themselves; recall the African squadron; give up the settlements on the West Coast of Africa';[2]

and Adderley, installed at last as Under-Secretary at the Colonial Office, quickly turned his attention to West Africa.

MacCarthy's Island

Adderley's first concern was the evacuation of MacCarthy's Island, which, though one of the few precise recommendations of his Committee, was proving difficult to effect. In August 1865, when this proposal was made known in Bathurst, there were protests from the merchants, and from 170 residents on the island itself. Even Elliot now thought the decision 'rather hard upon people who have settled on this spot on the faith of its occupation by Great Britain many years ago'; but the Parliamentary directive was too clear to be questioned, and the order to withdraw the garrison was confirmed.[3]

But the traders and settlers on the island showed no intention of withdrawing themselves, even though the neighbouring country was politically disturbed; to the concern of the Colonial Office, D'Arcy reported that they were planning to create a militia. Military withdrawal had merely revived the old problem of British responsibility for the physical protection of private

[1] Crooks, op. cit., pp. 371–4, Cardwell to Conran, 23 Nov. 1865; Wolfson, op. cit., pp. 129 ff.

[2] Moneypenny and Buckle, op. cit., Vol. IV, pp. 475–6, Disraeli to Derby, 30 Sept. 1866.

[3] C.O. 87/82, D'Arcy to Cardwell, 140, 21 Aug.; 141, 23 Aug. 1865, with minutes.

citizens trading outside the colonial boundary.[1] Cardwell's first
inclination was to leave the inhabitants of the island to look
after themselves; the Colonial Office, far from applauding the
enterprise of those who chose to trade in remote places, was
coming to regard their activities with suspicion.[2] But Forster,
who became Under-Secretary for a short period, pointed out that

'the information obtained since the Committee makes it impossible
for us to withdraw altogether from MacCarthy's Island without
disgraceful disregard of our responsibilities',

and eventually a precarious compromise was accepted, on lines
proposed by Blackall. A civil commandant was appointed to live
on the island, with a small detachment of civil police, and to
command the volunteer militia; the few remaining military
stores, together with the decrepit colonial steamer *Dover*, were
handed over to the merchants to use for their own protection.[3]

When Adderley discovered that the garrison but not the flag
had been withdrawn from MacCarthy's Island, he accepted
this interpretation of his Committee's recommendations with
very bad grace. Recognizing that so long as British subjects
continued to trade in the troubled country up-river there would
always be danger of a new frontier war, he began to talk wildly
of transferring sovereignty to 'the fittest neighbouring native
power'. At first he hoped to find a suitable Muslim state. Sharing
the fashionable belief that the 'Marabouts' were likely eventually to overcome the 'Soninkes', and that they would provide
stronger government and better markets, he was much perturbed by D'Arcy's hostility towards them; it seemed liable to
'rhodomontade us into another war'. When it proved difficult
to identify a Muslim state capable of co-operating in the protection of British trade, Adderley began to speak of 'cultivating
French intervention' in the Gambia, as well as in rivers further

[1] C.O. 87/84, D'Arcy to Cardwell, Mil. 6, 20 Jan.; 175, 23 April 1866,
with minutes.

[2] e.g. C.O. 267/275, minute by Elliot, 17 Nov. 1862, on F.O., 6 Nov.;
C.O. 267/290, minute by Adderley, 24 July 1867, on Blackall 29 June.

[3] C.O. 87/84, Blackall to Cardwell, 26 April 1866; Cardwell to Blackall,
19, 23 May; D'Arcy to Cardwell, 2, 21 May, minute by Forster; précis by
Elliot, 12 July 1866.

south. Such projects were not practical politics. In April 1867 Adderley's superior, the Duke of Buckingham and Chandos, decided it was impossible to restrict British responsibility for MacCarthy's Island any further; this opinion was confirmed by his Liberal successor in 1871.[1]

The Bulama arbitration

The Conservatives did eventually initiate a change of policy over Bulama. In the Colonial Office Elliot had already been willing to accept independent arbitration between the British and Portuguese claims; he believed that neither island nor mainland brought Britain anything 'except inconvenience and expense', and he was disturbed by his government's unctuous refusal to allow the Portuguese to question its claims.

> 'It may be troublesome to have to listen to their arguments, but if it were a more powerful nation, they might have used more forcible means of engaging our attention. . . . If . . . we really were in error in 1860, it may be a question whether National Honour is not only so delicate but so peculiar that it must be injured by frankly repairing an unintentional wrong.'

But Fortescue, Forster and Cardwell, impressed by Blackall's prophecy that the slave trade would revive under Portuguese rule, seemed determined to remain, insisting that the legal case was too good to send to arbitration — 'we are justified in holding Bulama if we think it expedient to do so'.[2]

It was Stanley who broke the deadlock in December 1866, urging the Colonial Office either to withdraw their claim or to submit it to arbitration. Adderley, insisting that 'we have no interest in Bulama but its being in the hands of a regular

[1] C.O. 87/84, précis by Elliot, 12 July 1866, minutes by Adderley, 12 July 1866, 20 March 1867, by Buckingham, 10 April 1867; C.O. 87/85, Blackall to Carnarvon, 7, 18 July; 9, 20 July 1866, minutes by Adderley, 21 Aug., 13 Oct.; cf. C.O. 267/287, minute by Adderley on Blackall, 11 Oct. 1866; C.O. 87/99, Kennedy to Kimberley, 9 June 1871; minutes by Knatchbull-Hughessen, Kimberley. On this question, see also J. A. B. Horton, *West African Countries and Peoples* . . . (London, 1868), pp. 83–6.

[2] C.O. 267/285, F.O. to C.O., 4 Jan. 1865, minutes by Elliot and Fortescue; 4 Dec. 1865, minute by Barrow; C.O. 267/287, Blackall to Cardwell, Conf., 17 April 1866, minutes by Elliot, Forster, Cardwell.

government', strongly recommended 'getting rid of this, and of everything on the West Coast that we can honourably escape from'.[1] But action was long delayed — due partly to inter-departmental misunderstandings and muddle, partly to the temperamental indecisiveness of the new Secretary of State, the Duke of Buckingham and Chandos, who displayed an excessive liking for the study of irrelevant details. Only on 27 June 1868, after more questions in the Portuguese legislature, did the British government formally agree to invite a foreign sovereign to arbitrate upon their claim to the island and the disputed mainland.[2]

This delay proved mildly unfortunate for Anglo-Portuguese relations. The military commander at Sierra Leone, while acting as governor in September 1867, withdrew the small garrison from Bulama; the Portuguese thereupon re-hoisted their flag at the points claimed by Britain on the mainland. The new Governor-in-Chief, Sir Arthur Kennedy, had acquired some regard for Bulama during earlier service at Sierra Leone: through another administrative oversight he was not informed of the decision to accept arbitration. In June 1868 he resumed the old game of hauling down the Portuguese flag; as soon as he left the Portuguese put it up again.[3] At first the Colonial Office seemed disposed to endorse Kennedy's defence of British rights; even Adderley took the initiative in sending a gunboat to Bulama.[4] But this comic melodrama did not prevent the completion in September of an agreement accepting the arbitration of President Grant of the United States. The Colonial Office felt so little interest that they left the preparation of the British case to the Foreign Office — a course they would hardly have

[1] C.O. 267/288, F.O. to C.O., 21 Dec. 1866, minutes of March 1867; C.O. 267/291, F.O. to C.O., 26 June 1867, minute by Adderley.

[2] C.O. 267/291, C.O. to F.O., 12 Sept. 1867; F.O. to C.O., 4 Dec.; C.O. 267/296, F.O. to C.O., 10 June; C.O. to F.O., 23 June; F.O. to C.O., 29 June 1868.

[3] C.O. 267/294, Kennedy to Buckingham, 62, 11 June; 113, 26 Aug. 1868; C.O. 267/296, F.O. to C.O., 24 July, 4 Aug. 1868.

[4] C.O. 267/294, minute by Adderley, 22 Sept. 1868 on Kennedy, 27 Aug.; C.O. to Admty, 26 Oct.; C.O. 267/295, Kennedy to Buckingham, 153, 14 Oct. 1868 and minutes.

taken where substantive interests were at stake. The Liberal victory of December 1868 brought no reversion to Cardwell's position; Granville, the new Colonial Secretary, light-heartedly wished the Portuguese good luck: 'if unfortunately we should win, we shall have justified our former conduct, and may then consider what course we will take.'[1] This embarrassment was spared him; in 1870 Grant decided in favour of the Portuguese, and Britain left Bulama amidst the most profound public indifference.[2]

The Liberian border

One other place where Adderley saw a real possibility of retracting British responsibilities was the coastline south of the Sherbro. In the matter of Liberian claims upon the territory of Prince Manna, he believed,

'we should take no part, neither refusing nor assenting. The more Liberia extends, the better the barrier against slave export.'[3]

Either Liberia or Manna might conceivably fill the role of 'strong native power'; Adderley's own preference was for Liberia, but events would show which offered the better prospects.

But events soon after Adderley left office made his policy of non-intervention difficult to maintain. Liberia found the *status quo* in the Gallinas irksome, not merely because it affronted her pride; British traders based in that river were evading payment of customs on indisputably Liberian coasts. Early in 1869 President Payne, hoping to further his chances of re-election by a spirited foreign policy, sent Liberian revenue officers into the Gallinas, where they impounded the small schooner *Elizabeth* and other property of Sierra Leonean traders. Kennedy was furious; he persuaded the British government to send a warship to Monrovia to demand compensation for the traders in the sum of £3370. In September 1869 the Liberian government,

---

[1] C.O. 267/296, F.O. to C.O., 26 Sept., 21 Dec. 1868, and minutes.
[2] E. Hertslet, *The Map of Africa by Treaty* (2nd ed. 1896) Vol. II, pp. 688–90.
[3] C.O. 267/291, minute by Adderley, 20 March 1867, on F.O. to C.O., 28 Jan.

under threat of bombardment, handed over produce valued at £500, and promised to pay the balance in six-monthly instalments.[1]

The Liberians, encouraged by the Bulama precedent, now proposed that the disputed boundary should be submitted to arbitration. The suggestion was seriously considered; the Liberians still had many British sympathizers, others besides Adderley had wondered whether self-governing settlements on the Liberian pattern might not provide the desired new order in West Africa.[2] Although the latest dispute made it more difficult for the Colonial Office to accept arbitration (since a decision in Liberia's favour would justify her proceedings against the traders and imply that British demands had been unwarranted), alternative procedures for amicable settlement were considered. During 1870 there was talk of a Joint Commission of British, French and Liberian representatives to settle Liberia's boundaries in both north and south; when France went to war with Prussia, a new Anglo-Liberian Commission was proposed instead.[3]

But now Liberia began to lose its sympathizers. After the Civil War there was an end to the financial support — never adequate for the founding of real governmental institutions — which the settlement had formerly received from the United States; observers began to report that the regime of the new President, Roye, was based insecurely upon a narrow oligarchy. During 1870 it became clear in London that this government was probably corrupt, and certainly bankrupt: it was incapable of meeting its commitment for compensation to the Sierra Leonean traders, or of facing new claims arising from

[1] C.O. 267/300, Kennedy to Granville, 71, 20 March; 72, 22 March; 114, 14 May 1869; C.O. 267/301, Kennedy to Granville, 148, 13 July 1869; C.O. 267/303, F.O. to C.O., 4 Aug.; Granville to Kennedy, 103, 11 Aug. 1869; C.O. 267/302, Kendall to Granville, 192, 17 Sept. 1869.

[2] Burton, Wanderings . . . Ch. 6; cf. 'African Discovery', The Quarterly Review, April 1861, pp. 527–8. P.P. 1865. V, pp. 257–61, evidence of Gerald Ralston. (Liberian Consul-General; an American 25 years resident in England; without experience south of Cape Verde Islands.)

[3] C.O. 267/303, F.O. to C.O., 14 Oct. 1869; C.O. to F.O., 12 Oct.; C.O. 267/309, F.O. to C.O., 8 June, 23 June, 31 Oct. 1870.

the plunder of a shipwreck in its territory, and could certainly not provide any satisfactory *pax*.[1] Meanwhile Kennedy was strongly championing Manna's claim to remain independent of Liberia, and binding him more closely to Sierra Leone by arranging free schooling in Freetown for two of his family.[2] The following year confirmed the view that Liberia was 'a helpless and hopeless place'; after more disturbances in the Gallinas, Roye was deposed in comic-opera fashion by a revolution led by ex-President Roberts, and drowned escaping through Monrovia harbour (weighed down, according to one malicious story, by the contents of the Treasury in a belt around his waist).[3]

Hopes that Liberia might play a constructive role in African development evaporated; when in December 1870 there was a curious rumour that Germany might buy the country, the Colonial Office felt pleased.[4] Only Winwood Reade, a faithful but eccentric disciple of Burton, still saw any hope of progress in the Liberians themselves — and then only under the informal protectorate and guidance of Sierra Leone. It was symptomatic of changing attitudes that the new Liberal Parliamentary Under-Secretary could for a moment take this idea seriously;

'If the policy of the Government is gradually to extend British possessions in Western Africa, with a view to the development of the resources of the country and the civilisation of its inhabitants, I should say that Mr. Reade's suggestion was excellent. But if our policy is rather to withdraw than to increase our hold upon the W. African coast, I doubt whether it will not be better to hold ourselves entirely aloof from Liberia, and certainly not to do

[1] C.O. 267/309, F.O. to C.O., 31 Oct. 1870; C.O. 267/307, Kennedy to Kimberley, 207, 7 Dec. 1870; C.O. 267/311, Kennedy to Kimberley, 69, 6 May 1871.

[2] C.O. 267/299, Kennedy to Granville, 24, 25 Jan. 1869; C.O. 267/307, Kennedy to Kimberley, 208, 7 Dec. 1870; cf. *Sierra Leone Studies*, n.s. 1 (1953) pp. 29–30.

[3] C.O. 267/310, Kennedy to Kimberley, 68, 14 April 1871, minute by Knatchbull-Hughessen; C.O. 267/311, Kennedy to Kimberley, 91, 5 June 1871, minutes by Holland, Herbert, Hughessen, Kimberley; C.O. 267/312, Kennedy to Kimberley, Conf., 14 Nov. 1871; cf. H. Johnston, *Liberia* (London, 1906) Vol. I, pp. 258–63, 268.

[4] C.O. 267/307, Kennedy to Kimberley, Conf., 28 Dec. 1870, minutes by Barrow, Hughessen.

anything which may lead to the expectation of a British Protectorate being established. But there can be no harm in ascertaining Sir A. Kennedy's opinion.'[1]

This decision was never in doubt. But if Britain could not accept Liberian rule, she would inevitably find herself exercising more active supervision over affairs on the Gallinas coastline.

★   ★   ★   ★   ★

These were minor issues. At Lagos a more portentous expansion of British influence was taking place, within the general limitations imposed by the Committee. With short intermissions J. H. Glover continued to administer this settlement until July 1872; since he was fairly successful in securing a prosperous trade and a buoyant revenue, his earlier indiscretions were largely forgotten. This energetic and humane man had served as a young naval lieutenant on the *Dayspring*'s Niger expedition of 1857; on this occasion he had become well acquainted with the routes between Nupe and Lagos by way of both Abeokuta and Ibadan.[2] As Administrator he worked to extend the colony's influence along these routes towards the Niger (but especially along the latter one), using such informal methods as the employment of regular messengers, the payment of stipends to chiefs who would guarantee 'open roads', the stationing of constables at important points. In the peaceful development of commerce under colonial influence he saw 'the means to a greater end'.[3]

But only partial success could be achieved by the methods open to Glover. The war between Abeokuta and Ibadan which began in 1860 dragged on until 1865, to the great detriment of trade. In March 1865 Glover, after some rather tortuous manoeuvring, engineered an opportunity to attack an Egba army which was besieging Ikorudu, a trading terminal on the

[1] Minute by Hughessen, 17 April 1871, on F.O. to C.O., 28 Feb., 14 April, encl. letters from Reade.

[2] A. C. G. Hastings, ed., *The Voyage of the* Dayspring (London, 1926) pp. 206–10; cf. Lady Glover, *Life of Sir J. H. Glover* (London, 1897).

[3] Hastings, *op. cit.*, p. 88, Glover's diary, 27 Sept. 1857; Gertzel, *op. cit.*, pp. 221 ff.

lagoon north of Lagos. Military success increased British prestige among the Yorubas, and enabled Glover to impose peace terms upon the Egba; but this pacification proved precarious. Glover was unable to convene the general peace conference of all Yoruba states which he desired; his subsequent policies made the Egba even more doubtful of his impartiality; and the Abeokuta missionaries warned the home government to be wary of their agent's schemes. In 1871, when war again threatened between Ibadan and the Egba-Ijebu alliance, Glover renewed his attempts at holding a general peace conference; but though representatives of the principal states actually met in Lagos, no settlement was achieved. The years of peace and prosperity did not long survive Glover's departure in 1872.[1]

*   *   *   *   *

If the Bulama question saw a limited and belated triumph for the ideas which Adderley had contributed to the Committee of 1865, the situation at Lagos, as well as the minor affairs of MacCarthy's Island and the Liberian boundary, demonstrated the difficulty of applying them. Towards the end of his term in office, Adderley had expressed his feelings of frustration:

> 'These horrible settlements, first occupied for slave trade and afterwards against it, are now merely pest holes for good English officers. . . . As to commerce, the Niger is proof that it does better without them, and the civilisation we occasion is *demoralising our men* and *winking at native practices*. . . . This, with occasional tribal wars from the Ashanti, which cost millions . . . is the result of the settlements in West Africa. The House of Commons Committee decided we should take every possible step in way of withdrawing; but Kennedy here talks of *the growing new settlement at Sherboro*, which I certainly hope to attack as soon as I'm free.'

But, since the letter on which he wrote these rather diffuse comments concerned the practical question of salary for the Chief Justice, Adderley had to conclude,

[1] For this period generally, see S. O. Biobaku and A. B. Aderibigbe, *op. cit.*

'But meanwhile we are *bound* to see that our officers are decently paid.'[1]

There was the crux: so long as Britain did retain responsibilities in West Africa, however reluctantly, her government had to take practical decisions, and devise arrangements for the immediate future of the settlements. By 1870 she was, in each territory, groping her way towards a new definition of local aims. And in the process she was encountering problems, albeit minor ones, which affected her relations with the other major power interested in West Africa.

[1] C.O. 267/296, minute by Adderley, 1 Sept. 1868, on Treasury to C.O., 28 Aug.

CHAPTER THREE

France and West Africa under the Second Empire

[1]

The Second Empire and African Policy

IT MIGHT, superficially, be expected that Imperial France would follow a more active policy in Africa than mid-Victorian Britain. Napoleon III's regime, owing its existence largely to its conscious appeal to the remembered glories of its predecessor, needed to justify itself by successes abroad and demonstrations of *panache*. Yet its ventures overseas did not follow any predictable pattern, or even concentrate on areas of established French interest. Mexico received attention disproportionate to any probable benefit to France; Algerian policy fluctuated; in West Africa, government initiatives were usually traceable to pressures from men on the spot.

Though not lacking in creative ideas for colonial policy, the Empire had no central authority capable of translating these into precise executive instructions, into a coherent policy. The *Direction des Colonies* was a small and insignificant organization, attached, except for one short interval, to the Ministry of the Marine; its views tended to become subordinated to those of professional naval officers, who might at heart regard African settlements and their commerce as regrettable distractions, really beneath their notice. This nautical supremacy over the colonies was relaxed only during the years 1858–60, when a Ministry of Algeria and the Colonies was formed. This experiment, however, represented no new approach to colonial administration, but chiefly an attempt to find suitable employment for the Emperor's cousin, Prince Napoleon — a man of vaguely liberal intentions, but without the application to build up a strong administrative machine. In any case the interlude was too brief to have much effect.[1]

If there was no strong and purposeful central administrative direction, neither could sectional interests command reliable means of controlling policy. In general, Napoleon aimed to satisfy Catholic missions and organized merchant interests; when such groups had African axes to grind they might well succeed in doing so. But even after the constitutional concessions of the 1860's, there was no reliable method of pressing home sectional pressure upon the government. Broad currents of popular opinion or sentiment the Emperor would recognize; but there were no such currents yet affecting tropical Africa. If high policy demanded the overriding of sectional interests, this was done. Thus, after the important commercial treaty with Britain in 1860, duties were abolished on most imported raw materials; this brought the end of many long-entrenched colonial privileges affecting, among many more important commodities, Senegalese gum. Although these changes were welcomed by many colonial merchants — the Marseille Chamber of Commerce favoured free trade on principle, and many of its members wanted free access to the home market for tropical imports not grown under the French flag — they represented less the victory of one group of interests over another than the imposition on all of a superior political objective.[2]

In Africa as well as in Paris, merchants who wanted political support for specific aims had to apply through the naval authorities. Until 1854 the Governor of Senegal was usually a naval officer; after that year all French settlements and interests south of St. Louis were placed under the supervision of the commander of the West African naval division.[3] Many naval

---

[1] A. Duchêne, *La Politique Coloniale de la France* (Paris, 1928) esp. Ch. II.

[2] A. Girault, *The Colonial Tariff Policy of France* (Oxford, 1916) pp. 66–70, 74–7; P. Masson (ed.) *Les Bouches-du-Rhône: Encyclopédie Départementale*; Tome IX, *Le Commerce* (Marseille, 1922) pp. 63 ff.

[3] But in 1859 Gorée and its 'dependencies', as far south as Sierra Leone, were restored to the government of Senegal; the naval commander was left with oversight of 'Les Etablissements du Côte d'Or et du Gabon'. C. Schefer, *Instructions Générales . . . aux Gouverneurs . . . en Afrique Occidentale* (Paris, 1927) Vol. II, pp. 250–1, 407, 447–8.

officers disliked service in these unhealthy waters, especially inshore service; they received requests to support traders without enthusiasm, suspecting that these *petits bourgeois* might be trying to use the French flag to further ignoble commercial intrigues. They themselves rarely felt patriotic compulsion to hoist their flag along the African coast, but more often shared the prevalent British desire for 'trade without dominion'. Many would have liked to bring all interested powers to accept a general neutralization of the West African coast south of the Gambia; this, they argued, had been the original purpose of Article XII of the Treaty of Versailles of 1783.[1] Thoughtful officers like Admiral Laffon de Ladebat were particularly attracted by the idea that the Crimean allies, renouncing territorial expansion, should jointly try to keep the peace in West Africa by prohibiting sales of firearms to Africans. Meanwhile the Navy hoped to fulfil its charge to 'protect the operations, encourage the development, and stimulate the efforts' of French commerce[2] without actually acquiring new responsibilities.

In the groundnut-producing districts between the Senegal and Sierra Leone, and for a time as far as the Sherbro, French traders operating under competitive conditions had some success. The island of Gorée, which many of them used as headquarters, also provided a seat of French authority to which they could appeal when in difficulties.[3] The French demand for groundnuts, which expanded considerably from the 1840's, was increasingly met by French traders, based in Bordeaux, in Senegal, and to a lesser extent in Marseille. They developed this trade in such readily accessible rivers as the Sine, Saloum, and Casamance; competed successfully with British traders in the Gambia and with Portuguese in the Guinea settlements; and gradually extended business in the *rivières du sud* — of which the

---

[1] For a typical statement of this view, see *MAE*, Afrique 86, Note for Challemel-Lacour, 1883. Article XII of the Treaty of Versailles reads, 'As for the remainder of the Coast of Africa, the English and French subjects shall continue to resort thereto, according to the usage which has hitherto prevailed.' cf. below pp. 114, 133–4.

[2] Schefer, *op. cit.*, II, p. 475; Chasseloup-Laubat to Didelot, 10 Oct. 1861.

[3] On its role, see *MMC*, Sénégal XIII, Report of Commission, 1851, Part I.

three most important were the Nunez, Pongos, and Mella-courie.[1]

These latter rivers, besides growing groundnuts (and some coffee in the Nunez) had a secondary importance as terminals for caravans bringing gold, ivory, and hides from Futa Jalon and the upper Niger. This was never a valuable trade — the ratio of these exports to those of local crops was of the approximate order of one to five — but the supposed potentialities of the interior trade gave these rivers an additional attraction. In the Nunez, French, British, and Belgian traders all tried to involve their governments in local politics; in 1849 French and Belgian warships forcibly installed the candidate favoured by a trading consortium as chief of the Landoumas.[2] In the 1860's French trade in the Mellacourie region overtook that in the Nunez, thanks largely to the Gorée house of Gaspard Devès; the Pongos was always a poor third. The total exports of the *rivières du sud* were probably worth considerably less than £500,000; though most of these went to France, the principal market for groundnuts, much of the business was handled by British or Sierra Leonean traders, who had long connections with these rivers. Still, this coast provided a modestly successful example of how French trade could expand in Africa without the formal intervention of state power.[3]

[1] There is no systematic account of the development of French trade on this coast; but cf. G. Hardy, *La Mise en Valeur du Sénégal, 1817–54* (Paris, 1921). On Marseille, see P. Masson, *op. cit.*, Tome VIII (1926) p. 93; Tome IX (1922) pp. 174–86.

[2] A. Demeugeot, 'Histoire du Nunez', *Bulletin du Comité d'Etudes Historiques et Scientifiques de l'A.O.F.*, Vol. XXX (Dakar, 1938); C. Monheim, *L'Affaire du Rio Nunez* (Louvain, 1931).

[3] Since no records were kept, only occasional estimates of the trade of these rivers can be found. These vary considerably from year to year, either because political or climatic conditions affected trade, or because of changes in its distribution. Among the sources used in reaching the above general conclusions are: *MMC*, Sénégal I/50, Laprade to Faidherbe, 14 April 1864 (report of tour in S. Rivers, with trade estimates); Sénégal III/9/b (Tour by Poisson, 1863); Sénégal IV/55/c, Requin to Laprade, 18 Dec. 1865 (Mellacourie trade); *MAE*, Angleterre (Freetown) 53, Braouezec to M.A.E., 18 Aug. 1865, encl. Dalmas, 13 Aug. (estimates of Mellacourie trade); Braouezec to M.A.E., 17 Aug. 1868 (French shipping calling at various points, 1865–7).

Further south the French government was less successful in avoiding territorial responsibilities; the reason lay essentially in the skill of a single Marseille merchant, Victor Régis the elder, in enlisting French power in support of his parochial interests. Régis first entered West African commerce through the Senegal gum trade about 1833; but about 1840 he withdrew, complaining that the mercantile regulations still enforced in that colony favoured the established privileges of Bordeaux,[1] and turned to the palm-oil coastlines further south. For a quarter of a century his was the only French house to achieve substantial business in these regions. In 1843 the French flag was hoisted on the Gabon estuary, and at Assinie, Grand Bassam, and Dabou on the eastern Ivory Coast; in each case, Régis was largely responsible for bringing this about. But he was a sharp and quarrelsome man, more interested in short cuts to high profits than in building up a steady turnover; he wanted not merely the French flag hoisted above his factories, but naval or military support in compelling African middlemen — the 'Jack-Jacks' to the west of Grand Bassam, or King Amatifou in the hinterland of Assinie — to trade with him on his own terms. Disappointed by the extent of his success in these matters, Régis withdrew his business in turn from each of these new French possessions; by 1856 he was interested chiefly in the oil trade of the Dahomey and Lagos area, and in a somewhat questionable scheme for shipping Africans as indentured labourers to the Antilles from the Congo and Angola. In these ventures also he sought government support, with some success, in whatever forms seemed expedient to him. Meanwhile, the only French traders who took his place at Gabon and the Ivory Coast commanded little capital, and achieved little trade. The navy was left in these places with the responsibility of protecting the trade of foreigners, in hope of better things.[2]

[1] See his pamphlet (in the Bibliothèque Nationale, Paris), *A Messieurs les Membres de la Commission*, 21 Sept. 1842.

[2] There is a favourable account of Régis' activities, based on his own papers, in P. Masson, *Marseille et la Colonisation française* (Marseille, 1906) Chs. XI, XII. But cf. *inter alia*, *MMC*, Gabon 1/2/b, Didelot to M.M.C., 12 Sept. 1862, 28 Sept. 1863; Sénégal XII/3/c, Report of Commission, 1851, Pt. 2.

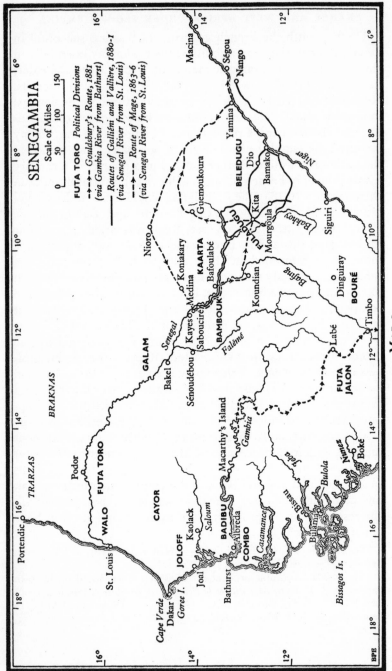

SENEGAMBIA

Scale of Miles

0   50   100   150

FUTA TORO *Political Divisions*

➤➤➤ *Gouldsbury's Route, 1881*
(*via Gambia River from Bathurst*)

——— *Routes of Galliéni and Vallière, 1880–1*
(*via Senegal River from St. Louis*)

———— *Route of Mage, 1863–6*
(*via Senegal River from St. Louis*)

MAP 2

The Senegal and Faidherbe's first governorship

On the lower Senegal, where French rule could be traced back to the seventeenth century, conditions and policies were quite different. After the Restoration there had been attempts to develop a proper colony, with a settled population engaged in commercial agriculture; though these were soon abandoned, St. Louis, whose population of up to 15,000 included 300 Europeans,[1] remained a colonial capital unlike any other on the coast. Governor D'Arcy, on a visit in 1860, was impressed by the schools, the hospital of four hundred beds, the military parade on the *Champ de Mars*, and by 'the ball at Government House, numbering at least forty ladies whose toilets might have done credit to a Paris ballroom'.[2] But the commercial fortunes of town and colony still rested precariously on the gum trade; groundnuts developed less impressively than in the other rivers. Although gum was required in the expanding calico-printing industry of Europe, the profits of the trade were declining; the development of chemical substitutes, and increased competition from Egyptian gum, were steadily depressing world prices. In addition to this, the organization of the trade posed problems which, until the 1850's, no Governor was able to solve.

There were continual controversies about the regulation within the colony of this trade, whose participants tended to employ stereotyped methods and expect fairly close protection by government regulation. Gum was obtained almost exclusively in exchange for blue cloths known as *guinées*, imported from India by European merchants. Europeans, however, were forbidden to engage directly in the river trade, which was largely reserved for the Eurafrican community, or *habitants*, some of whose families had enjoyed several generations of experience of Christianity and French culture. The *habitants* would proceed up-river at traditionally recognized trading

[1] *MMC*, Sénégal XIII, Report of Commission, 1851, gives the population of the colony as 282 whites, 17,976 *noirs*. Up to one-third of the latter would reside at Bakel and other trading posts up-river, cf. Cultru, *Histoire du Sénégal du xve siècle à 1870* (Paris, 1910) p. 355. On Senegal generally, see this work, and Hardy, *op. cit.*

[2] C.O. 87/89, D'Arcy to Newcastle, 56, 22 Dec. 1860.

seasons, to accredited markets known as *escales*, where gum
grown on the right bank of the river was brought for sale by
'Moorish' traders. This commerce would be profitable only if
there was some balance between the quantity of gum offered for
sale and the trade-goods available at the *escales*; a relatively
small increase in competition could easily glut these circum-
scribed markets. When new French houses tried to break into
the trade by employing free Africans from St. Louis as their
salaried trading agents, the income of the older merchants and
habitants fell sharply; and the Moors became more exigent, not
only in commercial bargaining, but in the imposition of political
conditions upon the market.

Successive governors tried various methods of attenuating the
consequences of this cut-throat competition; some favoured the
formation of monopolistic trading associations, others preferred
free competition, with the government imposing restraints only
in the interest of public order. In 1850 an inter-departmental
Commission met in Paris, representing the principal parties
interested in African policy. Its membership is revealing; senior
officials from the colonial directorate, the Customs, the
Ministries of Commerce and Foreign Affairs, were joined by
five naval officers, four parliamentarians, and a single merchant
— Régis. For the Senegal, they recommended freer trade and a
relaxation of many of the governmental controls hitherto imposed at the *escales*. But they also suggested building a fort at
Podor to protect traders on the lower river; and this suggestion
raised the even more intractable problem of France's political
relations with her Senegalese neighbours.[1]

One basic weakness in the whole French position was military; her governors were trying to support and protect traders
on the river without the means of making their power respected.
Thus military Moorish peoples — the Braknas, and more
particularly the Trarzas — could levy charges on the gum-
traders which they did not hesitate to describe as tribute.

---

[1] *MMC*, Sénégal XIII/3/c, Report of Commission, Part I, cf. Hardy, *op.
cit.*; and, for a contemporary discussion by a French official and a leading
habitant, F. Carrère and P. Holle, *De la Sénégambie Française* (Paris, 1855)
pp. 343–52.

Besides this, the Moors exercised influence among the Negro peoples across the river. A marriage alliance of 1832 gave them power within Walo, on the very borders of St. Louis; they also enjoyed political and religious influence in parts of Futa, in Cayor, and other Negro states. The effect of their policies, and probably their aim, was to encircle the French settlements with potential enemies, and to stultify attempts to broaden the Senegalese economy by encouraging the cultivation of groundnuts. The French looked for allies, but without sustained success; gradually they came to the conclusion that more direct measures would be needed to establish a favourable political order.

The first governor openly to advocate forceful policies was a future Admiral, Bouët-Willaumez, in 1844; but at that time French finances were still under Parliamentary supervision, and it was not practical to carry out his ambitious proposals for expansion. But an important preparatory step was taken by organizing a Bureau of External Affairs in St. Louis.[1] After Napoleon III became Emperor the political brakes were relaxed, and in 1853 Governor Protet received military reinforcements to help him carry out the Commission's proposal to occupy and fortify Podor, in Futa Toro. Protet did this in March 1854, but soon afterwards suffered heavy losses against the local Tokolors; he still felt too weak to withhold the customary payments of the Trarzas, and now there seemed dangers of reprisals from the Tokolor followers of El Haj Omar.[2]

The growing power of that prophet in the upper basin of the Senegal was the most disquieting feature of all in the middle fifties. French trade in his territories was not great, though ever since the early eighteenth century a few bold spirits had dreamed of tapping great sources of gold or produce in these countries; gold and ivory had never appeared in quantities sufficient to justify any considerable investment, either by the monopolistic

[1] Schefer, *op. cit.*, II, pp. 166–71, Bouët to Mackau, 6 Nov. 1844; cf. pp. 567 ff.

[2] *ibid.*, pp. 216–26, Ducos to Protet, 4 Jan. 1853; cf. pp. 246–50, and above, pp. 9–12.

Galam company before 1848 or by private traders thereafter. The highest French post of any size was Bakel; most of its 3,000 inhabitants remained chiefly dependent on the gum trade. At Medina, near the Félou rapids, a few Senegalese traders did some business with caravans from the interior, and a post was founded at Sénoudébou on the Falemé in 1845. But the reason why Omar's rise perturbed the French was at first not so much that he held the key to future commercial expansion towards the Niger; it was the fear that his religious authority, if used against the French, could imperil their security in the lower Senegal valley, and even in the largely Muslim town of St. Louis itself.

At this point Protet was succeeded as governor by an Engineer officer of thirty-six, with steel-rimmed spectacles and a reputation for being awkward to deal with. Captain Faidherbe, however, possessed admirable qualities, for which he is praised in general terms by almost every writer on French African policy. Hardworking and capable in administration, courageous in action, imaginative and scholarly when taking longer views, he has made a deep impression on historians, as he did on many of his collaborators.[1] Two qualities were particularly relevant to the situation he found in 1854; faith in the possibilities of penetrating the Sudan by the upper Senegal route, and a freedom from strong anti-Muslim prejudice, which he had apparently achieved during service in Algeria. Faidherbe applied these ideas enthusiastically but with some discrimination; it was in the hands of later successors that they tended to harden into dogmatic and sometimes illusory 'myths' no longer relevant to African realities.

Faidherbe's first governorship lasted from 1854 until 1861, providing a continuity of direction which the Senegal had

[1] e.g. G. Hardy, *Faidherbe* (Paris, 1947); A. Demaison, *Faidherbe* (Paris, 1932); R. Delavignette, 'Faidherbe' in C. A. Julien (ed.) *Les Techniciens de la Colonisation* (Paris, 1953); P. Cultru, *op. cit.*, Ch. XI; G. Hanotaux and A. Martineau (ed.) *Histoire des Colonies françaises et de l'Expansion de la France dans le Monde*, Tome IV, 'L'Afrique Occidentale', par M. Delafosse (Paris, 1931), Ch. V; H. Deschamps, *Les Méthodes et les Doctrines Coloniales de la France* (Paris, 1953), pp. 113–17. For a less favourable view, J. Suret-Canale, *Afrique Noire* (Paris, 1958) pp. 182–3.

previously unfortunately lacked. In administration, he distinguished priorities and allocated his limited resources with discrimination; he started new public works, and founded an *École des Otages* to train interpreters and other prospective emissaries of French influence in the interior.[1] But his first tasks were necessarily military. The limited forces at Faidherbe's disposal, strengthened in 1857 by the recruitment of a Senegalese battalion, were skilfully deployed in order to strengthen French prestige in the valley.[2] Walo was brought under direct French control in 1855; three years later the Trarzas, defeated in battle and deprived of their alliances on the left bank, agreed to respect French traders more fully, and to commute the controversial 'customs' charges into a fixed export duty of 3%. Britain's agreement in 1857 to renounce her right to trade on the Mauritanian coast at Portendic usefully complemented these operations by depriving the Trarzas of the only possible alternative market for their gum.

But these successes did not assure French authority in Futa, Cayor, or other states on the left bank of the Senegal. Here the ominous feature was the growing prestige of El Haj Omar, though he himself was still in distant Kaarta fighting pagan Bambaras. His prestige in the upper Senegal was believed to have encouraged local people to attack the French post at Sénoudébou in March 1855, and there were worries for the safety of Bakel. Even worse, early in 1855 the prophet issued a long-feared appeal to Muslims in St. Louis to join his Holy War against the unbelievers — which many Frenchmen interpreted to mean themselves. There were fears of a concerted onslaught by 'Muslim idolatry' against the whole French position — a religious war with terrifying social and racial overtones.[3]

Faidherbe, however, less influenced by anti-Muslim prejudice, would not be swept into accepting this gloomy prognosis. He

---

[1] For his administration generally, see Cultru, *op. cit.* For the *École des Otages*, L. L. C. Faidherbe, *Le Soudan Français*, 3e partie (Lille, 1885).

[2] For Faidherbe's military campaigns, see L. L. C. Faidherbe, *Le Sénégal; La France dans l'Afrique Occidentale* (Paris, 1889).

[3] Faidherbe, *Le Sénégal*, pp. 158–66, 180–1. The anti-Muslim view is expressed in Carrère and Holle, *op. cit.*

E

noted that Omar seemed to have no direct personal responsibility for the attack on Sénoudébou; that it seemed to be
his Tokolor followers with revolutionary aims in Futa Toro
who were most eager to turn against France and the lower
Senegal. It was also in 1855 that Omar issued a statement of
willingness to accept peaceful co-existence with the French,
Christians though they were:

> 'The whites are only traders: let them bring merchandise in their
> ships, let them pay me a good stipend [*tribut*] when I'm master of
> the Negroes, and I will live in peace with them. But I don't wish
> them to erect permanent establishments or send warships into the
> river.'[1]

Though Faidherbe could hardly be expected to accept such
terms literally and completely, they nevertheless suggested a
possible new policy. Instead of seeking Omar's downfall, an
object very difficult to envisage, might not France recognize his
power, and seek to develop commerce towards the Niger under
his sovereignty rather than her own? The Gallicized Christian
merchants of St. Louis, rigidly conservative in their commercial
outlook, might shrink from such a notion; but it was noticed
that the *jolas*, caravan traders with the Sudan, welcomed every
improvement in French relations with Omar.[2] The Tokolor
state might provide an excellent opportunity to try the policy of
collaboration with a 'strong native power'.

These, however, were long views. In 1855 Faidherbe understood that his first priority must be to restore France's military
prestige by proving himself capable of resisting the prophet's
power.[3] So he interrupted his campaign against the Trarzas to
establish a small fort at Medina, the most distant point of French
trade. In 1857 this was attacked by Omar's army, which may
by now have numbered 20,000. The tiny garrison, under the
Eurafrican trader Paul Holle, resisted bravely for three months,
and was then relieved by Faidherbe. Omar's subsequent strategy
confirms the view that he had been reluctantly persuaded to

---

[1] Cultru, *op. cit.*, p. 337, quoting *Annuaire Sénégalaise*.
[2] E. Mage, *Voyage dans le Soudan Occidental* (Paris, 1868) pp. 120, 247–9.
[3] *MMC*, Sénégal 1/45, memo. by Faidherbe, 5 Aug. 1856.

invade the French sphere of influence; his operations against them over the next two years were increasingly half-hearted. His own ambitions lay in the middle Niger, in Ségou and Macina, and those states now became his main military objective. By 1859 Omar was willing to negotiate a demarcation of spheres with France in the Senegal.

Faidherbe was willing to respond. Already, in a memorandum of 1858 which had won a somewhat vague approval from Paris, he had seemed to envisage advancing beyond Medina in association with the chastened Omar.[1] And in August 1860 he not only agreed with an emissary of the prophet on a demarcation of spheres of influence along the line of the upper Senegal and Bafing rivers, but provisionally promised to send his own ambassador to discuss the possibilities of further co-operation with Omar himself.[2]

Having eased the pressure in the lower Senegal, Faidherbe could look southwards along the coast, as well as inland towards the Niger. In 1859 Gorée and its 'dependencies' were restored to his government, and he began to act in support of French traders in the rivers. He established new forts at Joal in Sine and Kaolack in Saloum, and created difficulties with Portugal by sending a small expedition to the Casamance. Faidherbe also began to intervene more actively in Cayor (the key to overland communication between St. Louis and Dakar) and in 1861 deposed the *damel* Macodou. Some of his interventions roused much hostility, and the Cayor region was not subdued finally for a quarter of a century. But when Faidherbe's first governorship ended in 1861 he had sketched out lines for a considerable expansion, both inland and coastwise. And by doing so he had begun to infringe slightly on areas of marginal interest to the British. For the first time since the Napoleonic wars, the West African mainland stood to become a serious subject of international discussion.

[1] *MMC*, Sénégal 1/45, memo. by Faidherbe, 1 Oct. 1858; Schefer, *op. cit.*, II, pp. 306–14; Prince Napoleon to Faidherbe, 22 Feb. 1859; cf. *ibid.*, pp. 271–2.

[2] Mage, *op. cit.*, p. 404; Schefer, *op. cit.*, II, p. 327; Cultru, *op. cit.*, pp. 345–346; M. Delafosse, *Haut-Sénégal-Niger*, Tome II (Paris, 1912) pp. 310–17; Faidherbe, *op. cit.*, pp. 199, 237.

[2]

Background to Anglo-French Relations in West Africa

Although French and British settlements in West Africa were largely separated, and the one long-standing territorial dispute was settled in 1857, relations between Frenchmen and Britons on the coast were often strained. This is not surprising. Although for long periods the two governments were aligned in Europe by common policies, and during the Crimean war by military alliance, consciousness of cultural differences and memories of recent political traditions might still prevent mutual confidence between individuals. Englishmen, especially certain naval officers, were alert for a revival of Napoleonic ambitions; Frenchmen resented British maritime power, and interpreted every British move in Africa as part of some grand imperial design. Unfavourable stereotypes of the foreign nationality were handed on to colonial subjects. There was a well-known story of the Sierra Leonean policeman who arrested a Frenchman with the words, 'I tink you forget we win Waterloo'; and no British governor was more suspicious of French proceedings, whether naval or missionary, than Alexander Fitzjames, an Afro-West Indian.[1]

One cause of estrangement was a persistent British suspicion that French officials were half-hearted, or worse, in their efforts to suppress slave trading on land and sea. The Richardson-Barth expedition was largely inspired by fears that France, in her southward expansion from Algeria, might condone the Saharan slave traffic; it was in the hope of averting such a danger that Barth persuaded Sheikh El Bekkai to send a special embassy to London. By the time these messengers reached Tripoli France had become Britain's military ally, so this

[1] For Fitzjames, C.O. 267/263, Fitzjames to Lytton, Pte., 29 May 1859; C.O. 267/266, Fitzjames to Newcastle, Pte., 21 May 1860. For a typical French analysis of British policy, *MAE*, Afrique 58, M.A.E. to M.M.C., 25 Oct. 1862; cf. the account of Anglo-French relations elsewhere in R. Coupland, *East Africa and her Invaders* (Oxford, 1938) Ch. 14.

potentially embarrassing policy was discreetly dropped.[1] But the Colonial Office still viewed with deep distrust the contract granted to Régis by the French government in 1851 for the recruitment of African labour to work in the West Indies. Although the French government claimed that they supervised the conditions of transportation and service, some of Régis' agents still appeared to be using dubious practices; and in any case the very process of recruitment seemed certain to stimulate internal slave dealing and raiding. (These objections of the British were echoed by Faidherbe, who firmly refused to co-operate in the scheme.[2]) The British took the question up diplomatically, and in 1861 the French promised to suspend the scheme in return for facilities for recruiting indentured labour in British India.[3]

But while the British regarded the French as acting immorally in this matter, many Frenchmen were equally convinced that Britain was moved by false sentimentality, if not hypocrisy. Domestic slavery seemed to them 'one of the conditions of the social life of these peoples', and its opponents 'less concerned with facts than with a philosophical notion'. It seemed inconsistent to object to Africans labouring under conditions which were good enough for Britain's Indian subjects. Even before the Convention came into force the Ministry of Marine was contemplating the possibility of renouncing it.[4]

The other chief source of Anglo-French friction in West Africa in 1860 concerned the regulation of trade. One aspect of this was the question of navigation rights on those rivers whose mouths were under European control. On the Senegal France forbade foreign craft to pass above St. Louis; this relic of the restrictive colonial policy pursued by the Bourbons ensured that

[1] A. Boahen, *British Penetration of the Sahara and the Western Sudan* (Ph.D. Thesis, London, 1959). Barth, *op. cit.*, Vol. V, pp. 92–3, 117–18, 124–5.

[2] Faidherbe, *op. cit.*, pp. 382–6.

[3] W. L. Mathieson, *Great Britain and the Slave Trade 1839–65* (London, 1929) pp. 165–9; G. E. Marindin, *Letters of Frederic, Lord Blachford* (London, 1896) Ch. VI. P.P., 1865, V. qq. 2177–81; 2466–70; 3505; cf. Coupland, *op. cit.*, pp. 426–35.

[4] Schefer, *op. cit.*, II, pp. 466–9, 483–91; Chasseloup-Laubat to Didelot, 10 Oct. 1861.

French subjects continued to monopolize the trade of the river. For a time the British government tried to enforce the same prohibition in the rivers they controlled, although the greater part of the trade up the Gambia was already handled by French merchants. Early in 1861, when a Nantes vessel sought permission to go up the Rokelle river beyond Freetown, Governor Hill refused; and he was upheld by the home government, despite some doubts whether this attitude was consistent with 'the commercial principles which we now profess'.[1]

More serious were disputes over the incidence of colonial tariffs; ironically enough, the more serious charges of discrimination in the '60's were made against free-trade Britain. The well-known 'Cobden Treaty' of 1860 was followed by a great liberalization of French colonial trade. Duties in their West African possessions were either abolished or reduced to 4%; in 1866 the principal remaining British grievance, a heavy surcharge on colonial produce imported into France in foreign ships, was also removed. French colonial principles did not require dependencies to be financially self-supporting, and the metropolitan government could be persuaded, with but moderate difficulty, to subsidize colonial budgets; colonial governors were thus able to reduce tariffs in accordance with Imperial policy, or in hope of attracting foreign ships and traders to their ports.[2]

But a central principle of British colonial policy — *the* central principle, in the opinion of the Gladstonian Treasury, which during the 1860's was greatly tightening its control over departmental policies — was that every colony ought to meet the cost of its own administration. Since other British principles demanded that colonial governments should maintain quite considerable establishments of officials, tariffs had to be imposed to raise the necessary revenue. At Sierra Leone and Lagos in particular, these duties fell fairly heavily on imported alcohols

---

[1] C.O. 267/270, Hill to Newcastle, 43, 19 March 1861 and minutes; C.O. 267/272, F.O. to C.O., 25 June, 20 Dec. 1861; Newcastle to Hill, 23 Dec. 1861.

[2] A. Girault, *op. cit.*, pp. 66–80; Schefer, *op. cit.*, pp. 474–6; Chasseloup-Laubat to Didelot, 10 Oct. 1861.

and tobacco, but relatively lightly on textiles and other goods of British manufacture; French traders complained that these tariffs, though not differential in form, favoured British merchants in practice. Within established settlements foreign merchants tolerated these burdens in return for the added security which they might hope to enjoy; but when the Sierra Leone tariff was extended to the Sherbro in 1863, French traders there claimed that they suffered crippling losses without getting much additional protection in return. Their case had some substance; Russell in 1862 had thoughtlessly assured the French Ambassador that Frenchmen would be able to trade in the Sherbro 'as freely as in the past', but within a few years their trade had disappeared from the river.[1] French merchants, and some naval officers on the coast, resented this British action very keenly; they began to develop counter-action on their own, ineffectively in the Sherbro, more actively at Porto Novo.

But even though old political rivalries and prejudices were kept alive by these minor conflicts, France and Britain, holding their precarious footholds on the African continent, were repeatedly driven to co-operate in face of local African resistance. French troops assisted British operations in the Gambia in 1831 and 1855; twelve French artillerymen with two guns served as 'volunteers' in the Badibu campaign of 1861; later that year the French naval commander offered his services in Hill's Koya campaign 'on the principle that civilized nations should assist each other on this coast'.[2] In May 1860 Faidherbe was hospitably entertained by D'Arcy at Bathurst while returning from his outpost in the Casamance; in December D'Arcy repaid this visit. A French warship was sent to convey him to St. Louis, where he attended a military parade and travelled 150 miles up the Senegal. He was impressed by the amenities of the colony and by the personality and achievements of its governor, though

[1] *MMC*, Afrique IV/19/b, M.A.E. to M.M.C., 27 Jan. 1862; Brossard de Corbigny to Didelot, 25 Jan. 1863; Emparazanza to M.M.C., 21 July 1863; Brossard de Corbigny to Laffon de Ladebat, 4 Feb. 1865; Afrique VI/12/a, M.A.E. to M.M.C., 3 May 1864, and annotations. *MAE*, Angleterre (Freetown) 53, d'Elteil to Bourée, 10 June 1878.

[2] J. M. Gray, *History of the Gambia*, pp. 350–3, 394–5; C.O. 87/72, W.O. to C.O., 17 April 1861; C.O. 267/273, Hill to Newcastle, 76, 2 April 1862.

he noted that France's expensive policies had not produced any proportionate increase in trade.[1] This experience, and a realization that Gambian traders in the Saloum and Casamance rivers were benefiting from French protection, made D'Arcy an ardent francophil, urging that France and Britain should 'go hand and hand in trade and civilization as well as in war'. 'It is', he later wrote, 'a very great object on the northern coast to retain the Entente Cordiale in all its integrity.'[2]

The most obvious field in which these sentiments might be given practical application was the country between the Senegal and Gambia rivers. In particular, Faidherbe's intervention in Cayor in 1861 created difficulties; Madiodio, his nominee as *damel*, proved an unsatisfactory agent, and the rival claimants to the throne — first Macodou, and then his formidable relative Lat-Dior — found refuge and aid with Maba on the banks of the Gambia. From a series of difficult campaigns within Cayor, the French were drawn into conflict with Maba himself; and, in view of Maba's sympathies with El Haj Omar, there seemed some danger that they might find themselves involved in a general religious war with all the Muslims of Senegambia.[3] The most effective way of dealing with Maba would be to deny him the use of the Gambia river as a supply route; and better still, to use that river as a means of attacking him in his sanctuary. D'Arcy, who feared militant Islam more than Faidherbe did but lacked the resources to combat it, saw every advantage in co-operating with this plan.

Tentative suggestions on these lines were made to the British in 1862 and 1863; but only in March 1864, after Lat-Dior had taken refuge in the Gambia valley, did Faidherbe propose joint military operations to prevent Maba becoming another El Haj Omar. D'Arcy got his Executive Council to approve the principle of 'co-operation' with the French; but, to the relief of the Colonial Office, this proved to mean no more than providing facilities for supplying their military forces by the

[1] C.O. 87/69, D'Arcy to Newcastle, 27, 14 May; 56, 22 Dec. 1860.

[2] C.O. 87/71, D'Arcy to Newcastle, 52, 24 July 1861; C.O. 87/77, D'Arcy to Newcastle, 11, 25 Dec. 1863.

[3] Faidherbe, *op. cit.*, pp. 258–76.

Gambia route.[1] In January 1866 D'Arcy came up with a new proposal, on lines favoured by French 'neutralizers', for an embargo on the sale of arms and ammunition throughout the Senegambia region. But once again this came to nothing; the Foreign Office did not believe that the prohibition could be enforced on the Portuguese, and 'we should only be compelling our merchants to forego a lucrative trade for the benefit of other traders'.[2]

In fact, the authorities in London did not share D'Arcy's readiness to co-operate with the French. Of course, they wanted to reduce friction; but on the whole this seemed best attempted by keeping the two powers apart. This was the object of the agreement achieved in 1857, when the French withdrew from Albreda in return for Britain's formal renunciation of her right to trade for gum at Portendic.[3] But as regards positive co-operation, Newcastle commented:

> This growing habit on the W. Coast of Africa of 'going hand in hand in civilisation' with the French is dangerous, and if not checked will lead to complications. The 'Régis Contract' is a warning of the mode of civilisation in which we may involve ourselves.[4]

But this attitude seems to reflect distaste for French attitudes to questions of slavery rather than a positive antagonism. Although vaguely hostile towards France's expansionist tendencies,

[1] C.O. 87/74, D'Arcy to Newcastle, 153, 24 Nov. 1862; C.O. 87/76, same to same, 176, 24 March 1863; C.O. 87/79, same to same, Mil. 3, 25 June 1864; C.O. 87/80, same to same, Mil. 5, 16 Sept.; Mil. 6, 24 Oct. 1864; *MMC*, Afrique VI/11/f, M.M.C. to M.A.E., draft July 1864; 12 Aug.; 11 Nov. 1864.

[2] C.O. 87/84; D'Arcy to Cardwell, Mil. 4, 11 Jan. 1866; C.O. 87/90, F.O. to C.O., 5 Sept. 1868; *MMC*, Sénégal 1/50, Faidherbe to M.M.C., 204, 17 June; 428, 17 Nov. 1864.

[3] Little trade had been done there since 1847, but the Trarzas were able to obtain some fire-arms; and a British warship still paid a routine visit at the trading season. These visits actually continued until 1862, since nobody in the Foreign or Colonial Offices thought to tell the Admiralty to stop them. See Gray, *op. cit.*, pp. 406–9; P.P., 1865, V, qq. 4261–6; C.O. 87/73, D'Arcy to Newcastle, 109, 23 June 1862; C.O. 87/75, F.O. to C.O., 16 July, Admty to C.O., 30 July 1862.

[4] C.O. 87/71, minute by Newcastle, 20 Aug., on D'Arcy, 52, 24 July 1861.

E*

Newcastle had no intention of actively opposing them. Some politicians, like Adderley, agreed with D'Arcy that the protection which France could afford to British trade made her expansion positively desirable. The only participant in the proceedings of the 1865 Committee to express real concern about French proceedings was W. H. Wylde of the Slave Trade Department, and he was concerned mainly about the question of Porto Novo.[1]

[3]
French Policy in Porto Novo, 1862–8

The Anglo-French dispute over Porto Novo has already been mentioned, and it is now time to examine the case more closely. It does not fit readily into a discussion of French government policy, for the initiative was taken, as it had formerly been taken on the Ivory Coast and at Gabon, by Victor Régis, whose trade was by 1860 largely concentrated between the Volta and Niger rivers. Since 1841 his agents had occupied the former French 'fort' at Whydah, flying the national flag and representing themselves to the Dahomean authorities as direct agents of the Emperor. In return for annual payments (about 15,000 francs to the King of Dahomey, and a similar sum to his local officials), they enjoyed a near-monopoly of Dahomey's growing palm-oil trade.[2] Régis also had factories in the small autonomous principalities west of Whydah, known generally as the Popos; at Lagos; and, since 1855, at Palma. Here he hoped, by co-operating with Kosoko, to secure access to the important oil trade of Ijebu-Ode without danger of British interference.[3] But

[1] C.O. 267/279, minute by Newcastle, 31 Aug., on F.O. to C.O., 10 Aug. 1863; P.P. 1865, V, qq. 2758–9, 2915–17. For other references to French policy, see qq. 1846–9, 3664, 4027–35, 4407–15, 6664–9.

[2] MMC, Gabon 1/2/b, Didelot to M.M.C., 2, 27 March 1863; Afrique IV/10/d, Fleuriot de Langle to M.M.C., 8 Aug. 1866; Bonnaud to M.M.C., 25 June 1867.

[3] MMC, Gabon 1/2/b, Didelot to M.M.C., 54, 6 March 1863; Gabon IV/3/b, memo. by Zveppfel, 10 Feb. 1864; MAE, Afrique 55, M.M.C. to M.A.E., 15 Jan. 1862.

after the occupation of Lagos Régis quickly foresaw what actually happened in 1863: the imposition of a tariff bearing heavily on his imports of liquor and tobacco, and its extension to Kosoko's territories.[1] In the summer of 1862 Régis visited London and returned full of alarming rumours, suggesting that British aims might even include the conquest of Dahomey.[2]

Régis urged two steps to counter British policy. Firstly, he suggested that France should affirm her interest in Dahomey by appointing an honorary consular officer; his own agent, Marius Daumas, would be the obvious candidate.[3] His appointment would not only imply official recognition of the importance of Régis' interests on the Slave Coast, but would facilitate Régis' second aim, which was to bring Porto Novo under French protection. The independence of this small state was threatened by the kings of Dahomey, who raided its territory in 1850 and 1862; Soji, its ruler since 1848, could see that the support of a European power might be necessary to preserve his independence. He distrusted the British, who sought to control his trade in oil and to prevent that in slaves, and had attacked him so fiercely in 1861; he was therefore ready to look to France, who seemed less dangerously strong. On 18 May 1862 Régis informed the colonial department that Soji was willing to ally himself with France.[4]

Although Porto Novo was already exporting some 3,500 tons of oil a year, Régis at this time had no establishments there. But he had traded with a Brazilian resident named Carvalho, and shared his fears of British control. At Carvalho's suggestion Daumas travelled to Porto Novo on 5 July 1862, bearing a draft

---

[1] cf. above, pp. 58–9. According to Didelot's despatch cited in the previous note, French East Indian textiles accounted for about 12% of Régis' imports through Lagos; most of the rest seems to have been rum or tobacco, and so subject to specific duties.

[2] *MAE*, Afrique 51, Régis to M.A.E., 7 July 1862.

[3] *MAE*, Afrique 51, Régis to M.A.E., 7 July 1862.

[4] *MMC*, Gabon IV/3/b, Régis to M.M.C., 18 May 1862. On Porto Novo, see A. Akindélé and C. Aguessy, *Contribution à l'Etude de l'Ancien Royaume de Porto Novo* (Dakar, 1953); and C. W. Newbury, *The Western Slave Coast and Its Rulers* (Oxford, 1961).

appeal for the protection of Napoleon III.[1] To this document Soji duly made his mark, at the same time making a grant of land to Daumas on Régis' behalf.[2] In October Daumas returned, and concluded a new agreement. Régis agreed to open a factory for trade in palm-oil and other produce, and to pay the King 1,600 piastres a year; in return Soji agreed to permit the free passage of imports and exports, and not to vary the rates of duty charged upon them for ten years.[3] This was Régis' reply to the British occupation of Lagos. From a new base at Porto Novo he would seek to open new trade-routes into Yoruba country, protecting himself against high tariffs by agreement with Soji, and — since security guaranteed only by private treaties might prove precarious — fortifying himself as far as possible behind the authority of the French state.

There was one great weakness in this plan, which Régis failed to make clear; the difficulty of access to Porto Novo from the sea. Vessels drawing up to about ten feet of water could reach the town by way of Lagos bar; but this route was now under British control, and subject to any tariffs the colonial government might impose. The alternative was to unload imported goods by surf-boat on the long beach between Cotonou and Appa, at the risk of serious losses to the waves or the sharks. Thence they could either be man-handled across the coastal strip to the lagoon and ferried to the factories on its northern shores; or else loaded into canoes at Cotonou, and taken through Denham Water and certain small creeks. It was this last alternative which the merchants were eventually to find least unsatisfactory; but since Cotonou was still under the fiscal control of the King of Dahomey, it involved political as well as physical hazards.

Something of this and other difficulties was pointed out by

[1] *MMC*, Gabon IV/3/b, Régis to M.M.C., 18 May 1862; Gabon 1/2/b, Didelot to M.M.C., 25 Feb., 27 March, 7 Aug. 1863; Gabon 1/3/b, Laffon de Ladebat to M.M.C., 24 June 1864.

[2] *MAE*, Afrique 51, M.M.C. to M.A.E., 7 Sept. 1862, encl. Régis, 14 Aug.; Appeal of Soji to the Emperor, n.d.; Land concession to Régis; Daumas to Régis, 9 July 1862.

[3] *MAE*, Afrique 52, Régis to M.A.E., 21 March 1863 and enclosures, including Agreement between Soji and Daumas, 15 Nov. 1862.

Admiral Didelot, the naval commander, who was frankly contemptuous of the aims of Régis and Daumas; but neither foreign nor colonial officials fully grasped the point. Though they moved dilatorily, they eventually accepted the idea of acquiring a commercial foothold accessible to the rich basin of the lower Niger. In October 1862 a naval officer who accompanied Daumas to Porto Novo reported hopefully on the economic prospects; Cotonou, he thought, would offer an adequate outlet.[1] Meanwhile Régis returned to the offensive in Paris, visiting the Marine and Foreign Ministries in early December; his apprehension about British designs in the region was reinforced by Father Planque, Superior of the Society of African Missions, of Lyon, who had recently opened a mission at Whydah. Though Régis could not secure an immediate decision on Porto Novo, he did secure Daumas' nomination as Consular Agent; since his employee thus became entitled to advise the government on policy, this was to prove a decisive step.[2]

On 18 February Didelot, after installing Daumas as Vice-Consul at Whydah, accompanied him to Porto Novo town, where he was also to present his credentials. No sooner was Daumas officially installed there than he formally drew Didelot's attention to the danger of British encroachment upon French interests. The Lagos tariff had just been proclaimed; the occupation of Palma took place on 10 February, followed by the bombardment of Epe; McCoskry was reported to be heading for Porto Novo in the colonial steamboat; and the Sierra Leonean community in the town were said to be seeking a British protectorate.[3] Soji — encouraged by the Afro-Brazilians, great rivals of the Sierra Leoneans — asked for French support; and Didelot, despite his scepticism about new settlements, agreed that action was needed. His own preference was for an attempt

[1] *MMC*, Gabon 1/2/b, Didelot to M.M.C., 12 Sept., 4 Dec. 1862; Gabon IV/3/b, Libran to Didelot, 1 Nov. 1862.

[2] *MMC*, Gabon IV/3/b, Fr. Planque to M.M.C., 16 Nov. 1862; Régis to M.M.C., n.d. (rec. 2 Dec.); *MAE*, Afrique 51, Régis to Noel, 12 Dec. 1862; M.A.E. to M.M.C., 15 Dec.; Régis to M.M.C., 22 Dec. 1862.

[3] On the trading interests of Porto Novo, see Gellé's report of 25 Oct. 1863, *MMC* Gabon IV/3/b (partly printed in *Etudes Dahoméennes*, IX, pp. 15–20).

to neutralize Porto Novo and other African states in the region by negotiation with Britain; but to forestall the danger from Lagos he agreed to support Daumas in negotiating two treaties with Soji. The first, dated 23 February, defined the terms on which French subjects and *protégés* might trade at Porto Novo; one article reserved to the French government the right to confirm any alteration of customs duties. The second treaty, two days later, accepted (subject to confirmation by the Emperor) Soji's offer to place himself under French protection and leave the conduct of his foreign relations in French hands. Before leaving, Didelot detached Lieutenant Gellé to exercise French authority in this new protectorate in collaboration with Daumas, who might become suspected by foreign traders of confusing his commercial and political responsibilities.[1]

French authority was nevertheless precarious; if the Lagos government had really been as intent on expansion as Daumas believed, it is doubtful whether it could have been maintained. As it was, when Didelot proceeded to Lagos he found Governor Freeman much displeased, but willing to acquiesce on condition that the French co-operated in maintaining the blockade of Abeokuta.[2] Reactions in Paris to the new protectorate were mixed. Though officials were pleased to have placed a French foot inside one door opening, as they hoped, on the lower Niger, they correctly foresaw difficulty in maintaining it there. They regarded the protectorate less as a permanent acquisition than as a lever which might induce Britain to negotiate some sort of self-denying ordinance, neutralizing an extended line of coast under its African rulers and guaranteeing access to foreign traders.[3] But meanwhile the difficulties materialized.

Throughout 1863 French authority at Porto Novo, represented

---

[1] *MMC*, Gabon 1/2/b, Didelot to M.M.C., 25 Feb. 1863; Gabon IV/3/b, Treaty of Commerce, 23 Feb.; Protectorate Convention, 25 Feb.; Didelot to Gellé, 26 Feb. 1863; *MAE*, Afrique 52, Daumas to M.A.E., 9 March 1863.

[2] *MMC*, Gabon 1/2/b, Didelot to M.M.C., 6 March 1863; *MAE*, Afrique 52, Daumas to M.A.E., 6 April 1863; C.O. 147/3, Freeman to Newcastle, 23, 8 March 1863; cf. above, pp. 59-60.

[3] *MMC*, Gabon IV/3/b, M.M.C. to M.A.E., 7 July 1862, 20 April 1863; M.M-C. to Régis, 5 May 1863; M.A.E. to M.M.C., 3 June 1863; cf. Gabon 1/2/b, Didelot to M.M.C., 6 March 1863.

by one naval lieutenant and one trader accredited as Vice-Consul, remained tenuous, and liable to be endangered if serious hostility were shown from Lagos, from Dahomey, or from within. Even the slave trade, it appears, continued much as before.[1] Most serious of all, though some trade was carried by way of Porto Novo beach, no satisfactory outlet to the sea was secured. When the French tried to extend their control to Appa and its beach, Glover retaliated by cutting them off from Abeokuta — closing the most obvious, if not the only possible, route towards the Niger.[2]

In fact, British hostility proved the least serious. The Lagos government, once it had confirmed by the provisional boundary agreement of 1 August 1863 that France could have no access to Abeokuta, did not try to destroy the protectorate directly — though it still hoped eventually to control and tax its trade. In 1864 it agreed to a 'drawback' of 50% of the customs duty payable on goods passing through Lagos on the way to Porto Novo: no act of generosity, but an inducement to traders not to try and develop the hazardous beach landings which lay completely outside British control.[3] Disquieting rumours persisted that Britain would try to blockade these beaches under the pretext of preventing exports of slaves;[4] and some French suspicions went even further. Didelot, watching apprehensively the missions to Abomey undertaken by Wilmot in November 1862 and Burton in December 1863, feared that their real object might be, not merely to remonstrate with Gelele against his slaving raids and human sacrifices, but to obtain fiscal control over the Dahomean coastline.[5] But these fears did not materialize; and Didelot's successor, Laffon de Ladebat, soon found himself on friendly terms with Glover at Lagos.[6]

[1] *MAE*, Afrique 52, Daumas to Didelot, 6 Aug. 1863; *MMC*, Gabon IV/3/b, Didelot to M.M.C., 6 Oct. 1863; Gabon 1/3/b, Laffon de Ladebat to M.M.C., 28 Nov. 1863.

[2] *MAE*, Afrique 52, Daumas to M.A.E., 7 Oct. 1863; cf. above, pp. 60–1.

[3] *MAE*, Afrique 53, M.M.C. to M.A.E., 26 July 1864.

[4] C.O. 147/6, Freeman to Newcastle, 17, 7 April 1864.

[5] *MMC*, Gabon IV/3/b, Didelot to M.M.C., 6 Oct. 1863, encl. Brossard de Corbigny, 20 Sept.

[6] *ibid.*, Laffon de Ladebat to M.M.C., 3 Oct. 1864.

Dahomey was a more immediate menace than Britain, for in pressing her claims on Porto Novo she was not bound by European conventions of international behaviour. Gelele still regarded himself as rightful sovereign of Porto Novo itself, and of the whole coastline as far east as Appa. And during 1863 he was being incited to oppose French attempts to develop trade across these beaches by Domingo Martinez, a Portuguese who had hitherto held exclusive trading privileges, under Dahomey, at Cotonou.[1] Daumas visited Abomey and apparently secured some promise that the house of Régis might trade at Cotonou. But after Martinez died in January 1864 (according to Burton, in a fit of rage at the loss of his monopoly), Gelele sent a hundred soldiers to occupy the beach as far as Appa.[2] How far he would co-operate in maintaining Porto Novo's outlet to the sea soon appeared very doubtful.

On 26 May the mulatto Carvalho — now out of favour with the French authorities — was supervising the landing of rum at Porto Novo beach when two strangers invited him, in Gelele's name, to call on the Dahomean governor of Cotonou. Carvalho prudently declined, and fled to Porto Novo town; the Dahomeans impounded fifty-three barrels of his rum and refused all French requests for their return. Dahomean customs officers were designated to collect duties on all exports from the beach, as far as Badagry; and French attempts to secure confirmation of their landing rights at Cotonou came to a standstill. At best, this showed Gelele's intention of controlling the trade of Porto Novo; at worst it might foreshadow an attack on that state. Laffon de Ladebat warned his government to take a firm decision about their future plans for the protectorate, or risk a grave humiliation.[3] Though naval action could easily

[1] *MMC*, Gabon IV/3/b, Brossard de Corbigny to Didelot, 20 Sept. 1863; Gabon 1/2/b, Didelot to M.M.C., 28 Sept. 1863.

[2] *MAE*, Afrique 53, Daumas to M.A.E., 7 Oct. 1863; *MMC*, Gabon 1/3/b, Laffon de Ladebat to M.M.C., 9 March 1864; R. F. Burton, *A Mission to Gelele* (London, 1864) Vol. I, pp. 46–7, 104.

[3] *MMC*, Gabon 1/3/b, Laffon de Ladebat to M.M.C., 24 June 1864; Gabon IV/3/b, Brossard de Corbigny to de Ladebat, 12 June; de Ladebat to M.M.C., 4 July; Lefort to de Ladebat, 19 July; Daumas to de Ladebat, 31 July 1864.

eject Dahomey from the beaches, it could not defend Porto Novo against the famous Dahomean army, nor prevent reprisals against French property at Whydah. Laffon de Ladebat now declared that it had been a grave error to assume such a protectorate without assuring access to the sea; France could not make her authority respected, and seemed faced with the alternatives of paying duty to the British at Lagos or to Dahomey on the beaches. On 9 September he proposed to admit to the Porto Novans that a mistake had been made, and to withdraw.[1]

These reports at last shook the colonial department into a better appreciation of the precariousness of their protectorate; they urged the Admiral not to abandon French rights before a diplomatic attempt could be made to trade them to Britain, as part of a general adjustment of African territories, with mutual guarantees of fiscal equality.[2] But it was already too late. Though Gelele had been brought to a grudging and imperfect recognition of the French presence, the protectorate had been destroyed by developments in Porto Novo itself.

In October 1864, the naval Captain Desvaux accompanied Daumas to Abomey to negotiate with Gelele about the use of Cotonou. The French proposed that Cotonou creek should be recognized as the boundary between Porto Novo and Dahomey; that Dahomey should levy fixed rates of duty on exports from Cotonou; that she should evacuate the beaches further east, and restore Carvalho's rum. But their bargaining position was not strong. Military operations against Dahomey could not·be contemplated, and even a naval blockade would require British co-operation; their only real sanction was a threat to withdraw their merchants from Whydah. This would injure Gelele, but it would injure the house of Régis much more; it was not a winning card. Desvaux was detained in Abomey over a month without making much progress. Only on returning to Whydah was he curtly informed of Gelele's concessions. He

[1] *MMC*, Gabon 1/3/b, de Ladebat to M.M.C., 23 Aug., 9 Sept. 1864.
[2] *MMC*, Gabon 1/3/c, M.M.C. to de Ladebat, 22 Oct., 22 Nov. 1864; *MAE*, Afrique 53, M.M.C. to M.A.E., 14 Dec. 1864, 30 Jan. 1865; Afrique 47, Note pour le ministre, 28 Dec. 1864.

would not abate his territorial claims, but would agree to evacuate Porto Novo beach and allow the French to use it at his pleasure; as for the rum, he would restore thirty barrels to Carvalho — the unexpired portion of the fifty-three originally impounded.[1]

Meanwhile at Porto Novo the French position had been deteriorating since Soji's death on 23 January 1864. Daumas, hoping to keep the pro-French party in power, supported the succession of Dassi, the late king's son; but according to custom the office was due to pass to one of the other branches of the royal lineage; on 28 February their candidate, Mepon, was elected King, after an irate but ineffectual intervention against him by Laffon de Ladebat.[2] Mepon, encouraged by Carvalho, now began to treat the French with disrespect. In May they tried to fortify their authority by sending the warship *Dialmathe* to lie off the capital — Freeman admitted it to the lagoon without accepting this as a precedent — but it had little effect.[3] When Admiral de Ladebat revisited Porto Novo in mid-December he decided that France could save her prestige only by immediate withdrawal. (He had not yet received the despatch of 22 November, urging him to try to keep the protectorate as material for negotiation; but later he denied that it could have affected his decision.) Between 20 and 22 December the evacuation was carried out, despite anguished protests from Régis' agents and a few other traders.[4]

*   *   *   *   *

Now the authorities at Lagos might have had the opportunity to complete their fiscal control over the lagoon — had they been

---

[1] *MMC*, Gabon 1/3/b, de Ladebat to M.M.C., 3 Oct., 21 Nov. 1864.

[2] *MAE*, Afrique 53, Daumas to M.A.E., 7 Feb. 1864; *MMC*, Gabon 1/3/b, de Ladebat to M.M.C., 9 March 1864; Akindélé and Aguessy, *op. cit.*, pp. 35, 75 ff.

[3] C.O. 147/6, Freeman to Newcastle, 29, 9 May 1864; *MMC*, Gabon IV/3/b, de Ladebat to M.M.C., 8 May 1864; M.M.C. to M.A.E., 24 Aug. 1864.

[4] *MMC*, Gabon 1/3/b, de Ladebat to M.M.C., 22 Dec. 1864; 2 Jan. 1865; Gabon IV/3/b, Note by Lefort, 10 Dec. 1864; Lefort to de Ladebat, 1 Jan. 1865; Régis to M.M.C., 8 Feb. 1865.

left more free to act by their political masters in London. In January 1865 Glover visited Porto Novo and found King Mepon chastened and unusually compliant. He dealt with several detailed complaints, reaffirmed the commercial treaties of 1852 and 1861, and seemed to acquiesce in Glover's announced intention of appointing a British Resident.[1] Clearly Glover wished to bring about British control. In April 1865 he angered the French by declaring a blockade of Cotonou (ostensibly to tighten up that directed against Abeokuta); simultaneously he withdrew the 'drawback' allowed by Lagos customs regulations on imports destined for Porto Novo, and began staking-up the channels leading to Porto Novo from Cotonou and Godomey. Unfortunately the navy insisted on withdrawing its blockading ships before this attempt to assume full control of Porto Novo's maritime trade could have any important effects.[2]

In August Glover made a more direct attempt to get control of Porto Novo by espousing the claim to the throne of Dassi (who, having found the French a broken reed, had been looking for support in Lagos). After the failure of hopes that Mepon might be deposed from within, Glover sailed up to his capital in a gunboat, fined him seventy puncheons of oil as damages claimed by British subjects, and renewed his proposal for a British Resident. When Mepon rejected this last demand, Glover contemplated a new bombardment. According to local tradition he was dissuaded by Dassi, out of patriotic feeling; Glover himself said it was British merchants who advised against such action. Back in Lagos, Glover wrote to ask permission to annex the state, on the grounds that Mepon was incapable of maintaining order, respecting treaties, or preventing human sacrifice. Since the year was 1865, this proposal was almost automatically rejected.[3]

Even from the viewpoint of Anglo-French relations, still more from that of the future of British Nigeria, this decision proved

---

[1] C.O. 147/8, Glover to Cardwell, 19, 31 Jan. 1865.
[2] C.O. 147/8, Glover to Cardwell, 36, 9 April; 47 and 48, 8 May 1865.
[3] C.O. 147/9, Glover to Cardwell, 87, 7 Sept. 1865; Cardwell to Glover, 273, 23 Oct. 1865; C.O. 147/10, F.O. to C.O., 29 Nov. 1865; Akindélé and Aguessy, op. cit., p. 77.

unfortunate. Though France's immediate reaction would have been resentful, much subsequent trouble would have been prevented. Régis and his agents continued to work to frustrate Glover's attempts to channel all trade in the lagoon through the Lagos customs-sheds, and though de Ladebat warned his governmer.t against accepting their advice, his successors took the danger seriously. With their support Régis' agents, still holding the consular appointment, began to build up their interests at Cotonou, which, they alleged, Gelele had ceded to Desvaux in 1864.[1] (On 13 October 1867 the British were informed of this claim, but failed to note its significance.)[2] On 19 May 1868 Régis' agent Bonnaud, acting as Vice-Consul, signed a Treaty with the Yavogan of Whydah on behalf of Dahomey; this confirmed the cession to France of territory at Cotonou about six kilometres square, but left it under Dahomean administration until such time as France chose to occupy it.[3] The Ministry of the Marine felt apprehensive about this new attempt to raise paper claims against British encroachments; de Ladebat, now serving there as Director of Personnel, doubted whether Gelele could have assented to such a treaty, and became most alarmed when Bonnaud spoke of obtaining a new concession of land at Porto Novo itself.[4] But since no immediate commitments seemed involved, the French government eventually decided to confirm the Cotonou treaty. The rights it conferred remained latent, as weapons for future use, and had no immediate relevance to the negotiations which by now had been opened with Britain.[5]

---

[1] *MAE*, Afrique 53, Béraud to M.A.E., 1 May, 2 Sept. 1865; *MMC*, Gabon IV/3/b, Régis to M.M.C., 8 Feb. 1865; Gabon 1/3/b, de Ladebat to M.M.C., 2 Feb. 1865, de Langle to Bonnaud, 8 May 1867; *MAE*, Afrique 53, M.M.C. to M.A.E., 11 July, 16 Aug. 1867, encl. de Langle, 22 May, 8 June.

[2] *MAE*, Afrique 53, Baude to Moustier, 13 Oct. 1867.

[3] Treaty printed in *Etudes Dahoméennes*, IX, pp. 26–8; *MAE*, Afrique 53, Bonnaud to M.A.E., 22 May 1868.

[4] *MMC*, Gabon IV/3/c, Note pour le Directeur des Colonies, 20 July 1868.

[5] *MAE*, Afrique 53, M.A.E. to M.M.C., 11 July 1868; M.M.C. to M.A.E., 30 July, 23 Oct.; Afrique 54, M.M.C. to M.A.E., 11 Feb., 5 March 1869; M.A.E. to Daumas, 9 April.

[4]
Faidherbe's Second Governorship

Relations with El Haj Omar

In 1863 Faidherbe returned to Senegal, after another tour of service in Algeria. This second governorship lasted only two years and produced fewer striking results than the first. Militarily Faidherbe still found himself occupied in the lower basin of the river, trying to pacify Futa, and dealing with the strong resistance of Lat-Dior and Maba in Cayor and its vicinity. Economically too the immediate prospects did not seem encouraging. The gum trade continued to decline; groundnut production flourished less than in the rivers further south; hopes of growing cotton, stimulated once more during the American Civil War, proved as illusory as the legendary 'mines of Bambouk'. Faidherbe remained convinced that the colony could command a great future, but increasingly he concentrated his hopes on plans for extending French influence into two adjacent regions. One was that of the groundnut-producing *rivières du sud*; the other, even more fascinating since Barth's publication, was the middle Niger basin.

One of Faidherbe's first actions was to obtain the services of Lieutenant Mage, a courageous naval officer who had already served five years ashore in Senegal, to lead a mission to the Niger. His instructions were far-reaching; if possible, he was to follow Mungo Park's route to Boussa and to emerge in the Bight of Benin.[1] Faidherbe had long been interested in the possibility, remote though it seemed, of developing a waterborne trade along the whole length of the Niger; in 1858 he had contemplated occupying a post in the delta in order to preclude any danger of British control.[2] But he did not build concrete hopes on this project, nor even on the commercial treaty which he signed in St. Louis with a relative of El Bekkai of Timbuktu, in

[1] *MMC*, Sénégal III/9/c, Faidherbe to Mage, 7 Aug., 7 Oct. 1863, printed in E. Mage, *Voyage dans le Soudan Occidental* (Paris, 1868) pp. 12–18.

[2] Schefer, *op. cit.*, II, p. 313; Prince Napoleon to Faidherbe, 22 Feb. 1859.

1863.[1] Before France could develop any sort of Niger policy she would have to face the outstanding problem of relations with El Haj Omar and the Tokolor empire.

Although the information available in St. Louis was patchy, it was clear that the prophet had greatly extended his power since turning towards the Niger. In 1861 the Bambaras of Ségou, in 1862 the Fula state of Macina, were subjected. Faidherbe continued to glimpse possible benefits in a policy of co-operating with this strong Muslim power: as Tokolor power advanced down the Niger, might it not prepare the way for French trade and influence? Mage's primary role was to explore these possibilities 'in the capacity of ambassador to El Haj Omar'.

Co-operation would of course not be easily achieved, and one of Faidherbe's proposals was certain to raise difficulties. Hoping to encourage African traders to visit Senegal rather than Morocco, Faidherbe wished to construct a line of fortified posts beyond the frontier provisionally accepted in 1859, covering the route from Bafoulabé (where Bafing and Bakhoy join to form the Senegal river) to Bamako on the Niger. Omar had declared in 1855 that he would not welcome such encroachments on his territory. But to secure his acquiescence and appease his fears Faidherbe was willing to go a considerable way towards meeting his desire to impose customs duties on French traders, and would even promise to place no artillery in the projected forts.[2]

That Faidherbe should be willing to consider co-operation on such terms is a tribute to Omar's success in creating a state. The original foundation of the prophet's power was the authority which he commanded among Muslims, by virtue of preaching which was at once rigorous in its demands and egalitarian in its doctrine. But as a political and military leader he necessarily had to introduce or accept hierarchies of authority. An *élite* group of *talibés*, or disciples, provided the leadership of his army

[1] Delafosse, *op. cit.*, II, p. 407 n.

[2] *MMC*, Sénégal III/9/c, Register, Conseil d'Administration, 25 March 1864, quoting supplementary instructions to Mage; cf. Faidherbe, *op. cit.*, p. 170; above, pp. 102–3.

and the instrument for the government of his conquests; many
of these were Tokolors who had come from Futa to join him. In
his conquered territories Omar established chosen lieutenants
in selected centres, where they built stone forts and dominated
the surrounding country, maintaining armies and levying
taxation more in the manner of feudal barons than of military
governors. Usually Omar ruled through members of his own
family, Tokolors from Futa, or Africans who had some experience in the European settlements; but sometimes he maintained
conquered chiefs as his own agents.[1]

So long as Omar led a victorious army, this machinery of
government worked efficiently. Most of the *talibés* seem to have
given him their full loyalty; the conquered provinces provided
slaves (or conscripts) to serve in his army, and taxes in kind with
which to buy arms and powder at the coast. Defeat naturally
weakened the prophet's prestige, and Mage claimed that
desertions after the relief of Medina in 1857 reduced Omar's
army from 23,000 to 7,000.[2] But by 1862 the conquests on the
Niger had apparently raised the Tokolor empire to its greatest
strength.

But even as Mage left St. Louis in October 1863, some of the
conquered peoples were beginning to revolt. The general causes
seem clear enough: resentment of the restrictions which religion
sought to impose upon their conduct, patriotic resistance to the
rule of an alien aristocracy and to its exactions. In 1863 Fulas
and Bambaras of newly-conquered Macina began the revolt;
El Bekkai of Timbuktu, who did not welcome powerful neighbours, gave them some assistance. When Mage reached Ségou
in February 1864 Omar was absent, and many conflicting
rumours were circulating on the military situation. Amadu, son
and heir-presumptive to the prophet, would not allow Mage
and his colleague Quintin to proceed towards Macina, but
detained them in the capital for more than two years. Gradually the Frenchmen realized that the route to Macina was no
longer under Tokolor control; that Omar was dead (though

---

[1] The best European account of Omar's empire and its institutions is
Mage, *op. cit.*

[2] Mage, *op. cit.*, p. 248.

Amadu could not afford to let this be known) and his army defeated.

Amadu, lacking his father's religious authority, now used all his considerable political skill to hold the Tokolor empire together. Even his title to succeed was disputed by his half-brothers, Abibou and Moktar, the viceroys of Dinguiray and Koniakary. Only in 1873 was Amadu able to defeat them in battle and assert control over their provinces.[1] Even more serious were the signs of revolt or dissension among the conquered peoples — not only in Macina but also among Mandinkas and Bambaras of the upper Senegal basin. Mage now understood that it was the dissension of these peoples which had led the Tokolors to divert him to a circuitous route through Kaarta and Nioro. Even here, he had detected signs of discontent with the Tokolors. As for the army, he put its strength in 1866 at only 4,000 talibés, their discipline and loyalty weakened by defeat, supported by 11,000 unreliable slaves and conscripts. Reflecting somewhat sourly on the prospects, Mage decided during his captivity at Ségou that Amadu's alliance should not be relied upon too heavily.[2]

Nevertheless, when he finally agreed to negotiate with Mage in February 1866, Amadu was not at all eager to accept French terms for an alliance. His paramount aim was to secure armaments which might ensure the submission of his enemies. Two howitzers captured by Omar in the Senegal had already proved decisive weapons,[3] and Amadu insisted on a promise of more artillery of this type. Mage eventually gave him a rather imprecise assurance, which was never fulfilled. But even in return for military supplies Amadu would not admit French influence to his country without strict conditions. He refused to agree to the proposed forts in his dominions, and insisted that French traders should pay, like any others, an import duty of 10%. It was a somewhat general treaty of peace and commerce which Mage was finally allowed to take back to St. Louis in May 1866.[4]

---

[1] Capt. Piétri, *Les Français au Niger* (Paris, 1885) pp. 101–24.

[2] *MMC*, Sénégal III/9/c, Report by Mage, n.d. [1866].

[3] Delafosse, *op. cit.*, II, p. 313.

[4] Mage, *op. cit.*, pp. 572–3 (Faidherbe to Mage, 30 Nov. 1865) 587–9, 608.

Had Faidherbe still been governor, it is likely that some attempt would have been made to develop relations with Amadu from this disappointing starting-point. But his successor, Laprade, seems to have been influenced by the anti-Muslim prejudices common in St. Louis; and Mage, after his harrowing stay in Ségou, was in no mood to argue otherwise. Political conditions in the Tokolor empire, he argued, would not encourage commerce. On the other hand, Amadu was still strong enough to resist any attempt to build the proposed chain of forts against his will; any such attempt would be dangerous, costly, and unremunerative. France should welcome Sudanese traders who continued to come to the Senegal, but to go out to meet them would mean giving hostages to fortune.[1] For more than a dozen years, then, nothing was done to advance Faidherbe's hope of contact with the Niger. But the hope itself was not forgotten by all.

The idea of an exchange

Along the coast, Faidherbe wanted to see French authority exercised at least as far as the river Nunez, whence he hoped to develop caravan routes to the upper Niger.[2] Beyond Sierra Leone Faidherbe had no interest. On the Ivory Coast trade was still disappointing; the mythical 'mountains of Kong', as marked on contemporary maps, seemed to preclude any chance of deep inland penetration; and Faidherbe himself, while building a fort at Dabou in 1853, had formed highly unfavourable opinions of the climate and the local political situation. These opinions were largely shared by the naval officers responsible for the oversight of these troublesome and unprofitable settlements.[3] Faidherbe did remain interested in the possibility of acquiring a territorial stake near the lower Niger which could prevent any British monopoly on that river: an attitude which made the Ministry of the Marine more

[1] *MMC*, Sénégal III/9/c, Brief report by Mage, 1866.
[2] See within, pp. 129–32.
[3] Schefer, *op. cit.*, II, pp. 474–9, Chasseloup-Laubat to Didelot, 10 Oct. 1861, pp. 495–500; C-Laubat to de Ladebat, 26 Sept. 1863; *MMC*, Gabon 1/2/b, Didelot to M.M.C., 13 May 1863.

sympathetic to Régis' venture at Porto Novo.[1] But territories south of the Nunez had little intrinsic value in Faidherbe's eyes.

Thus Faidherbe came to advocate the view that France could usefully abandon all her existing territorial claims south of Sierra Leone, if thereby she could secure Britain's withdrawal from the Gambia valley. Commercially, British rule here seemed anomalous; groundnuts constituted over 90% of the colony's exports, and about three-quarters of these were sent to France, though not all by French merchants. More important, under British control the Gambia valley made France's military campaigns in the Cayor region much more difficult; her enemies used it both as a market for buying firearms and as a sanctuary where the French could pursue them only with the reluctantly-conceded co-operation of the British. Finally, and most tempting to Faidherbe, the Gambia offered a route, more easily navigable than the Senegal, towards Omar's empire and Futa Jalon, the organized states whence he hoped that France's African empire might draw its future wealth.

While preparing to embark for Senegal in 1863, Faidherbe drafted a far-reaching proposal which he hoped would receive the attention of the Emperor. He began by pointing out that France's trade at Gabon and the Ivory Coast was negligible, while that further north was increasingly taking place outside her own jurisdiction; French imports from the Gambia and the 'free rivers' were as great as from the Senegal colony. This position might be rationalized by an agreement with Britain, more extensive than the neutralization and free-trade agreement currently adumbrated in connection with Porto Novo. France should aim at securing the Gambia, so that she could organize a large and compact colony as a base for penetration towards the upper Niger. In return she could offer to withdraw in Britain's favour from the Ivory Coast, Gabon, and the new protectorate of Porto Novo, while stipulating that there should

---

[1] Schefer, *op. cit.*, II, p. 313, Prince Napoleon to Faidherbe, 22 Feb. 1859; *MMC*, Sénégal 1/50, Faidherbe to M.M.C., 23 April 1863; Afrique IV/12/b, M.A.E. to M.M.C., 3 Aug. 1864, minutes by Zveppfel and C-Laubat; cf. above, pp. 113-4.

be no inequalities in customs or navigation duties in these territories. If further inducement seemed necessary, she might offer to open the Senegal to foreign shipping. On such terms, Faidherbe concluded rhetorically but sincerely, the two civilized powers might succeed in co-operating in a common policy for the development of Africa.[1]

Chasseloup-Laubat, the Minister responsible for the colonies since 1859, was temperamentally inclined to favour bold schemes of this sort; but he lacked the strength of purpose necessary to carry them through. Though he supported such a plan in a minute of June 1863,[2] many of his officials were critical of Faidherbe's enthusiasm, and opposed any withdrawal from the Bight of Benin — especially from Gabon, which many naval officers judged a useful base. In 1862 the Department had ruled that,

'far from seeking to exchange the territories which we possess in the Gulf of Guinea, we must apply ourselves to developing our influence in those waters';[3]

and once Faidherbe was back in Africa official objections to the plan began to shake the conviction of Chasseloup-Laubat, himself a former bureaucrat. Faidherbe's report never reached the Emperor; and policy over Porto Novo vacillated between the new idea of using French rights as material for a territorial exchange, and the earlier one of trying to negotiate for neutralization and free trade. Thus, a letter to the Foreign Ministry of 28 July 1863, originally drafted so as to favour the latter aim, was so amended as to give equal emphasis to the exchange proposal — and lost much coherence in the process. At the same time the Ministry of the Marine promised a considered opinion on the exchange question; but it was long delayed.[4]

[1] *MMC*, Afrique VI/11/a, Rapport à l'Empereur, July 1863. This copy is not in Faidherbe's hand, but is attributed to him in Afrique VI/15/a, Note, Nov. 1871.

[2] *MMC*, Gabon IV/3/b, minute by C-Laubat on M.A.E. to M.M.C., 3 June 1863.

[3] *ibid.*, M.M.C. to M.A.E., 7 July 1862.

[4] *MMC*, Gabon IV/3/b, M.M.C. to M.A.E., 28 July 1863; cf. the long and indecisive Note on Porto Novo by Zveppfel, 10 Feb. 1864.

In May 1864 Faidherbe's paper was taken from the files and re-drafted as a departmental Note, without its peroration or the suggestion of admitting foreign shipping to the Senegal.[1] Its original author now had new grounds for pressing his scheme, for military operations in Cayor were again being hindered because France could not operate in the Gambia valley without British co-operation. Lat-Dior, after a defeat by Faidherbe's forces, had taken refuge there and made an alliance with Maba, who was to prove most troublesome to the French until he died in July 1867. For his immediate operations, Faidherbe successfully asked D'Arcy's co-operation; and on 21 May he got his *Conseil d'Administration* to add their authority to the exchange proposal.[2] At the same time he extended his ideas to embrace possible negotiations for the cession of the other foreign enclave in Senegambia — Portuguese Guinea.

But these arguments did not overcome the objections of officials, nor complete the conversion of the wavering Minister. In a long manuscript letter to Faidherbe, Chasseloup-Laubat explained that he felt unable to offer the British any compensation which might induce them to give up the Gambia. Because the question of labour recruitment might need to be re-opened, he would not offer the Gabon; he hesitated to offer Porto Novo, because he still hoped it might afford a practical route towards the Niger. And the Ivory Coast settlements alone, the Minister rightly concluded, would hardly tempt the British. Hence they would be likely to retain the Gambia for its nuisance value. The Portuguese were even less likely to respond to an exchange proposal; their strong national pride in their African possessions was notorious, and 'it is often more difficult to deal with a secondary government than with a great power'. Chasseloup-Laubat thus concluded, with profuse expressions of sympathy and esteem, that the time was unripe for any diplomatic initiative.[3] By the time the idea was revived France had abandoned

---

[1] *MMC*, Afrique VI/11/a, Note sur nos établissements . . . May 1864.

[2] *MMC*, Sénégal 1/50; Faidherbe to C-Laubat, 27 May, 17 June 1864; cf. Faidherbe, *Le Sénégal* . . . pp. 277 ff; above, p. 108.

[3] *MMC*, Afrique VI/11/a, C-Laubat to Faidherbe, 23 July 1864 (copy of extract); cf. Schefer, *op. cit.*, II, pp. 377–81; Afrique VI/11/f, M.M.C. to M.A.E., July 1864 (cancelled draft); 12 Aug. 1864 (amended draft).

one possible bargaining counter, at Porto Novo; but she had also acquired a new one.

[5]
French Occupation of the Mellacourie, 1865–7

Faidherbe's growing interest in the *rivières du sud* led him to propose, as early as 1860, the establishment of a military post in the river Nunez, and of a political resident in the Pongos. His object was partly to provide better protection of French trade — though he noted that the traders were often not anxious for French protection — partly to develop a base from which French political influence might spread towards Futa Jalon (whither he sent Lieutenant Lambert on a mission in 1860). But it was only in December 1863 that Chasseloup-Laubat author- ized Faidherbe to take these steps, and only on condition that the expenses should be met out of local revenue. This delayed action for a further two years; it was Faidherbe's successor, Pinet-Laprade, who eventually, between November 1865 and February 1866, signed a number of treaties of protection with rulers in these two rivers, and established a military post at Boké in the Nunez.[1]

In these two rivers British trade was small, and no inter- national complications were expected; in fact, the only immedi- ate complaints about the French occupation came from fifteen small Creole traders in the Nunez, and three others in the Pongos.[2] But the third of the principal *rivières du sud*, the Mella- courie (together with the Fouricaria and Bereira, whose estuaries merged into an extensive area of inshore navigation) was more important to Sierra Leone. Since the 1820's the colonial

---

[1] Schefer, *op. cit.*, II, pp. 337–40, C-Laubat to Jauréguibery, 17 Dec. 1861; cf. pp. 366, 371–2, 375–7, 384–5; *MMC*, Sénégal 1/50, Laprade to Faid- herbe, 14 April 1864; Faidherbe to C-Laubat, 23 April; *MAE*, Afrique 47, M.M.C. to M.A.E., 5 April 1866. For Futa Jalon, see Colonel Lambert, 'Voyage dans le Fouta Djallon' *Bulletin de la Société Languedocienne de la Géographie*, 1889, pp. 1–28; cf. below, pp. 267–71.

[2] C.O. 267/290, Blackall to Carnarvon, 28, 22 March 1867; to Buckingham, 67, 27 June; Separate, 29 June 1867; C.O. 267/291, F.O. to C.O., 30 April 1867.

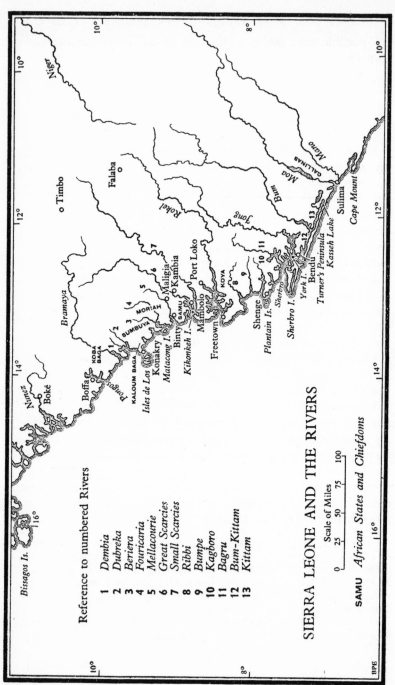

Reference to numbered Rivers

1   Dembia
2   Dubreka
3   Beriera
4   Fouricaria
5   Mellacourie
6   Great Scarcies
7   Small Scarcies
8   Ribbi
9   Bumpe
10 Kagboro
11 Bagru
12 Bum–Kittam
13 Kittam

SIERRA LEONE AND THE RIVERS

Scale of Miles

0   25   50   75   100

SAMU   *African States and Chiefdoms*

MAP 3

BPE

government had worked to preserve peace and encourage legitimate commerce in this district; in 1826 an acting Governor signed treaties ceding a strip of seaboard one mile wide, but was disavowed by London. In 1845 new and less drastic treaties were made at the instance of Charles Heddle, a wealthy Eurafrican merchant of Freetown, who was developing a large export trade in groundnuts; these provided the basis for British influence during the next twenty years. The chiefs of the region agreed, in return for small stipends, to suppress the slave trade, to protect the persons and property of British subjects and refer litigation affecting them to Sierra Leone, and to preserve order and the free movement of commerce.[1] The Mellacourie thus provided a small but reasonably successful example of the classical policies of 'informal empire'.

During the early 1860's there seems to have been appreciable growth in the Mellacourie trade. This was partly because the river attracted more caravans from Futa Jalon; some were diverted from the Great Scarcies, the estuary immediately to the south, by a prolonged war between the Temne and Susu peoples (in which Susus from the Mellacourie joined). Another reason was increased export of groundnuts, stimulated by increasing competition among foreign traders. For the first time, French traders became active in this district; about 1864 the Gorée house of Gaspard Devès opened several factories under the direction of their Freetown agent, Felix Dalmas, a forceful young mulatto from Guadeloupe. Devès was affiliated with the Bordeaux firm of Chaumel and Durin, and soon the Bordeaux Chamber of Commerce was urging the French government to protect the coasts between the Gambia and the Sherbro — 'exploited almost exclusively by French commerce' — against further British encroachments. Specifically, they suggested establishing a base to watch French interest on the coast in the

---

[1] The treaties are printed in A. Montagu's *Ordinances of Sierra Leone*, and in C.O. 806/346. The main ones were signed between 20 and 28 May 1845 with Bay Sherbro, Chief of the Samo country and Morie Bokkary, Chief of Moricania; Mori Lahai, Chief of Malaghea; Alimami Ali, Chief of the Fouricaria country; and Alimami Morie Mussa, Chief of Berieira; cf. C.O. 267/187, Ferguson to Stanley, 18 July 1845.

Mellacourie region.[1] There was some support for this idea in Paris, but Faidherbe, with his eyes on the Nunez, thought it would be offensive to Sierra Leone to intrude politically so far south, and dismissed the idea as originating in the self-interest of some small group.[2]

But in May 1865 a destructive war broke out in the Mellacourie which gave French and British merchants alike strong reason for desiring foreign intervention. In the Susu chiefdom of Moriah the office of chief customarily passed to the oldest male member of the royal family. On the death of Alimami, Foday Wise the heir-apparent renounced his claim in favour of Maligy Gbele, a junior member of his own Touré family; his right to do this was questioned by his cousin Bokkari, who enlisted the support of some rather unruly Temne warriors from the Scarcies district, and of Chief Yemba Lamina of Samu.[3] Their armed conflicts disrupted trade and cultivation; there was looting of produce and trade-goods from ships and stores. Most merchants favoured Maligy Gbele, whom they expected to co-operate more readily with their trading practices, and for a time they supplied him with arms; but soon they concluded that peace was unlikely to be achieved quickly by the outright victory of either party, but only through the intervention of external power.

At first both French and British merchants looked for resolute action to the government of Sierra Leone. But the acting

[1] *MMC*, Sénégal IV/55/b, Bordeaux Chamber of Commerce to M.M.C., 12 Dec. 1864; cf. J. D. Hargreaves 'The French Occupation of the Mellacourie', *S.L.S.*, n.s. 9, 1957; and above, p. 94.

[2] *MMC*, Sénégal 1/50, Faidherbe to C-Laubat, 15 Feb. 1865; Sénégal IV/55/b, M.M.C. to Bordeaux Chamber, 12 April 1865; cf. Schefer, *op. cit.*, II, p. 342; C-Laubat to Jauréguibery, 17 Dec. 1861.

[3] Strictly speaking, Yemba Lamina was chief of Moricania, not of Samu. This territory between the Mellacourie and Great Scarcies rivers was predominantly Bullom in population; and the chief of the indigenous 'Samu Bulloms' bore the title of Bai Sherbro. The Moricanians were Muslim immigrants, described by T. G. Lawson as 'Mandingo Susus', who had acquired territorial jurisdiction within the same area. But Yemba Lamina, until his death in 1868, seems to have had power to commit the Samu Bulloms as well as his own people; cf. C.O. 806/279, memo. by Parkes (really by Lawson), Feb. 1887; *MMC*, Senegal IV/56/a, Poutot, 14 June 1868; Trimingham and Fyfe, *loc. cit.*, pp. 35–7.

governor, Colonel Chamberlayne, knowing that no strong initiative would be approved in London, only sent colonial officials on missions of mediation, and asked the warship *Zebra* to watch over European interests. In August Chamberlayne did suggest to the Colonial Office that Britain might undertake some responsibility for the region under the inoperative treaties of 1826–7, appointing a resident agent and meeting the cost by imposing customs duties; but this recommendation, arriving shortly after the Parliamentary Committee's report, was rejected almost automatically. Indeed, Cardwell and the Admiralty, though not the Foreign Office, even seemed to doubt whether the *Zebra* should have visited the disturbed area. The only action seriously discussed in the Colonial Office was the imposition of duties on transit trade through Freetown to the Mellacourie.[1] Any action Britain might take seemed likely to cost the traders more in taxation than it would immediately bring them in improved security.

After the ineffective visit of the *Zebra*, the French in the Mellacourie ceased to look for support from Britain. Braouezec, French Vice-Consul in Freetown — an ambitious ex-naval officer, with a strong though concealed dislike of the British and their perfidious fiscal policy — decided to work for French intervention, operating through the trader Dalmas in order to avoid compromising his official status. The firm of Devès demanded action, both in Senegal and in Paris; on 28 July a landing-party from a French warship compelled Bokkari to admit responsibility for losses suffered by Devès. Its commander, Requin, next proposed to make a treaty of protection with Maligy.[2]

In October Laffon de Ladebat, as French naval commander, visited Sierra Leone and the rivers to investigate Braouezec's reports of an imminent British occupation. Aware that, what-

---

[1] C.O. 267/284, Chamberlayne to Cardwell, 19 July; 90, 19 Aug.; 107, 18 Oct. 1865; Huggins to Chamberlayne, 31 July; C.O. 267/285, Admty to C.O., 20 Sept.; F.O. to C.O., 9 Oct. 1865 and minutes.

[2] *MAE*. Angleterre (Freetown) 53, Braouezec to M.A.E., 18 Aug., 20 Oct. 1865; 4 July 1867; *MMC*, Sénégal IV/55/b, Chaumel and Durin to M.M.C., 20 July 1865, encl. Dalmas, 21 June, Devès (Gorée) 1 July; Bordeaux Chamber of Commerce to M.M.C., 19 Sept. 1865; Requin to Laprade, n.d. [Aug.], Devès to Laprade, 1 Sept. 1865; Braouezec to M.A.E., 19 Sept. 1865.

F

ever plots might be formed locally, the general trend of British
policy made such action unlikely, de Ladebat was anxious that
his government should not once more be drawn by intriguing
traders into establishing territorial claims where they would
provoke British resentment; he would have preferred a diplomatic negotiation to neutralize the rivers, on the lines he had
already suggested at Porto Novo. Laprade, more deeply suspicious of British designs, disagreed; he preferred to stake
claims in the Mellacourie at the same time as in the Nunez and
Pongos. With these cards in her hand, France might have better
hopes of securing the cession of the Gambia.[1] By maintaining
warships in the Mellacourie he reinforced the diplomacy of
Braouezec and his allies; on 20 November the leading Mellacourie merchants, with the important exception of Messrs.
Broadhurst and Frame, signed a letter inviting Laprade to
continue to show his solicitude for the protection of the Mellacourie and Fouricaria rivers. Of the nineteen signatories between six and nine were Frenchmen or agents of French firms;
most of the others were British or Sierra Leonean merchants
from Freetown, or their resident agents. No doubt many of
these signatories expected that French protection would continue to be given informally, by the timely despatch of warships; they may not have noticed that the French word used for
protection was *protectorat*. But armed with their letter Requin
proceeded to sign a treaty by which Maligy Gbele accepted
French protection and suzerainty in return for recognition of
his title as chief of Moriah.[2]

Before publicly acknowledging their *protégé*, the French
government waited to see him prove his strength. In fact the war
went well for Maligy during 1866, and in September the commander of one of the French warships in the river published the
treaty. But this proved to be premature. Within a few weeks

[1] *MMC*, Sénégal IV/55/b, de Ladebat to M.M.C., 29 Sept., 30 Oct. 1865;
Laprade to de Ladebat, 26 Oct.; Sénégal 1/51, Laprade to M.M.C., 31 Oct.
1865.

[2] *MMC*, Sénégal IV/55/b, merchants to Laprade, 20 Nov. 1865 (Copy).
For a slightly different list of signatories, A. Arcin, *Histoire de la Guinée
Française* (Paris, 1911) p. 317 n; C.O. 267/290; Blackall to Buckingham, 67,
27 June 1867, enclosing copies of treaties.

Maligy was captured and killed; though his brother carried on the war, he was much less successful, and the acting French Consul suggested that France should change horses by seeking a treaty with Bokkari. While the Colonial department was still wondering whether this would be logical, Laprade himself went to Sierra Leone in December 1866 with the intention of finally clearing up the political status of all the *rivières du sud*.[1] Although Blackall was too much under the influence of the Parliamentary Committee to object to French protectorates,[2] Laprade encountered resistance from Mellacourie traders resident in Freetown. The danger that the British tariff might be imposed seemed to have passed; if France intervened on behalf of the 'Maliguistes', this now seemed likely to prolong hostilities; and when peace was ultimately restored there might prove to be inconveniences attached to a permanent French presence. But Laprade indicated that if he was not supported in bringing pressure on Bokkari he would intervene in the war more violently; hence, at Fouricaria on 30 December four traders, French and British, stood by while Bokkari was coerced into signing a treaty with the acting Consul, containing the same obligations as that with Maligy.[3]

Now the French gradually asserted their authority. In February 1867 a military post for twenty-five men was established on a site just outside Heddle's factory at Binty; on the south bank of the Mellacourie, it actually lay outside Moriah, in Samu chiefdom. Soon afterwards a supplementary agreement with Bokkari regulated the payment of stipends and the conditions of trade; the French were to collect anchorage dues but for the present no customs duties. (They hoped thus to avoid antagonizing British merchants, and to attract trade away from Freetown.)[4] Their power was still very limited; the succession

[1] *MMC*, Sénégal 1/51, Laprade to M.M.C., 19 May 1866; Sénégal IV/55/d; Suarez to M.M.C., 14 Nov. 1866; Laprade to M.M.C., 23 Jan. 1867.

[2] C.O. 267/287, Blackall to Cardwell, 72, 11 Oct. 1866; *MMC*, Sénégal IV/55/c; Suarez to M.M.C., 13 Oct. 1866.

[3] *MMC*, Sénégal IV/55/d, Report by Suarez, 4 Jan. 1867; C.O. 267/290, Blackall to Buckingham, 67, 27 June 1867, encl. copy of treaty.

[4] *MMC*, Sénégal IV/55/d, Flize to Laprade, 6 March 1867; Treaty with Bokkari, n.d.; Sénégal 1/51, Laprade to M.M.C., 23 Jan. 1867.

war was still unsettled, and French trade in 1867 was only about one-sixth the level of 1865.[1] But they had established a title which it would be difficult to dispute if the normal canons of international relations were applied.

Their ultimate purpose in acquiring it was still uncertain. Devès, Braouezec, and the naval officers with whom they had collaborated, clearly intended that the protectorate they had helped to create, for reasons of patriotism and self-interest, should be permanent. But their political influence in France was insufficient to determine that it should be so. Laprade and the Ministry of the Marine valued the Gambia far more highly than the Mellacourie, and had been contemplating a possible exchange. Yet they had not conceived the occupation *solely* as a bargaining counter. Both governor and ministry believed that French trade was capable of more rapid development under French rule; their newly acquired rights had a value of their own. And it was still not clear that Britain was in the exchange market at all.

[6]

Early British Reactions to the Exchange Proposal

Apparently the idea of a territorial exchange was first suggested to the Colonial Office in 1861, when D'Arcy returned from his visit to St. Louis with the idea that the Gambia might be exchanged for Gabon; later, French naval officers on the coast occasionally raised the question. Two witnesses before the 1865 Committee mentioned the idea, and in 1864 Blackall suggested that it might be beneficial to remove sources of Anglo-French friction 'even at the cost of an exchange which might in the first instance prove disadvantageous'.[2] All these

---

[1] *MAE*, Angleterre (Freetown) 53, Braouezec to M.A.E., 17 Aug. 1868.

[2] C.O. 87/72, F.O. to C.O., 4 Oct. 1861; *MAE*, Afrique 51, Didelot to M.M.C., 2 May 1862; Afrique 53, de Ladebat to M.M.C., 19 May 1865; P.P. 1865, V, qq. 4027 ff. (Edmonstone); 6664 ff., 6782 ff. (Robertson); cf. Burton, *Wanderings* . . . I, pp. 184 ff.; C.O. 267/281, Blackall to Cardwell, 129, 21 Sept. 1864.

references were vague about the terms of such an agreement; but when in November 1865 the French Ambassador at last raised the subject semi-officially, Lord Clarendon, after consulting the Cabinet, invited him to make formal proposals.[1]

After reflection, the Ministry of the Marine decided to begin by offering only the three settlements on the Ivory Coast; if this inducement seemed inadequate they agreed to offer to surrender their new rights in the Mellacourie, and even in the Nunez. On 2 March 1866 this first offer was commended to Clarendon as providing a formula by which the two powers would concentrate their political influence in the respective areas of commercial interest.[2] French control of the groundnuts which went into French soap, British control of the palm-oil which went into British soap: there was a tidy, quasi-mercantilist logic about the proposal which appealed to those who did not realize to what extent the interests of traders, missionaries and other private citizens already straddled the proposed line of partition.

The immediate reaction in the Colonial Office was to welcome this prospect of getting rid of the Gambia. D'Arcy's clashes with the 'Marabouts', and the difficulties currently being experienced in evacuating MacCarthy's Island, confirmed the opinion that this was a dangerous colony, as well as an insolvent one. Nor were many hopes placed on its future development; any attempt to develop trade with the Sudan was likely to bring major political and military entanglements. The French were welcome to these. There would need to be safeguards for the Protestant missions, and for any British traders who objected to working under French rule; otherwise there seemed nothing to prevent British withdrawal.

Except one seemingly minor obstacle: the difficulty of finding any acceptable compensation. About the Ivory Coast little was known in London, and nothing good; since there was current a plan for an exchange of forts with the Dutch on the Gold Coast

[1] *MAE*, Afrique 47, Tour d'Auvergne to Drouyn de Lhuys, 18 Nov. 1865.

[2] *MMC*, Afrique VI/11/a, M.M.C. to M.A.E., 15 Feb. 1866; C.O. 87/86, F.O. to C.O., 10 March 1866, encl. Tour d'Auvergne to Clarendon, 2 March.

under which Britain would withdraw from the more westerly ones, Grand Bassam and Assinie would not even give Britain control of a continuous stretch of coastline. Blackall's comments on the French proposal confirmed this view, though he regarded the cession of Gabon and an assurance of French co-operation at Porto Novo as objects worth asking for. He also suggested that, in view of Sierra Leone's interest in what Freetown called the *northern* rivers, the dividing line in any partition of influence might be drawn near Bulama; but since little was yet known of Laprade's recent activity in this region, no definite claim was formulated here. The Colonial Office, in fact, regarded the problem as being less the negotiation of an even bargain than the decision whether a unilateral cession of the Gambia would be politically expedient. Elliot commented:

'The only use of an exchange with the French would be to pre-clude any mistaken annoyance of public opinion at a pure cession of territory to them. Otherwise it appears certain that anything we accept from them will be a loss and not a gain.'[1]

This anticipated public reluctance to abandon even a terri-tory so widely unpopular may seem rather curious. Cessions of territory as such were not invariably condemned. The Orange River Territory was abandoned in 1854, the Ionian Islands transferred to Greece in 1863; even the Republic of Honduras received the cession of the Bay Islands Colony in 1859 — though the Colonial Office was unlikely to accept the latter as a happy precedent.[2] It may well have been the idea of surrendering a British colony to *France*, the historic rival, which was expected to stick in the public throat. The moment when Blackall's report was received, in July 1866, was certainly inauspicious. The Austro-Prussian war had been decided by the battle of Sadowa on 3 July, and Napoleon III was interesting himself in the peace negotiations with the fairly obvious hope of making territorial gains in Belgium or Luxembourg as compensation for

[1] C.O. 87/86, F.O. to C.O., 10 March 1866, minutes by Barrow, Elliot, Forster; Blackall to Cardwell, Conf., 4 June 1866, minute by Elliot, 21 Aug.

[2] D. Waddell, 'Great Britain and the Bay Islands, 1821–61', *Historical Journal*, II, 1959.

the increase in Prussian power. Though these events were not directly mentioned in the Colonial Office discussions, they may well have made the government hesitate in contemplating any public generosity to France.[1]

Nevertheless, Adderley, on his arrival at the Colonial Office, urged that the opportunity to get rid of the Gambia should not be lost; and in November 1866 a letter to the Foreign Office was drafted, agreeing to the French proposal in principle but suggesting that the line of partition of interest should be at Bulama. The idea now was to negotiate this exchange concurrently with another negotiation, intended to redistribute and consolidate the British and Dutch possessions on the Gold Coast; the Ivory Coast posts might thus be passed on to the Dutch as an additional inducement.[2] But for some reason this letter was never sent, and during 1867 officials continued to look wistfully for ways of getting rid of the Gambia. Although that colony's finances improved considerably, peace in the river seemed as far away as ever, and the merchants as embarrassingly importunate for protection. Moreover Laprade, possibly intending to add to Britain's problems, twice asked permission to send warships into the river to attack Maba. The Colonial Office refused the more formal of these requests, but the incident confirmed Adderley's opinion that

'the future lies between French and Mahometan conquest — and we should not lose time in honourably getting out of the way'.[3]

But still he could take no active steps to do so.

During this long British silence the French were reconsidering, not for the last time, the expedience of including Gabon in their offer. Few Frenchmen seem to have felt much philanthropic interest in the tiny settlement of freed slaves established at Libreville since 1849; and commercially their position was

[1] For the Foreign Office attitude, cf. M. R. D. Foot, 'Great Britain and Luxembourg, 1867', *English Historical Review*, LXVII (1952) pp. 352–6.

[2] C.O. 87/85, Blackall to Carnarvon, 7, 18 July 1866; 9, 20 July, minutes by Adderley; C.O. 87/86, draft to F.O., November 1866.

[3] C.O. 87/87, Patey to Carnarvon, 8, 19 March 1867, minute by Adderley, 9 April; Blackall to Buckingham, 15, 2 May; 18 May 1867, minutes by Elliot, Adderley.

disappointing. Produce reached this coast from a restricted area, and until 1875 attempts to find routes to the interior by the Ogoué or other rivers had little success. Such trade as there was was largely handled by British firms, notably Hatton and Cookson of Liverpool and their experienced agent R. B. N. Walker; in 1874, for example, only two of the twelve trading houses were French, and they were struggling.[1] Apart from the possibility of renewing the recruitment of 'indentured labour' in the area, the settlement's main use to France was as a coaling and victualling station for warships.[2] After the Ministry of the Marine decided to retain Gabon in 1866, its agents began to carry out explorations and sign treaties in the Ogoué valley; Walker, hitherto satisfied with French rule, feared their intention might be to raise revenue by taxing trade currently carried on outside the range of the modest French tariff.[3] But in 1867 the Ministry changed its mind again, and decided that Gabon might if necessary be included in an exchange.[4] On 26 August it was formally offered in a letter to the Foreign Office.

The Colonial Office was still not tempted; indeed, their comments on the new French proposal betray no appreciation that something new had been added to the offer. Elliot repeated his opinion that the cession of the Gambia would be a positive gain, and — though still uncertain of what was happening in the Nunez and Mellacourie — suggested an agreement that the two powers would abstain from interfering with native chiefs north and south, respectively, of the parallel of Bulama. But again he asked, what of public opinion? This was

'a question which can only be judged by politicians; as the subject has never been publicly agitated, there are no *data* for forecasting the manner in which it would be viewed; and I fear there must be grave doubts as to its reception by those who have never had

[1] P. Masson, *Marseille et la Colonisation française* (Marseille, 1906) p. 385; Hanotaux and Martineau, *op. cit.*, IV, pp. 373–82, 431.

[2] *MMC*, Afrique VI/11/a, M.M.C. to M.A.E., 15 Feb. 1866; notes by Zveppfel, 13 Feb.; de Ladebat, 17 Feb. 1867.

[3] Hanotaux and Martineau, *op. cit.*, IV, pp. 379–81; F.O. 84/1336, Walker to Wylde, 28 July, 23 Oct. 1867; C.O. 267/296, F.O. to C.O., 11 Aug. 1868.

[4] *MMC*, Afrique VI/11/a, M.M.C. to M.A.E., 5 Aug. 1867.

occasion to acquire information or form an opinion on the measure before, but would be sure to have a strong one the moment that it was announced'.

Adderley was at first less apprehensive, believing that if the Commons were consulted, whether by debate or through a Committee, their opinion would be favourable.[1] But he later modified this opinion, possibly after sounding fellow-Members, or even reflecting on the recently-passed Reform Act. When the French sent a reminder in May 1868, Adderley agreed that it might be necessary to accept some visible though useless equivalent on the Ivory Coast; and Buckingham closed the discussion by declaring it inopportune to unsettle people in the Gambia by further discussion.[2]

Under the new Liberal government the idea was momentarily revived of accepting the Ivory Coast posts in order to facilitate the re-grouping of British and Dutch interests on the Gold Coast. After 1865 the Colonial Office, tiring of attempts to get the Dutch to agree on a common tariff for the whole coast, decided to seek an exchange of forts, with the Dutch controlling all those to the west of the Sweet River, the British those to the east. This would mean no net increase of responsibility, and, since each power would be able to impose its own tariff in its own sector without inviting evasion, there would be some chance of making the British settlement solvent. An agreement on this basis was duly concluded in March 1867, and the Dutch handed over their four forts in the east. But the negotiators had not taken into account the opinions of the Fanti states of the British 'protectorate' in the west; they were unwilling to be transferred to a sphere of Dutch influence, fearing their neighbours would favour the power of Ashanti and the trade of Elmina. The inhabitants of the western forts resisted the transfer to Dutch control; and when a Dutch warship bombarded the

---

[1] C.O. 87/88, F.O. to C.O., 26 Aug. 1867, minutes by Elliot, 9 Sept., Adderley, 11 Sept.

[2] C.O. 87/90, F.O. to C.O., 5 May 1868, minutes by Elliot, Adderley, Buckingham; C.O. 87/91, minute by Barrow, April 1869 on Kennedy to Granville, 13 March 1869; *MAE*, Afrique 48, Tour d'Auvergne to Drouyn de Lhuys, 23 May 1868.

F*

town of Kommenda, representatives of Wassaw, Denkyera, Assin and many Fanti states met to form a military alliance and confederation.[1]

At first the British tried to remain neutral and disclaim responsibility for the acts of their former *protégés*, but this attitude proved untenable. During 1868 trade was stopped over much of the Gold Coast, or diverted to Assinie, and there seemed a growing danger of Ashanti intervention against the new Fanti confederacy. Despite the Parliamentary Committee, the government could not limit their attention to the forts in the face of such disorder. By early 1869 Granville, the new Colonial Secretary, had reluctantly accepted the necessity of buying the Dutch out altogether and taking over responsibility on the whole coast between Half Assinie and Keta. It was to avoid the necessity of asking Parliament to vote money for this unpopular purpose that he toyed again with the idea of accepting the French posts on the Ivory Coast to pass on to the Dutch instead of cash.[2] But these places did not appeal to the Dutch either, and this plan fell through. British Ministers, though well aware that 'Parliament would prefer to sell over ours to buying others',[3] decided that Dutch withdrawal was the only immediate solution, irrespective of Britain's ultimate future on the Gold Coast. 'They are in our way whether we stay or go,' Granville concluded.[4] In February 1871 the Dutch agreed to transfer all their rights on the Gold Coast in return for a cash payment, and certain concessions in Sumatra.

Having accepted one extension of responsibility, the government was more reluctant than ever to consider another on the Ivory Coast, even if they could get rid of the Gambia in exchange. For want of anything to ask in return for that unwanted colony they remained speechless in face of the French proposal.

---

[1] On this negotiation, see Wolfson, *op. cit.*, pp. 186 ff; Gertzel, *op. cit.*, pp. 76 ff.

[2] C.O. 87/91, minutes by Monsell, Granville, April 1869 on Kennedy to Granville, 15, 3 March; cf. *MMC*, Afrique VI/11/a, de Langle to Dauriac, 26 Feb. 1868.

[3] P.R.O. 30/29/55. (Granville Papers) Clarendon to Granville, 5 Oct. 1869.

[4] *ibid.*, Granville to Clarendon, 1 Dec. 1869.

Only as they began to appreciate the implications of events in the northern rivers did any incentive to negotiate appear.

Reactions on the Mellacourie

The Colonial Office at first attached little importance to Laprade's advances in the Nunez, Pongos, and Mellacourie. In November 1866 Elliot remarked about the reported treaty with Maligy,

'The French ought not to be coming in with Protectorates or other pretensions so near our settlement of Sierra Leone. Friendly European nations ought to avoid *elbowing* each other . . . in such countries as Africa.'

But Adderley merely rejoined,

'What could we wish for more than that the French should establish their Protectorates, and run their heads instead of ours against them?'[1]

Later the Foreign Office, examining complaints about French behaviour in the Nunez and Pongos, could find no basis for protest in existing treaties, and hoped that French expansion would hasten the final end of the slave trade in these rivers. Adderley did wonder vaguely whether the question could be linked with the Gambia proposal, but nobody defined clearly what Britain ought to ask for.[2]

In June 1867 the Sierra Leone government for the first time received texts of the French treaties in the Mellacourie, and soon afterwards both Bokkari and Yemba Lamina wrote seeking British support against French pressure. The acting governor was careful not to encourage them to resist, but he expressed his fears that France might next extend her control to the Scarcies, and further threaten Sierra Leonean commerce.[3] The British government still hoped to be able to leave the northern rivers

[1] C.O. 267/287, minutes by Elliot, Adderley, 14 Nov. 1866, on Blackall to Buckingham, 72, 11 Oct.

[2] F.O. 84/1336, C.O. to F.O., 27 April 1867, minutes by Wylde and Stanley; C.O. 267/291, F.O. to C.O., 30 April 1867 and minutes.

[3] C.O. 267/290, Blackall to Buckingham, 67, 27 June 1867; Yonge to Buckingham, 81, 12 July; 79, 15 July 1867 [sic].

under African rulers, whose behaviour could be informally supervised by the navy and the Sierra Leone authorities; their first thought was to propose to France some general agreement to preserve free trade and political neutrality along this coast.[1]

But although French officials had formerly desired some neutrality agreement of just this nature, this was not their object in occupying the northern rivers. Hoping to exploit their new rights in the Mellacourie to make Britain cede the Gambia, they rejected a British invitation to restore the *status quo* in that river, and vigorously asserted their right to be there.[2] The British therefore sought some legalistic doctrine which might protect their trade. The Colonial Office proposed the convenient doctrine that France was not entitled to levy any duties at all in protectorates where Britain possessed treaty rights of free trade granted by African rulers: an ideal doctrine for merchants, who would stand to gain security without paying for it. The French, however, would only promise to treat foreign merchandise and shipping in the Mellacourie on the same basis as their own, not to exempt them from duty.[3] If France's right to do this were admitted, then the only way to be sure of protecting British commerce in the Mellacourie would be to negotiate for a renunciation of French sovereignty. But the Colonial Office had not decided whether they wished to attempt this when the Conservatives left office in December 1868.[4]

[1] F.O. 84/1336, C.O. to F.O., 27 July 1867, minute by Wylde; C.O. 267/292, Blackall to Elliot, 26 Aug. 1867, minute by Adderley; F.O. 84/1336, C.O. to F.O., 29 Sept. 1867, minute by Wylde.

[2] F.O. 84/1336, F.O. to C.O., 22 Nov. 1867, minute by Stanley; C.O. 267/291, minutes on the same; *MMC* Afrique VI/11/g, M.M.C. to M.A.E., 19 March 1868; F.O. 84/1336, F.O. to C.O., 30 March 1868.

[3] C.O. 267/296, C.O. to F.O., 21 May 1868, minutes on draft; F.O. 84/1336, minute by Wylde, 22 May 1868; *MMC* Afrique VI/11/g, M.M.C. to M.A.E., 24 June 1868.

[4] F.O. 84/1336, F.O. to C.O., 11 Aug. 1868, minutes on draft; C.O. 267/296, minutes on above, Nov. 1868; C.O. to F.O., 27 Nov. 1868.

CHAPTER FOUR

Towards a Territorial Exchange, 1869–76

[1]

Sir Arthur Kennedy's Policies at Sierra Leone

THE GLADSTONE ministry formed in December 1868 had one asset denied to its predecessors since 1846; a Parliamentary majority, not indeed wholly reliable at all times, but based on a reasonably coherent party organization. But whether it would produce a more decided policy in West Africa was uncertain. Most of the new Cabinet lacked experience of African affairs; with Palmerston and Russell gone, only W. E. Forster, and possibly Cardwell, held fixed opinions extending beyond the comfortable slogan of 'peace and retrenchment'. Earl Granville, the new Colonial Secretary, was a charming aristocrat, whose early actions seemed to justify his reputation as a colonial 'separatist'; of Africa he knew little. If West African policy did in fact for a time show signs of rather clearer direction, this was largely due to Sir Arthur Kennedy, whom Buckingham had appointed as Governor-in-Chief.

Kennedy's objectives were clearest in the area of Sierra Leone, which he had previously governed in 1852–4; he knew its possibilities, and avoided the fashionable error of despising its people. Instead of mocking Sierra Leoneans for borrowing institutions and values from Victorian England, or despising them for not doing so more completely, Kennedy appreciated realistically the great cultural adaptation made by liberated Africans who had become successful traders, clerks, teachers, and clergymen, and by the new generation of Creoles, who were beginning to qualify as doctors or lawyers. He had not abandoned the old ideal of 'commerce and civilization', and believed that Sierra Leone could do much to extend both. European merchants and missionaries would necessarily tend to concentrate near the coast or major rivers; Sierra Leoneans, satisfied with smaller remuneration, could range further afield, taking into relatively small and remote villages not only the trade goods of Europe, but something at least of its religious and cultural values. As Braouezec reported in 1865 of Sumbuya, eighty miles north of Freetown,

'Almost all the inhabitants speak English, and use merchandise threequarters of which is English; the most petty chief has, when it pleases him and he cannot write himself, a little Negro from Sierra Leone who serves him as secretary, and writes English correctly enough. But these districts are in no way dependent upon the Sierra Leoneans, who have been able to impose their language over a radius of eighty miles by exploiting their advantage of primary education, which is widespread in the colony.'[1]

Kennedy's primary aim in Sierra Leone was to maintain commercial prosperity: because trade was proving beneficial in itself, and also because he wished to command sufficient revenue to make some modest public investment in education and public works. For this, order was essential in a wide surrounding area; for much of Freetown's prosperity depended on its role as *entrepôt*, offering facilities for safe storage in bonded warehouses to merchants trading far beyond the colonial boundary. Soon after returning to Freetown, Kennedy addressed a circular letter to all chiefs who had treaties with the colony, inviting their co-operation in his policy of peacefully developing the resources of the region, and announcing his intention to 'protect and foster those chiefs who are peaceably disposed, and to exert all the influence I possess to punish any disturber of the peace'. The replies suggested that Kennedy could expect some co-operation from many chiefs between the Nunez and the Gallinas.[2]

Though this appreciation of Sierra Leone's interdependence with its commercial hinterland led Kennedy to resist Liberia's

[1] *MMC*, Sénégal IV/55/b, Report by Braouezec, *c.* Oct. 1865; cf. Arcin, *op. cit.*, p. 264.

[2] C.O. 267/293, Kennedy to Buckingham, 14, 5 March; 45, 15 May; 59, 27 May 1868; C.O. 267/294, Kennedy to Buckingham, 83, 13 July 1868.

claims to the Gallinas and Portugal's to Bulama, he did not seek
to extend the colonial boundaries. In fact, after consultation and
reflection, he set on foot the retrocession to the chiefs of part of
the territory in Koya annexed in 1861. Except for a limited area
where some Creoles had settled, Kennedy saw little hope of
agricultural or educational progress in this territory of small
villages and low fertility. It had proved hard to find a suitable
Resident Manager; and the taxes, which the inhabitants paid
with bitter resentment, did not cover the cost of their collection.
But since Koya still occupied the same potentially important
position across the trade routes, British withdrawal was not
complete. The treaty of retrocession, concluded in 1872, reserved
to the British Crown ultimate sovereignty over all Koya; British
subjects were to be exempt from the chief's taxes, and any death
sentence pronounced by him was to be reviewed by the
Governor.[1]

Kennedy was looking far beyond Koya, to the caravan trade
with the savanna belt. One relatively minor element in the
'informal empire' of nineteenth-century Freetown was the success of its shops and warehouses, its modest urban amenities, in
attracting caravan traders to bring gold or hides from Futa
Jalon or the Sudan. The government's Aborigines Department
extended a little hospitality to these men, with the triple aim of
encouraging their return to Freetown, advertizing the colony in
the interior, and obtaining political and economic information;
but since Major Laing's journeys in the 1820's no agent of the
government had travelled far towards the Niger, though W. C.
Thompson visited Futa Jalon in 1843. Kennedy, attracted by
these distant countries, encouraged Winwood Reade, a restless
young intellectual looking for somewhere to explore, to come to
Sierra Leone in 1868, and to go and look for the source of the
Niger. Reade, who as a traveller showed more determination
than foresight, went twice to Falaba in 1869, and on the second
visit was permitted to proceed to the Niger, below its source,
and to the gold-bearing country of Bouré, over four hundred

[1] C.O. 267/294, Kennedy to Buckingham, 112, 24 Aug. 1868; C.O.
267/301, Kennedy to Granville, 162, 23 July 1869; C.O. 267/315, Kendall
to Kimberley, 46, 2 Feb. 1872.

miles north-west of Freetown. Though this country was previously unvisited by Europeans, Reade met many people speaking a smattering of 'coast English'; he reported hopefully on the prospects for developing trade in gold and hides, and for navigating the Niger still further down its course.[1]

Kennedy was already thinking on similar lines, and incorporated some of Reade's ideas in his reform of the Aborigines Department, which under the experienced Government interpreter, T. G. Lawson, was already developing into a kind of parochial foreign office. A 'Protector of Strangers' was appointed to look after the welfare of caravan traders in Freetown, and prevent them from being exploited by their 'landlords'; later an able young Muslim scholar, Mohamed Sanusi, was appointed Arabic writer.[2] In 1871 Kennedy sent a further mission to Falaba and beyond under Samuel Bowling,[3] there was another in 1872 under E. W. Blyden, an acute and articulate Afro-West Indian who had recently moved to Freetown from Monrovia after a quarrel with President Roye. Another Afro-West Indian went as far as Kankan. Kennedy's successor gave Blyden a permanent appointment as 'Agent to the Interior'; and though he did not hold this post long, Blyden made an important journey in 1873 to Futa Jalon, where he secured a treaty of trade and friendship in return for an annual stipend of £100.[4]

This use of annual payments to perpetuate the friendly relations established by official messengers, on condition that the recipients provided facilities for the conduct and transit of trade, was a major feature of Kennedy's policy. The system had been

[1] C.O. 267/302, Reade to Kimberley, 21 Dec. 1869; cf. W. Winwood Reade, *The African Sketch-Book* (London, 2 Vols., 1873); J. D. Hargreaves, 'Winwood Reade and the Discovery of Africa', *African Affairs*, LVI (1957) pp. 309–13.

[2] J. D. Hargreaves, 'The Evolution of the Native Affairs Department', *Sierra Leone Studies*, n.s. 3 (1954).

[3] C.O. 267/310, Kennedy to Kimberley, 59, 29 March 1871; C.O. 267/315, Kennedy to Kimberley, 28, 17 Jan. 1872.

[4] C.O. 267/315, Kennedy to Kimberley, 7, 3 Jan. 1872; C.O. 267/316, Hennessy to Kimberley, 110, 1 Sept. 1872; C.O. 267/320, Harley to Kimberley, 25, 22 May 1873, Report by Blyden.

employed in some areas for many years,[1] but it was now extended, and given some publicity as a possible instrument for the pacific development of Africa. Reade's books, like some of Burton's, pointed out that wars in Africa, commonly dismissed as displays of primitive bellicosity, were often caused by the desire of middlemen states to monopolize, or of inland peoples to share in, the profits of trade. Kennedy hoped that a discriminating use of stipends might create a more general interest in keeping trade-routes open, and so help to push Sierra Leone's commercial frontier further inland.[2]

One of the reasons why Kennedy's views commanded respect in London was that, despite his pugnacity at Bulama, his policies did not envisage much use of military force.

> 'The Negroes', he told a French naval officer, 'are becoming cultivators, are planting cotton. They know that we don't want to fight them, but to buy their produce. Military expenses, henceforth, are unnecessary.'[3]

To the delight of the War Office he prepared to withdraw the garrisons, not only from Bulama and Koya, but from Sherbro, and later from the Gambia and other stations. Eventually, by recruiting armed police forces in Africa, he hoped to reduce the total of Imperial forces stationed on the coast.[4]

However, a policy of withdrawing military detachments implied as corollary an increased dependence upon naval assistance, to show the flag in the out-stations, and to convey troops rapidly to the scene of any emergency. This did not please the Admiralty. Now that slave exports had finally ceased, they were anxious to reduce drastically the number of ships stationed on the unhealthy West coast. In 1869 they agreed, after round table discussion, to station two cruisers between Lagos and Bathurst,

[1] For a list of stipends payable in 1886, see C.O. 806/279, pp. 53 ff.

[2] C.O. 267/300, Kennedy to Granville, 103, 7 May 1869; C.O. 267/310, Kennedy to Kimberley, 38, 22 March 1871; C.O. 267/314, Reade to Kimberley, 2 Feb. 1871.

[3] *MMC*, Afrique VI/11/a, Duperré to M.M.C., 3 Jan. 1870.

[4] C.O. 267/294, Kennedy to Buckingham, 115, 27 Aug. 1868; C.O. 267/304, Kennedy to Granville, 29 Sept. 1869; W.O. to C.O., 3 March 1869.

'with instructions to their commanding officers to attend to any requisitions they may receive from the Governor at Sierra Leone for their co-operation and assistance on any necessary service'.[1]

This sounded satisfactory, but the Admiralty spokesman had in fact only accepted this role subject to important reservations. In July 1870, when Kennedy asked for naval assistance in punishing a chief who had attacked a trading settlement in the Sherbro, his request was refused on the grounds that neither life nor property was in danger; and while he was still complaining that inaction would jeopardize British authority, the warships left Sierra Leone altogether. The Admiralty, it now appeared, did not intend to station any warships on that part of the coast during the six rainy months of the year.[2] Kennedy's bitter complaint that he would never have agreed to withdraw the Sherbro garrison under such conditions did not succeed in inducing any substantial modification of this policy.

Here was one weakness in Kennedy's attractive chain of reasoning. Without fuller naval support, further military withdrawals became difficult; even that from the Sherbro proved only temporary.[3] It was a first warning of the fragility of the fashionable hopes that treaties, stipends, and moral influence could provide an adequate basis for an expanding 'informal empire' of West African trade. These hopes had always been pitched higher in London than on the coast; Kennedy himself knew that moral influence required a backing of power. Even so, his policies still seemed to contain the best prospects of extending the influence of the settlements without new military or financial commitments; their success seemed to be reflected in Kennedy's annual Blue Books of colonial accounts for Sierra Leone; and Kennedy himself (whose daughter was married to

---

[1] C.O. 267/303, Admty to C.O., 19 April, 10 May, 29 Sept., 12 Oct., 5 Nov., 15 Nov. 1869; Kennedy to Rogers, 19 Oct. 1869.

[2] C.O. 267/305, Kennedy to Granville, 59, 19 April; 83, 23 May 1870; C.O. 267/306, Kennedy to Granville, 108, 4 July 1870; C.O. 267/308, Admty to C.O., 14, 25 July, 13 Aug. 1870; C.O. 267/313, Admty to C.O., 14 Feb. 1871.

[3] C.O. 267/313, W.O. to C.O., 3 May, 13 July 1871; C.O. 267/311, Kennedy to Kimberley, 99, 9 June 1871.

Robert Meade, a rising official in the Colonial Office) continued to command confidence in London. Hence, when his appreciation of British interests led him to support a territorial exchange with France, his proposals were quickly adopted.

[2]

The Exchange Negotiations of 1870 and the Origins of the Gambia Lobby

In Kennedy's opinion, founded on his previous experience, the Mellacourie region formed a natural part of Sierra Leone's commercial hinterland. Refusing to accept the legitimacy of French claims there, he continued to play the role of paramount power. In May 1868 he went to Fouricaria and pronounced judgment in Bokkari's favour in the succession dispute, giving a reasoned opinion which he claimed was received with acclamation. Bokkari, who had not allowed his treaty with the French to interrupt military operations against his domestic enemies, was already receiving more help from foreign traders, and encouragement to resist the rather minatory demands of the newly-appointed French commandant at Binty. With Kennedy's support behind him, he wrote to London, appealing for help under the Treaty of 1826, and contrasting 'the just, honourable and kind behaviour' of the British with that of the 'unjust, lawless, and wicked French'. Simultaneously Kennedy denounced the French encroachments, which he feared might soon extend to the Scarcies; he suggested appointing a political agent for the northern rivers.[1]

The Colonial Office hesitated to challenge French expansion in this area. Granville's intention was, not to embark upon long and probably fruitless discussion of treaty rights, but to con-

---

[1] C.O. 267/293, Kennedy to Buckingham, 47, 15 May; 58, 27 May 1868; C.O. 267/294, same to same, 77, 3 July 1868; *MMC*, Afrique VI/11/g, M.M.C. to M.A.E., 24 June, 20 Aug. 1868; C.O. 267/296, F.O. to C.O., 11 Aug. 1868; Buckingham to Kennedy, 227, 8 Dec. 1868; C.O. 267/299, Kennedy to Granville, 15, 22 Jan. 1869; C.O. 267/300, same to same, 85, 13 April 1869.

centrate on securing commercial guarantees, preferably through some formula of reciprocity which the two powers could apply elsewhere on the coast. To avoid further collisions he proposed 'to draw a line round Sierra Leone embracing all that we desire to retain or acquire as dependency', and to use this as a basis for demarcating spheres of political influence.[1] But Kennedy insisted that this line could be drawn no further south than the Isles de Los; though the Nunez and Pongos were expendable, French rule in the Mellacourie would jeopardize Freetown's trade and her food supply, and would be resisted by the natives. If such a line was indeed necessary, there was only one simple way to secure it. On 4 August the Colonial Office suggested that the French government might be sounded about accepting such a demarcation in exchange for the Gambia.[2]

Kennedy, who shortly afterwards returned to London on leave, welcomed this proposal enthusiastically. The Gambia had never seemed to him a satisfactory colony; in his zeal to recover the Mellacourie he now overstated its disadvantages. He claimed that it was chronically and hopelessly insolvent; that the total profits of its trade (which was in any case largely in French hands) did not equal the cost of its defence; that the risk of involvement in local wars was not offset by any real possibility of spreading civilization. None of these allegations was wholly groundless, but none can be accepted as a proper gubernatorial summing-up. Throughout the discussions, Kennedy based his financial calculations on 1869, which cholera and a bad groundnut harvest had made an exceptionally poor year; his opponents replied by citing good trading years, such as 1867. To persuade the Colonial Office to accept expansion in the Mellacourie, Kennedy appealed to their anti-expansionist instincts elsewhere: besides the Gambia, he was prepared to renounce all British rights north of the Dembia river, including any which might be recognized in the Bulama

[1] C.O. 267/299, minute by Rogers, 21 Feb. 1869, on Kennedy to Granville, 15, 22 Jan.; C.O. to F.O., 9 March; Granville to Kennedy, 35, 1 April; cf. above, pp. 143–4.
[2] C.O. 267/300, Kennedy to Granville, 98, 29 April 1869; Kennedy to Meade, Ptc., 29 April; C.O. to F.O., 4 Aug. 1869.

arbitration; he was willing to forego the French offer of 'expensive and unmanageable incumbrances' on the Ivory Coast or Gabon.[1] On this basis a proposal was at last made to the French government in February 1870.[2]

French officials, who must have given up hope of receiving any reply to their own proposals for an exchange, were mostly delighted to receive it. Although some of them hesitated slightly about giving up the Mellacourie rather than the Ivory Coast, the suggested agreement seemed to offer great advantages, not only to the Senegal, but also from a diplomatic point of view. On 31 March acceptance in principle, subject only to certain stipulations of detail, was communicated to the British Ambassador. All seemed clear for a rapid conclusion.[3]

*   *   *   *   *

While the British were formulating their proposals, rumours of what they intended to do had roused opposition among the Gambia merchants. Four British houses of some standing were represented at Bathurst. The London firm of Forster and Smith had been active there since the 1820's; since the recent deaths of its senior partner, the ex-M.P. Matthew Forster, and its local agent, W. H. Goddard, its business had been reduced, and was about to be transferred to the firm of Lintott, Spink and Co.[4] The other three houses were small family concerns, built up by

[1] C.O. 87/93, Kennedy to Granville, 54, 9 Aug. 1869; Kennedy to C.O., 23 Sept. 1869. The latter document is published in *P.P.*, 1870, L, as are most of the more important British official documents cited in this section. However, departmental minutes are not printed, and personal references are usually excised.

[2] C.O. 87/94, F.O. to C.O., 23 Oct. 1869; Otway to Rogers, 23 Oct.; C.O. to F.O., 10 Nov., C.O. 87/98, F.O. to C.O., 11 Feb. 1870, encl. Clarendon to Lyons, 11 Feb.

[3] *MMC*, Sénégal IV/56/a, M.M.C. to M.A.E., 9 Feb. 1869; Afrique VI/11/a, Note relative à l'échange, 17 Feb. 1870; M.A.E. to M.M.C., 23 Feb.; M.M.C. to Dauriac, March 1870; M.M.C. to M.A.E., 17 March; C.O. 87/98, F.O. to C.O., 2 April 1870, encl. Lyons to Clarendon, 31 March, minute by Rogers.

[4] *P.P.*, 1842, XI, p. 717, evidence of Matthew Forster; *P.P.* 1870, L, No. 34, Forster and Smith to C.O., 18 June 1870; C.O. 87/101, Pamphlet by Brown, Chown and Quin.

men who had later introduced a son and, in the case of the
Chown family, a grandson into the business.[1] The most recent
comer was T. F. Quin, formerly in government employment; in
1860 he had been 'perhaps the most substantial man in the
Colony', but since then his fortunes appear to have declined.[2]
Thomas Brown, Member of the Legislative Council, had, like
the Chowns, traded in the Gambia since the 1830's; in 1854 he
thought he had made enough money to retire to England, but
by 1859 he was back, trying to make more.[3] Brown wrote many
long and polemical letters and petitions to the Colonial Office,
which were often read with surprisingly patient attention; such
a man, it was felt, could be 'very useful as a watchdog, though
he may sometimes bark without necessity'.[4]

Since 1866 these merchants had often acted together in
criticism of their governors. Their grievances included the withdrawal of the garrison from MacCarthy's Island, the increasing
reluctance of government to protect their agents in the river,
the union with Sierra Leone (whose interests seemed to receive
precedence over their own) and, symptomatic of them all, the
reduction of commercial representation in the Legislative
Council from three members to one. D'Arcy had sometimes felt
uncertain of a majority in that Council, and had treated the
unofficial members almost as respectfully as if the Gambia were
still controlled by a company of merchants;[5] now the British
merchants received less consideration, and resented it. In their
complaints[6] they were often joined by the French firms, mostly
from Bordeaux, some from Marseille. Commercially, the French
were formidable rivals of the British; by paying cash for their

---

[1] C.O. 806/57, No. 7, T. C. Chown to C.O., 9 Feb. 1876.

[2] C.O. 87/69, D'Arcy to Newcastle, Conf., 24 Feb. 1860; C.O. 806/36,
No. 5, Kortright to Carnarvon, Conf., 19 June 1874.

[3] C.O. 87/71, D'Arcy to Newcastle, 28, 24 April 1861; C.O. 87/109,
Cooper to Carnarvon, 3, 9 March 1876.

[4] C.O. 87/102, minute by Kimberley, 21 May 1872, on Callaghan to
Hennessy, 24, 8 March.

[5] C.O. 87/73, D'Arcy to Newcastle, 92, 14 March 1862; 25 June 1862;
C.O. 87/75, Admty to C.O., 4 Dec. 1862; C.O. 87/76, D'Arcy to Newcastle,
172, 21 Feb.; 23 April 1863.

[6] e.g. C.O. 87/87, Blackall to Buckingham, 15, 2 May 1867; C.O. 87/92,
Kennedy to Granville, 44, 12 July 1869.

groundnuts while the latter stuck to barter, they made such rapid progress during the 1860's that some officials believed they might soon monopolize the trade.[1] But their political interests were similar to those of their British competitors: to get the maximum protection from the colonial government at the minimum cost in taxation and supervision. In 1869 both groups joined in opposition to Administrator Patey; in 1870 they joined in opposing the exchange proposal.

★   ★   ★   ★   ★

The first enquiry about the negotiations was despatched by Quin, from his London office, on 12 January 1870. The Foreign and Colonial Offices now discussed for the first time whether Parliamentary consent, or even legislation, would be required for the cession of a colony; though undecided about the legal position, they agreed to tell Quin that the 'intervention' of Parliament would be necessary before anything was done. This represented a political, rather than a constitutional, judgment;

[1] P.P. 1870, L, No. 7, Patey to Monsell, 1 Oct. 1869; No. 15, memo. by Fowler, 12 March 1870. These accounts seem deliberately pessimistic. A very rough index of the level of activity of the various groups in the river between MacCarthy's Island and Bathurst in 1876 may be gathered from the following figures, supplied by the merchants themselves, for traders working in their interests. But it must be remembered:

  (i) That these figures give no indication of the amount of business done by each trader.
 (ii) That they do not include business done in Bathurst. Most of this seems to have been in French hands; one important firm, C. A. Verminck, did no trade up-river.
(iii) That they do not include trade above MacCarthy's Island, which is said to have been wholly in the hands of British subjects.

French firms		British firms		British-African	
Maurel frères	42	Thomas Brown	33	J. D. Cole	8
Maurel & Prom	21	Lintott, Spink & Co.	28	E. J. Nicol	8
V. Barrère	16	T. F. Quin	15	J. D. Jones	5
A. Minville	6	T. C. Chown	13	P. A. Cole	5
	—		—	S. F. Owens	5
	85		89	J. D. Richards	3
	—		—		—
					34
					—

Consolidated from C.O. 806/107, No. 1.
Cooper to Kortright, 33, 6 July 1876.

and Clarendon added a further point, that Parliament would doubtless require evidence that the natives of the Gambia were willing to be transferred.[1] Although the resistance of the people of the western Gold Coast against transfer to Dutch control had demonstrated the importance of assent in Africa, Monsell, the Liberal Under-Secretary, saw no reason for consulting African opinion; and Rogers thought the consent of the 1,500 families affected 'might be procured by no very great expenditure of *dash*'. But he also foresaw that,

> '. . . if one or two merchants desire to thwart the transfer, it is hardly conceivable that they would find any difficulty in getting up such a black opposition as could be paraded in Parliament, and it is not very easy for the English Government to counter-work such a movement'.

A proviso requiring the consent both of Parliament and of the natives was added to the draft proposal to the French; meanwhile Kennedy was asked to report on the extent of local opposition and the best means of overcoming it.[2]

Kennedy, determined that the exchange should go through, belittled this opposition; he repeatedly declared that it was being synthetically created by the merchants, whose ultimate aim was not to stop the transfer but to secure compensation for their businesses. Nevertheless, a petition against cession was presented in April, bearing the names of more than five hundred Africans.[3] Kennedy insisted that these were men of straw: 'its innate absurdity', he wrote, 'and the entire absence of the names of any educated or responsible persons, render it of little weight'. He quickly set out for Bathurst, where he addressed a meeting of about eighty signatories, and later interviewed

---

[1] C.O. 87/98, Quin to C.O., 12 Jan. 1870; F.O. to C.O., 22 Jan., 11 Feb.; C.O. to Quin, 3 Feb.; F.O. 84/1318, Note on draft of Clarendon to Lyons, 128, 19 Feb. 1870.

[2] C.O. 87/98, minutes by Rogers, 25 Jan., Monsell, 27 Jan. 1870 on F.O. to C.O., 22 Jan.; Granville to Kennedy, 21 Feb. 1870; F.O. 84/1318, Clarendon to Lyons, 128, 19 Feb. 1870.

[3] C.O. 87/96, Kennedy to Granville, Conf., 29 March; 17, 18 April; Conf., 23 April; 20, 30 April 1870 (encl. petition). Kennedy to Bravo, 34, 30 April 1870.

Messrs. Brown, Chown, and Quin. These consultations did not alter his opinion that the opposition could be overcome, or with propriety discounted; while in Bathurst he openly received a representative from the Senegal to discuss arrangements for the transfer.[1]

Major Bravo, Administrator of the Gambia, was less willing to ignore the petition; while not accepting its arguments, he pointed out that its supporters did in fact represent 'whatever intelligence, respectability, property or feeling there may be in the natives of these settlements'. In June the King of Combo added his protest against being transferred to French protection;[2] and simultaneously the merchants opened a public campaign of protest in Great Britain. On 30 May a letter to *The Times*, signed by 'An English Colonist', protested that British subjects should not be placed under French rule against their will; other letters to other newspapers followed. First Forster and Smith, then Brown, Chown and Quin, singly and in combination, in writing and by personal visits to the Colonial Office, presented reasoned objections; they pleaded the interests of the African inhabitants as well as the extent of their own investment and their fears for its future under the French flag.[3] Forster and Smith obtained the support of forty-one other London firms for one of their protests; the Manchester Chamber of Commerce was moved, first to seek information, then, after hearing a statement by Brown, to send a Memorial of objection. Later the Bristol Chamber of Commerce joined in.[4] Some of

---

[1] C.O. 87/96, Kennedy to Granville, 5 May; 28, 10 May; 32, 10 May (encl. memo. by Lawson); 36, 2 June; 39, 2 June 1870; *MMC*, Afrique VI/11/a, Note by Joubert, 19 May 1870.

[2] C.O. 87/96, Bravo to Kennedy, 2, 13 May 1870 (minutes by Rogers, Granville); Kennedy to Granville, 42, 10 June 1870.

[3] C.O. 87/98, Forster and Smith to C.O., 18 June (minute by Monsell); 4 July; 3 Aug. 1870; Brown to C.O., 12 July (minutes by Herbert, Monsell); Quin and Brown to C.O., 21 July; Printed memo. for M.P.s, by Brown and Quin, 26 July; T. and T. C. Chown to C.O., 3 Aug. 1870 (minute by Kimberley).

[4] C.O. 87/98, Manchester Chamber of Commerce to C.O., 23 June; 4 July 1870 (with Memorial). Memorial of London merchants, rec. 15 July; Bristol C. of C. to C.O., 30 July 1870; cf. P.R.O. 30/29/55, Clarendon to Granville, Pte., 4 June 1870.

these arguments succeeded in impressing both officials and Members of Parliament.

*   *   *   *   *

The years 1869–70, it has been argued, saw the beginning of a conscious reaction against the 'separatist' tendencies attributed to some leading politicians, concerned primarily about the colonies of European settlement. Although its spokesmen criticized chiefly Liberal ministers actually in office, they were not a partisan group; more of their leaders were Liberals than Conservatives, and W. E. Forster, now a member of Gladstone's cabinet, was associated with them. This was not in any sense a mass movement; its principal manifestations were a modest increase in press and Parliamentary interest, and the formation of the Royal Colonial Institute as a centre for discussion and study of colonial problems.[1] But even this relatively small ripple of informed opinion meant that politicians became rather more receptive to the arguments raised by the Gambia merchants.

Yet these 'new Imperialists' would hardly have taken up the Gambia question unprompted; but for the merchants' campaign, the transfer might have been quietly and speedily effected. Why then did they raise objections? Kennedy believed throughout that they were deliberately exaggerating the importance of their businesses in the Gambia in order to claim financial compensation for them from either the British or French government; as early as March 1870 he put the Collector of Customs to work calculating possible bases for such compensation.[2] Though it cannot be proved beyond doubt, there is much evidence to support his interpretation. All the merchants submitted precise, though doubtless inflated, estimates of their investments in the Gambia, and either asked

[1] cf. C. A. Bodelsen, *Studies in Mid-Victorian Imperialism* (N.Y., 1925) Ch. 2; . R. M. Butler, 'Imperial Questions in British Politics, 1868–80', *Cambridge History of the British Empire*, III (Cambridge, 1959) pp. 26 ff.

[2] C.O. 87/96, Kennedy to Granville, Conf., 29 March; 17, 19 April; Conf., 23 April; 32, 10 May 1870; C.O. 87/97, Kennedy to Kimberley, 68, 16 Aug.; 82, 20 Sept.; 85, 24 Sept. 1870; C.O. 87/98, Fowler to C.O., 12 March 1870.

explicitly or hinted broadly that, if any sacrifices had to be made for the sake of Imperial interests, the expense should be borne by the public rather than by individuals. In the Legislative Council, Brown openly admitted that he had no objection to the transfer, 'provided equitable terms are arranged and all rights respected'.[1] Brown, Chown, and Quin, it is true, all spoke of handing on their business in the Gambia to their children; but there is no reason to suppose that these children would not have preferred to reside in England on comfortable endowments provided at public expense. T. F. Quin and both Chowns ceased to live in the Gambia shortly after this time, the latter leaving the conduct of their interests to a highly efficient German agent; and Brown's premature attempt at retirement does not suggest that he was sentimentally attached to African soil. A Paris firm with correspondents in the Gambia asserted that opposition would cease if satisfactory compensation were assured; later, well-informed British merchants repeated that this had been the sole purpose of the British opposition.[2]

Desire for compensation, however, will not explain one curious feature of this opposition to the exchange: that the British merchants claimed to speak also in the name of their French competitors. These men were not planning to leave the Gambia; it was generally assumed that their trade would continue to expand. For them it seems to have been a matter of weighing the additional protection which their trade might expect from the more militarily-minded government of the Senegal against the danger that this goverment would exercise closer supervision of trading practices; it was King Log against King Stork. The decisive factor in leading them to prefer King Log may well have been the British tariff, which in the Gambia still weighed more heavily on imported goods than on exports of groundnuts, and so did not touch the currency which French

---

[1] C.O. 89/3, Gambia Leg. Co., 5 May 1870.

[2] *MMC*, Afrique VI/11/a, Creton et Cie to M.M.C., 12 July 1870; Afrique VI/24/a, Montebello to Freycinet, 15 Nov. 1879; C.O. 806/203, National African Co. to C.O., 28 Feb. 1883; C.O. 806/214, memo. by Meade, 29 Sept. 1883. On the desire of Gambia merchants to live well in London, see J. Whitford, *Trading Life in Western and Central Africa* (Liverpool 1877) pp. 21–2.

traders largely used. Their tactical co-operation with their British competitors did not imply unity of interests and objectives.

One body which might have been expected to oppose the cession of the Gambia was the Wesleyan Church, the largest Christian communion in the colony. Their West African missionaries, in particular their militant and authoritarian Chairman, Benjamin Tregaskis of Freetown, had many grievances against the government of the British settlements; perhaps for this reason, their fear of French Popery did not at this time dominate their attitude. One of the general secretaries of the parent Society, Rev. W. B. Boyce, who was later to denounce the transfer of Protestant Africans to a Roman Catholic power, in 1869 was commenting privately that,

> '. . . the French are *on the whole* better administrators than we are for Colonies like ours in West Africa. . . . As an instrument of civilisation and national progress I do not undervalue Missionary labours or Education, but good rational government in which the rulers *bear not the sword in vain* but are *a terror to evil-doers* (Romans XIII) is equally an Ordinance of God . . .'[1]

When H. J. Quilter, minister in charge of the Gambia mission, first heard the possible transfer discussed in May 1870, his immediate reaction was merely to think of safeguarding the small grant which his mission received from the government for educational purposes; and Tregaskis only added that it was necessary to look to the protection of other established interests, such as titles to land and 'all our religious privileges'.[2] Early in 1871 Tregaskis presided over a District meeting in Bathurst; a minute was passed, drafted in his distinctive style, which obliquely deplored any cession, but chiefly emphasized the need for an early and definite decision one way or the other, so as to settle the prevailing uncertainty. Tregaskis then wrote to

[1] C.O. 87/98B, Boyce to Dr. Rigg, 17 Sept. 1869.
[2] W(esleyan) M(issionary) S(ociety). Quilter to Perks, 13 May 1870, Tregaskis to W.M.S., 11 May 1870. In Sierra Leone Tregaskis was shortly to raise the influence of his mission to its peak under a Roman Catholic Governor, whom he regarded as a natural ally against the Anglican Establishment.

urge the parent society to publicize this minute in order to thwart Kennedy's plans.[1] This marks a moderate hardening of the Wesleyan attitude, which may be attributable to the influence of Thomas Brown; though not, apparently, a deeply religious man, he had long cultivated good relations with the mission.[2] At this stage, it seems that Wesleyan fears for religious liberty were muted, and such protests as they made co-ordinated with those of the merchants.

The people with the deepest interest in preventing the Gambia from becoming French were undoubtedly the African townspeople of Bathurst, whose livelihood depended on their education in the English tongue, and their acquaintance with British law or commercial practice. Some were qualified, under British rule, for employment in government or mercantile offices, and a few for local legal practice; small shop-keepers could order and import merchandise from their British suppliers — so long as the subsidized mail-steamer continued to call at Bathurst. Moreover, though a small minority of the 13,000 inhabitants of the Gambia might in time aspire to rights of French citizenship, for the great majority French rule was liable to mean deterioration in personal status and loss of legal rights. As early as December 1864 a French official noted that the class of 'black gentlemen — more English than the English, more Protestant than the Protestants', would certainly oppose any transfer to France.[3]

These very real dangers, however, were not described with much clarity in the petition of April 1870, with its five hundred signatories; this consisted largely of general rhetorical arguments against the transfer. Kennedy claimed, not implausibly, that Brown was the chief sponsor of this document, acting through W. C. Walcott, a West Indian lawyer, and Harry Finden, owner of a small African store (which Kennedy sneeringly

[1] *WMS*, Tregaskis to W.M.S., Feb. 1871; the minute is quoted by Gray, *op. cit.*, p. 440.

[2] *WMS*, Tregaskis to W.M.S., 5 March 1869; Tyas to W.M.S., 18 March 1869; Brown to Tregaskis, 6 May, 20 June 1872; Adcock to W.M.S., 15 Sept. 1873.

[3] *MAE*, Afrique 47, Note pour le Ministre, 28 Dec. 1864.

called a 'grog shop').[1] If this was indeed the case, it rather weakens the hypothesis that Brown's only real aim was to secure compensation. For the African opposition would not be so easy to buy off as Kennedy imagined; it might not include many men of property and learning, but once it succeeded in convincing British politicians that the good faith of the Empire, or the reputation of British philanthropy, required the retention of the Gambia, it would become impossible to make the transfer, with or without compensation. It may of course simply be that Brown miscalculated the potential strength of the opposition he was encouraging in this quarter; certainly the African petitioners brought new allies into the field whom the government would find it hard to disregard.

*   *   *   *   *

To judge from their official files the French government, even under the liberalized Empire, had less need than the British to worry about public pressure on such questions. The one merchant interested in the Ivory Coast, Verdier of la Rochelle, did enlist the support of his local Chamber of Commerce in 1869 in urging that the French posts there should not be ceded; but these representations had little effect.[2] Devès and his Bordeaux allies do not appear to have made any move· to defend the Mellacourie at this stage. Nevertheless on 1 July the French Foreign Minister, probably hoping to expedite progress, asked the British for an early reply to his Note of 31 March so that he could reply to questions in the Chamber.[3]

This made the British take stock of their attitude to the opposition. On 10 June Gladstone, replying to questions in the Commons from two Conservative Members, had promised that the Gambia would not be ceded without Parliamentary consent;[4] the question therefore was whether that consent could be

[1] C.O. 87/96, Kennedy to Granville, 20, 30 April 1870, encl. petition; 5 May; 32, 10 May; 36, 2 June (encl. notes on signatories); Bravo to Kennedy, 2, 13 May 1870; cf. *MMC*, Afrique VI/15/a, Note by Bourgois, Nov. 1872.

[2] *MMC*, Afrique VI/11/a, La Rochelle Chamber of Commerce to M.M.C., 16 March 1869.

[3] F.O. 84/1318, Lyons to Clarendon, Tel., 3 July 1870.

[4] *Hansard*, 3rd series, CCI, 1842–3, 10 June 1870.

quickly obtained without political difficulties. It was still assumed that the opposition was basically inspired by the merchants' desire for compensation and that this could quite easily be met; the French were therefore warned to expect 'some additional representations', possibly involving 'slight expenditure'. This hint was poorly received in Paris; since under the draft terms British subjects in the Gambia were to be guaranteed against loss of privileges, the Ministry of the Marine could see no grounds for paying compensation as well. A Note to this effect was returned on 20 July.[1]

But meanwhile the British government had discovered new and more serious difficulties. On 13 July the Law Officers of the Crown delivered their opinion that formal Parliamentary consent for the proposed cession of territory ought to be expressed in the form of a Statute rather than a simple resolution. It was late in the Parliamentary session to introduce new legislation, and Rogers thought this opinion must mean postponing the agreement, though Monsell preferred to press ahead.

> 'Delay', he wrote, 'will intensify opposition among the natives, and encourage resistance here — It will be taken as an admission that there is a degree of public feeling here against the cession far greater than, as I believe, really exists.'[2]

But on 15 July the subject was discussed in both Houses of Parliament. Sir John Hay introduced a short debate in the Commons by expressing concern at the idea of transferring British subjects to France against their will; he was supported by six other Conservative Members and four Liberals, and by the Duke of Manchester in the House of Lords. Only Adderley supported Monsell in arguing the case for transfer.[3] Although the British Parliament was notoriously ill-informed on African questions, the opponents of transfer had still been able to find ready sympathizers there.

[1] F.O. 84/1318, Clarendon to Lyons, S.T. 7, 4 July; S.T. 9, 4 July 1870; Lyons to Granville, S.T. 17, 21 July; *MMC*, Afrique VI/11/a, M.A.E. to M.M.C., 7 July 1870; M.M.C. to M.A.E., 14 July.

[2] C.O. 87/98, Law Officers to C.O., 13 July 1870, minutes by Rogers, 13 July, Monsell, 14 July 1870; cf. F.O. 84/1335, memo. by Meade, 13 July.

[3] *Hansard*, 3rd series, CCIII, 339–42, 351–67.

There was now a new Colonial Secretary. The Earl of Kimberley was one of the abler administrators among the Whig aristocrats; though not prone to sentimentalism, he took Britain's responsibilities to colonial peoples seriously. On 16 July he decided that 'we cannot proceed with the Bill this Session'. Though the reason given to France was the pressure of business on Parliamentary time, the opposition in the Gambia largely explains Kimberley's reluctance to find time. Eventually, he hoped, Kennedy might succeed in reconciling this opposition to the resumption of negotiations; but unlike Monsell, Kimberley was unwilling to over-ride it.[1] For the present, France's declaration of war on Prussia on 15 July, and her subsequent defeat at Sedan on 2 September, would prevent negotiations in any case.

Kennedy, who still regarded the exchange as urgently desirable, continued to point out the great importance of the Mellacourie region to Sierra Leone; and it seems that he deliberately set out to make things difficult in the Gambia. Already he had withdrawn the small garrison, leaving the colony to defend its territory and uphold its prestige in the river out of its own resources, with the possibility of an occasional naval visit. Undecided whether it would be less unsatisfactory to rely upon an armed police force or a colonial militia, the settlement remained impotent beyond its frontiers and insecure within. When the merchants protested through a newly-organized Chamber of Commerce, Kennedy angrily belittled their grievances, and added a new one by exacting an annual subsidy towards new mail-boat services which served the needs of Freetown much better than those of Bathurst.[2]

[1] C.O. 87/98, minute by Kimberley, 16 July, on Law Officers, 13 July 1870; F.O. 84/1318, Granville to Lyons, S.T. 13, 20 July; S.T. 14, 27 July; S.T. 15, 13 Aug. 1870; cf. *MMC*, Afrique VI/11/a, M.A.E. to M.M.C., 25 July; 30 July; 20 Aug. 1870; M.M.C. to M.A.E., 5 Aug. 1870. For a comment on Kimberley as Colonial Secretary, C. Gertzel, *op. cit.*, pp. 136 ff. On these negotiations, cf. R. Catala, 'La Question de l'Echange de la Gambie Britannique contre les Comptoirs français du Golfe de Guinée, de 1866 à 1876', *Revue d'Histoire des Colonies françaises*, XXV (1948).

[2] C.O. 87/97, Kennedy to Kimberley, 97, 3 Nov. 1870; C.O. 87/99, same to same, 32, 9 June 1871; C.O. 87/104, Cooper to Kimberley, 1, 9 April 1873.

Nevertheless, during 1871 Kimberley increasingly came to doubt the justice, as well as the expediency, of exchanging the Gambia, even when conditions in France might permit it; instead he began to review arrangements for its future administration.[1] His new Under-Secretary, Knatchbull-Hughessen, was a forthright squire with a robust view of Imperial responsibilities; he favoured more energetic protection of the river trade, and even support of the Soninkes of Combo against the 'Marabouts'.[2] Twice it was denied in Parliament that there was any intention of resuming exchange negotiations; and when Thiers' provisional government tentatively raised the question in August 1871, Kimberley replied that opposition within the settlement made it impossible to proceed. The original draft of this reply again included the qualifying phrase 'at present'. Kimberley struck these words out; and on 15 September he informed Quin by letter that the government had abandoned the projected exchange.[3]

[3]
The Ashanti War of 1873–4, and its Effects on British Policy

Inevitably the Franco-Prussian war acted as a brake upon French policies overseas. In West Africa a brake might have been applied in any case, for since 1869 Valière, the new Governor of Senegal, had proposed to relax French control over much of Cayor and Futa Toro in favour of looser forms of suzerainty;[4] but the tendency to retrench was greatly increased

[1] C.O. 87/98, minute on Chown to C.O., 30 July 1870; C.O. 87/99, minutes on Kennedy to Kimberley, 2, 9 Jan. 1871; 4, 9 Feb.; on Anton to Kimberley, 4, 17 April 1871.

[2] C.O. 87/102, minutes by Hughessen on Fowler to Hennessy, 34, 1 May 1872; Simpson to Hennessy, 46, 5 June; 56, 4 Aug. 1872; C.O. 87/103, minute on Admty to C.O., 5 Sept. 1872.

[3] *Hansard*, 3rd series, CCVI, 153, 4 May 1871; 1806–23, 9 June 1871; *MAE*, Afrique 48, M.M.C. to M.A.E., 20 July 1871; C.O. 87/101, F.O. to C.O., 14 Aug. 1871 and minute by Kimberley; Kimberley to Quin, 15 Sept. 1871.

[4] Schefer, *op. cit.*, II, pp. 398–402, 589–90.

G

by the shattering impact of the Prussian victory. Until post-war antagonisms had been appeased and the future régime in Paris decided, politicians could not be expected to direct attention and resources towards consistent policies overseas. French garrisons were withdrawn completely from the Ivory Coast, and the flag left in charge of Verdier's commercial agents, while in Senegal Valière began a policy of somewhat uneasy co-operation with Lat-Dior (who, in common with the French, was disturbed by the growing influence in the lower basin of the river of Amadu Cheikou, a Tokolor 'marabout' of the Tijaniyya fraternity). However, this temporary change of policy in no way destroyed France's desire to control the Gambia; since peace in Senegal was her aim, it was all the more important to be able to control the import of firearms by this route.

Despite Kimberley's unfavourable attitude, then, the French Embassy in London continued to watch for opportunities to revive the exchange proposal; Charles Gavard, its ambitious Counsellor, and Admiral Véron, the naval attaché, both held informal instructions from the Ministry of the Marine on the subject.[1] In April 1873 Britain's difficulties in the Gambia seemed to offer hopes for a new sounding; but Kimberley again declared that local opposition precluded any negotiation. French officials were irritated, for they believed that most of this opposition was attributable to Brown; they decided their best hope would be to make British agents on the coast urge the merits of an exchange as strongly as Kennedy had done in 1870.[2] The outbreak of a new Ashanti war seemed to offer means of making them do so.

* * * * *

The Colonial Office had not regarded the agreement of 1871, by which they took over the Dutch possessions on the Gold

---

[1] *MMC*, Afrique VI/15/a, Note for Vérou, Nov. 1872; *MAE*, Afrique 48, M.M.C. to M.A.E., 5 March, 2 May, 16 June 1873.

[2] *MMC*, Afrique VI/15/a, Note du Cabinet du Ministre, 27 March 1873; Gavard to d'Azy, 6 April; M.A.E. to M.M.C., 30 April; C.O. 87/106, F.O. to C.O., 23 May 1873, minute by Kimberley; *MMC*, Afrique VI/15/a, M.A.E. to M.M.C., 5 July; M.M.C. to M.A.E., 27 Sept. 1873. For a hint of French pressure on Brown, C.O. 87/104, Cooper to Harley, 61, 29 April 1873.

Coast, as violating the Parliamentary Committee's doctrine of non-extension. Only control of a continuous coastline, it seemed, could make the British settlements fiscally self-supporting; the agreement clearly came under the dispensation for 'measures . . . necessary for the more efficient and econo-mical administration of the settlements we already possess'. Kimberley could in good faith disclaim all idea of 'the acquisi-tion of territory or the extension of British power'.[1] The one possible risk attached to the transaction seemed that of conflict with Ashanti over her claims to suzerain rights at Elmina; but only after obtaining evidence which appeared to show that the Asantehene had renounced such rights did the British govern-ment proceed, early in 1872, to ratify the agreement and take over the forts.[2]

Trouble with Ashanti was the last thing they wanted; she seemed to offer a fine example of a 'strong native power', capable of providing an ordered market for an expanding British trade. If this analysis were correct, the great danger would be to commit British power to supporting weak and 'degenerate' coastal peoples against her. In 1869-70, when attempts by Administrators Simpson and Ussher to open the Volta river to trade and navigation seemed to be leading them into hostility towards Ashanti and her allies in the lower part of the valley, the Colonial Office disavowed their policy; and Rogers commented,

'I cannot see why we should attempt to thwart the Ashantis in carrying out their traditional policy of reaching the sea by the valley of the Volta. It seems to me a very sensible policy, just the thing which is most likely to civilize them and bring them under our influence, commercial and military.'[3]

When Ashanti forces engaged in these operations took four European members of the German missions as prisoners to Kumasi, the British government avoided taking any strong or

---

[1] Crooks, *op. cit.*, p. 405, Kimberley to Hennessy, 12 Feb. 1872.

[2] Ward, *op. cit.*, pp. 245-50.

[3] C.O. 96/79, minute by Rogers, 4 May 1869, quoted Wolfson, *op. cit.*, p. 146; Wolfson, pp. 129 ff., gives the best discussion of the Volta question.

hostile line in negotiating for their release; instead, they soon afterwards proposed to increase the stipend of Kofi Karikari, the new Asantehene.

This policy of appeasement culminated while John Pope Hennessy was acting as Governor-in-Chief in 1872. An Irish Catholic lawyer and former Conservative M.P., Hennessy has strong claims to be regarded as the worst colonial governor of the century; from Hong Kong to Barbados he was to display his gifts for quarrelling with subordinates and stirring up communal dissension, often in well-intentioned but maladroit attempts to improve the status of under-privileged groups. During his one short visit to the Gold Coast he reversed the attitude of previous Administrators towards the Mankessim confederacy, which by 1871 had evolved from a defensive alliance against Dutch and Ashantis into an attempt by chiefs and educated men to erect a federal government over the Fanti states of the former British 'protectorate'. British attitudes towards this practical essay in African self-government had hitherto been curiously inconsistent, implying that it violated Imperial authority in countries where the nature and basis of that authority was extremely uncertain; but Hennessy's encouragement of the confederacy, constructive though it may have been in intention, was in practice confined to unctuous generalities, and had no permanent effects.[1] However, at the same time as he was encouraging this anti-Ashanti grouping, Hennessy went further in appeasing the Ashantis. He sent presents to Kumasi, and re-opened the frontier to trade, just in time to allow Kofi Karikari to buy arms for the purpose of renewing the invasion which had been checked in 1864.

Even after Ashanti armies began their advance towards the coast in December 1872, the British government hesitated to offer whole-hearted resistance. It was painful to abandon the casting of Ashanti in the role of strong African collaborator, still more painful for a Gladstonian government to contemplate the expense of a major military campaign in Africa. But by July 1873, after news of Ashanti victories had damaged British prestige, the government reluctantly decided to send a sub-

[1] Ward, *op. cit.*, pp. 251–61.

stantial expeditionary force under Sir Garnet Wolseley to undertake an invasion of Ashanti itself. Perhaps Pine had been right in 1863 when he urged that a decisive military victory in Ashanti was a necessary condition for the maintenance of even limited British authority on the Gold Coast. The campaign proved successful; superior British fire-power drove the Ashantis back across the Pra with heavy losses, and Wolseley entered Kumasi on 4 February 1874 (though anxiety for the health of his troops led him to withdraw after thirty-six hours).

The campaign marked the beginning of certain changes in British attitudes towards African problems. The operations were reported in British newspapers, along with accounts of Ashanti itself, by a surprisingly large and talented group of war correspondents,[1] and the war seemed to prove less unpopular with the British public than with many members of the Liberal Cabinet. Disraeli's references to Imperial questions in his Crystal Palace speech of 1872 had revealed the premonition of a shrewd politician that the enlarged electorate was becoming bored by Cobdenites and separatists, and ready to listen sympathetically to leaders who talked more about British power. How many votes this speech actually influenced is of course uncertain; but as a result of the election of February 1874 it was a Disraeli ministry, supported by a clear Conservative majority in the House of Commons, which faced the problems of peace-making in the Gold Coast.

Despite Disraeli's new fascination with problems of Imperial power, his government was not notably more interested or better informed in African matters than its predecessor. Adderley was kept discreetly away from colonial affairs; but Stanley, now fifteenth Earl of Derby, returned to the Foreign Office, and continued to express pacific, anti-expansionist views very unlike those of his leader. The new Colonial Secretary, Lord Carnarvon, was, like Derby, thoughtful, conciliatory and indecisive. During his short tenure of office in 1867 he had presided over the federation of Canada, and he showed some interest in

[1] Extracts from some of their reports are collected in F. Wolfson, *Pageant of Ghana* (London, 1958). For a convenient summary of operations, see Ward, *op. cit.*, pp. 265–84.

repeating this trick in South Africa. Like most of his colleagues, Carnarvon was not opposed in principle to expansion in the tropics, as he soon showed by sponsoring, rather reluctantly, the annexation of the Fiji Islands; but the Cabinet was certainly not 'imperialist' in the sense of regarding increases of territory as bringing increments of power. Over the treatment of the Gold Coast after the Ashanti war they were divided, on practical grounds. But Carnarvon was soon convinced that any retraction of British responsibilities was no longer conceivable: a view in which he was encouraged by a forceful new official, Augustus Hemming, who argued that the 'vague and inconclusive' resolutions of 1865 had prevented any firmness of policy.[1] Parliamentary discussion soon showed that politicians too were changing their attitudes.

On 27 April a Conservative M.P., R. W. Hanbury, opened a debate, which was continued a week later, on the motion

> 'That in the interests of civilization and of commerce, it would not now be desirable to withdraw from the administration of the affairs of the Gold Coast.'

The pacific radical Sir Wilfrid Lawson moved an amendment in favour of withdrawing from 'all equivocal and entangling engagements'; and four other Liberals spoke in his support — J. Holms, Sir F. Goldsmid, H. Richard (a Welsh Nonconformist, of the Peace Preservation Society) and the notable old Yorkshireman J. A. Roebuck. This group raised 75 votes when they forced a division, but 311 Members voted against them. The tone of the speeches ranged from patient acceptance of the impossibility of withdrawal — voiced by Hay and Mills, two survivors of the 1865 Committee, and most reluctantly by the new Under-Secretary, James Lowther[2] — to confident appeals, many by Liberals, to 'the honour and dignity of the Empire'. William Macarthur, a Liberal, a Wesleyan, and a London merchant with a large Australian trade, argued that

---

[1] *D(israeli) P(apers)* XII, Carnarvon to Disraeli, 6 March 1874; C.O. 806/12, memo. by Hemming, *Gold Coast: Enquiry of 1865*, 1 April 1874.

[2] cf. his minute in C.O. 96/119, quoted Wolfson, *British Relations . . .*, p. 384, on 'old women of both sexes' who insist on maintaining 'these undesirable possessions'; cf. also Ward, *op. cit.*, p. 262.

'we were destined not only to confer still greater blessings upon the Gold Coast, but to carry them far into the interior'.

Even more interesting was the speech of Knatchbull-Hughessen, who while in office had been arguing that Britain's contribution to civilization and Christianity in West Africa made her 'continued presence and action . . . most desirable in the interests of West Africa and of the world'.[1] In his speech Hughessen, after defending Liberal policy in Ashanti, turned to attack Adderley and his school.

'They did not think that England ought to interfere anywhere excepting where it could be shown that direct and substantial advantage would accrue, and they would never annex an acre or add a foot to British territory except in such a case. He need hardly point out to the House that if these principles had guided the past policy of this country we should have had no colonial Empire to speak of today.'

The Liberal leaders might privately despise Hughessen's speeches as 'the Bunkum in which . . . the House too much delights', but in doing so they admitted the growing popularity of such views.[2]

At the time of this debate the Cabinet had still taken no final decision about the future of the Gold Coast; but eight days later Carnarvon announced in the Lords that, judging it impossible to withdraw, the government had desired to exercise more direct authority in the protectorate. For the Liberals, Kimberley agreed that this represented the least unsatisfactory course.[3] Now the government had to decide how to wield this authority, for conceivably some attempt might still have been made to work through the agency of the Mankessim confederacy. Instead, Carnarvon decided to annex the former 'protectorate' by Royal Proclamation and make it a Crown Colony, independent

[1] C.O. 267/316, minute by Hughessen, 3 Oct. 1872, with Hennessy to Kimberley, 110, 1 Sept. 1872; cf. his minute of 18 Feb. 1873 in C.O. 96/104.

[2] A. Ramm (ed.), *The Political Correspondence of Mr. Gladstone and Lord Granville* (London, 1952) No. 914, Gladstone to Granville, 21 Oct. 1873, No. 983, Granville to Gladstone, 4 May 1874. For the debate, *Hansard*, 3rd series, CCXVIII, 1204–25 (27 April 1874); 1592–1664 (4 May 1874).

[3] *Hansard*, 3rd series, CCXIX, 152–73, 12 May 1874.

of Sierra Leone though still united with Lagos. This raised another problem: could domestic slavery be tolerated on what was now British soil? Carnarvon was at first disposed to do so, regarding its local form as a relatively harmless and deeply entrenched 'native custom'; but soon pressure from British philanthropists made him legislate for its early abolition.[1] This social revolution by ordinance, if less than revolutionary in its immediate effects, demonstrated very clearly that Britain was in the Gold Coast to stay. Soon proposals for improving education and public works showed that there was some intention of making her presence beneficial. But the financing of such development schemes raised yet further problems which affected the new Colony's relations with its neighbours.

One method of increasing the prosperity of the Gold Coast might be to apply there also the magic formula of 'trade with the Sudan'. Now that Ashanti was out of favour as a 'strong native power', many people turned their attention further north, and specifically to Salaga, a noted market-town in Gonja. This was one of the centres from which kola-nuts grown in Ashanti had long been distributed through the savanna belt; access from the south had formerly been tightly controlled by the Ashanti, who did not want European firearms to find their way to their northern neighbours. Now this obstacle was removed people like Winwood Reade, formerly pro-Ashanti, suggested encouraging Muslims from the north to come down the Volta valley to trade at the coast.[2] In 1876 Captain Gouldsbury was sent by the colonial government to visit Salaga; but his report on the prospects was rather discouraging, and no other official mission was sent so far inland until 1882.[3]

Since trade with the distant interior could not be easily or quickly increased, it was all the more tempting to try to increase the revenue which the new colony could collect from customs duties on the coast. The Dutch exchange permitted the enforce-

[1] *D.P.* XII, Carnarvon to Disraeli, 28 June 1874; cf. Ward, *op. cit.*, pp. 262–4, 393–5.

[2] P.R.O. 30/6/46 (Carnarvon Papers) Reade to Carnarvon, 8 July 1874; W. W. Reade, *The Story of the Ashanti Campaign* (London, 1874) p. 144.

[3] Wolfson, *Pageant of Ghana*, pp. 24, 167–9, Report by Gouldsbury, 27 March 1876.

ment of a common tariff along some two hundred miles of coastline, but the old problem of evasion had not been removed. Trade-goods could still enter through ports immediately east or west of the colony, and, free from serious duties, find their way round into what British administrators regarded as their rightful hinterland. Some of this trade, too, was in firearms: a fact which added political to fiscal reasons for desiring to extend colonial control. Governors were soon coveting fiscal control of the 'Slave Coast' — the littoral of the Popos states and of Dahomey, separating what were commonly referred to as 'the two parts of the Gold Coast Colony'. In 1875 Administrator Rowe estimated the additional revenue which might be collected on this coast at £46,000 — including £17,150 at Cotonou. Their new position on the Gold Coast also gave the British, for the first time, some interest in taking over from France on the Ivory Coast. Rowe believed £20,000 in additional revenue might be collected here.[1] Moreover, much of this trade consisted of renewed imports of firearms into Ashanti; the central authority and power of the Asantehene, which had seemed to be fatally weakened by the fall of Kumasi, were slowly and painfully being re-established. In 1883 the French believed that three or four thousand guns might be reaching Ashanti each year through the hands of their Agni kinsmen on the Ivory Coast.[2]

The logic of the changed situation in the Gold Coast gradually led Carnarvon to favour the idea of acquiring sovereign rights over narrow strips of neighbouring coastline — a notion which was simultaneously being advocated for the region of Sierra Leone. This does not mean that he had become a territorial expansionist; his hope was to collect revenue without assuming administrative responsibility for the interior districts where many of the dutiable goods would be consumed. This was a weak compromise, of questionable morality, justifiable only by the worthy motives of the Colonial Office; they hoped that the extra revenue might provide finance for those schools and roads which the peoples of the Gold Coast desired for their

[1] C.O. 806/40, Nos. 1, 2, memo. by Rowe, c. 1 April 1875.
[2] *MAE*, Afrique 78, Bories to M.M.C., 20 March 1883.

G*

betterment. Moral arguments apart, however, the Colonial Office now had a new interest in negotiating the surrender of those French rights and territories which stood in the way of this new policy.

[4]

The Revival and Extension of the Exchange Proposal, 1874–5

The British began to take an interest in the Ivory Coast while attempting to blockade Ashanti during the war; they discovered that the French house of Verdier and the British factory of F. and A. Swanzy at Assinie were supplying arms. The French Admiral agreed on his own responsibility to co-operate in preventing the disembarkation of more arms, and temporarily assigned the warship *Prégent* to lie off Assinie. In Paris, this seemed a good opportunity to press the cause of the exchange. Véron, calling on Goschen at the Admiralty on 29 October 1873, contrasted this co-operation with Britain's failure to control imports of arms through the Gambia; but he hinted that it might not last, since French merchants were exerting pressure for the lifting of the blockade.[1] (In fact Verdier, the only Frenchman affected, was more interested in demanding compensation from the British than in resuming his not very profitable operations; and though Deputies from la Rochelle supported his complaints, these were still not treated very seriously by the government.[2]) But Goschen, instead of showing interest in the possibility of taking over Assinie, seemed more disposed to divert discussion to the subject of possible joint control of the African arms traffic.[3] On 19 December Gavard

[1] *MAE*, Afrique 54, du Quilio to Mathieu, 22 Aug. 1873; *MMC*, Afrique VI/15/a, M.M.C. to M.A.E., 27 Sept. 1873; Swanzy to M.M.C., 6 Nov.; M.M.C. to Swanzy, 18 Nov. 1873.

[2] *MAE*, Afrique 54, M.M.C. to M.A.E., 16 Jan. 1874; A. Verdier, *Trente-cinq Ans de Lutte aux Colonies* (Paris, 1896) pp. 12–29.

[3] *MAE*, Afrique 48, Dutreuil to de Broglie, Pte. 29 Oct., 11 Nov. 1873; M.M.C. to M.A.E., 5 Dec. 1873; cf. C.O. 806/40, Strahan to Carnarvon, Conf. 23 March 1875.

had an informal talk with Herbert at the Colonial Office, and reluctantly concluded that the exchange question would have to wait.[1]

At the end of the war, in April 1874, Gavard proposed to the new British Ministers an exchange of the Gambia against the Ivory Coast and the Mellacourie. The advantages to Britain seemed much greater than in 1870.[2] Besides the new fiscal needs of the Gold Coast there were comparable arguments for coastwise extension from Sierra Leone; in 1873 that Colony had run into financial difficulties, and control of the Mellacourie trade now seemed doubly desirable.[3] And the outlook for the Gambia itself was still extremely gloomy. Recent shortcomings of trade had affected colonial finances; in April an attack on one of Brown's vessels above MacCarthy's Island re-emphasized the dangerous ambiguity of the situation in the upper river; the advance of the 'Marabouts' in Combo seemed liable to threaten Bathurst itself, where many Muslims were known to sympathize with them; the problem of local defence was still unsolved; and the formidable sanitary problem of the swamp on St. Mary's Island was again causing alarm.[4] The case for ceding the Gambia, in return for concessions so beneficial to the other settlements, seemed to Carnarvon unanswerable.

On the other hand, the experience of 1870 showed the need for careful political preparation. It was now accepted that Parliamentary legislation was necessary for the cession of a colony, and clearly this might not be unopposed. But C. H. Kortright, Administrator of the Gambia, reported hopefully on local opinion. The merchants, he declared, would simply calculate losses and gains. Quin, whose trade was now small, and

[1] *MMC*, Afrique VI/15/a, M.A.E. to M.M.C., 23 Jan. 1874 and minute.
[2] *MMC*, Afrique VI/15/a, M.A.E. to M.M.C., 14 April 1874, encl. Gavard to Decazes, 12 April; F.O. 27/2226, Derby to Lyons, 11 April 1874, memo. by Hill, Wylde, 20 April; Note left by French Ambassador, 27 April; C.O. 87/107, F.O. to C.O., 27 April 1874, minutes.
[3] See below, pp. 214-8.
[4] For all these questions, see P.P., 1876, LII, *Correspondence respecting the Affairs of the Gambia and the Proposed Exchange with France* . . . (C. 1409). This was hurriedly published in February 1876 in hope of demonstrating the case for exchange.

Brown, who had recently had to resign from the Legislative Council after a public scandal, would both welcome an opportunity to retire; neither Lintott and Spink, the successors of Forster and Smith, nor William Goddard, a relative of the latter's ex-agent, would press their opposition. Only the Chowns were now doing much business: they themselves do not seem to have been in Bathurst since 1870, but their interests had prospered in the hands of their agent Henry Helm, an enterprising Prussian who had been locally naturalized and now sat in the Legislative Council. On African opinion, too, Kortright was moderately complacent.

> 'The shopkeepers and small traders fear that they may be supplanted by Frenchmen of the same class; and they also feel the same disinclination as the native inhabitants to pass from mild British sway to French military rule. I do not believe that this feeling would be more than temporary, as the greater activity introduced by a French occupation would speedily reconcile them to the change.'[1]

(Kortright might also have added that the resident French merchants had now withdrawn their former opposition to the transfer. The deterioration of local government since 1870 had convinced them that they would be better off under Senegal, even though they might expect increased interference from 'une administration méticuleuse et parfois tracassière'.[2])

But though the French continued to press for a reply, the British Cabinet was not consulted until a year after Gavard's original proposal. First there was the long Parliamentary recess; then, early in 1875, Carnarvon was largely withdrawn from public business for several weeks by the fatal illness of his wife.[3] He had already decided that an exchange was desirable, as much for the sake of avoiding trouble in the Gambia as because of the positive advantages elsewhere. Worried by what he quaintly described as 'this conquering tribe of Mohammedan

---

[1] P.R.O. 30/6/8, Carnarvon to Derby, 13 May 1874; Derby to Carnarvon, 14, 22 May; C.O. 87/107, Carnarvon to Kortright, Pte. 21 May 1874; Kortright to Carnarvon, 19 June.

[2] *MAE*, Afrique 48, Besnard to du Quilio, 5 April 1873.

[3] A. Hardinge, *Life of Carnarvon* (London, 1925) Vol. II, pp. 80–1.

Marabouts who are already on our frontier and are absorbing our allies', and all too mindful of the way his predecessor had stumbled into the Ashanti war, Carnarvon was anxious to get out of the firing-line.[1] Derby accepted his conclusions, though with lukewarm enthusiasm:

'as far as the interests of the Empire are concerned, I see no harm in it; and after Fiji and the Gold Coast we are not likely to be reproached with a policy of colonial surrender'.

But, speaking as one only too familiar with the strong feelings which could be aroused on colonial questions, he advised careful consultation with the Prime Minister about probable Parliamentary reactions. He recalled the opposition raised in 1870, and added,

'the present Parliament is likely to be inspired with at least as much zeal for the integrity of the British possessions.'[2]

Nevertheless, the Colonial Office did not expect a serious renewal of opposition. Though Kortright reported in November 1874 that rumours of an impending transfer to France were again circulating in Bathurst, he did not seem greatly perturbed; Brown, he added, was negotiating to sell his business to a French firm, and would again be chiefly interested in compensation claims.[3] As a means of buying off the merchants the Colonial Office decided to suggest that France should pay a lump sum for government property when she took over the Gambia, and that this should be used to settle compensation claims.

They were also considering taking the opportunity to ask for something more than the Ivory Coast and Mellacourie. In December 1874 Carnarvon suggested disposing of France's somewhat obscure rights at Porto Novo and Cotonou by inviting her to renounce all territorial claims between the Gold Coast and Lagos. In March, when under pressure from Hemming he

[1] P.R.O. 30/6/8, Carnarvon to Derby, 31 Aug.; 12 Dec. 1874.
[2] P.R.O. 30/6/8, Derby to Carnarvon, 16 Dec. 1874.
[3] C.O. 87/107, Kortright to Carnarvon, Conf., 6 Nov. 1874, minute by Herbert, 30 Nov. On Brown's plans, cf. P.R.O. 30/6/24, T. Gibson (Bathurst) to Carnarvon, 29 March 1875.

finally formulated a definite proposal, it was in still wider terms; the French were now to be asked to accept a far-reaching division of the west coast into spheres of influence. France would leave the way open for fiscal expansion from the Gold Coast and Sierra Leone by renouncing all claims between the Benin river and some point north of Sierra Leone such as the Pongos; Britain would do likewise from this latter point up to the Moroccan border. On 17 April 1875 the British Cabinet agreed that negotiations might be opened on this basis.[1]

But even now, despite the need to synchronize negotiations with Parliamentary timetables in both countries, progress was very slow. This was partly due to bureaucratic delays in Whitehall, and to the loss of the Note in which the French very promptly agreed to receive proposals.[2] But also the British were still enlarging their demands. The Foreign Office decided that it was desirable to get France formally to disinterest herself in the vital area of the Niger delta; hence it was decided to extend the southern border of the proposed British sphere from the Benin river to the borders of Gabon.[3] At the same time, the sphere offered to France was contracted, so that it would stop at 'the northern limit of the existing French possessions' (wherever that might be) rather than the southern border of Morocco. This change was prompted by representations which Carnarvon received in support of a fantastic scheme for cutting a canal inland from the Mauritanian coast in order to flood the Sahara

[1] P.R.O. 30/6/8, Carnarvon to Derby, 12 Dec. 1874; C.O. 87/107, minute by Hemming, 20 Feb. 1875; C.O. 267/328, minute by Hemming, 13 Feb. 1875, on French, 8, 13 Jan.; C.O. 87/107, C.O. to F.O., 5 March 1875. (The text given in *P.P.* 1876, LII, is not accurate.) *D.P.* XII, Carnarvon to Disraeli, 13 April 1875; F.O. 27/2226, F.O. to C.O., 21 April 1875; *MMC*, Afrique VI/16, M.A.E. to M.M.C., 12 April 1875. It is a curious point that Carnarvon — not, as might have been expected, the Foreign Office — insisted on a wording which would exclude any recognition of French claims in Morocco. C.O. 87/108, memo. by Fairfield on F.O., 25 June 1875.

[2] F.O. 27/2226, Derby to Gavard, 30 April 1875; Gavard to Derby, 3 May; Note by Tenterden, June 1875; cf. *MMC*, Afrique VI/16, M.A.E. to M.M.C., 3, 4 May 1875.

[3] F.O. 27/2226, memo. by Wylde, 7 May 1875, C.O. 87/108, F.O. to C.O., 15 May 1875, minute by Meade; C.O. to F.O., 17 May; F.O. to C.O., 25 June 1875.

and allow sea-going ships to sail to Timbuktu. Although the British government gave little encouragement to this plan, even after it was modified into one for a trading-station at Cape Juby, Carnarvon thought it better to word his offer to France in terms which would not prejudice its future.[1]

So it was only on 23 July 1875 — less than three weeks before both French and British Parliaments were due to rise — that the French at last received a concrete British proposal. Nevertheless, Carnarvon still hoped to complete negotiations and put the agreement through in a hurry. Reflection had convinced him that there was no need for legislation, or even a vote in the House of Commons, in order to effect a transfer of territory; formal consultation would suffice. His intention was, if France accepted the offered terms, to make a brief announcement of the government's decision, trusting that no effective opposition could be organized before the adjournment of the House.[2]

★   ★   ★   ★   ★

The British terms came as an unpleasant surprise to the French colonial department. They regarded their posts on the Ivory Coast and Mellacourie — attenuated though French control might be in both areas[3] — as ample value for the Gambia. The notion of giving financial compensation to British merchants in that colony seemed to carry derogatory implications — 'they would lose nothing by becoming French'.[4] But their strongest objection was to the proposed renunciation of

[1] C.O. 267/328, Mackenzie to C.O., 24 June 1875 and minutes. F. V. Parsons, 'The North-West African Company and the British Government', *Historical Journal*, I, 1958. For the process of amendment of the British draft, C.O. 87/108, minute by Carnarvon on Cooper, 6, 20 June 1875; minute on F.O. to C.O., 25 June; F.O. 27/2226, amended copy of F.O. to C.O., 25 June, minute by Wylde, 9 July. In *P.P.* 1876, LII this letter is printed in its later, amended, form.

[2] C.O. 87/107, Carnarvon amendments to draft of C.O. to F.O., 5 March 1875; *MMC*, Afrique VI/16, D'Harcourt to Decazes, 26 July 1875; F.O. 27/2226, minutes by Tenterden, 23, 24 June 1875; F.O. to Law Officers, 14 July; Derby to D'Harcourt, 23 July 1875.

[3] *MMC*, Afrique VI/15/a, M.M.C. to Ministry of Agriculture and Commerce, 16 April 1874; Afrique VI/16, Bourgois to D'Azy, 9 Sept. 1875.

[4] *MMC*, Afrique VI/16, M.M.C. to M.A.E., 1 May 1875.

French influence in the Slave Coast and Niger delta. This would mean permanent exclusion from the lower Niger, which they still envisaged rather vaguely as a route for future political penetration towards both Senegal and Lake Chad. It would also mean renouncing political influence in Dahomey, Porto Novo and the Popos, and leaving an established French commerce at the mercy of Britain and her colonial tariffs.

Two new Marseillais firms had now entered this area, breaking away from Régis. The first, Lasnier, Daumas et Cie, had opened business in 1866, with one former Régis agent among the partners and another, Béraud, as their agent at Whydah. Régis reacted acrimoniously, using the influence of the consular agency (which had become virtually entailed upon his representative) to hinder his competitors; for two years prices were driven up by fiercely competitive buying. But in 1868, when Régis' nephew and former associate, Cyprien Fabre, also entered trade at Whydah, Régis resigned himself to the loss of his monopoly. Cut-throat competition was called off, and the three firms attempted to maintain a common front in matters of common interest.[1] After the Ashanti war they sought government support in resisting the apparent designs of the Gold Coast authorities upon their trade. The Ministry of the Marine regarded their interests as important enough to merit support — especially since they were backed by the Marseille Chamber of Commerce; in the summer of 1875 the warship *Diamant* was sent to cruise along the Slave Coast, calling at the Popos, Whydah and Cotonou, and sending a party to Porto Novo.[2] Since the British terms would mean abandoning these traders, the Colonial Department would have preferred to confine the agreement with Britain to a simple exchange of territories

[1] *MMC*, Gabon IV/3/b, de Langle to M.M.C., 6 Sept. 1866; *MAE*, Afrique 53, M.M.C. to M.A.E., 11 July, 16 Aug. 1867 (encl. de Langle, 22 May, 8 June); Daumas to M.A.E., 26 Nov. 1868; Afrique 54, M.M.C. to M.A.E., 23 Oct. 1868, 25 March 1869 (encl. Dauriac, 22 July, 22 Dec. 1868); Masson, *Marseille et la Colonisation française*, p. 382.

[2] *MAE*, Afrique 54, Ministry of Agriculture and Commerce to M.A.E., 11, 26 Jan. 1875, encl. Marseille Chamber of Commerce, 22 Dec.; M.M.C. to M.A.E., 3 April 1875, encl. Pilandrin, 1 Dec. 1874; Report by Capt. Cantaloube (extract) 14 Aug. 1875.

actually held. If France did renounce political intervention on the Slave Coast, wrote Benoît D'Azy, Director of Colonies, she should insist that Britain did likewise, as part of some neutralization agreement.[1]

The Foreign Ministry, however, was prepared to sweep such objections aside for the sake of a speedy agreement. Ever since 1871 they had sought good relations with Britain as part of the re-establishment of France's position in Europe, and they were particularly anxious to stand close to her in 1875. In May Derby had succeeded in giving Gavard an impression of cordial support during a period of acute Franco-German tension, though without any definite commitment; as he himself admitted:

'We have been lucky in our foreign policy; for what we did involved no risk and cost no trouble, while it has given us an appearance of having helped, more than we really did, to bring about the result.'[2]

But even the appearance of British support was valued by French diplomatists; this suggestion of a possibly incipient *entente* encouraged them to persevere in any colonial negotiation which might improve Anglo-French relations. The London embassy besought the colonial department to accept the British terms immediately, so that they might be ratified by both legislatures before the recess. On 27 July Gavard even told Carnarvon semi-officially, on his own initiative, that his terms would be accepted; he cannot have read them very carefully, since he described them as 'merely the reproduction of our own'.[3] Such zeal might well have rushed the French into hasty acceptance, but they were saved from this by the ineptitude of British ministers.

★ ★ ★ ★ ★

[1] *MMC*, Afrique VI/16, Draft Note, July 1875; Note by D'Azy, Aug. 1875; M.M.C. to M.A.E., 21 Aug. 1875.

[2] *D.P.* XII, Derby to Disraeli, 20 May 1875; cf. D(*ocuments*) D(*iplomatiques*) F(*rançais*) 1st series, Vol. I, Nos. 400, 403, 410, 420; Gavard to Decazes, 2, 6, 9, 12 May; 429, Decazes to Gavard, 19 May; C. Gavard, *Un Diplomate à Londres* (Paris, 1895) p. 258.

[3] *MMC*, Afrique VI/16, Gavard to (?) D'Azy, 25 July 1875; *MAE*, Afrique 48, D'Harcourt [Gavard] to Decazes, 26, 27 July 1875; *D.P.* XII, Carnarvon to Disraeli, 28 July.

On 22 July, the day before the British terms were handed over, Disraeli had informed the Commons that, in order to avoid sitting too far into August, the government would not proceed with its controversial Merchant Shipping Bill that session. Thereupon Mr. Samuel Plimsoll M.P. created a distressing and unprecedented scene upon the floor of the House, declaring this decision to be a betrayal of British seamen. The government was much embarrassed; there was some outcry in the country, many Conservative supporters shared Plimsoll's concern for marine safety, and there seemed some danger of a concerted opposition attack. On 26 July the responsible Minister — somewhat ironically, it was Adderley — introduced a 'stop-gap' Bill, simpler but less effective. This gesture appeased the dissidents, at the price of a very slight prolongation of the parliamentary session; but Disraeli now viewed with great distaste the possibility of further trouble from spokesmen of the Gambia interest.[1] On 28 July Carnarvon was persuaded to postpone his statement on the exchange until 3 August; soon afterwards Disraeli let it be known he would prefer the matter to stand over until the next session. This also Carnarvon rather weakly agreed to accept.[2] The French, when told of this decision, blamed the postponement on Disraeli's weakness as Premier; but they could only accept it and agree to try and avoid public discussion.[3]

It was already too late. On 29 July a note appeared in *Le Moniteur* announcing that negotiations had been completed; it gave a fairly accurate account of the proposed exchange of territory, but did not mention the proposals for spheres of influence along the coast. Decazes denied that this statement had any official authority, but the damage was done. On 30 July Knatchbull-Hughessen enquired about the report in the Commons; and on 3 August Carnarvon, instead of announcing the completion of agreement, had to deny the *Moniteur* report as

[1] Moneypenny and Buckle, *op. cit.*, V, pp. 381–7; Pemberton, *op. cit.*, pp. 219–22.

[2] *D.P.* XII, Carnarvon to Disraeli, 28 July, 5 Aug. 1875.

[3] F.O. 27/2226, Derby to Lyons, Conf., Tel. 29, July 1875; *MAE*, Afrique 48, D'Harcourt to Decazes, 30 July; cf. C.O. 806/45, Carnarvon to Rowe, Cooper, Secret, 30 July 1875.

'wholly inaccurate'. He said that negotiations were 'very far from conclusion'; that he hoped eventually for full Parliamentary discussion; that nothing would be done until the new session of 1876. He added that the 'mere handful' of British subjects in the Gambia would have their interests fully respected;[1] but this assurance, instead of satisfying the merchants, encouraged them to seek full publicity.

[5]
The Failure of the Exchange Negotiations, 1876

Although Kortright had reported that rumours of the exchange were current in Bathurst in November 1874, there had so far been little overt opposition. The *Moniteur* report of 29 July stimulated the house of Swanzy to make immediate anxious enquiries, but their interest was less that the Gambia should remain British than that Assinie should not become British.[2] In the Gambia itself, the only significant move had been a letter written by the three Wesleyan missionaries on 29 June to their parent society, urging resistance to a plan which might prove 'destructive to the commercial, civil and religious privileges of its inhabitants'.[3] The reasons for this hostility, much more marked than in 1870, are not clear. It may simply be that these men, all fairly recent arrivals, feared the rule of the nascent Republic more than their predecessors had feared that of the Empire; or possibly Brown had something to do with the change. (Next year he got up a somewhat sanctimonious round robin, in which the leading merchants thanked the Wesleyans for opposing the exchange.[4]) On 7 October Adcock, the most unstable of the missionaries, was one of two Europeans who

[1] F.O. 27/2226, Lyons to Derby, Tel. 30 July 1875; *Hansard*, 3rd series, CCXXVI, 222, 30 July; 436–8, 3 Aug.

[2] C.O. 806/45, No. 63, F. and A. Swanzy to C.O., 29 July 1875.

[3] *WMS*, Babcock, Adcock and Fieldhouse to W.M.S., 29 June 1875.

[4] *WMS*, Brown and 33 others to Boyce and Bunting, 24 Feb. 1876. This letter is written on the distinctive foolscap used by Brown for official correspondence.

joined 150 Africans in signing a petition against transfer; it was even reported that he presided over the drafting meeting.[1]

The merchants were slower in organizing direct opposition. There were a few letters in *The Times* during August,[2] but when Lintott, Spink and Co. made the first direct representation to the Colonial Office on 8 September, they did not oppose the transfer at all, but demanded indemnification for their prospective losses.[3] The other merchants seem to have been discussing tactics with the Manchester Chamber of Commerce, their allies in 1870. On 15 September Thomas Bazley, Liberal M.P. for Manchester, asked Carnarvon to receive a deputation from that body. Soon afterwards Brown launched a new series of letters, featuring two new arguments: the danger of France introducing protective and discriminatory colonial tariffs, and the more positive possibility of opening British trade-routes through the Gambia valley to Ségou and the Niger.[4] Later J. F. Hutton, an influential Manchester merchant with a keen interest in all West African questions, developed similar arguments at greater length, and announced that the Chamber of Commerce had set up a committee to study the Gambia question.[5] These representations had every appearance of genuine opposition.

Nevertheless, Carnarvon was not deterred. Hemming wrote a long and eloquent minute on Hutton's letter, refuting some of his arguments, and seeking to set the proposed exchange in perspective.

'The whole question appears to be one of expediency and compromise,' he wrote. 'If we could acquire the French possessions and at the same time retain the Gambia it would probably be desirable to do so, even though the settlement is of little value, and is a constant source of danger and anxiety. But it is a question of comparative advantages. Public attention has recently been strongly

[1] C.O. 806/45, No. 98, Rowe to Carnarvon, 75, 29 Oct. 1875, encl. petition; No. 100, Cooper to Carnarvon, 23 Nov. 1875. On Adcock, cf. *WMS*, Adcock to W.M.S., 15 Sept. 1873, Tregaskis to Perks, 20 Dec. 1874.

[2] *The Times*, 7, 13, 16, 27 Aug., 17 Sept. 1875.

[3] C.O. 806/45, No. 78. Lintott, Spink and Co. to C.O., 8 Sept. 1875.

[4] C.O. 806/45, No. 79, Bazley to C.O., 15 Sept. 1875; Nos. 82, 85, 93, Brown to C.O., 24 Sept., 7 Oct., 1 Nov. 1875.

[5] C.O. 806/45, No. 86, M.C.C. to C.O., 13 Oct. 1875, encl. Hutton, 27 Sept.

directed to the West Coast of Africa, and a feeling of astonishment has been displayed that, after so long, so little has been affected in the way of advancement in civilisation. We are now apparently, particularly on the Gold Coast, committed to a policy of development and improvement, a policy of real and earnest efforts to raise the natives of our settlements from the slough of ignorance and barbarism in which they are sunk.'

This meant providing schools and roads, which could be financed only by collecting more customs revenue on the Gold Coast; it followed that

'the interests of the few British merchants at the Gambia are hardly to be weighed against the possibility of providing the means of carrying the blessings of civilisation and importing the advantages of education to thousands of British subjects.'[1]

Affairs in Sierra Leone, without moving Hemming to such rhetorical heights, pointed in the same direction; Creole merchants were urging colonial control over the northern rivers, and this required agreement with France.[2] Carnarvon, though probably moved most by his negative desire to be rid of the Gambia, therefore agreed to try to circumvent the opposition. Discussing tactics with Derby during the recess, he suggested that France should be invited to tempt the opposition by concrete offers of compensation; and during October he devised a 'fresh scheme' for satisfying Parliament by submitting the proposed agreement to a Joint Committee of both Houses.[3] In the informal atmosphere of a Committee room, Carnarvon doubtless anticipated little difficulty in convincing reasonable men of the merits of the bargain.

He did consider extending the British terms still further, to include the Gabon area. A Glasgow merchant had recently asked that a British Consul might be appointed there, and R. B. N. Walker, who for twenty-five years had got on well with

[1] C.O. 87/108, minute by Hemming, 14 Oct., on Hutton, 27 Sept. 1875.

[2] P.P. 1876, LII, Rowe to Carnarvon, 153, 11 Sept. 1875, encl. petition; Kortright to C.O., 13 Oct. (minutes may be found in C.O. 267/328).

[3] P.R.O. 30/6/8, Carnarvon to Derby, 9 Oct.; Derby to Carnarvon, 11, 16 Oct.; Carnarvon to Derby, 19, 27 Oct. 1875; D.P. XII, Carnarvon to Disraeli, 23 Nov. 1875.

the French authorities, solicited the appointment. Describing the neglected state of this settlement since 1871, Walker expressed the opinion that its trade might greatly expand under British rule.[1] Seeing that the inclusion of Gabon in the exchange would tilt the balance of actual territory more strongly in Britain's favour, and might influence politicians to whom flags were important, Carnarvon asked the Foreign Office whether France was likely to agree.[2] French officials had in fact been expecting such a request; and although some of them were beginning to see possibilities of developing the Ogoué basin, where de Brazza was now starting his first journey, a determined British request might still have succeeded.[3] But none was made; Carnarvon was now wavering about the whole agreement, and the Foreign Office would make no further approaches without a clear decision as to policy.[4]

★   ★   ★   ★   ★

During the early weeks of 1876 opponents of the exchange intensified their activities in preparation for the new Parliamentary session. The Manchester Chamber of Commerce sent their deputation to Carnarvon on 31 January. It was notable that their President went out of his way to ask how the interests of British subjects would be safeguarded if the exchange went through.[5] On the same day the Liverpool Chamber, at an

[1] F.O. 84/1425, Scott to F.O., 25 Oct. 1875; Walker to Wylde, 14 Nov.; C.O. 806/45, No. 97, Walker to C.O., 11 Dec. 1875; C.O. 806/57, No. 15, Walker to C.O., 19 Feb. 1876; F.O. 27/2226, Admiralty to F.O., 3 Feb. 1875 [sc. 1876]. French fiscal control at the Gabon was impaired by Spain's sovereign rights over the off-shore Corisco and Elobey Islands; several of the British factories were here. Spain had refused to cede these to France, but Wylde believed she might let them go to Britain.

[2] F.O. 27/2226, C.O. to F.O., 29 Dec. 1875.

[3] MMC, Afrique VI/16, M.A.E. to M.M.C., 17 April 1875; M.M.C. to M.A.E., 10, 15 April, 29 Nov. 1875.

[4] F.O. 27/2226, minute by Wylde, 31 Dec. 1875; Tenterden to Herbert, 6 Jan. 1876.

[5] A report of the deputation, with a letter of 11 Feb. from Hutton to the C.O. were printed in Hutton's pamphlet, The Proposed Cession of the British Colony of the Gambia to France (Manchester, 1876). A copy is enclosed in C.O. 87/109, Cooper to Herbert, Pte., 21 March 1876.

annual meeting attended by two M.P.s, asked the government to suspend negotiations pending further enquiries.[1] Individual merchants and commission houses also sent in representations; those from Swanzy were discounted in the Colonial Office, since his self-interest was evident, but some attention was paid to a long letter from T. C. Chown.[2] Since the Chown business was now prospering sufficiently to support three generations of the family in the United Kingdom, they had the strongest interest in stopping the exchange rather than securing compensation; it is probably no coincidence that their letter contained the most convincing argument which had yet reached the government about the possibly harmful effects of French rule on African traders, clerks, and professional men. One official, after discussing this problem with Wylde of the Foreign Office, suggested stipulating for the temporary maintenance of the English language and British law in the Gambia, and perhaps for the equal treatment of French and British imports in all African possessions of the two powers. But Meade still believed that all this opposition could be removed by offers of compensation, belatedly lamenting that this had not been discreetly arranged at an earlier stage.[3]

Brown too was still prepared to use the argument of African opposition — imprudently so, if his intention really was simply to raise his terms for compensation. Officials had not been impressed by the number and quality of the supporters of the petition of 7 October; but in February Brown organized another one, with 121 signatures, and also drafted a letter which was signed by the nineteen principal non-French merchants.[4] Such methods aroused interest among British philanthropists, and

[1] *The Times*, 1 Feb. 1876; *MMC*, Afrique VI/17/a, Pernette to M.A.E., 1 Feb. 1876.

[2] C.O. 806/57, Spartali and Co. to C.O., 31 Dec. 1875; Swanzy to C.O., 3 Feb. 1876; C.O. to Swanzy, 9 Feb. 1876; C.O. 87/109, Swanzy to C.O., 12 Feb., minute by Hemming; T. C. Chown to C.O., 9 Feb., minutes by Fairfield, Meade, Herbert.

[3] C.O. 87/109, Walcott to C.O., 15 Feb. 1876, minutes by Fairfield, Meade.

[4] C.O. 806/57, Nos. 42, 43, Cooper to Carnarvon, 4, 9 March 1876, and enclosures. On the petition of October 1875, see P.P. 1876 (C. 1498).

among those beginning to take a constructive interest in Imperial affairs: influential men whose opposition could not be easily called off. In January the Royal Colonial Institute published a *Report on the Gambia Question*, which evoked some newspaper comment; on 16 February the Duke of Manchester, as its President, presented to Carnarvon five objections to the transfer. Native subjects of the Crown should not be abandoned against their will; they should not be transferred to a state with a different religion; the transfer was likely to cause wars in the Gambia; the river was potentially an important route to the interior; and, 'except for advantages of the highest and most undoubted Imperial importance . . . it is most undesirable to part with any of the territories of the Empire.'[1]

The spearhead of the opposition was the Gambia Committee, a new organization working from the office of the Aborigines Protection Society. Its senior officers were mostly representatives of that established group of philanthropists; William Macarthur M.P. was among its ten ordinary Committee members. The other nine were all West African merchants, including T. T. F. Quin, T. C. Chown, Brown's son David, and two or three representatives of Swanzy. On 1 February the Committee went as a deputation to see Carnarvon, reinforced by other missionary and humanitarian spokesmen, including Dr. Moffat of the London Missionary Society, Boyce of the Wesleyans, and three more Liberal M.P.s. Their arguments were similar to those of the Royal Colonial Institute, beginning with 'the integrity of the empire', and combining religious with commercial arguments. Next day *The Times*, in a pontifical though somewhat inconclusive leading article, questioned the desirability of completing the exchange.[2]

Although he must already have felt apprehensive about Parliamentary reactions, Carnarvon still intended to go ahead;

[1] Royal Colonial Institute, *Proceedings*, 1875–6.

[2] C.O. 87/109, Gambia Committee to C.O., 31 Jan. 1876. *The proposed Cession of the Gambia.* Report of the Proceedings of a Deputation to the Earl of Carnarvon . . . (London, 1876). *The Times*, 2 Feb. 1876; cf. C. Fitzgerald, *The Gambia and its Proposed Cession to France* (London, 1875). Fitzgerald, an ex-West Indian Regiment officer and one of the Secretaries of the Gambia Committee, was talking of an expedition from Bathurst towards Timbuktu.

he assured both deputations that the terms would be much more advantageous than a simple comparison of the territories to be ceded might suggest. Derby reminded him that the government was pledged to proceed, unless some new reason for withdrawal appeared; and Carnarvon accepted this position.[1] Hemming wrote a powerful memorandum, later printed for circulation, re-affirming his criticisms of the 'undecided policy' which the 1865 Committee had induced; comparing Britain's position to that of the magician in *Aladdin* who offered to exchange new lamps for old, he asserted that the transaction would greatly strengthen the Empire.[2]

On 17 February the proposed exchange was debated in the House of Lords, and the confidence of Ministers began to weaken. Carnarvon's arguments were supported by three Liberal peers with Colonial Office experience — Granville, Blachford (formerly Under-Secretary Rogers) and, more hesitantly, Kimberley. But the other five speakers — the Conservative Dukes of Somerset and Manchester, the Earl of Lauderdale, the Liberals Fortescue and Stanley of Alderley — all declared their opposition to any cession of the Gambia.[3] Two days later Carnarvon found the Cabinet 'as usual averse to a bold course': which appears to mean, that they refused to risk submitting the agreement directly to Parliament. On 21 February, Disraeli announced instead a proposal to appoint a Select Committee of the House of Commons.[4] But shortly afterwards Ministers began to fear that the Commons might rebuff them by rejecting even this procedure.[5] Carnarvon, plagued by apprehensive colleagues, was beginning to waver when a final blow was struck at the negotiation by a curiously devious route.

★   ★   ★   ★   ★

[1] P.R.O. 30/6/8, Derby to Carnarvon, 1 Feb. 1876; *MAE*, Afrique 49, D'Harcourt to Decazes, 12 Feb. 1876.

[2] C.O. 806/60, memo. by Hemming, 7 Feb. 1876.

[3] *Hansard*, 3rd series, CCXXVII, 374–97, Lords, 17 Feb. 1876.

[4] Carnarvon's diary, 19 Feb. 1876 (Hardinge, *op. cit.*, II, p. 144). *D.P.* XII, Carnarvon to Disraeli, 20 Feb.; *Hansard*, 3rd series, CCXXVII, 561, Commons, 21 Feb. 1876; *MMC*, D'Harcourt to Decazes, 18, 19 Feb. 1876.

[5] *MAE*, Afrique 49, D'Harcourt to Decazes, 15 March 1876.

During 1875 French merchants raised little effective opposition against the proposed exchange. In September 1875 J. F. Hutton, remembering the attitude of French Gambia merchants five years earlier, had tried to excite resistance from two leading Bordeaux houses, Maurel Frères and Maurel & Prom. But since 1870 their opinions had been altered by the deterioration in political conditions and by increases in customs duties; instead of supporting Hutton they reported his overture to the Ministry of the Marine.[1] The French Mellacourie merchants, apparently, raised no resistance; their business was not flourishing. Verdier did renew his pleas for the retention of the Ivory Coast, but little notice was taken of them.[2] The only prospective sufferers who had even a moderate political influence were Régis and his two rivals on the Slave Coast. But despite their strong fears of British fiscal expansion, it was only in November 1875 that, realizing that this might be authorized in the proposed agreement, they renewed their representations through the Marseille Chamber of Commerce.[3]

It was not certain that the Ministry of the Marine would heed even these objections. Past experience had taught French officers on the coast to distrust Régis' political initiatives. The commanding Admiral feared that the traders on the Slave Coast might involve France in war with Dahomey; in any case, their commerce should count for less than the political interests of the Senegal government.[4] If Britain was really intent on occupying the Slave Coast, French objections might not stop her; and her presence there might well lead to political improvement. Civilian officials attached more importance to the probable loss of French trade under the Lagos tariff; they had

---

[1] *MMC*, Afrique VI/16, Maurel to Roy, 6 Oct. 1875, encl. Hutton to Maurel and Prom, 11 Sept., Maurel and Prom to Hutton, 24 Sept. 1875.

[2] *ibid.*, Verdier to M.M.C., 30 July, 22 Oct. 1875; M.M.C. to Verdier, 6 Nov.; Note pour le ministre, 28 Dec.; Afrique VI/17/a, Verdier to M.M.C., 30 March 1876, encl. his pamphlet, *Echange de Territoire Coloniale* (La Rochelle, 1876).

[3] *MAE*, Afrique 48, Note by Régis, 22 Nov. 1875; *MMC*, Afrique VI/16, Marseille Chamber of Commerce to M.A.E. (copy received, 29 Nov. 1875); cf. above, pp. 180–1.

[4] *MMC*, Afrique VI/16, Bourgois to M.M.C., 9 Sept. 1875.

never approved of extending the territorial exchange to include a very unequal partition of unoccupied coasts, except on the improbable condition that Britain would agree to impose no new tariffs.[1] In December they asked the Foreign Ministry to try to meet the fears of Marseille by excluding the Slave Coast (and if possible the Niger delta also) from the proposed British sphere; failing this, they suggested returning to the old idea of some sort of neutralization agreement. But Gavard, realizing that such an amendment, removing the principal attraction of the agreement in the eyes of the British government, would almost certainly cause Carnarvon to yield to the growing opposition, asked his government to reconsider this suggestion.[2] Thus in January 1876 the French government reviewed the balance of advantages offered by the British terms.

The Foreign Ministry and the London Embassy desired the agreement for essentially diplomatic reasons: 'to maintain the *entente* which exists between the two governments of France and Great Britain.' With the increasing danger of a European crisis in the Balkans, this aim seemed more central than ever.[3] As for the Slave Coast, it would be a long time before France could afford the luxury of protectorates in such places; even if Britain was planning an offensive against Dahomey, as the Ministry of the Marine feared, France could not effectively resist her.[4] It would be better to recognize British supremacy in that region while the Gambia negotiation offered an opportunity, seeking guarantees for the position of French merchants under the future fiscal régime. Since France herself, under pressure from her textile manufacturers, was about to impose protective duties in the Senegal, it would be wise to secure the best terms possible for French merchants on the Slave Coast before there could be any question of reprisals.

[1] *MAE*, Afrique 54, M.M.C. to M.A.E., 29 Jan. 1875.

[2] *MMC*, Afrique VI/16, Note by D'Azy for the Minister, 28 Dec.; M.M.C. to M.A.E., 28 Dec. 1875; M.A.E. to M.M.C., 31 Dec., encl. Decazes to D'Harcourt, 31 Dec. 1875; Afrique VI/17/a, Gavard to D'Azy, Pte., 19 Jan. 1876.

[3] *MMC*, Afrique VI/17/a, Note by M.A.E. [early] Feb. 1876.

[4] *MAE*, Angleterre 771, Decazes to D'Harcourt, 13th, 20th Jan. 1876; cf. below, p. 201.

Speaking from the African point of view, Benoît d'Azy still disliked the proposed terms. Disadvantageous in themselves, they might have the further effect of encouraging an aggressive British imperialism. Prompted, perhaps, by Disraeli's recent purchase of Suez Canal shares, d'Azy attributed to him vast schemes of tropical expansion which had never entered his head, or Carnarvon's:

'Is it not clear that British policy aims at securing control in turn over Egypt and over Zanzibar (where she is pushing armed reconnaissance parties into the interior)? Meanwhile at Natal and the Cape her explorations and conquests are extending daily. If she is allowed to subject Dahomey, the most formidable and war-like state of central Africa, her influence will soon spread over the whole southern portion of that great continent, and we shall eventually find our role restricted to Senegal and Algeria.'

But even if d'Azy's information had been better, these fears could not justify an anti-British African policy at this date. Reluctantly the colonial department agreed that superior political considerations made it necessary to conclude the agreement, even at some risk to French traders.[1] On 11 February the French Ambassador left a Note at the Foreign Office seeking further elucidation of British intentions for the territories between the Gold Coast and Lagos; but his instructions made it clear that the aim was to negotiate temporary guarantees for French traders passing under British rule, not to jeopardize the agreement.[2]

This enquiry threatened to cause difficulty and delay, for of course the British did intend eventually to impose tariffs along the Slave Coast. But in view of the prospective advantages of uniting the Gold Coast fiscally with Lagos, it is hard to believe that they could not have offered concessions satisfactory to the French government, if necessary by paying compensation in some form to the firms affected. Unfortunately the Foreign

[1] MMC, Afrique VI/17/a, Note by D'Azy, given to the Minister, 19 Feb. 1876; MAE, Afrique 54, Note by D'Azy, 12 Feb. 1876.
[2] MMC, Afrique VI/17/a, M.A.E. to M.M.C., 12 Feb. 1876, encl. Decazes to D'Harcourt, 10 Feb.; C.O. 27/2227, D'Harcourt to Derby, 11 Feb. 1876.

Office failed to communicate the French enquiry to Carnarvon until 1 March, by which time opposition to the agreement was weakening his nerves.

On 17 February a British Parliamentary Paper, hastily published to influence opinion, revealed for the first time the full extent of the proposed renunciations by the French. Although this made the terms much more attractive,[1] J. F. Hutton nevertheless decided to stimulate opposition in Marseille by sending a translation of a relevant document to Régis.[2] The latter replied on 21 February, claiming that the Ministry of the Marine had promised him that France would not surrender her rights on the Slave Coast. When Hutton communicated this letter to the Colonial Office, it created alarm and despondency; it suggested that Carnarvon might have undertaken to persuade a Parliamentary Committee to accept the French terms under a false impression of what those terms involved. On 29 February the Foreign Office was asked to clarify the French position;[3] this request stimulated them to find and forward the French Note of 11 February. To the somewhat demoralized Colonial Office this document seemed to confirm Régis' interpretation of the French position. Although Hemming noted that the British terms were not directly rejected, Carnarvon feared that the delay in communicating this Note might have caused him to mislead Parliament as to the French position in his statement of 17 February. Fearing that he had put himself in a false position, he was anxious to escape from it before his critics discovered his error.[4]

[1] Twelve years later Hutton claimed that the mercantile opposition had not understood what benefits were being offered on the Slave Coast. C.O. 806/299, Hutton to C.O., 15 Oct. 1888.

[2] *MMC*, Afrique VI/17/a, Régis to D'Azy, 23 Feb. 1876, encl. translation of Strahan to Carnarvon, 22 Nov. 1875; cf. *Hansard*, 3rd series, CCXXVII, 394, Lords, 17 Feb. 1876. The letter quoted may be earlier correspondence between Régis and Hutton.

[3] C.O. 87/109, Hutton to C.O., 24 Feb. 1876, encl. letter from a Marseille correspondent, 21 Feb., minutes by Hemming, Meade, Herbert; C.O. to F.O., 29 Feb. 1876 (two letters).

[4] C.O. 87/109, F.O. to C.O., 1 March 1876, minutes by Hemming, 2 March, Carnarvon, 3 March; cf. Carnarvon's minute of 14 May on F.O. to C.O., 8 May 1876.

Meanwhile the Foreign Office had asked the French whether or not they were willing to 'consent to the . . . entire relinquishment in favour of Her Majesty's Government of political influence or protection along this line of coast'. Lyons submitted a Note on 2 March, and was told to press for an answer before the question of the Parliamentary Committee was due to come up on 13 March.[1] The French replied on the 8th; they closed no doors, but expressed their hope that, for the sake of the Marseille traders, the British would not take advantage of France's renunciation of Cotonou, Porto Novo and Whydah to impose their own fiscal control. This of course was exactly what Carnarvon proposed to do — and with patience he could almost certainly have secured French acquiescence; but in his agitation he decided to take the occasion to drop the whole embarrassing project. On 15 March he advised the Foreign Office that, since 'nothing short of the power to control and regulate all tariffs, and in case of need even to prohibit absolutely the importation of arms and ammunition' in the Slave Coast area could be accepted as adequate compensation for the Gambia, 'the present negotiations' should be broken off.[2]

Lyons' Note announcing this decision was an unwelcome surprise to the French; they believed that Carnarvon had been motivated by fears of public criticism, and protested when, in a speech to the House of Lords, he tried to blame France for the failure. Derby himself thought his colleague had been hasty in ending the negotiation, and Hemming concluded from the French protest that they would eventually have accepted Britain's terms. There even seems to be regret in Carnarvon's own comments, and his rather petulant attempt to blame the Foreign Office.[3] But there was no thought of reviving the

[1] F.O. 27/2227, Derby to Lyons, 1 March; 7 March (Tel.) 1876.

[2] *MMC*, Afrique VI/17/a, M.A.E. to M.M.C., 8 March 1876; C.O. 87/109, F.O. to C.O., 10 March, encl. memo. by the French govt., 8 March 1876; minutes by Fairfield, Herbert, Meade; C.O. to F.O., 15, 18 March 1876.

[3] *MAE*, Angleterre 771, D'Harcourt to Decazes, 21 March 1876; Decazes to D'Harcourt, 27 March; F.O. 27/2227, Notes by Tenterden, Derby, 24 April 1876; C.O. 87/109, F.O. to C.O., 8 May 1876; minutes by Hemming, Carnarvon; *Hansard*, 3rd series, CCXXVIII, 264–5, Lords, 20 March 1876.

question immediately, and facing Parliamentary opposition once more.

This failure left the Colonial Office still facing severe questions, economic, fiscal, and military, on the frontiers of all the West African colonies, and not least in the Gambia itself. To solve them, French co-operation seemed in varying degrees necessary. But without the tempting inducement of the Gambia, the French had much less interest in co-operating; if anything, their interest lay in increasing Britain's difficulties so that she would come back to the idea of a comprehensive settlement. Yet such a settlement would never again seem so near. A negotiated partition of influence on the West African coast could have saved both powers much trouble and anxiety during the rest of the century; and in particular it could have strengthened immeasurably the future British African empire. If, as seemed possible at this time, a single British administration had been permitted to control the coast, and develop the hinterlands of modern Ghana, Togo, Dahomey and Nigeria the political geography of twentieth-century Africa would have been strikingly different. Carnarvon's nervous ineptitude had wasted an extraordinary opportunity.

CHAPTER FIVE

The Development of Anglo-French Conflicts, 1876–81

[1]

General Attitude of British and French Governments towards West Africa, c. 1876

ALTHOUGH THE Gambia negotiation aroused a certain amount of patriotic feeling in both countries, neither government was moved by its failure to embark on any consciously expansionist policy. Disraeli's new willingness to talk about Empire in political speeches and to pursue spirited policies in the Eastern Question did not imply any new attitude towards tropical Africa. Nor was his Colonial Secretary — who had been initiated into the Colonial Office in the days of Merivale and Rogers, and whose temperamental indecisiveness earned him the nickname of 'Twitters' — much more purposeful. Carnarvon's ideas on a constructive African policy hardly went beyond his plans to collect customs duties along hitherto unappropriated stretches of coastline; his hesitancy at the crisis of the exchange negotiation shows how little he appreciated his opportunities.

True, advice was sometimes heard from men with a clearer sense of purpose. Hemming, of the new Colonial Office generation, consistently supported such extensions of British authority as might increase her capacity to develop resources and conduct 'civilizing' policies. Governors like Kennedy and Glover, a few publicists like Reade, continued to advocate peaceful expansion towards Hausaland and the western Sudan; and during the 1870's a few more merchants and industrialists, facing increased competition in export markets, began to pay some attention to African possibilities. But men with formed opinions on such subjects were few. The Gambia affair had shown that public sentiment might impose limits on the government's freedom to dispose of its existing responsibilities; the formation of the Royal Colonial Institute, an invitation from the Royal Society of Arts to Hennessy to address their 'African section' in 1874, suggested that interest was beginning to extend beyond the old circle of traders, missionaries and philanthropists. But an informed and disinterested public opinion which might urge definite policies upon the government was nowhere in sight.

Hence West African policy remained governed by the old principles of limiting the exercise of direct authority, and relying where possible on African rulers to provide such protection as British interests might require. On the Niger and the Oil Rivers, although commercial expansion might require some change in the methods by which the government provided support, there was no essential departure from the old system of 'informal empire'. Wylde reflected in 1876 that,

> 'Where there is money to be made our merchants will be certain to intrude themselves, and . . . if they establish a lucrative trade public opinion in this country practially compels us to protect them.'[1]

Merchants certainly freely sought physical protection in local difficulties; but that did not mean that they desired permanent supervision by a colonial government, and there was no pressure on the Colonial Office to provide one. Thus the attempt to collaborate with the Emir of Nupe, the annual expeditions to coerce the middlemen of Brass, represented logical developments of the principles formulated in 1865, not any decisive departure from them. Even the Order-in-Council of 1872, which gave the British Consul in the Bight of Biafra extensive magisterial powers over British subjects, marked a 'consolidation' of British power only on the old informal basis. The great event of these years in the Oil Rivers, the rise of JaJa to political power at Opobo, took place, not only without any intervention by the British government, but against strong initial opposition

[1] Minute by Wylde, 6 Aug. 1876, quoted Diké, *op. cit.*, p. 205.

H

from the Consul.[1] Only occasionally, and always on the frontiers of existing colonies, was there any real pressure to seek formal extensions of British power.

*　*　*　*　*

In France, also, public and official opinion converged to preclude any expansionist policy in West Africa, and to restrain the pugnacity of local agents. Until 1881 the colonial department remained attached to the Ministry of the Marine, with its traditional aims of maintaining French honour and rights rather than serving the interests of local traders. And the Ministry for Foreign Affairs continued to insist on the paramount importance of maintaining friendly relations with Great Britain, as the starting-point for the re-establishment of France's international position.[2] The perils of isolation were somewhat relieved in July 1878, when the Treaty of Berlin ended the prolonged Near Eastern crisis; but the Quai d'Orsay still urged that local colonial interests should be subordinated to the cause of Anglo-French relations.

Specifically, they desired a general settlement of all West African disputes, possibly embracing other colonial questions also: preferably a broadly-conceived exchange agreement which would give France the Gambia, but in any case one bold enough to have international as well as African significance. Such local conflicts as might meanwhile occur should be smoothed over in the cause of Anglo-French amity; the elimination of their causes, however, was not to be sought by discussing the merits of individual cases — who in London or Paris *really* understood the legal and political issues at Matacong, Assinie or Cotonou? — but as part of a comprehensive agreement, in which each side could gracefully surrender unprovable claims in return for concessions elsewhere. Piecemeal settlements might prejudice this objective by reducing the incentive for the British to negotiate. Thus in May 1877 a British request that the Gold Coast

---

[1] These events are fully described, but differently interpreted, by Diké, *op. cit.*, Ch. 10.

[2] C. Bloch, *Les Relations entre la France et la Grande-Bretagne, 1871–78* (Paris, 1955) esp. p. 278.

boundary near Assinie might be moved three miles to westward was left in abeyance by Decazes, in the hope that concessions there might be traded for a more conciliatory British attitude in the Mellacourie. The French government did not, apparently, understand at this time that the British purpose was to control duty-free imports which were reaching the Gold Coast hinterland through Assinie; their stations on the Ivory Coast, left in Verdier's charge, were judged of no intrinsic value. It was simply a question of conserving all French rights until a comprehensive negotiation could again be opened.[1]

During the 1870's there was little pressure within France of sufficient force to convert the Ministry of the Marine to a forward policy in West Africa, or to turn the diplomatists away from their aims. All Frenchmen still gave first priority in foreign policy to the recovery of power and prestige in Europe after the catastrophe of 1870-1, and many expressed positive hostility to such a diversionary activity as colonial expansion.[2] Until 1877, red republicanism and clerical reaction alike seemed (to those who feared them) active and dangerous forces; most politicians therefore remained absorbed in constitutional disputes and in the underlying questions concerning the social order of France. In that year the electoral victory of the 'Opportunists' — conservative Republicans devoted to the protection of property at home, and equally hostile to a militantly Catholic foreign policy and to aggressive ideas of *revanche* — produced conditions in which French interests overseas might hope to secure a more active protection; but they did not at once succeed in doing so.

Some writers regard the year 1879 as opening a new period in French colonial policy, even attributing the change to the appointment of Jules Ferry as Minister — of Public Instruction![3] But it remains difficult to identify any change of public

[1] C.O. 806/194, No. 1, Report by Tyrrell, 15 Jan. 1877; No. 4, C.O. to F.O., 26 May 1877; No. 9, F.O. to C.O., 13 Aug.; *MAE*, Afrique 49, M.A.E. to M.M.C., 26 June 1877; Afrique 76, M.M.C. to M.A.E., 18 April 1878.

[2] cf. Déroulède's well-known, later, reproach to Ferry: 'I have lost two children and you offer me twenty domestics'.

[3] e.g. H. Blet, *Histoire de la Colonisation française*, Tome III, *France d'Outremer* (Paris and Grenoble, 1955) pp. 10 ff.

attitudes or of general African policy. A few geographers and publicists, notably Leroy-Beaulieu, had already begun to discuss the advantages of colonies, but a careful student of the press has observed no active or enthusiastic support for colonial expansion in its columns before the occupation of Tunis in 1881.[1] Widespread and deep public mistrust of colonial expeditions persisted until such time as 'colonial conflicts came to appear as an aspect of European rivalries'.[2] The hostility of Royalists, who grudged the Republic any access of prestige, and of many Radicals, would at any hint of a colonial *débâcle* be reinforced by that apprehensive caution which characterized so many politicians of the Republican majority.

Even when the general hostility to colonial activity began to weaken, the first results appeared in Indo-China and the Mediterranean rather than in tropical Africa. Algeria, indeed, was already so closely linked with metropolitan France as to be partially exempt from the reaction against overseas commitments. It was as a by-product of Algerian interest in a trans-Saharan railway that a forward policy in Senegal was authorized in 1879, though by a divided and often hesitant Assembly.[3] This new departure, however, still implied no change of policy in countries south of Sierra Leone. Here French interests were represented principally by the Marseille traders. But their political influence, as was shown in 1876, was only moderate. Marseille, like some other ports, tended to elect Radical Deputies; and it was only gradually that the Radicals acquired a commanding position in the politics of the Third Republic.[4] In the 1870's French governments, like British, could take a reasonably detached view of the demands of their 'frontiersmen' in West Africa; there were still fair prospects that some division of influence could be negotiated without interference from French politicians or pressure groups.

[1] E. M. Carroll, *French Public Opinion and Foreign Affairs* (N.Y., 1931) pp. 84–6; cf. A. Murphy, *The Ideology of French Imperialism, 1871–1881* (Washington, 1948).

[2] Blet, *op. cit.*, p. 7.

[3] Below, pp. 253–5.

[4] F. Goguel, *Géographie des Elections françaises* (Paris, 1951) Carte 21.

[2]
Friction on the Slave Coast, 1876–9

The British Blockade of Dahomey

Those who exercised authority on the coast were not always so ready to accept compromise. For three distinct reasons, British officials during the 1870's were anxious to extend their control to Porto Novo and the rest of the Slave Coast. Anti-slavery zealots, in the Navy and elsewhere, wished to place more direct pressure upon Dahomey; officials in Accra and Lagos coveted the additional customs duties; and Porto Novo remained an essential link in Glover's old plan for bringing all the Yoruba states under the paramount influence of Lagos. Having failed to secure Porto Novo in 1865, Glover made another attempt to intervene in its succession dispute in 1867; in 1871 he once more argued strongly for annexation, pointing to the continuance of slave-dealing and human sacrifice within its boundaries. But Kimberley not only returned a firm refusal; he suffered many of Glover's policies to be reversed by Pope Hennessy, during a brief visit to Lagos in April 1872. This new Governor-in-Chief, obtuse and sentimental by turns, objected to Glover's attempts to prevent arms from reaching Abeokuta; backed by merchants whose trade was suffering he took a dog-matically pro-Egba line, lifted the blockade, and virtually provoked Glover's retirement. But this arbitrary shift of policy failed to appease the Egba or re-open the trade-routes; the revenue dropped sharply in 1873 (though partly because of low palm-oil prices abroad) and for the first time Lagos required an Imperial loan. Although the colony's finances had recovered by 1875 (thanks partly to the development of an easterly trade-route to Ibadan through Ondo, which Glover had pioneered) their brief crisis provided a sharp reminder of the advantages of controlling the Slave Coast.[1]

Early in 1876, while the negotiations with France were breaking down over this very point, a possible pretext for direct intervention appeared. The Yavogan, or viceroy, of Whydah

[1] cf. Aderibigbe, *op. cit.*, Chs. 1 and 2; also Biobaku, *op. cit.*, Ch. 7.

fined a mulatto trader, José Santos, and attempted to distrain upon goods which Santos had obtained on credit from European merchants. H. C. Turnbull, Swanzy's agent at Whydah, believed that the da Souza family had instigated this action out of commercial jealousy; on 23 January he protested violently to the Yavogan, who replied by having Turnbull stripped of his trousers and confined in a midden for two hours. Naval officers sought redress for this outrage, but found the Yavogan evasive. On 26 February Commodore Sir William Hewett therefore demanded from Gelele a fine of 500 puncheons of oil (eighty thousand gallons, worth about £6,000) threatening to blockade Dahomey if full payment was not received by 1 June.[1] It seems likely that Hewett named such a high figure in the hope of finding a pretext, in default, for an attack on Abomey which would put an end to Gelele and his 'diabolical practices'.[2]

Derby, however, wanting nothing less than to mount another military expedition in Africa, regretted Hewett's action; the previous blockade of 1852 did not encourage hopes of Gelele's repentance. His Under-Secretary thought the fine exorbitant: 'a tyrannical use of the opportunity for punishing the Dahomans for being savages . . . a gunboat policy to back a trade quarrel.'[3] But Derby admitted to the French Ambassador that he could not disavow Hewett's ultimatum without endangering British prestige along the whole coast.[4] Gelele's reply reached London about 2 May; it bluntly refused to accept foreign intervention. Expressing the shrewd opinion that the palaver originated with the Commodore rather than the Queen, Gelele disingenuously suggested that Hewett should

'stop all war palavers and be a merchant, turning his vessels into sailing ships, and, loading them with rum, cloth, and other merchandise, come to trade with him.'

[1] F.O. 84/1464, Admty to F.O., 6 April 1876 and enclosures.
[2] *ibid.*, Hewett to Admty, 21 March 1876. For hints of Hewett's intentions, see *MMC*, Afrique IV/10/c, Note du 2e bureau, 20 Jan. 1876; de Jaille, 5 July 1876.
[3] F.O. 84/1464, minutes by Wylde, Tenterden, Derby, on Admty to F.O., 6 April 1876; by Derby on C.O. to F.O., 14 June 1876.
[4] *MAE*, Afrique 54, D'Harcourt to Decazes, 14 May 1876.

This defiance deprived the government of any possible pretext for discreetly climbing down; on 10 May a Cabinet meeting, after mildly rebuking Hewett for not referring the matter home, authorized him to enforce the threatened blockade. This was eventually done on 1 July.[1]

Although the French agents at Whydah seem to have supported Turnbull in his original dispute with the Yavogan, Hewett's action greatly alarmed them.[2] A protracted blockade of itself would injure their trade; but if the dispute ended with a British occupation their fate would be far worse. Régis, who claimed to have twenty-one ships actually en route for the Slave Coast, cancelled further shipments and travelled to Paris early in May. He told the colonial department that he was willing to help avert the immediate danger by supplying palm-oil to help Gelele pay the fine; for the future he suggested that France should herself obtain the sovereignty of the Dahomey coastline, if necessary financing her occupation by a light export duty. At last the danger of a British tariff seemed to outweigh the attractions of continuing to trade under the relative freedom offered by African rule.[3]

The Foreign Ministry had little respect for Régis, and did not intend to take control of the Slave Coast either temporarily or permanently. With their eyes still focused on Europe and the Near East they wanted no new complications with Britain. But they did recognize some obligation to safeguard Marseillais trade in the area, as they had finally done during the exchange negotiation. Since Dahomey was an independent state, they could not deny Britain's right to blockade it. But Hewett had extended his blockade to the whole Slave Coast, between Lagos and the Gold Coast; since Dahomey traded along this whole stretch this measure seemed necessary for effective control, but it raised political questions concerning which the British govern-

[1] F.O. 84/1464, Admty to F.O., 2 May 1876, encl. Gelele's reply. 'Decisions of the Cabinet,' 10 May 1876.
[2] F.O. 84/1464, Admty to F.O., 6 April 1876, and encl.; *MAE*, Afrique 54, Régis to M.A.E., 12 May 1876.
[3] *MMC*, Afrique IV/10/c, Régis to D'Azy, 9 April 1876; *MAE*, Afrique 54, Régis to M.A.E., 5, 12, 23, 30 May 1876.

ment had little information. On 9 June the French presented two objections; in the west Little Popo, Porto Seguro and Aghwey should be excluded as independent principalities, in the east Cotonou should be excluded as French territory under the Treaty of 1868.[1] Régis himself went on to London, hoping to guide the French Embassy in its representations; but, though he secured interviews with Tenterden and Meade, he returned complaining that Gavard was more concerned to avoid troubling the British than to protect French merchants.[2]

Régis' objections succeeded in increasing British embarrassment; as Tenterden complained, matters were 'in a very great mess'. Enquiry quickly confirmed that the Popos were not part of Dahomey; the Law Officers therefore ruled that they could not be included in the blockade; and while the Foreign Office was still searching for expedients to circumvent this difficulty, Hewett reported that he had himself re-opened them to trade in the first days of the blockade.[3] Over Cotonou, on the other hand, neither Hewett nor the government proposed any concession; the French claim to sovereignty came as a disagreeable surprise, and it was agreed they should be required to substantiate it. Nor was there any disposition to admit French claims at Porto Novo, which Régis had mentioned to Meade.[4] But if the British were reluctant to be drawn into complicated African negotiations, so were the French. Although Decazes suggested 'a distinct understanding upon the territorial question upon the West coast of Africa', he showed no more readiness than Derby to enter into details.[5] From this indecision, Lagos seemed likely to benefit. Fabre and Daumas seemed resigned to

[1] *MMC*, M.A.E. to M.M.C., 27 May; M.M.C. to M.A.E., 31 May 1876; F.O. 84/1464, Decazes to D'Harcourt, 3 June, comm. to Derby, 9 June 1876.

[2] *MAE*, Afrique 54, Decazes to D'Harcourt, 3 June; Régis to (?) Bourée, Pte., 14, 15 July 1876; *MMC*, Afrique IV/10/c, Régis to M.A.E., 3 July 1876.

[3] F.O. 84/1464, minute by Hertslet, 12 June; F.O. 84/1465, minute by Wylde, 4 July; L.O. to F.O., 12 July and minutes; F.O. to L.O., 27 July; L.O. to F.O., 16 Aug.; Admty to F.O., 12 Aug. 1876, encl. Hewett, 6 July.

[4] F.O. 84/1464, minute by Hertslet, 13 June; F.O. 84/1465, C.O. to F.O., 3 July 1876.

[5] F.O. 84/1465, Lyons to Derby, Conf., 72, 18 July 1876.

accepting a British occupation of Dahomey, which would at least relieve them from Gelele's arbitrary exactions.[1]

Lagos was certainly gaining even from the blockade. The closure of Cotonou meant that all trade with Porto Novo — and possibly even some with Dahomey itself — now passed through its customs-houses. The colonial revenue jumped from £43,366 in 1875 (itself a good year) to £46,448 in 1876 and £59,389 in 1877;[2] this underlined the benefits to be expected from permanent fiscal control of the Slave Coast. While Hewett (according to the French) was studying plans for a landing in Dahomey, the Administrator of Lagos was reconnoitring a lagoon which seemed navigable to within twenty-three miles of Abomey.[3] Even the French government seemed to accept a military expedition as inevitable, and concentrated on discussing the personal safety of the twenty or so French subjects detained within the blockaded state.[4] But in fact British Ministers wanted no military campaigns in Africa; Derby's pacific instincts and pre-occupation with the Near East were reinforced by fears of alienating French sympathy. On 27 December D'Harcourt spoke gravely about public reactions if the French hostages should be killed; even though public opinion had for some years been pre-occupied elsewhere, he said, national susceptibilities were still alive.[5] Even the Colonial Office, where there was most sympathy with the fiscal ambitions of Lagos, was anxious to find an honourable escape from their apparent commitment to coercive policies.

There was therefore much interest when, in December 1876, Régis forwarded a letter in which Gelele apparently offered to receive a British envoy at Abomey. Herbert, glimpsing a possibility of 'reversing the unjust and impolitic acts of foolish

[1] *MAE*, Afrique 54, M.M.C. to M.A.E., 26 Oct. 1876, encl. report from de Jaille.

[2] C.O. 806/130. 'Information respecting the Settlement of Lagos, June 1879.' cf. *MAE*, Afrique 76, Report by Serval, 23 April 1878.

[3] F.O. 84/1466, C.O. to F.O., 21 Oct., 8 Nov., 24 Nov. 1876.

[4] *ibid.*, Derby to D'Harcourt, 4 Oct. 1876; cf. C.O. 147/32, minute by Strahan, 18 Oct. 1876.

[5] F.O. 84/1466, C.O. to F.O., 9 Dec. 1876, minute by Derby; *MAE*, Afrique 54, D'Harcourt to Decazes, 28 Dec. 1876.

H*

officers', hopefully suggested offering to remit the fine in return for the cession of fiscal control over the whole Dahomey coastline — an alternative certainly envisaged by neither Gelele nor Régis.[1] Wylde thought more modest demands would be realistic; but he doubted whether any at all would be acceptable to Gelele.

'I have no faith,' he added, 'in any measures being effective, short of completely breaking up the king's power, which we shall sooner or later be compelled to do.'

Derby too was sceptical, fearing that such a negotiation might end in the African war which he dreaded:

'. . . we shall have Abyssinia on our hands again if we send an officer up into the interior. He will be detained — and what then? Annexation of more W. African coast will be very unpopular.'

Yet the Colonial Office remained ready to consider even this approach.[2]

Régis, however, was working along an alternative line. On 3 December he suggested somewhat indiscreetly to Meade that, if the British would drastically reduce the amount of their fine, he himself would provide the oil, in the form of an advance on Gelele's trading account. The British were not willing to accept the direct intervention of Régis, nor, at this stage, to reduce the fine; but this idea, more discreetly handled, held possibilities of face-saving.[3] Early in January Germa, Régis' agent in Whydah, suggested to the Yavogan that a letter might be sent to Carnarvon expressing Gelele's regret for the ill-treatment of Turnbull and requesting a reduction of the fine. If this reduction was secured, Régis would discreetly provide the oil to be handed over in Gelele's name. Gelele apparently hesitated to accept even this compromise, insisting that Turnbull's punishment had been justified. Like his predecessors, Gelele set the

[1] C.O. 147/32, Régis to Meade, 3 Dec. 1876, minute by Herbert.
[2] F.O. 84/1466, C.O. to F.O., 13 Dec. 1876, minutes by Wylde, Pauncefote, Derby; F.O. 84/1467, C.O. to F.O., 14 Feb. 1877, minute by Derby; C.O. 147/32, minute by Hemming, 26 March 1877.
[3] C.O. 84/1466, C.O. to F.O., 13 Dec. 1876; *MAE*, Afrique 54, Régis to M.A.E., 4 Dec. 1876.

independence and prestige of his state higher than commercial profit. (In any case, since Dahomey could trade through the Popos and perhaps at Lagos he was injured less by the blockade than were the French merchants, whose capital was fruitlessly tied up.) But eventually the King agreed that Germa himself should write such a letter and append a cross.[1] When this document reached London in mid-March it was welcomed without enquiry into its authenticity, and there was little demur about reducing the fine.[2]

The officer in charge of the blockade, Captain G. L. Sulivan, believed this compromise would be regarded in Dahomey as a success for the French merchants; nevertheless, the arrangements were quickly carried through by a new Commodore, F. W. Sullivan. On 12 May the Yavogan signed a treaty, which for the most part re-affirmed old unkept promises to prohibit slave exports and protect British traders; two hundred small puncheons of oil were paid, and the blockade was at an end. Sixty of the puncheons were provided by Fabre, the rest by Régis; the boat taking them to England was wrecked at Cape Palmas and all were lost.[3] A second instalment of two hundred puncheons was to be paid a year later; it was not forthcoming, and the British government never agreed on any method of exacting it. The saving of British face had been most perfunctory. It is not clear how much Gelele knew of what was being done in his name; certainly he did not regard himself as having apologized or paid compensation. British prestige in Dahomey must have been weakened by this outcome. But it was not therefore easy for the French to strengthen theirs.

The French at Cotonou and Porto Novo, 1878-9

The French were greatly relieved that the British had concluded their blockade without extending their territory; many of them remained convinced that Britain nevertheless planned

[1] *MAE*, Afrique 76, Ribourt to M.M.C., 30 Dec. 1876; Régis to Bourée, 21 Feb., 6 March 1877; cf. E. Foà, *Le Dahomey* (Paris, 1895) p. 35.

[2] F.O. 84/1467, C.O. to F.O., 13 March 1877 and minutes.

[3] *ibid.*, Admty to F.O., 18 April 1877, encl. G. L. Sulivan, 18 March; Admty to C.O., 3, 5 July 1877 and encl.; *MAE*, Afrique 76, M.M.C. to M.A.E., 15, 28 June, 12 July 1877 and enclosures.

to occupy by force the coast which she had failed to secure in negotiation. Even from the diplomatists' point of view such an occupation would have been unwelcome, for it would weaken France's hand in the eagerly-awaited revival of the Gambia negotiation. It was therefore decided to negotiate a new treaty with Dahomey, to appoint a salaried Vice-Consul to the Slave Coast, and to confirm those French rights at Cotonou which the blockading British had refused to recognize.[1] The importance of Cotonou as an entrance to Porto Novo and to Egba country was still increasing; Germans and Brazilians, besides the three French firms, now operated there in order to avoid the Lagos tariff. French exports alone were said to amount to 670,000 gallons of oil and 2,000 tons of kernels annually, compared with figures for the three Dahoman ports combined (Whydah, Godomey, and Abomey-Calavi) of 740,000 gallons and 3,700 tons. Régis, who claimed half of the Cotonou trade, was anxious that France should provide effective safeguards against British action at both Cotonou and Porto Novo.[2]

The cession of territory approximately six kilometres square at Cotonou was confirmed, along with other provisions, in a treaty signed at Whydah on 23 April 1878 by the Yavogan and the headman of Cotonou, acting in Gelele's name. Whether the King had in fact agreed to this cession is very doubtful, in view of later events; it is noteworthy that one of the messengers who announced his consent was an African employee of Régis.[3] This acquisition made it more urgent to appoint a salaried Vice-Consul; the Ministry for Foreign Affairs always disliked leaving national interests in the care of private traders, but their earlier experience at Porto Novo had shown the special dangers of doing so when territorial rights were involved. In November 1878 they appointed Lieutenant-Colonel Ardin d'Elteil,

[1] *MAE*, Afrique 76, Allemand to M.M.C., 4 June 1877; M.A.E. to M.M.C., 16 July; Note pour le ministre, 23 July 1877; Note by Serval, 30 April 1878; *MMC*, Afrique IV/10/c, Note pour le directeur, 23 July; draft of 9 Aug.; M.A.E. to M.M.C., 8 Sept.; M.M.C. to Allemand, 29 Sept. 1877.

[2] *MAE*, Afrique 76, Report by Serval, 23 April 1878; cf. Note by d'Elteil, 28 Sept. 1879.

[3] *ibid.*, Report by Serval, 23 April 1878. Text of treaty printed in *Etudes Dahoméennes*, IX, pp. 28–9.

formerly in the Senegalese forces, to be Resident at Cotonou and Vice-Consul at Whydah, with a watching brief over French interests between Senegal and the Gabon.[1] Before leaving France d'Elteil conferred in Marseille with Régis and Fabre, and secured their approval for a plan to avert any future blockade by placing a corporal's guard at Cotonou; this was to be financed by a small export duty. Régis in turn urged the reestablishment of the Porto Novo protectorate; Cotonou alone would be useless if the British succeeded in occupying the routes or sources of its trade.[2]

D'Elteil reached Porto Novo by way of Lagos on 16 February 1879; he lodged with J. A. Colonna di Lecca, an independent Corsican trader whose cousin Bonaventura was Régis' chief agent in Dahomey. The dynastic question was still causing dissension. Mepon had died, supposedly poisoned, in May 1872; the short reign of his successor, the aged Messi, was a period of internal strife. In September 1874 Prince Dassi, Soji's capable but ruthlessly ambitious son, at last succeeded in securing the throne, at the age of thirty-four, in the name of Tofa. His attempts to impose a strong monarchical government were opposed by his many enemies within the kingdom — supported, apparently, by some of Tofa's former friends in Lagos. Against them he relied heavily on the support of French merchants, especially J. A. Colonna di Lecca, who apparently provided him with money in order to secure his candidature.[3] D'Elteil's arrival thus provided a convenient opportunity to seek French support against British encroachments from Lagos and against rival claimants to the throne, to obtain endorsement of his son's title to the succession, and to put the state's revenues on a sound basis; on 4 March Tofa wrote to the Vice-Consul offering to renew the protectorate of 1863. D'Elteil procrastinated, seeing the danger of being drawn into commitments against Lagos; but he did urge his government, when occupying Cotonou, to guard

---

[1] *MAE*, Afrique 76, M.A.E. to M.M.C., 27 Nov. 1878; Decree, 4 Feb. 1879.
[2] *ibid.*, Note by d'Elteil, 29 Nov. 1878; d'Elteil to Bourée, 23 Dec.; Régis to Bourée, 30 Dec.
[3] Akindélé and Aguessy, *op. cit.*, pp. 77–86.

against British reprisals by renewing the Porto Novo protectorate at the same time.[1]

Proceeding to Cotonou, d'Elteil discovered that the Dahomean authorities were resisting any imposition of French
authority, and that the Yavogan was disclaiming his signature
of 1878. These difficulties, and rumours of a renewed British
offensive against Dahomey, led d'Elteil to suggest sending
sizeable garrisons to the coast: 50 troops to Cotonou, 100 to Porto
Novo, 350 to Whydah.[2] The French government would not
consider this; yet without some such manifestation of power
their treaty rights appeared precarious. And it was not only
Dahomey and Lagos that threatened the merchants. In April
1879 sharks became particularly active at Cotonou beach; the
sixty-three canoemen hired from Elmina, on whose seamanship
all landing operations depended, deserted to Lagos, where the
government naturally declined to encourage them to return.
Consequently all trade was stopped. (Later in the year some
captains improvised a method of landing rum and embarking
oil by a form of ropeway, but this proved only moderately
satisfactory.) Cargoes destined for Porto Novo now had to pass
by Lagos, whose revenue began to rise towards the record figure
of the blockade year.[3]

The British occupation of Ketenou

The sharks, however, could not be expected to assist the
Lagos Treasury indefinitely. Ever since 1865 British officials had
been hoping to find some way of controlling the trade of Porto
Novo and so increasing their revenue. In 1874–5 there were
hopes of persuading Tofa voluntarily to enter the British fiscal
system; but Tofa seemed more concerned to improve his independent access to the sea.[4] During the blockade of 1876
Administrator Dumaresq noted that he was clearing the old

---

[1] *MAE*, Afrique 76, d'Elteil to Waddington, 22 Feb., 6 March 1879, encl.
Tofa to d'Elteil, 4 March.

[2] *ibid.*, d'Elteil to Waddington, 1 May 1879.

[3] *ibid.*, d'Elteil to Waddington, 14 Aug.; 15, 28 Sept. 1879. Figures of
Lagos annual revenue (C.O. 806/130 and annual Blue Books): 1876:
£46,448. 1877: £59,389. 1878: £50,889. 1879: £54,939. 1880: £47,987.

[4] C. W. Newbury, *The Western Slave Coast . . .* , pp. 92–3.

road to Appa beach with the evident aim of by-passing Cotonou. Dumaresq's reply was to procure secret offers of territorial cession from the chiefs of both Appa and Ketenou. This latter place lay on the creek between Cotonou and Porto Novo, at a point where tolls were customarily payable. It was commonly assumed to be subject to Porto Novo, but the old Lagos hand Thomas Tickel wrote a paper arguing that Ketenou was an independent state, originally founded by refugees from Whemi, and that its rightful chief, Seton, now resided in British territory near Badagry. The significance of all this was, that by extending its territory through Appa to Ketenou, Lagos could interrupt Porto Novo's access to the sea. The Colonial Office was tempted by this idea, but feared Dahomey might have claims over the area which could involve them in the very military campaign that they were so anxious to avoid. They therefore took no action during the blockade, but later invited a new Governor to investigate the possibilities very cautiously.[1]

The renewal of war between Abeokuta and Ibadan in 1877 made Porto Novo doubly important to Lagos, as a key centre of arms import as well as a source of revenue. In January 1878 Dumaresq asked permission to occupy the town. His principal grievance was that Tofa had chartered a British steamer in order to bombard certain towns in Whemi which had supported the Porto Novan opposition; he fortified this with complaints of ill-treatment of traders, slave-dealing, and generally atrocious practices. Hicks Beach, the new Secretary for the Colonies, was attracted by the proposal, and optimistically suggested a mission to Abomey to invite Gelele to renounce his claims on Porto Novo and Cotonou in lieu of the second instalment of his fine.[2] But Salisbury, the new Foreign Secretary, was determined to authorize no forward colonial policies which might complicate

[1] C.O. 147/32, Dumaresq to Lees, 96, 29 June; 103, 5 July; 135, 12 Sept. 1876, encl. memo. by Tickel, 7 Sept.; minutes by Hemming, Meade, Carnarvon, Strahan, Nov. 1876–March 1877; Carnarvon to Freeling, 129, 6 April 1877.
[2] C.O. 147/35, Dumaresq to Freeling, 11, 23 Jan. 1878, minutes by Hemming, Meade, Beach; C.O. 147/36, F.O. to C.O., 28 Feb., C.O. to F.O., 20 March 1878.

his European diplomacy; by procrastination and suggestions of reference to the Cabinet he successfully prevented any action before October. And then the French gave notice of their new treaty at Cotonou.

Herbert was so discouraged by this as to suggest a complete change of policy, by which Britain would cease to try to improve her West African colonies but instead would actually encourage French expansion. Hicks Beach, fortified by Hemming's bolder advice, refused to consider this: 'our merchants would complain, and I think Parliament would support them.' Instead he proposed that, while a 'friendly remonstrance' against the Cotonou treaty was addressed to France, the government of Lagos should retaliate by occupying Appa and Ketenou.[1] To this rather bold suggestion, Salisbury said nothing at all for five months; in May 1879 his stock reply went back: any such proposal was a Cabinet matter, and in view of a new dispute with France at Matacong the Foreign Office could not regard the suggestion as opportune.[2] The Foreign Office believed that France's real aim was still to re-open the Gambia negotiation; and Salisbury himself was increasingly coming to favour such a course.[3]

While Salisbury was still stonewalling, news arrived from Lagos that Tofa had been punishing British subjects for trading with his enemies in Whemi. Hicks Beach (not appreciating that their trade was in fire-arms) authorized the new governor, Ussher, to protest at Porto Novo; his despatch also rehearsed the old charges of slave-dealing and human sacrifice. This forceful language suggested to Ussher that he was expected to deal firmly with Tofa, 'who by his arbitrary and barbarous conduct is considered to have placed himself beyond the pale of ordinary international law'. He took a gun-boat to Porto Novo, and on 21 September obliged Tofa to agree to meet the compensation claims of British and German traders, and to

---

[1] Correspondence between F.O. and C.O., with minutes, July–Dec. 1878, in C.O. 147/36.

[2] C.O. 147/39, C.O. to F.O., 12 April 1879; F.O. to C.O., 21 May 1879.

[3] F.O. 27/2414, Salisbury to Lyons, S.T. 3, 11 Feb. 1876; Lyons to Salisbury, S.T. 5, 31 March 1879, minute by Wylde.

guarantee future security to foreign commerce.[1] But d'Elteil's presence led Ussher to fear that the French were planning to intervene at Porto Novo; he therefore went on to Ketenou and hoisted the British flag. The French, he wrote, could now gain nothing by occupying Porto Novo; indeed Tofa himself might, 'by skilful and tricky diplomacy,' be induced to offer his state to the British.

The Colonial Office viewed the seizure of this strategic position with much pleasure concealed beneath their disapproval. Strictly, Ussher should not have acted without authority; but to disavow him would involve a serious loss of prestige in the Lagos area — and would also throw away a card of vital importance for the future of the British colony.[2] This veiled satisfaction was not shared by Salisbury, who commented angrily that such unauthorized acts were liable to 'produce resentment on the part of the Power with whom more than any other it is the interest of the country to live on terms of friendship'.[3] Ussher's deliberate thwarting of French designs seemed likely to produce some violent retaliation which might complicate Anglo-French relations during a difficult period.

★   ★   ★   ★   ★

But the French government also remained anxious to avoid serious quarrels on the West African coast. Waddington, the anglophil Premier and Foreign Minister, had already refused d'Elteil's request for the despatch of garrisons and a new protectorate at Porto Novo, insisting that considerations of general policy must take priority.[4] Nor was the Ministry of the Marine anxious to take up combative positions on behalf of traders whose real desire was clearly still 'to operate in free territory, dealing directly with the negroes without European supervision'. Neither department could see any national interest on

[1] C.O. 147/39, F.O. to C.O., 3 June 1879; Beach to Ussher, 140, 11 July 1879; C.O. 147/38, Ussher to Beach, 19 Aug. 1879; Beach to Ussher, 27 Sept.; Ussher to Beach, 154, 29 Sept.

[2] ibid., Ussher to Beach, 155, 29 Sept.; 165, 7 Oct. 1879, minute by Hemming, 10 Nov.

[3] F.O. 27/2418, F.O. to C.O., 22 Nov. 1879 (from Salisbury's draft).

[4] MAE, Afrique 76, Waddington to D'Elteil, 1 May, 12 July 1879.

the Slave Coast which would justify them in stationing troops in such dangerously exposed and unhealthy positions.[1] Quite apart from the friction with Britain, the military power of Dahomey was to be regarded with cautious respect; French officials were still quite happy to assume that it would eventually be British forces which undertook its inevitable destruction.

France could only impose her will upon Africans, reasoned the Ministry of the Marine, by exciting cupidity or inducing fear. Since it was inexpedient to commit sufficient forces to the Slave Coast to induce fear, French merchants would do best to rely for their security on the self-interest of their customers. Hence the government, while making diplomatic representations to Britain over Ketenou, should avoid allowing its own authority to become involved in such an exposed position.[2] Protests and hard bargaining were certainly called for; but the rights which would form the subject of the bargaining could still be regarded as expendable in the cause of a more broadly-based African settlement.

[3]

Friction near Sierra Leone, 1876–9

Sierra Leone's fiscal problems and attempts to solve them

About 1873 Sierra Leone began to decline from that modest fiscal and commercial prosperity which it had enjoyed under Kennedy. There were at least three reasons for this; the first and most important was largely beyond local control. World prices for palm-oil began to fall sharply, partly as a result of increased competition among exporters in Sierra Leone and elsewhere, but also because of changing patterns in the world demand for vegetable oils.[3] Secondly, the elaborate system of informal influence on which Kennedy had relied to maintain order and tranquillity in the productive hinterland began to reveal its

---

[1] *MAE*, Afrique 76, M.M.C. to M.A.E., 5 July, 30 Sept., 18 Nov. 1879.

[2] *MAE*, Angleterre 782, M.M.C. to M.A.E., 18 Nov. 1879.

[3] cf. A. McPhee, *The Economic Revolution in British West Africa* (London, 1926) pp. 32–4.

deficiencies. Paying stipends could secure peace only so far as the recipients possessed the power and the will to enforce it; yet the expansion of foreign commerce might itself make it more difficult for them to do so. The more an African state profited from the presence of European factories or the regular visits of Creole traders, the greater the risk of internal conflicts or attacks from jealous neighbours. The outbreak of war did not necessarily kill trade — in some ways it might even stimulate it — but the effect of prolonged fighting could only be to reduce the amount of produce available for export. The 'tribal wars' of the Sherbro hinterland during the last quarter of the century received more than their share of the blame when trade was slack, but sometimes at least they deserved it.

The third cause of commercial decline was a new fiscal policy introduced by Hennessy in 1872. By abolishing duties on all imports except tobacco, liquor, arms and ammunitions, and by greatly increasing the rates payable on these staples of the inland trade, Hennessy hoped to 'shift the incidence of taxation from the settlements to the consumers in the interior'. But these consumers were not so easily fleeced. Dutiable imports were increasingly consigned to rivers outside the colonial boundary, where any loss of physical security for the merchandise was outweighed by the absence of high tariffs; African traders and producers began to frequent these rivers at the expense of Freetown. Shop-keepers and merchants who had hitherto operated chiefly within the colony were badly hit; and the government's revenue declined steeply, at a time when heavy capital charges had been incurred for projected harbour works. In 1873 receipts fell short of the estimate by £10,882, or 20%; further increases in taxation only reduced takings still further, while drastic cuts in expenditure failed to meet the deficit.[1]

As at the Gold Coast, officials hoped to retrieve the position by extending British authority along the neighbouring coastline and collecting duties in new areas; merchants in the rivers, they held, profited from the proximity of British authority at Sierra Leone, and their trade should contribute to the colonial revenue. The case for coastwise expansion was strongly supported by

[1] C.O. 267/326, Berkeley to Kimberley, 35, 3 Feb. 1874.

leading Sierra Leoneans. William Grant, a wealthy Creole who himself traded in the northern rivers, developed it in a letter to Carnarvon in October 1874, and a year later promoted a petition whose three hundred signatories were broadly representative of Freetown's African businessmen.[1] After some discussion the Colonial Office agreed that the Governor should try to obtain the right to collect duties along additional stretches of coast; and in March 1876 it was announced that the chiefs of Ribbi, Bumpe, and Kagboro, between Sierra Leone and its Sherbro dependency, had agreed to this.

The trade of the northern rivers was potentially more valuable; but much of it was in French hands. Charles Heddle, the most important merchant there, sold his factories about 1877 to C. A. Verminck, an able and enterprising Marseillais, who had first gone to Africa about 1844 in Régis' service, and had built up an independent business in the Gambia and elsewhere.[2] In 1878 Governor Rowe reported that only the Manchester house of Randall and Fisher represented British trade in the Mellacourie (but he cannot have been counting Creole merchants shipping through Freetown, like Grant and William Lewis).[3] Even in the Scarcies direct exports to Europe were all handled by French houses. There were many Sierra Leoneans there, shipping smaller quantities of produce to Freetown; but they faced hostile competition not only from the French, but from local Temnes who had recently learned to build sea-going boats and wished to keep coastal trade in their own hands.[4]

Despite this French predominance it was widely assumed in Freetown that the whole coast south of the Pongos fell within Sierra Leone's sphere of political influence. Samuel Rowe, a

---

[1] *P.P.*, 1876, LII, C. 1409, No. 20; Grant to Carnarvon, 6 Oct. 1874; C. 1402, No. 10, Rowe to Carnarvon, 11 Sept. 1875, minutes in C.O. 267/328; cf. J. D. Hargreaves, *A Life of Sir Samuel Lewis* (London, 1958) Ch. 2.

[2] P. Masson, *Marseille et la Colonisation française* (Marseille, 1906), pp. 398, 402, 473; P. Masson (ed.) *Les Bouches-du-Rhône: Encyclopédie Départementale*, Tome 8 (1926) pp. 184, 264; Tome 9 (1922) pp. 365 ff., 386, 398–9.

[3] C.O. 806/114, Rowe to Beach, 104, 1 July 1878; C.O. 806/129, Rowe to Beach, 7 April 1879.

[4] C.O. 806/114, Rowe to Beach, 100, 28 June 1878.

forthright and energetic army surgeon who became Administrator in 1875 and Governor in 1877, had no doubt that this
claim was justified by historic connections and fiscal necessity,
and that speedy action should be taken to exclude the French,
despite their territorial toe-hold at Binty. At first Carnarvon
hesitated on account of the exchange negotiations; only on 16
June 1876 did he authorize Rowe to negotiate for permission to
collect customs duties in territories bordering the two Scarcies
rivers. (At the same time he provisionally authorized the
establishment of British jurisdiction on the island of Matacong,
under an inoperative treaty of 1826, hoping to derive a revenue
from the trade which Randall and Fisher conducted from this
base.)[1] By this time, however, Rowe had found an opportunity
to obtain fiscal control by a different method. On 10 June he
attended a meeting of Temne chiefs from the Scarcies who had
recently raided the Mellacourie and now feared reprisals from
Bokkari or his French protectors; they secretly offered to cede a
strip of their seaboard to the British government.[2]

Many officials in London preferred this method of securing
revenue to Carnarvon's plan of negotiating for fiscal rights
alone; they feared that such rights would not be recognized by
other powers unless accompanied by some assumption of
responsibility, and they also wondered whether customs officers
would be entitled to visit vessels lying offshore. But Carnarvon,
apprehensive as ever about political repercussions, saw in
Rowe's proposal 'a distinct acquisition of territory'; it took
three months to convince him that any method of acquiring
extra revenue was liable to involve some additional responsibility towards those who paid the duties. On 24 October Carnarvon reluctantly agreed to seek Cabinet approval for the
annexation of Rowe's coastal strip in the Scarcies.[3]

But fiscal control of the Scarcies alone might not solve the

[1] C.O. 806/94, Rowe to Carnarvon, 21 March 1876; C.O. 267/329,
minutes on above; Rowe to Hemming Pte., 22 May 1876; C.O. 806/94,
Carnarvon to Kortright, 16 June 1876. On Matacong, cf. C.O. 267/328,
French to Carnarvon, 8, 13 Jan. 1875.

[2] C.O. 806/94, Rowe to Carnarvon, 89A, 19 June 1876.

[3] C.O. 267/329, minutes on Kortright to Carnarvon, 89, 20 June 1876;
C.O. 806/94, C.O. to F.O., 24 Oct. 1876.

problem. Some revenue would be collected there, and some trade might move back to Freetown; but more was likely to move north to the Mellacourie. Carnarvon still hoped to deal with this river by agreement with the French — if not by an exchange, then by some arrangement for equalizing rates of duty. But Rowe, while reluctantly prepared to recognize that French control of the Nunez and Pongos would be permanent, regarded all the coastline south of the latter river as part of Sierra Leone's legitimate sphere of influence. In this view he was encouraged by T. G. Lawson, the Government Interpreter, whose strongly anglophil and Protestant sympathies were leading him to resist France's advance in the northern rivers with all the very considerable personal influence which he commanded there.[1] (It was due to his initiative that on 4 September 1876 the chiefs of Sumbuya, north of the Mella-courie, offered to cede their territory.)[2] Rowe and Lawson believed that control of the Mellacourie region, besides bringing in more revenue and arresting the decline of Freetown, would give the colony a new base for commercial expansion inland towards the upper Niger; and both insisted that French rights south of the Pongos were confined to Binty fort alone. Rowe therefore planned to encircle that French outpost by a network of British treaties; this would make it simple either to negotiate satisfactory terms for the French withdrawal, or to neutralize the position.[3] The attitude of the Colonial Office towards these plans was naturally cautious; but while they were leisurely reviewing the legal and political difficulties their hands were forced by developments on the coast.

Anglo-French conflicts in the Mellacourie and the Scarcies

Late in March 1877 the government of Sierra Leone began

[1] *S.L.S.* (n.s.) III, p. 172 n for Lawson's opposition to a Roman Catholic mission at Port Loko, November 1876. The G(overnment) I(nterpreter(s) L(etter) B(ook) in the Sierra Leone archives contains many examples of Lawson's fear of French activity after 1875.

[2] C.O. 267/329, Kortright to Carnarvon, 133, 14 Sept. 1876; G.I.L.B., 12 Sept. 1876.

[3] C.O. 806/70, Rowe to Meade, Pte., 14 Aug.; Rowe to Hemming, Pte., 16 Aug. 1876.

open preparations to collect customs duties on Matacong.[1] This led Colonel Brière de l'Isle, the active new Governor of Senegal, to take counter-measures; French authority in the Mellacourie had not been much in evidence since 1867, and there seemed a danger that even the exchange value of her rights might be lost by default. Armed with a draft Proclamation affirming that France held 'undivided sovereignty' from the Pongos to the south bank of the Mellacourie, the political director of Senegal, Boilève, set out to sign a new treaty with Bokkari.[2] But before his arrival the acting Governor of Sierra Leone (Horatio Huggins, who knew the Mellacourie well) sent Lawson to bring Bai Sherbro and the chiefs of Samu to Freetown. They were hospitably treated, and on 2 May they signed a treaty ceding to Britain the whole coastline between the Mellacourie and Great Scarcies rivers, together with several islands (including Kakoutlaye, which lies opposite Binty).[3] The French reacted violently, sending a small military detachment to occupy Kakoutlaye; Boilève issued his Proclamation, and Brière de l'Isle asked permission to start collecting customs duties as proof of sovereignty.[4] Here were all the elements of a bitter local feud.

Both the metropolitan governments instructed their governors to exercise restraint; but neither was in a hurry to enter into definitive negotiations, for neither had decided its ultimate intentions for the rivers. The French government, still hoping that possession of the Mellacourie might eventually help them to secure the Gambia, approved Brière de l'Isle's policy of resisting encirclement.[5] But French influence was weak, especially in Samu, and her title to the small fort at Binty was admittedly unsatisfactory.[6] Bokkari signed a new treaty on 7 June 1877, re-affirming and strengthening that of 1866; but his influence over his own subjects in Moriah seemed to be weaken-

---

[1] C.O. 806/94, Huggins to Carnarvon, 73, 7 April; 79, 16 April 1877.

[2] *MAE*, Afrique 49, M.M.C. to M.A.E., 20 June 1877.

[3] C.O. 806/94, Huggins to Carnarvon, 89, 4 May; 91, 7 May 1877.

[4] *MAE*, Afrique 49, M.M.C. to M.A.E., 24 June, 31 July 1877 and enclosures.

[5] *MAE*, Afrique 49, M.A.E. to M.M.C., 22 June; M.M.C. to M.A.E., 19 July 1877.

[6] *ibid.*, M.M.C. to M.A.E., 19 July; de l'Isle to Roy, Pte., 7 July 1876.

ing, and he again seemed to be looking for support towards Freetown and the Aborigines Department. The trader Valantin, who had abetted French policy in 1865–7, also seemed to be using his considerable local influence against Boilève, who at first believed he had entered British service; later, however, it appeared that he had changed his attitude out of disappointed pride — 'to prove his importance and oblige us to make use of his influence rather than to favour the British'.[1] He was induced to change sides again: and by March 1878 three important sub-chiefs had signed treaties recognizing France as protecting power. Brière de l'Isle would have liked to strengthen French prestige by reinforcing the garrison at Binty, but the government in Paris did not wish to go beyond a diplomatic offensive in the rivers.[2]

Carnarvon personally would have preferred not to go even so far; but his responsibility for Sierra Leone prevented him from washing his hands of the northern rivers. On 20 July 1877 a Committee of senior officials representing Colonial Office, Foreign Office, and Treasury reported on the financial plight of the Colony. The possibility of abandoning Sierra Leone altogether, attractive though it seemed, was excluded, in anticipation of objections from

> 'the merchants interested in the West Africa trade, the philanthropists (an important factor in West African politics), and the various Chambers of Commerce throughout the country which they would set in motion.'

The resistance offered to the cession of the Gambia would certainly be surpassed in the case of Sierra Leone, where British trade and philanthropic interest were both greater, and where the opposition would be powerfully sustained by Creole spokesmen like Grant and Lewis. The Committee therefore concluded that 'either some means must be found of recruiting the colonial finances, or . . . considerable pecuniary assistance must be afforded by the Imperial Government'. Since the former course

[1] *ibid.*, M.M.C. to M.A.E., 31 July, 20 Oct. 1876, encl. de l'Isle, 7 July, 16 Sept.

[2] *ibid.*, M.M.C. to M.A.E., 24 April 1878, encl. de l'Isle, 6 March; M.A.E. to M.M.C., 15 May.

was undoubtedly preferable, they recommended confirmation of Rowe's Scarcies treaties of 1876, and the conclusion of similar treaties ceding the littoral of the Ribbi-Kagboro area.[1] And, when relations with France permitted, Samu and Moriah chiefdoms should also somehow be brought within the system; for the present, therefore, it would be inexpedient to take any final decision about Huggins' treaties.

The Ministers received this report unenthusiastically. Northcote and Derby both regretted any extension of British territory, however nominal or limited; they would even have preferred a temporary Parliamentary subsidy, to allow a reduction of duties in the hope of developing Freetown into a free port serving a wide area, like Hong Kong or Singapore. Meade was sceptical about this plan, pointing out that Hong Kong served a vastly greater established market than Freetown, while Singapore was supported by concealed duties on opium and spirits; coastal extension of colonial jurisdiction, he argued, might eventually become unavoidable. Eventually there was a temporary compromise. The suggestion of a continuing subsidy was to be examined by a Parliamentary Committee during 1878; the Foreign Office would resume the process, abandoned in 1869, of testing France's claims in the Mellacourie; meanwhile the Scarcies and Samu treaties would be neither implemented nor renounced.[2]

1878 was a quiet year in Sierra Leone. Rowe, like Boilève, was active in the rivers; he secretly visited Bokkari in the Mellacourie in November 1877, went to the Great Scarcies in April 1878, and to Fouricaria in June. Further north he continued to send stipends and messengers to chiefs of Sumbuya and Baga country.[3] There was no conflict; but also there was no Parliamentary Committee (probably on account of the Near Eastern crisis), and so there was no radical improvement in the financial

---

[1] This proposal was not acted upon immediately, nor quite in this way. cf. C.O. 806/129, No. 190, Rowe to Beach, 20 July 1879; C.O. 806/158, Rowe to Beach, 10 March 1880.

[2] C.O. 806/94, Appendix, Report of Committee and minutes; C.O. to F.O., 2 Nov. 1877.

[3] These activities may be traced in C.O. 806/94 and C.O. 806/114.

position. The Colonial Office therefore went back to the proposals of the inter-departmental committee; and eventually, on 16 October, Rowe was authorized to accept sovereignty over coastal strips in the Scarcies, although without founding any new 'establishments for the exercise of jurisdiction'.[1] The Foreign Office remained sceptical about the wisdom and the justice of this expedient. Wylde foresaw dangers of retaliation elsewhere by other European powers; Salisbury expected resistance from the chiefs, 'who are presumably free traders.'[2] Rowe, he commented, seemed to believe

> 'that we can take fiscal, without taking political possession; that he can get the money without risking the war; but this is probably impossible.'

But Rowe went enthusiastically about his task, and on 25 February 1879 announced that customs duties would be collected after the end of May.

French merchants in the Scarcies at once protested, and the government of Senegal reacted vigorously by sending, on March 14, a corporal's guard to occupy the island of Matacong. Rowe had not yet acted on the notification of British sovereignty which he had issued in 1877, fearing that to collect duties here only would simply drive trade to the mainland; he none the less regarded the French action as sheer aggression.[3] Soon afterwards it was announced that France would collect at Binty and Fouricaria the normal Senegalese export duty of 5%, together with differential anchorage dues of fifty centimes per ton on French ships, one franc on foreign ones.[4] Her object here was less to raise revenue than to assert title. Thirdly, Boilève launched a new diplomatic offensive among the chiefs: on 30 April there was a new treaty with Bokkari, aimed at ending the civil war, on 2 May two new treaties of protection with sub-

[1] C.O. 806/114, C.O. to F.O., 20 April 1878; F.O. to C.O., 11 June; Treasury to C.O., 7 Sept.; Beach to Rowe, 119, 18 Oct. 1878.

[2] F.O. 27/2413, minutes by Wylde; F.O. 27/2414, F.O. to C.O., 8 Jan. 1879 (draft by Salisbury).

[3] C.O. 806/129, Rowe to Beach, 64, 3 March; 87, 24 March 1879.

[4] *MAE*, Afrique 50, M.M.C. to M.A.E., 11 Sept. 1879; Afrique 56, M.M.C. to M.A.E., 28 July 1879.

chiefs. Even Bai Sherbro, though he still refused to recognize French suzerainty, was induced by Valantin to admit that he had ceded both Binty and Kakoutlaye to the French.[1]

Rowe was even more embarrassed by African opposition in the Scarcies. In part at least it was stimulated by French merchants, who stirred up resentment among Temne traders (already jealous of Creole competition) by using the British duties as a pretext for halving the quantities of liquor and tobacco which African brokers received in return for their produce. Nor was it difficult to create anxiety among the chiefs about the future of their domestic slaves.[2] On 17 March the leading Scarcies chiefs subscribed a letter of protest against British encroachments on their independence. Popular feeling also ran so high that a British naval officer judged it prudent not to carry out his orders to land constables on Kikonkeh island, site of the proposed customs house.[3] Even though it did eventually prove possible to start collecting duties on 1 June, African opposition persisted for several weeks — lubricated, Rowe, insisted, by liberal doses of French spirits. Rowe reacted vigorously to this challenge to his policy, even visiting Dakar to protest personally; it seems that only the prudence of the commander of the Freetown garrison restrained him from landing on Matacong with an armed party.[4] Armed conflict in the rivers seemed a real possibility.

[4]

The Salisbury-Waddington Discussions, 1879–80

These local conflicts did not immediately alter the aims and priorities of the governments in Europe. For France, the ob-

---

[1] *ibid.*, copies of treaties; C.O. 806/129, Rowe to Beach, 104, 16 April 1879.

[2] C.O. 806/129, No. 177, Rowe to Beach, 151, 9 July 1879.

[3] *ibid.*, Sattan Lahai *et al.*, to Rowe, 17 March 1879; No. 46, Admty to C.O., 11 April 1879.

[4] *ibid.*, No. 37, Rowe to Beach, 88, 26 March 1879; No. 98, W.O. to C.O., 8 May 1879.

jectives most desired were still friendship with Britain and, if possible, the Gambia; no local interests at Matacong or Cotonou took priority over these. In December 1877 W. H. Waddington became Minister for Foreign Affairs, and remained so for two years; after February 1879 he combined the office with that of President of the Council. An archaeologist and numismatist of repute, Waddington was the son of a British industrialist established in France since 1780; educated at Rugby School and the University of Cambridge, he had opted for French nationality only since coming of age. Although it would have been indiscreet for a politician of British descent to avow it too openly, Waddington strongly favoured co-operation with Britain (a policy which, since the Congress of Berlin, held prospects of support for French policy in Tunis); he would very gladly have furthered it by a comprehensive West African agreement. When appointing d'Elteil as Vice-Consul at Whydah, Waddington signed instructions making it clear that his aim should not be to found 'distant establishments in unhealthy regions', but rather to increase France's bargaining power in the Gambia question; in order to avoid unnecessary conflicts with Great Britain he rejected the proposed renewal of the Porto Novo protectorate.[1] He was even less disposed to engage in fierce controversy over Matacong or the Mellacourie.

In London, too, there was much desire to settle minor African disputes speedily and amicably. Salisbury had as yet little knowledge of African problems, and less sympathy for the local difficulties of Sierra Leone or Lagos; with the aftermath of the Near Eastern crisis still undispersed, and serious colonial campaigns pending in Afghanistan and Zululand, there was nothing he wanted less than 'a nigger war for the sake of settlements which commercially represent but little profit, and financially represent only a deficit'. His instinct was to distrust all advice on frontier questions offered by governors of small colonies; thus he expressed shrewd though imperfectly informed scepticism about Rowe's fiscal plans for the Scarcies, warning the Colonial

[1] *MAE*, Afrique 76, Waddington to d'Elteil, 27 Nov. 1878, 1 May 1879; Bloch, *op. cit.*, pp. 21–3.

Office against complications with the local rulers.[1] When faced
with any proposal from the Colonial Office, however apparently
trivial, which might produce military or diplomatic complications, Salisbury's standard reaction was to suggest referring it to
the Cabinet — a course which, as the Colonial Office well
realized, was calculated to prevent any decisive action at all.
Infuriating as it often was, this contempt for the African settlements and their problems represented the obverse side of
Salisbury's greatest quality as a statesman: his capacity for clear
definition of priorities. Few things ranked higher in his scale, in
1879, than good relations with France; all African disputes had
therefore to be considered in this context.

Both foreign ministers therefore approached the obscure and
often incomprehensible problems of the African coast from
fundamentally congruent standpoints. Both were resolved to
avoid serious conflict; both would welcome a comprehensive
agreement based on the principle of exchange. Salisbury's
private conversations with Waddington at the Berlin conference, and again in Paris in October 1878, which appear to have
touched on colonial problems generally as well as Tunis and the
Near East, showed Salisbury the advantages of dealing with 'a
French minister who works on principles intelligible to the
English mind'.[2] These meetings were followed by new attempts
to settle the old and thorny problem of French fishing rights in
Newfoundland: not a matter of vast intrinsic importance, but
one which affected influential groups in both countries and was
thus especially liable to damage relations. Negotiations on
Africa were expected to follow in due course, as part of some
'comprehensive' bargain.[3]

Diplomatic handling of the Matacong incident

The French 'encroachments' at Cotonou and Matacong were

---

[1] V. Hicks Beach, *Life of Sir M. Hicks Beach* (London, 1932) vol. I, p. 72,
Salisbury to Beach, 10 Oct. 1878; cf. above, p. 222.

[2] Newton, *Lord Lyons* (London, 1913) vol. II, pp. 197, 201.

[3] F.O. 27/2413, minute by Wylde, 30 Aug. 1878; F.O. 27/2414, minute by
Pauncefote, 30 April 1879; C.O. 147/39, minute by Meade, 9 May, on
Fitzgerald, 26 April 1879.

at first interpreted by the Foreign Office as part of a single consistent policy, whose purpose was 'by checkmating our policy on
the African coast, to force us to re-open negotiations for an
exchange of territory'.[1] But the announcement of the Matacong
landing happened to coincide with the much graver news that
the Khedive Ismail had dismissed his French and British
Ministers, who represented the visible means by which the two
powers controlled Egyptian financial policy. French newspapers
reacted fiercely, even talking of military intervention. The
British government, less committed than France to the protection of private investments, refused to consider this; and
Waddington agreed to keep in line with their calmer approach,
believing with *The Times* that the prime necessity was 'to maintain unbroken and efficient the French alliance, which has become so potent a factor in world affairs since the fall of the
ministry of 16 May [1877]'.[2] This Egyptian crisis underlined the
futility of Anglo-French quarrels over what Salisbury called 'a
desert island at the mouth of a pestilential river'.[3] Waddington
hastened to assure Britain that Matacong had been occupied
without authority from Paris and to withdraw the troops, having
first received a British promise not to occupy the island during
negotiations.[4]

The British, however, envisaged a more limited negotiation
than the French. *Le Temps* of 9 April had carried an apparently
'inspired' suggestion that the opportunity should be taken to
negotiate a general settlement, embracing the Newfoundland
fisheries, the frontier in Guiana, the French position in Tonkin
and Cambodia, and 'the West African question'. In particular,
the article hinted, the exchange of the Gambia should be discussed; previous failures were attributed to Protestant fears of
Catholic influence, which could have no foundation now that

[1] F.O. 27/2414, Lyons to Salisbury, S.T. 5, 31 March; Tel., 6 April; S.T.
10, 7 April 1879, minutes by Wylde.

[2] Newton, *op. cit.*, II, pp. 175–82; Salisbury to Lyons, 10, 16 April; 6 June
1879; *The Times* (Leader) 10 April 1879.

[3] S(alisbury) P(apers), A. 26; Salisbury to Lyons, Pte., 4 April
1879.

[4] F.O. 27/2414, Lyons to Salisbury, Tel. 9, April; S.T. 15, 12 April; S.T.
18, 16 April; S.T. 20, 22 April 1879.

good Republicans held office. But the Foreign Office were not convinced that it would be politically expedient to include the Gambia in a comprehensive deal; their preference was for a straightforward delimitation of disputed frontiers.

> 'If the present policy of the two governments is to be carried out,' wrote Wylde, 'we shall each go on annexing until the greater portion of the African Coast is divided between us, and unless we lower our duties or the French raise theirs to an equality with ours, these annexations will only lead to increased expenditure without a proportional increase of revenue or an increased trade.'

This point was immediately underlined by news that Rowe was seeking new acquisitions between the Mellacourie and the Pongos; Pauncefote therefore tentatively suggested to the Colonial Office an attempt to secure a boundary line along the Mahniah river (just north of the Mellacourie system) with Britain abandoning the Isles de Los in exchange for French withdrawals south of the line.[1]

The idea of a limited demarcation agreement was put to Waddington on 11 June, with no specific line mentioned. Waddington, still anxious to revive the Gambia question, commented that he would 'infinitely prefer a resumption of the negotiations for an exchange of territory'.[2] But the Colonial Office had burned its fingers badly over the exchange negotiation of 1876, and only Hemming was prepared to try again. Meade warned the government that they would 'only damage themselves politically in the country', and Hicks Beach refused to re-open the question.[3] Failing this, on 30 June Waddington showed interest in the demarcation suggestion.[4] But if the French had to discuss the rivers questions without the inducement of the Gambia in view, they intended to be exacting

[1] F.O. 27/2414, Lyons to Salisbury, S.T. 22, 26 April 1879, minute by Wylde, 29 April, C.O. to F.O., 30 April encl., Rowe 69, 5 March; Conf., 6 March; memo. by Pauncefote, 30 April.

[2] *MAE*, Angleterre 780, Waddington to Montebello, 77, 20 May 1879; Montebello to Waddington, 51, 31 May; F.O. 27/2415, Lyons to Salisbury, S.T. 36, 11 June 1879.

[3] C.O. 267/339, minutes on F.O., 12 June 1879; C.O. to F.O., 20 June.

[4] F.O. 27/2416, Lyons to Salisbury, S.T. 41, July; 42, 10 July 1879.

bargainers. They had already made this clear by progressively associating themselves with objections raised by their merchants against the application of the Freetown tariff in the Scarcies.[1]

The French claimed, with increasing plausibility, to be acting under some public pressure on commercial questions like this. Lyons had long been complaining of protectionist tendencies among Republican politicians; and although his own free trade convictions may have made him over-sensitive, his fears seemed partly confirmed when the French government failed to renew the Commercial Treaty with Great Britain at the beginning of 1879.[2] But those forces which were later to bring about openly differential and protectionist tariffs in French colonies had not yet gained decisive strength.[3] The merchants of Marseille — though not all the industrialists or shipowners — remained free traders;[4] in the name of principle the same merchants who objected to British duties in the Scarcies also opposed French duties in the Mellacourie. But though they might not demand fiscal protection, merchants did continue to seek government support for their special interests, and many found that the structure of Republican politics enabled them to do so with increasing success. Verminck in particular (who had now taken over the important Senegalese interests of his townsfellow J. B. Pastré) enlisted the co-operation of Maurice Rouvier, deputy for Bouches-du-Rhône.

Rouvier, who was twice to be Prime Minister at critical points in the history of the Republic, was a man of strong personality, still under forty. A rough-hewn, self-made businessman and banker, not over-scrupulous in some of his financial

---

[1] *MAE*, Angleterre 780, Waddington to Montebello, 58, 17 April; Montebello to Waddington, 45, 15 May; 51, 31 May 1879; F.O. 27/2415, Note by Pauncefote, 29 May; Montebello to Pauncefote, Pte., 2 June; Note by Salisbury, 16 June 1879.

[2] Newton, *op. cit.*, II, pp. 3, 163.

[3] A. Girault, *The Colonial Tariff Policy of France* (Oxford, 1916) pp. 81–4; H. Brunschwig, *Mythes et Réalités de l'Impérialisme colonial français* (Paris, 1960) Ch. 6.

[4] P. Masson (ed.), *op. cit.*, Tome 9, 1922; pp. 63 ff, 82 ff, 382; cf. *MAE*, Afrique 77, Verminck to Rouvier, Feb. 1880.

and political methods, Rouvier had been closely associated with Gambetta since 1867. Though an ardent Republican, even with Radical tendencies, he took a hard-headed and unsentimental view of such political issues as might affect business interests. Caillaux said he had all the qualities of a born financier, notably 'imagination combined with an exact comprehension of realities'.[1] Rouvier was to play an important role in Republican expansion in Africa; it seems likely that his initiation into colonial affairs came from such pressures as this, from constituents with concrete interests in danger. When such substantial political figures began to take an interest in the rates of duty payable by French traders in the Scarcies, they were bound to hamper diplomatic efforts to negotiate a speedy settlement. By the end of July Salisbury was urging the Colonial Office to deal with the tariff complaints speedily and generously; otherwise he feared hostile discussion in the French Chamber, which 'could hardly fail to increase the difficulty, already considerable, of adjusting the relations between the French and English Governments on the West Coast of Africa'.[2] Waddington on his side used the emergence of this political pressure as an argument in favour of a comprehensive exchange agreement.[3]

An even stronger reason for settling African disputes was provided by the uncertain European situation; the growth of Russo-German tension and the rumours surrounding Bismarck's relations with Austria-Hungary were alarming the French. On 19 September Waddington visited Salisbury at his vacation home at Puy near Dieppe. Their conversation ranged widely over high policy in Europe and the Near East, and Waddington expressed his strong desire for 'a close *entente* with Britain'. They also discussed co-operation in Egypt, and briefly reviewed colonial questions; besides the African disputes, these included the old question of the Newfoundland fisheries, and the new French desire to annex Raiatea and other Leeward Islands

[1] J. Caillaux, *Mes Mémoires*, Vol. I (Paris, 1942) p. 109.

[2] F.O. 27/2416, F.O. to C.O., 30 July 1879 (draft by Salisbury); C.O. to F.O., 2 Aug.; F.O. 27/2417, F.O. to C.O., 11 Oct. (amended by Salisbury); C.O. to F.O., 17 Oct. 1879.

[3] F.O. 27/2415, Lyons to Salisbury, S.T. 36, 11 June 1879; F.O. 27/2416, Montebello to Salisbury, 14 July 1879.

I

north-west of Tahiti.[1] Salisbury, unbriefed, avoided discussing details, but Waddington returned hopeful that the friendly spirit of this hasty exchange of views would facilitate future colonial negotiations.[2]

★   ★   ★   ★   ★

Meanwhile in Freetown Rowe was considering the Foreign Office's suggestion of a demarcation line along the Mahniah, and the implied abandonment of the Isles de Los. These islands, which had formed part of Sierra Leone Colony since 1818, were chiefly valued for the good anchorage of Factory Island; as at Matacong, warehouses could be securely located there, and merchandise trans-shipped into small craft for distribution along the neighbouring coasts. During the 1870's this site was occupied by Gaillard, a Frenchman naturalized in Sierra Leone (who about 1880 sold out to Verminck); in 1879 his trade was estimated at £63,000 annually. Before 1874 British rule was usually nominal, but in that year the financial crisis led to the enforcement of the Sierra Leone tariff on the islands; although Gaillard thereupon transferred much of his dutiable business to mainland sites, the islands yielded £1,834 in revenue in 1878. Rowe's inclination was therefore to incorporate the neighbouring coasts into the Colony, rather than to surrender the islands. He had recently urged the Colonial Office to accept an offer of the sovereignty of the Koba Baga country,

---

[1] cf. C. W. Newbury, 'Aspects of French Policy in the Pacific, 1853–1906', *Pacific Historical Review*, XXVII (1958) pp. 50–3. France was about to annex her Tahitian protectorate, and wished to forestall any German designs on these islands. But their independence was guaranteed by an Anglo-French agreement of 1847. Though the British government had no substantive objection to French annexation, her Australasian colonies were always opposed to foreign imperialism in the Pacific, and Protestant missionaries wished to keep the islands out of France's Catholic hands. The role played by Protestant sentiment in the Gambia question made Salisbury hesitate to flout 'ancient prejudices' over Raiatea. (*S.P.* A. 26, Salisbury to Lyons, Pte., 29 Nov. 1879.)

[2] *MAE*, Angleterre 781, Waddington to Pothuau, 149, 30 Sept. 1879; cf. G. Cecil, *Life of Salisbury*, II, pp. 363–4; *MAE*, Angleterre 782, Pothuau to Waddington, 30, 11 Oct. 1879.

further north;[1] and he hoped to complete his encirclement of the French position by similar diplomacy among the Kaloum Bagas, immediately opposite the Isles de Los, and in Sumbuya, to the south. If only the cession of the islands could secure French withdrawal from the Mellacourie, Rowe would reluctantly accept it; but his own strong preference was to affirm Sierra Leone's influence as far north as possible, building on old treaties, stipend payments, and general goodwill, and to offer France only cash compensation for Binty.[2]

The Colonial Office passed on this appreciation, with the additional suggestion that the Dubreka river might form the demarcation line. This the Foreign Office regarded as frivolous. Since the Admiralty had reported that the Isles de Los — of some potential value in the days of sail — no longer interested them,[3] there seemed no valid reason why the islands should not be treated as material expendable in negotiation. To propose the Dubreka line to the French (who were actually hoping for a line between the Great and Little Scarcies[4]) would invite angry rejection; the Foreign Office themselves could see little serious basis for British claims on the mainland north of the Mellacourie. They therefore proposed to keep to their suggestion of the Mahniah line, but to ask for a substantial makeweight elsewhere on the coast: the withdrawal of French claims at Cotonou. This alternative basis the Colonial Office accepted on 27 September.[5]

But early in November, before negotiations began, news reached Europe of Ussher's seizure of Ketenou. Salisbury's first reaction was one of extreme anger against the 'insupportable pro-consul' who was thus complicating Anglo-French relations.[6]

---

[1] F.O. 27/2414, C.O. to F.O., 30 April 1879, encl. Rowe, 69, 5 March; Conf., 6 March.

[2] C.O. 806/129, No. 153; Rowe to Beach, Conf., 20, 16 June 1879.

[3] C.O. 806/129, Admty to C.O., 3 July 1879.

[4] *MAE*, Angleterre 780, Montebello to Waddington, 45, 13 May; 86, 18 June 1879.

[5] F.O. 27/2416, C.O. to F.O., 14 Aug. 1879, minute by Pauncefote; F.O. 27/2417, F.O. to C.O., 4 Sept.; C.O. to F.O., 27 Sept. 1879.

[6] *S.P.* A. 26, Salisbury to Lyons, Pte., 12 Nov. 1879 (quoted Cecil, *op. cit.*, IV, p. 251). Salisbury was too angry to identify the pro-Consul and, out of habit, blamed Rowe.

But even the Foreign Office could not avoid some suppressed satisfaction at the potential improvement in the condition of Lagos; and since British prestige on the coast would have suffered from a withdrawal, Salisbury did not insist on one, but contented himself with censuring Ussher for 'unauthorized and dangerous exercise of power'. Indeed the episode seemed to improve the prospects for a comprehensive negotiation, combining Ketenou and Cotonou, Matacong and the Scarcies, and possibly other questions arising outside Africa.[1]

Waddington, anxious to promote negotiation on the broadest possible basis, protested only in restrained terms against the occupation of Ketenou. On 24 November Salisbury suggested that the cause of many territorial disputes might be removed by an agreement to assimilate French and British tariffs along the West African coast; this idea had been tentatively advanced by Meade during the Dahomey blockade, examined in passing by the Inter-Departmental Committee of 1877, and discussed at length between Foreign Office, Colonial Office, and Rowe during 1879. Waddington welcomed the suggestion in principle, and sought to enlarge the scope of negotiation still further. Whereas Salisbury had suggested disarming missionary opposition over Raiatea by linking a British concession there with a settlement of the Newfoundland fisheries, Waddington (who could expect trouble from Breton and Norman Deputies over the Newfoundland question) preferred to find compensation for Raiatea within the African agreement. And — although he discreetly dropped no hint of this — he still hoped to enlarge the negotiation by including the Gambia.[2]

The Gambia in 1879

There seemed to be some basis for this hope. Early in November Montebello, French chargé d'affaires in London, reported conversations with a man called Speer, who had entered the

---

[1] F.O. 27/2418, minute by Wylde on C.O. to F.O., 13 Nov. 1879; F.O. to C.O., 22 Nov.; *S.P.*, A. 26, Salisbury to Lyons, Pte., 29 Nov. 1879.

[2] *MAE*, Angleterre 782, Waddington to Pothuau, 176, 21 Nov. 1879; Pothuau to Waddington, 45 Conf., 25 Nov.; 49 Conf., 12 Dec.; 51, 13 Dec.; Waddington to Pothuau, 188, 20 Dec. 1879.

Gambia as a doctor in 1876, gone into trade, and attempted unsuccessfully to induce a more active British policy up-river.[1] Speer asserted that the merchants who had opposed the exchange in 1876 would no longer do so, in view of the depressed state of the settlement, and the lack of security inland. If the French government approached them discreetly through the French merchants, all (possibly with one exception) would sell their businesses, and articulate opposition to the exchange would disappear. £80,000 to £100,000 would suffice! After returning to Bathrust Speer reiterated this opinion in letters, adding the advice, 'the more uncomfortable France makes it for Great Britain down the coast, the more willing Great Britain will be to cede the Gambia.'[2]

Speer seriously misled Montebello about his own standing and influence with the Colonial Office, where he was regarded as an 'Irish-Yankee adventurer . . . a person who has no position in the Colony, and less character'.[3] His own concern was evidently to secure heavy compensation for an unhealthy business. But conditions in the Gambia did lend some plausibility to his story. Temporarily commerce was prospering; but its future prospects would remain precarious so long as the government lacked effective means of controlling the 'Marabouts', Foday Kabba and Foday Silla, in the lower river, or of ensuring protection to traders higher up. Uncertainty about the future was inhibiting investment by traders and by government alike. Of the older British residents, only Brown remained; when a second Legislative Councillor had to be appointed in 1878 it was necessary to turn to a locally-naturalized alien.[4] Even the Bathurst Africans, a French naval officer reported in 1880, were beginning to regret their opposition to transfer in 1875, 'and are

[1] C.O. 806/85, Cooper to Rowe, 7 April 1876; C.O. 87/114, Speer to C.O., 12 Aug., 14 Aug., 2 Oct. 1879, etc.; Herbert to Speer, 16 Oct. 1879.

[2] *MAE*, Afrique 50, Montebello to Bourée, Pte., 11 Nov. 1879; Speer to Montebello, 2 Dec. 1879, 18 Feb. 1880.

[3] C.O. 87/116, minute by Hemming on Speer to C.O., 21 Nov. 1879.

[4] C.O. 806/107, No. 22, Rowe to Beach, 8 July 1878; cf. Gray, *op. cit.*

not far from petitioning in the opposite sense.'[1] From a British point of view, the recently-renewed French advance on the upper Senegal was liable to render the Gambia 'more worthless and more burdensome than it is even now'.[2] But these very operations made the French more anxious than ever to control the Gambia valley; hence the Ministry of the Marine welcomed the apparent opportunity to re-open the question, and offered to consider providing monetary as well as territorial compensation.[3]

Discussion of a 'comprehensive agreement' 1880

But although Salisbury himself was very willing to re-introduce the Gambia into the negotiations, he was prevented from doing so by the stubborn refusal of the Colonial Office.[4] When on 9 January 1880 he replied to a French protest about Ketenou, he could only suggest linking that question with the Cotonou and Matacong-Mellacourie questions, in hope of reaching 'some arrangement securing in both localities the greatest practical freedom for European commerce'.[5] In subsequent conversations he enlarged on that formula, developing ideas which he had discussed with Hicks Beach at the close of a Cabinet meeting. Britain, Salisbury suggested, might abandon her claim to Matacong (of its legal basis he felt extremely dubious) and renounce any further expansion north of the Scarcies (presumably meaning the Great Scarcies). In return, France should renounce all expansion south of that river, and abandon Cotonou. If these terms were accepted, Britain would probably agree to the French annexation of the Tahitian Leeward Islands; and to disarm the principal French objection Salisbury even offered a pledge to impose no new duties at

[1] MMC, Afrique IV/14/c, Report by Thierry, 9 April 1880. But in Afrique IV/17/c, Capt. Ferrat, 19 Feb. 1878, says Akus still hostile to transfer.

[2] C.O. 87/114, minute by Hemming on F.O. to C.O., 31 Dec. 1879; cf. below. Ch. VI, [1].

[3] MAE, Afrique 56, M.A.E. to M.M.C., 7 Jan.; M.M.C. to M.A.E., 15 Jan. 1880.

[4] F.O. 146/2679, C.P. 4418, No. 19, Ussher to Beach, Conf., 28 Oct. 1879; C.O. 147/39, F.O. to C.O., 20 Dec. 1879, minute by Meade, 26 Dec.

[5] MAE, Afrique 77, Salisbury to Pothuau, 9 Jan. 1880.

Ketenou. This condition would remove much of the advantage which Lagos hoped to draw from Ussher's action,[1] and the Colonial Office complained that these terms had not received full examination. Salisbury rejoined that he personally had been 'disposed to make them more liberal'. He did not conceal from the French Ambassador that his more liberal terms would have included an offer of the Gambia, and that he hoped that this might become feasible after the General Election.[2]

Immediate French reactions were rather favourable. Although Waddington had resigned at the end of 1879 — partly, at least, because he was suspected of excessive anglophilia — his successor, Charles de Freycinet, was also anxious to co-operate with Britain, and took some personal interest in Salisbury's overture.[3] His officials believed that a British promise to levy no new duties on the Slave Coast would protect French commerce more effectively than the precarious retention of Cotonou, while Matacong would give France 'the key to the Mellacourie'; if the Leeward Islands were really to be thrown in, there seemed no reason to hesitate. The suggestion that France and Britain should seek no new territory south and north, respectively, of the Scarcies needed clarification; and the Ministry of the Marine thought it would be imprudent to take such commitments until Britain seemed definitely willing to offer the Gambia. But they too were willing to exchange Cotonou for Matacong and the Leeward Islands, provided that the guarantees to French commerce seemed sufficiently precise.[4]

These appreciations proved to be over-sanguine in assuming that the Marseillais merchants would acquiesce in French withdrawal from the Slave Coast. On 2 February Rouvier wrote to

[1] Salisbury himself seems to have been under the misapprehension throughout that 'the only object of the annexation was to obtain a screw over Dahomey' (*S.P.* A. 26, Salisbury to Lyons, 29 Nov. 1879).

[2] F.O. 27/2480, Salisbury to Lyons, 17, 21 Jan. 1880, Note by Pauncefote, 28 Jan.; Pauncefote to Herbert, Pte., 31 Jan.; *MAE*, Angleterre 783, Pothuau to Freycinet, 3, 12 Jan.; 6 Conf., 12 Jan.; 12 Conf., 18 Feb. 1880.

[3] cf. his minute on Pothuau, 6 Conf., 20 Jan. 1880; C. de Freycinet, *Souvenirs, 1878–1893* (Paris, 1914) pp. 87–8, 95–8, 108.

[4] *MAE*, Afrique 77, M.A.E. to M.M.C., 31 Jan. 1880 (cf. draft at fo. 96); *MAE*, Afrique 56, M.M.C. to M.A.E., 9 Feb. 1880.

Freycinet strongly supporting protests from that city against British policy at Sierra Leone and Lagos; at a time when all European states were seeking new markets, France must not be excluded from lands where her traders had been the pioneers. On receiving this letter Freycinet invited Rouvier to sound Marseillais opinion on the Cotonou-Matacong proposal; the replies were discouraging. Not only Fabre and Régis, who had much to lose on the Slave Coast and nothing to gain in the northern rivers, but also Verminck, regarded the proposed exchange as equivalent to 'un boeuf contre un oeuf'. Since Verminck traded in both Scarcies and Mellacourie, but not as yet on the Slave Coast, his opinion sounded impressively disinterested. (However, his desire seems not to have been the permanent retention of Cotonou, but its eventual use as bait to secure the Gambia.)[1]

Despite these opinions, Courcel, Freycinet's new *Directeur Politique*, still thought that Salisbury's proposals should be welcomed as an advance towards a more comprehensive settlement. Since this modification of British policy was attributable to France's tenacity in defending her local interests since 1876, it was certainly pertinent to consider

> whether, in agreeing to what is expected of us, we should not risk reducing the value of those material guarantees which we still hold, and whose surrender might one day be bought by the cession of the Gambia.

But for the sake of a free hand in the Leeward Islands it would be worth accepting the British terms, provided that the guarantees for trade on the Slave Coast proved genuinely satisfactory.[2]

However, when the French Ambassador tried to advance the discussion on 18 March, Salisbury said little that was precise and, under Colonial Office pressure, even denied having made a firm offer to accept the Great Scarcies demarcation line. He then left for a holiday in Biarritz, leaving the French to hope the

[1] *MAE*, Afrique 56, Rouvier to Freycinet, 2 Feb. 1880; Afrique 77, Rouvier to Freycinet, 3 March 1880, encl. letters from Régis, Fabre, Verminck.

[2] *MAE*, Afrique 77, Freycinet to Pothuau, 6 March 1880, from draft by Courcel (cf. earlier draft by Bourée). Printed in part in *D.D.F.*, III, No. 52.

Cabinet would feel freer to raise the Gambia question in the new Parliament which was about to be elected.[1] But, contrary to Salisbury's confident hope, the new Parliament had a Liberal majority. Montebello hopefully commented that a Whig government could hardly prove less co-operative in West Africa than the Conservatives had been;[2] but the new Colonial Secretary appointed in late April proved to be Kimberley — of all leading politicians, the man most firmly committed against the cession of the Gambia. Hopes of a comprehensive colonial agreement began to recede into the background.

[5]
The Growth of New Difficulties

The Ivory Coast Border

Failing a comprehensive settlement, the diplomatists could only try to deal with particular disputes: a thankless task, for they were handicapped by imperfect knowledge of local conditions, and by increasing pressure from interested parties. Even the apparently trivial question of the Ivory Coast boundary was already presenting new problems; although the disputed area was small, the minor gold-rush of Europeans into the western Gold Coast after 1877 gave it additional significance, and produced some frontier incidents. In April 1880 the British proposed to appoint a Joint Commission locally; the French agreed in principle, hoping that a speedy settlement might facilitate the Cotonou-Matacong negotiation.[3] But in October the British had to request postponement on the grounds that their proposed representative had been invalided home, and this Commission could not meet until December 1883.[4]

[1] F.O. 27/2480, Pothuau to Salisbury, 18 March 1880; *MAE*, Angleterre 783, Pothuau to Freycinet, 18 March 1880.

[2] *MAE*, Afrique 50, Montebello to Bourée, Pte., 3 April 1880.

[3] C.O. 806/194, No. 11, Ussher to Beach, 40, 4 Feb. 1880; F.O. 27/2480, C.O. to F.O., 19 March 1880, minute by Wylde; Salisbury to Lyons, 375, 17 April; *MAE*, Afrique 77, M.M.C. to M.A.E., 4 June 1880; F.O. 27/2481, Lyons to Granville, 30 June 1880.

[4] F.O. 27/2481, C.O. to F.O., 14 Oct. 1880.

I*

In the meantime Verdier's interests began to expand. Hitherto his ambitions had been confined to the creation of a modest but steady trade in the coastal area, using rather restrictive methods. In 1867 he had reached a gentleman's agreement with Swanzy to share the trade of Grand Bassam and Assinie;[1] this probably involved price-fixing, certainly common action against interlopers. Their agents, a French naval officer reported, 'seem to maintain a good understanding, and work together wonderfully to defend the privileged situation which circumstances have given to them.' By the early 1880's the total trade of the two firms was said to be worth about £60,000 annually. But they encountered difficulties in such attempts as they made to develop new markets. They failed to break into the lucrative palm-oil trade of the coast immediately to the west; this was still controlled by sailing-ships from Bristol which, as in the days of the slave trade, would anchor offshore and deal directly with the 'Jack-jack' brokers, without any need for land establishments.[2] Nor could Verdier and Swanzy establish much regular trade with inland states. Even their trade with Ashanti was subject to regulation by the commercially astute Amatifou, ruler of the kingdom of Kinjabo since 1843.[3] As for penetration towards the savanna belt, it was still generally assumed that this would always be blocked by the 'mountains of Kong', so conspicuously marked by contemporary cartographers.

During the early 1880's these pessimistic views began to be questioned, and Verdier began to apply his profits to new and more enterprising purposes. In 1881 he founded a substantial coffee plantation and, joining the gold-rush, secured a mining concession at Mafari. He also began to sponsor reconnaissances of possible routes for inland penetration.[4] His government at

[1] A. Verdier, *Trente-Cinq Ans de Lutte aux Colonies* (Paris, 1896) pp. 196–7.

[2] *MAE*, Afrique 78, Report by Dislère, 30 May 1883, encl. Bories, 20 March 1883.

[3] H. Mouëzy, *Assinie et le Royaume de Kinjabo* (Paris, 1953) pp. 76 ff, 96 ff; Winwood Reade, 'La Côte d'Or', *Bulletin de la Société de Géographie*, Paris, May, 1869; *idem, African Sketch-book*, II, pp. 73–6.

[4] *MAE*, Afrique 77, Observations by Bonnat, 18 Feb. 1881; Bonnat to Nisard, Pte., 10 April 1881; M. A. Bretignère, *Aux Temps Heroïques de la Côte d'Ivoire* (Paris, 1931) *passim*.

first took only slight interest; naval officers on the coast echoed the old view that Verdier was merely an unpatriotic monopolizer, and thought he would be well-advised to abandon his dreams of tapping the Ashanti trade.[1] Nevertheless, these developments in the French settlements were bound to make an abandonment or exchange of the Ivory Coast more difficult to justify — especially since Verdier himself was becoming active in local Republican politics.[2]

The eastern border of the Gold Coast

Between Lagos and the Gold Coast conditions remained unsettled. The Liberal government did not take up Salisbury's proposal of exchanging Cotonou against Matacong; and the French, possibly discouraged by Rouvier's report on Marseillais opinion about these two places, did not raise the subject. The British detachment remained at Ketenou, though without collecting duties; and there were signs that the government of Lagos might be planning further advances.[3] At the other end of the Slave Coast French merchants were afraid of British designs against the Popos states. Rumours of this were based upon a strictly limited advance which Ussher carried out from the Gold Coast; in December 1879 he obtained the cession of the towns of Denu and Aflao, a few miles east of Keta, where Europeans had been trading in order to avoid customs duties.[4] The French need not have worried about the Popos; Salisbury was just as anxious as they to prevent any major territorial expansion. His renewed warnings against unauthorized advances moved Hemming to complain that 'the Foreign Office are apparently determined on throwing every possible hin-

[1] *MAE*, Afrique 77, d'Elteil to M.A.E., 28 April 1880 and minute; Afrique 50, M.M.C. to M.A.E., 23 April 1881, encl. Mottez, 5 April; *MMC*, Gabon VI/2/a, Note on the Appollonia frontier, 5 March 1881.

[2] Verdier, *op. cit.*, p. 185. (He became President of the Republican Committee of La Rochelle in 1885.)

[3] *MAE*, Afrique 77, d'Elteil to M.A.E., 20 Aug. 1880.

[4] F.O. 84/1581, C.O. to F.O., 9 Jan., 17 Jan. 1881, and encl.; *MAE*, Afrique 77, d'Elteil to Freycinet, 2 Jan. 1880; Scotter, *op. cit.*, pp. 194–5; P. E. Schramm, *Deutschland und Übersee* (Braunschweig, 1950) p. 255; Ward, *op. cit.*, pp. 309–10.

drance in the way of our attempts for the development and progress of the West African colonies'.[1] But naturally this was not publicly known; d'Elteil, left in uncertainty, urged his government to take direct action to protect their interests, at least at Porto Novo and Cotonou.[2]

The Sierra Leone-Liberia frontier

South of Sierra Leone it was the British who felt insecure; the area disputed with Liberia was unsettled throughout the 1870's, and French intervention seemed a real danger. The commercial depression of 1873 interrupted a period of expansion in the Sherbro region; competition, already intense, became quite bitter as prices fell. In 1878 seven European houses were trading in the Sherbro, together with some substantial Creole merchants; smaller Sierra Leonean traders of both sexes, as agents or pedlars, were extending the commercial frontier into Mende country, and Rowe was beginning to interest himself in routes towards the Konos and the Kissis. The region came to resemble 'a kind of Australia'. This keen competition on a falling market produced new political tensions; there were frequent wars in the producing areas inland, which destroyed Mafwe and other trading centres of the Bum.[3] On the coast, that portion of Turner's Peninsula immediately adjoining British Sherbro remained peacefully ruled by W. E. Tucker, a capable chief believed to be pro-British (though back in 1863 even he had discussed the possibility of a French protectorate).[4] But southwards, as far as the acknowledged limit of Liberian authority at Cape Mount, the seaboard had many rulers, some of whom were trying to cut out Creole traders by enforcing commercial monopolies; and petty wars were frequent. Prince Manna had died in 1873; his successor, Jaia, was a blind old man, little respected outside his own chiefdom (nor indeed, within it).[5] Rivalries

[1] C.O. 96/133, minute by Hemming, 9 Feb., on F.O. to C.O., 7 Feb. 1880.
[2] *MAE*, Afrique 77, d'Elteil to M.A.E., Oct. 1880.
[3] C.O. 806/118, Rowe to Beach, 182, 9 Nov. 1878, and encl. pp. 17, 19, 45–6; cf. C. H. Fyfe, *op. cit.*, pp. 399–404, 410–12.
[4] *MMC*, Afrique IV/19/b, Emparanza to M.M.C., 21 July 1863; C.O. 806/118, pp. 35–6.
[5] *ibid.*, pp. 36–42, 45–6, and map.

among African rulers were complicated by traders who sought to draw business to their own factories, and to avoid customs duties; they, in turn, drew in the colonial authorities.

While competition was intensifying in the Sherbro, J. M. Harris continued to enjoy a profitable monopoly at Sulima, where since 1860 he had consolidated a very influential position among the local people. Although direct embarkations through the surf of the Moa estuary were still extremely hazardous, and the overhead costs of his shore establishments were high, Harris seems to have drawn substantial profits from a fairly modest turnover. His liquor and tobacco competed as far afield as the Kittam with similar goods cleared through the Sherbro customs. Late in 1879 the jealousy of the Sherbro traders turned to alarm, when it became known that Harris planned to expand this Kittam trade by landing goods through the surf directly on to Turner's Peninsula, within a short haul of Kasseh Lake, source of the river Kittam. These traders (led by Verminck, who had taken over Heddle's interests here) urged Rowe to prevent this, threatening that otherwise they also would attempt to develop customs-free landings on that part of Turner's Peninsula ruled by Tucker. Rowe needed little urging, for the Kittam trade provided about 80% of the Sherbro's revenue; he was doubly apprehensive, since a new Anglo-Liberian Boundary Commission was slowly being constituted. Although neither Harris nor his rivals seemed likely to seek Liberian protection (for that government might well prove even more avaricious for revenue than Sierra Leone, and more arbitrary in its demands), Rowe thought it essential to secure at least the Peninsula, and preferably Sulima also, against any possible Liberian claim. If Liberian rights to these back-doors to the Sherbro hinterland were by any mischance recognized, it would mean both a 'loss to civilization' and a loss to the Sierra Leone Treasury of some £10,000 a year.[1]

The Colonial Office did not welcome Rowe's proposal to take control of Turner's Peninsula; but the prospect of losing revenue was more unwelcome still. They searched feverishly for some

[1] *ibid.*, pp. 3, 46–7; C.O. 806/129, Nos. 15, 16, 22, Rowe to Beach, 4 Jan., 5 Jan., 18 Feb. 1879.

less drastic expedient, but finally decided, on legal advice, to regard the Peninsula as already British, under Turner's Treaty of 1825.[1] Meanwhile the new Boundary Commission had assembled, only to break up on 24 April 1879; the British Commissioners defended all their claims intransigently and refused to refer disputed points to the American arbitrator, although the Liberians had been obliged to agree in advance that *they* would abide by his final decision.[2] Some unilateral extension of British power on the disputed coast now seemed certain.

At this point rumours began to circulate of an impending French protectorate over Liberia. These are not confirmed by the French archives, and appear to have been started by E. W. Blyden during a visit to Grant and other old friends in Freetown. (A romantic dialogue to the same effect in the Monrovia *Observer* of 25 September 1879 also seems to reflect Blyden's classical erudition.)[3] This attempt to frighten the British into a more conciliatory attitude towards Liberian claims was unsuccessful; instead, it led them to approach the United States government, which responded by expressing its 'peculiar interest' in Liberian independence.[4] So far as Turner's Peninsula was concerned, the Colonial Office now felt confident that British rights were safeguarded by the Treaty of 1825; if they were slow and cautious in asserting those rights, this was out of fear of exciting African opposition like that in the Scarcies.[5] But in October 1880 Rowe reported that Verminck was trying to lease a landing-place on the peninsula with the object of avoiding customs. This information came from Harris (who, according to Rowe, had just negotiated unsuccessfully to sell his own

[1] C.O. 267/339, Law Officers to C.O., 14 March 1879, and minutes; L.O. to C.O., 16 July; C.O. to F.O., 15 Aug. 1879.

[2] C.O. 267/339, F.O. to C.O., 4 July 1879, encl. F.O., Conf., Print, 'Further Correspondence respecting the Liberian Boundary Commission 1878–9'; minute by Meade, 18 July.

[3] C.O. 806/151, No. 9, Rowe to Beach, Tel., 28 Aug. 1879; No. 26, F.O. to C.O., 27 Sept.; No. 42, C.O. to F.O., 31 Oct.; No. 56, Rowe to Beach, Conf., 4 Nov. 1879; F.O. 84/1581, C.O. to F.O., 26 Feb. 1880.

[4] H. H. Johnston, *Liberia*, I, p. 247 n.

[5] C.O. 806/151, No. 28, Beach to Rowe, 30 Sept. 1879; C.O. 806/158, No. 84, Streeten to Kimberley, 11 June 1880.

business to Verminck) and it had an effect which that gentleman cannot have foreseen. The Colonial Office finally decided that the time had come to establish a conterminous boundary with Liberia; and that, in view of the evidence of anti-Liberian feeling among the peoples north of Cape Mount, such a boundary ought not to recognize any new Liberian claims.[1]

Although much more official ink was to be used on the subject of the Liberian boundary, this proved a decisive definition of policy. In March 1882 Governor Havelock went to Monrovia with a naval escort, and browbeat President Gardner into agreeing orally to a frontier just north of Cape Mount; in return Liberia secured only the renunciation of those financial claims which Britain had kept carefully on file since 1860 and 1871. Popular indignation in Monrovia prevented the Liberian authorities from ratifying this *diktat*, even when Havelock decided that British interests permitted the moving of the frontier as far north as the Mano river (thus leaving to Liberia responsibility for controlling the powerful chief Moranna Sando). Final agreement on the Mano line was not signed until 1885, nor ratified until 1888.[2] Nevertheless Havelock, on his voyage home, signed treaties with Jaia and other Gallinas chiefs which ceded half-mile strips of coast to Sierra Leone. In 1883 these treaties were enforced, in face of Liberian protests, and the collection of duties began. There were equally fierce protests from Harris (who recruited no less a person than ex-Governor Hill as chairman of his newly-formed company);[3] and soon military operations were needed to enforce British authority in this new dependency. But by this time diplomatic precautions had removed any danger of France fishing in these troubled waters.

The rise of Samori: first effects on Anglo-French relations

Although Rowe's plans for restoring the prosperity of Sierra

---

[1] C.O. 267/343, Rowe to C.O. (two letters) 21 Oct. 1880, minute by Hemming; C.O. to F.O., 5 Nov. 1880.

[2] C.O. 806/195, *passim*; Johnston, *op. cit.*, I, pp. 277 ff.

[3] J. M. Harris, *Annexations to Sierra Leone and their Influence on British Trade with West Africa* (London, 1883).

Leone may seem somewhat myopic, based as they were on attempts to collect customs duties in small coastal states, the older tradition of looking towards the savanna states of the western Sudan had not been forgotten. The Aborigines Department continued to encourage caravan trade with this region, and 1877 and 1878 were excellent years for it. But this trade depended on political conditions beyond the Colony's control; early in 1879 many roads were closed by internal wars, and the number of caravans visiting Freetown dropped by 80%.[1] To restore this situation Rowe turned to the old idea of finding 'strong native powers' with whom it might be possible to collaborate. In April 1879 he despatched the government messenger Sanoko Madi with friendly greetings and modest presents to the three principal states within three hundred miles of Freetown. Their rulers were the Alimamies of Futa Jalon; Aguibou of Dinguiray, brother to Amadu of Ségou; and a new potentate, of whom little was yet known at the coast beyond his name of Samadu or Samori.[2]

Samori is one of the most remarkable figures in modern African history.[3] He appears to have been born about 1835, son of a Mandinka herdsman from Sanankoro, in Wassulu. He was apparently enslaved in adolescence (some accounts say he bound himself to slavery to redeem his mother), and during this period began to engage in trade. About 1871 he began an armed revolt, and during the next ten years created a powerful state around the towns of Kankan and Bissandugu. He proved a

---

[1] Figures from Sierra Leone archives, summarized in *S.L.S.* (n.s.) III, p. 171.

[2] Rowe's letters, dated 12 April 1879, are copied in C.O. 267/341, Streeten to Kimberley, 231, 3 Oct. 1880.

[3] Samori's career is being studied by M. Yves Person, to whom I am grateful for some interesting suggestions. There is much material in print about Samori, none of it wholly satisfactory. Two accounts by African contemporaries are to be found in C.O. 806/279, and in Amadou Kouroubabi, 'Histoire de l'Imam Samori', *Bulletin de l'IFAN*, xxi, 1959 (this account was first recorded by Delafosse about 1901). A. Mévil, *Samory* (Paris, 1899) is competent journalism, based on narratives by French officers like Binger and Péroz. For a strongly anti-colonialist reconsideration, see J. Suret-Canale, 'La Guinée dans le Système Coloniale,' *Présence Africaine*, XXIX, 1959–60, pp. 18–24.

military commander of considerable ability, and his army, built round a cadre of professional soldiers called *sofas*, made good use of cavalry. The causes for which he stood proved attractive enough to bring him many willing recruits. In the first place he was a devout Muslim, claiming the title of *Imam*; he built mosques in conquered territory, and compelled pagan peoples to observe some at least of the Koranic usages. Though he and his followers were less learned in Islamic law and tradition than the Tokolor leaders, and less exacting in their disciplinary demands, those observers who doubted the sincerity of Samori's religious fervour seem to have been unnecessarily sceptical.[1] But he also had more worldly sources of appeal, to Mandinka solidarity, and to social egalitarianism. El Haj Omar too had preached the equality of all the faithful before God, but Samori seems to have gone further in attacking the worldly position of the Mandinka chiefly caste. No doubt, too, some of his followers were motivated by hopes of loot — or of slaves. Many thousands of Africans were ruthlessly and sometimes brutally enslaved by Samori's army. But this was not purposeless cruelty. Slaves were still a highly marketable commodity in the Sudan, especially for the Saharan trade; they therefore represented the easiest means for Samori to obtain the equivalent of foreign exchange with which to purchase the European fire-arms he needed to consolidate his power.

Doubtless it was largely in hope of obtaining arms that Samori welcomed Sanoko Madi's visit of 1879 so warmly. He entertained the messengers for about a fortnight, and sent a plenipotentiary to accompany them on their return journey to Freetown. The party was detained for about a year at Dinguiray because Aguibou was at war with the predatory group of Fulas called Houbous (and also, it seems, because of tension with Futa Jalon); but they eventually reached Sierra Leone in September 1880. Samori's messengers, and others sent by Aguibou, were given an impressive reception at Government House; they in return were sincerely profuse in expressing their

---

[1] A. Gouilly, *L'Islam en l'Afrique Occidentale française* (Paris, 1952) pp. 77–82; cf. Binger, *Du Niger au Golfe de Guinée* (Paris, 1892) I, pp. 90, 150; Pietri, *Les Français au Niger* (Paris, 1885) p. 277.

desire for friendship and commerce.[1] For Samori, regular contact with the port of Freetown might prove the key to continuing success.

But the colonial government could do little except reciprocate these friendly sentiments, and hope that caravans would continue to arrive. They lacked the means to intervene effectively beyond the fall-line of the rivers, or to undertake military action to open the roads. And as yet too little was known about Samori for him to seem attractive as an ally; there seems to have been no further contact with him until 1885.

The French were nevertheless alarmed by even these spasmodic signs of a more active British policy. It was doubtless suspicion of British motives which led Verminck, in 1879, to send two of his local agents on a mission to Falaba and the Niger sources. The party left Freetown in July, without the government's knowledge; numbering seventy-five men, it represented a considerable investment of commercial capital. Its purpose was described as geographical and commercial — but essentially French.[2] After its return, French traders joined in demanding that the Mellacourie should be developed by France as a terminal for the caravan trade, and kept free of customs duties so that it could compete with Freetown and the Scarcies in this role.[3] This theme was elaborated by d'Elteil, during a consular tour of the coast. Rowe, he declared, was planning to station a Resident at Falaba, and to send an exploring party down the Niger into Bouré; to prevent the diversion of Bouré's existing trade with the French rivers, d'Elteil recommended the despatch of a French officer to Bouré through Futa Jalon, with a return route through Ségou and the Senegal valley.[4] The Ministry of the Marine rejected this plan, chiefly on the grounds that such funds as the Chamber might be induced to vote for penetration towards the Niger would be better em-

[1] C.O. 267/341, Streeten to Kimberley, 231, 3 Oct.; 240, 16 Oct. 1880, and encl.

[2] J. Zweiffel and M. Moustier, *Expédition C. A. Verminck: Voyage aux Sources du Niger* (Marseille, 1880) esp. pp. 1–4, 9, 148–9; A. Arcin, *op. cit.*, pp. 359 ff.

[3] *MAE*, Afrique, 56, M.M.C. to M.A.E., 17 April 1880, and encl.

[4] *MAE*, Afrique 77, d'Elteil to M.A.E., 28 April 1880.

ployed in the Senegal.[1] But they showed themselves far from satisfied with the *status quo* in the Sierra Leone region, and increasingly sympathetic with Brière de l'Isle's impatience to settle the status of the rivers.[2]

[6]
The Sierra Leone Boundary Commission of 1881

Neither Rowe nor Brière de l'Isle was content with the *modus vivendi* which their metropolitan governments had established after the Matacong incident. The French were eager to assert their authority and recover the 'face' they had lost locally by withdrawing from the island; Rowe still wanted the Mella-courie, and abstained with great reluctance from responding to Bokkari's new overtures for British support.[3] Forbidden to intervene in that river, he sought to encircle the French position by vigorous diplomacy further north. On the Tumbo peninsula, immediately opposite the Isles de Los, Rowe began to cultivate the chief of a small village called Konakry; to forestall his plans Brière de l'Isle signed a treaty of protection with the superior chief, Balla Demba of the Kaloum Bagas, in June 1880.[4] Rowe angrily claimed that this violated the *modus vivendi*; and even Kimberley, commenting 'we had better bestir ourselves and try to counterwork the French', agreed that he should send political messengers to forestall any similar action in the Koba Baga or Sumbuya countries.[5]

[1] *ibid.*, M.M.C. to M.A.E., 31 July 1880.

[2] *MAE*, Afrique 50, M.A.E. to M.M.C., 31 Aug.; M.M.C. to M.A.E., 6 Sept., 20 Oct. 1880.

[3] C.O. 806/158, No. 49, Rowe to Kimberley, 25 May 1880; No. 64, Streeten to Beach, 15 May 1880; No. 104, Streeten to Kimberley, 16 July 1880.

[4] *ibid.*, No. 5, Rowe to Beach, 27 Dec. 1879; *MAE*, Afrique 56, Verminck to Gasconi, 9 March 1880; cf. Arcin, *op. cit.*

[5] C.O. 806/158, No. 96, Streeten to Kimberley, 5 July 1880; No. 107, Streeten to Kimberley, 23 July, minute by Rowe; C.O. 267/343, Rowe to C.O., 19 Aug., minute by Kimberley; C.O. 806/158, No. 124, Kimberley to Streeten, 27 Sept. 1880; C.O. 806/170, No. 18, Streeten to Kimberley, 30 Dec. 1880; No. 19, minute by Rowe, 17 Jan. 1881.

These conflicts, and the French decision to levy customs duties in the Mellacourie from July 1880, made the British government doubly anxious to dispose of the whole troublesome question by negotiation. But although the French, still with their eyes on the Gambia, dropped new hints about '*un arrangement d'ensemble*', the Foreign Office under Granville was reluctant to embark on any such negotiation without previously clarifying the legal basis of French presence in the Mellacourie. To expedite Lyons' handling of this unfamiliar question, Pauncefote suggested that Hemming and Rowe might visit Paris.[1] But this suggestion was misinterpreted by the French as a proposal to appoint the two men to a Joint Commission; to the British surprise, a Note of 14 September accepted the 'proposal' and named d'Elteil and Roy of the *Direction des Colonies* as French Commissioners.[2]

Such a Commission did not seem the most promising procedure. Many British officials would still have preferred a last attempt to link an African agreement with a concession over Raiatea. In April 1880 the French authorities in the Pacific had prematurely hoisted their flag in the Leeward Islands, wrongly assuming that Britain had formally consented; the French government, admitting that this violated the 1847 Convention, wished to avoid a formal British demand for withdrawal. The Foreign Office, disinclined to help the French out of this predicament without compensation, asked the Colonial Office whether they would prefer to obtain concessions in Africa or in Newfoundland. Hemming argued forcefully the claims of Sierra Leone, but his seniors agreed with Meade that Newfoundland was more important 'both from a colonial and Imperial point of view'.[3] This was an unfortunate choice — for no Newfoundland agreement could be concluded until 1904 — and it left the Foreign Office unhappy about considering the northern rivers in isolation.

[1] F.O. 27/2481, C.O. to F.O., 6 July 1880, minute by Pauncefote.

[2] *MAE*, Afrique 56, M.A.E. to M.M.C., 22 June, M.M.C. to M.A.E., 1 July, 13 Aug. 1880, F.O. 27/2481, Adams to Granville, 854, 16 Sept. 1880.

[3] F.O. 27/2475, Adams to Granville, 760 Conf., 20 Aug.; 787, 28 Aug. 1880 and minutes; C.O. 225/6, minutes by Hemming, Meade, Herbert, Kimberley on F.O. to C.O., 16 Sept. 1880.

Indeed, it seemed doubtful whether there could ever be real agreement on the *rights* of the Mellacourie question; only by setting aside the conflicting evidence of treaties, disregarding the tangled questions of African politics and customary law, and seeking a workable compromise at the diplomatic level was the dispute likely to be settled. In January 1881, Lyons urged the importance of excluding French colonial officials from negotiations:

> 'Such chances as there may be of a satisfactory issue must depend in very great measure upon the considerations of general policy which will have weight with the Minister of Foreign Affairs, and may induce him to overrule the colonial, and, so to speak, technical, views which are apt to prevail in the Department of the Marine here.'

Instead of a formal Joint Commission, Lyons preferred that,

> 'one or two officials on each side, practically acquainted with the matters in discussion, should meet at Paris, and that the instructions to them should be to endeavour to fix, without reference to questions of right or of present possession or occupation, a practically satisfactory line of demarcation. . . .'[1]

This was a diplomatists' solution, unlikely to satisfy colonial enthusiasts on either side. For Rowe, such an approach would mean abandoning any hope of encircling Binty with a new series of treaties; for the French, it would set back any hope of trading the Mellacourie for greater advantages elsewhere. Negotiations restricted to the northern rivers, argued the Ministry of the Marine, could do nothing except confirm rights which France already held — or else take them away without compensation.[2] The following undated Note, classified in the colonial archives for 1881, suggests that they might still have been ready to make very considerable concessions on the Slave Coast for the sake of a comprehensive agreement:[3]

[1] F.O. 27/2551, Lyons to Granville, 55, V. Conf., 18 Jan. 1881.
[2] *MAE*, Afrique 57, M.A.E. to M.M.C., 17 Feb. 1881; M.M.C. to M.A.E., 15 March 1881.
[3] *MMC*, Afrique VI/27/a, Undated Note, *Bases du Négociation à engager avec l'Angleterre*. The limitation to a period of five years of the proposed pledge not to alter customs rates is inserted in the document as an afterthought.

'On the one hand, France cedes:

    (i) her rights of sovereignty over Cotonou, Grand Bassam, Assinie and Dabou.

    (ii) a portion to be determined of the rights reserved to her on the Newfoundland coast by the Treaty of Utrecht (1713).

On the other hand, England

    (i) cedes her right of sovereignty over the Gambia.

    (ii) renounces the reservations laid down in the Convention of 19 June 1847 with regard to the Leeward Islands.

To put an end to all disputes as to their reciprocal rights on the west coast of Africa, the two nations make the following declarations:

England renounces all claim to sovereignty over all parts of the said coast between the northern limits of the Senegal and the Scarcies. France makes a similar renunciation with regard to that portion of the coast between the Scarcies and Cape St. John, which is considered as the northern frontier of our establishment of Gabon. . . .

It is also agreed, in order to safeguard the interests of their respective subjects at present established in the territories exchanged, that each of the two nations promises to make no modification in the customs tariff at present existing during a period of five years.'

But since the British government seemed to have set its face against such a combination, the more limited form of boundary Commission was eventually established and met, with no great enthusiasm, on 16 May 1881. France was represented by Brière de l'Isle and Roy, Britain by Hemming and Sir Arthur Havelock, Governor-designate of Sierra Leone. As Lyons had feared, the deliberations of these 'colonial men' were sometimes acrimonious; at one point Hemming was accused of tampering with the minutes on instructions from the Colonial Office.[1] The British delegates began by emphasizing that their instructions precluded any discussion of the Gambia; the French retorted, tongue in cheek, that since Frenchmen already did all the trading they were quite content that Britain should continue to

[1] The French records of meetings are in *MAE*, Afrique 57; the British, in C.O. 806/177.

bear the cost of administration. The British then proposed the Mahniah line as boundary, with the Isles de Los exchanged against French rights in the Mellacourie; the French, after a formal reference to their government, offered instead a line between the Mellacourie and the Great Scarcies. Without strong objections the British agreed to proceed on this basis, provided that France would formally renounce all claims between the Sherbro and the Liberian border, and would promise to treat British subjects and British commerce in their territories as favourably as French.

The British minutes suggest that the French delegates seemed ready to consider these conditions in return for the cession of the Isles de Los; but French evidence suggests that commercial equality was never a possibility. The Ministry of the Marine were determined to apply in the Mellacourie their new Senegalese tariff, which discriminated in favour of French cotton-goods, disregarding a plea from the Foreign Minister that 'in the interests of our general policy, and on the eve of negotiations for a commercial treaty, we ought to march in accord with the British as far as possible'.[1] It was Britain that compromised, on the assumption that if France was really resolved to apply protective tariffs in her empire, all that could be achieved in the Mellacourie was 'a tolerably satisfactory boundary line'.[2] They dropped their demand for commercial equality, and kept the Isles de Los; by June a boundary line had been roughly drawn through the middle of Samu chiefdom. Except at the Isles de Los, Britain agreed to exercise no political influence between this line and the Nunez, while France would exercise none between the line and the Liberian border.[3] A few details remained for definition; but it did appear that one Anglo-French dispute had been roughly but peacefully settled.

Settling it in isolation from other interests of the two powers in Africa had not been easy, and might have proved impossible

[1] *MAE*, Afrique 57, St. Hilaire to Cloué, Pte., 24 May; Cloué to St. Hilaire, Pte., 25 May 1881.

[2] C.O. 267/347, minute by Herbert, 26 May, on F.O. to C.O., 25 May 1881.

[3] F.O. 27/2551, C.O. to F.O., 25 May; F.O. to C.O., 2 July 1881.

had not diplomatic caution restrained the enthusiasm of colonial authorities. In retrospect, it seems that Sierra Leone lost most by this procedure. France's abandonment of the Scarcies, though a real blow to her traders there, had perhaps been foreseeable; Britain's loss of the Mellacourie might, up to the last, have been averted by shifting the discussion on to a wider basis. This renunciation was to weaken the future state of Sierra Leone, both by restricting the line of coast from which immediate revenue could be drawn, and by reducing the area of hinterland where it was possible to develop a dominant influence. And the agreement was not even destined to improve Anglo-French relations, inside or outside Africa.

CHAPTER SIX

The Beginning of the Scramble

[1]

The French Advance from the Senegal, 1879–82

The Senegal railway schemes

WHILE THESE relatively minor disputes were simmering in coastal districts, in both Britain and France interest was slowly reviving in schemes for penetrating inland. Faidherbe's immediate successors had not developed any clear Sudanese policies; after Mage's return, relations with the Tokolors remained in a condition of mistrustful suspense. After 1857 they made no direct military threat to the French colony, but Amadu's influence in Futa remained disturbingly strong; and the presence of Tokolor garrison-colonies at Koniakary to the north-east of Medina, and at Koundian and Mourgoula to the south, threatened to impede any advance of the traders' frontier. But the Senegalese traders were traditionally conservative, and showed no eagerness to advance beyond their established positions up to Medina. Nor did Governor Valière, who in 1874 proposed a treaty to Amadu on terms intended to encourage Sudanese caravans to visit Senegal rather than to facilitate Senegalese penetration of the Sudan.[1]

Policy began to change when Valière was succeeded by Colonel Brière de l'Isle. Known as a disciple of Faidherbe, and an exponent of *le go-ahead des Américains*,[2] he planned to combine resistance to Rowe's policy on the coast with a bold extension of French influence towards the Niger. This was to include bold schemes of railway construction. In 1878 Brière de l'Isle

---

[1] *MMC*, Sénégal III/10 bis, Galliéni to de l'Isle, 18, 16 Nov. 1880, enclosing a copy of these proposals communicated by the Tokolors at Nango. Galliéni does not recall having seen these before.

[2] J. S. Galliéni, *Voyage au Soudan Français* (Paris, 1885) p. 1.

submitted a triple programme to Paris: one railway to connect St. Louis with the rising port of Dakar, a connecting line to Medina or Kayes, which would carry traffic hitherto dependent on the unsatisfactory river navigation, and a third section on to the Niger near Bamako. These proposals, though ambitious and costly, were well-timed, for Algerian interest in the even more extravagant plan for a Trans-Saharan line was making politicians still indifferent to colonial expansion think seriously about railway construction in Africa.

In April 1878 the explorer Paul Soleillet arrived at St. Louis for the purpose of locating possible southern terminals for a Trans-Saharan railway; after visiting Ségou he returned to France advocating the Senegal-Niger line instead. Though this alternative was unsatisfactory to the Algerian interest, who hoped to draw such riches as the Sudan might contain in their own direction, it was clear that the dangers, difficulties and expense of this plan would at least be less than those of the Trans-Saharan. In 1879 the Minister of Public Works approved the simultaneous study of both projects; next year a Committee report presented by Rouvier successfully recommended a vote of 1,300,000 francs for preliminary studies on the upper Senegal.[1] Meanwhile Jauréguibery (a former Governor of Senegal now become Minister of the Marine) introduced a Bill authorizing all three of de l'Isle's proposed lines, at a cost hopefully estimated at 120,000,000 francs.

These schemes did not have a happy history; severe natural difficulties were reinforced by political ones. At first, the native prudence of the Deputies was reinforced by advocates of the rival Trans-Saharan project; but the influence of the latter group was weakened by an unfavourable report from the Austrian traveller Lenz, who in 1880 travelled from Morocco to St. Louis by Timbuktu, and was finally quenched when a French expedition under Colonel Flatters was destroyed at Bir-el-Gharama on 16 February 1881. In December 1880 a much-reduced Senegal programme was approved. The Dakar-

[1] A. Terrier and C. Mourey, L'Expansion française et la Formation territoriale (Paris, 1910) pp. 53 ff. See also an official publication of the Ministry of the Marine, Sénégal et Niger: La France dans l'Afrique Occidentale (Paris, 1884).

St. Louis line was to be built by contractors (it was opened in 1885); but the branch to Medina was not approved, on the grounds that it would duplicate the Senegal navigation; and the line from Kayes was authorized only as far as Bafoulabé. This was a senseless and costly compromise. In the first place, it overestimated the navigable capacity of the Senegal. Unusable for eight months of the year, the river proved quite inadequate as feeder to a major commercial railway, and in 1907 it was necessary to begin the railway link between Kayes and the Dakar line after all. Meanwhile climatic and medical problems, added to the difficulty of transporting all material and equipment by water as far as Kayes, delayed construction and increased the cost. By 1883 Deputies, sometimes prompted by disillusioned Senegalese officials, were tiring of the commitment and its ever-increasing expense; in December, many Radicals and Republicans joined the monarchist opposition in rejecting a demand for more credits by 234 votes to 197, and Ferry's government suffered the humiliation of using its majority in the Senate to induce the Chamber to provide another small and grudging instalment.[1] Not until 1890 did the first train reach Bafoulabé (which itself had little economic significance), and only in 1905 was the link with the Niger finally achieved. Long before this it became clear that the immediate economic potentialities of the Sudan had been much exaggerated, and that some of them could in any case be more easily developed by other routes.

Galliéni and the Tokolors

Plans for penetrating the Sudan revived a major political dilemma which Faidherbe had faced but not finally resolved: was Amadu's Tokolor empire to be regarded as an obstacle in the path of France's 'civilizing mission', to be eventually removed by force, or could this 'strong native power' be accepted as a possible associate in the task of advancing French trade and influence in the Niger valley?[2] This problem fell to the new

[1] *Journal Officiel, Débats: Chambre*, 4 July, 18 Dec. 1883, 1 April 1884; *ibid.*, *Débats: Sénat*, 23 Jan. 1884.
[2] cf. above, pp. 121–5.

Directeur Politique at St. Louis, J. S. Gallieni, a marine captain of Italian descent. This future pro-consul, at the age of thirty, was ardent, impulsive, physically courageous, but inexperienced and unstable in political judgment. He had little information on Amadu's empire more recent than Mage's rather unflattering reports; the unfavourable dispositions which these tended to create were reinforced by anti-Muslim prejudices, and by a soldier's impatience at being confined in the Senegal valley by the Tokolor garrisons. Initially therefore Gallieni regarded the Tokolors as an obstacle in the way of France's advance to the Niger.

October 1878 saw the first step in that advance (against the wishes of traders on the river, who feared that military action might jeopardize the modest commerce which they already enjoyed). Logo and Natiaga, two small districts of Khasso immediately above Medina, were brought back under French influence by a limited military operation against the Tokolors at Sabouciré. This forceful action, Gallieni claimed, greatly encouraged Mandinka resistance to Tokolor rule — a 'national' movement which fitted into Mage's picture of an empire mortally threatened by the revolt of its subject peoples. In 1879 Gallieni travelled as far as Bafoulabé, at the confluence of the Bafing and Bakhoy rivers, and reported more evidence to support this view. The Tokolor-protected chief was hard pressed by an army which Gallieni believed to represent Mandinka national resistance.[1] While professing his strict neutrality, Gallieni surreptitiously began to favour the insurgents, drinking African beer to demonstrate his sound religious principles and accompanying their messengers back to St. Louis. He returned convinced that the Mandinkas, good economic men (*économes et même avares . . . et âpres au gain*) would be better partners and customers for France than the Muslim Tokolors, so lamentably inclined to waste time in the mosque and the harem.[2] This was a curious inversion of the fashionable pro-Muslim school of thought.

In these circumstances, French professions of neutrality

---

[1] Other causes for the war are suggested in Pietri, *Les Français au Niger* (Paris, 1885) pp. 152–6.

[2] *MMC*, Sénégal III/10 bis, Galliéni to de l'Isle, 17 Nov. 1879.

sounded unconvincing to Amadu. Even if Gallieni's blandish-
ments to the Mandinkas could have remained secret, his action
at Sabouciré seemed clearly hostile, and so did the fort which
he began to construct at Bafoulabé in October 1879. Amadu
claimed sovereignty of these territories under his father's
agreement of 1860, and in his negotiations with Mage he
expressly refused to accept French forts. Nevertheless, the
commandant at Bafoulabé was still instructed to pursue a two-
faced policy: while Tokolor officials were to be told that French
relations with Amadu were excellent, the subject peoples were
to be encouraged to look to France as their protector.[1] Then, in
January 1880, Gallieni, with four European officers and 150
men, set out to explore the largely unknown country beyond
Bafoulabé, with the urgent aim of forestalling the British on the
Niger. Gallieni's published account makes it appear that this
mission's aims were ambiguous and contradictory: that it was
intended at the same time as a 'solemn embassy' to win
Amadu's favour, and as an attempt 'to exploit the seeds of
discord which exist between the Tokolor conquerors and their
discontented tributaries'.[2] But his contemporary reports show
that initially the latter aim predominated. Relying on the
advice of his guide Abderrahman, who came from a chiefly
trading family of Bamako but had been absent from there some
years, Gallieni hoped to find in that city a prosperous trading
centre where he could station a French Resident, and to secure
serious allies for a more openly anti-Tokolor policy. But by
June these assumptions had proved unjustified, and Gallieni
was drifting back towards the idea of some alliance with
Amadu.[3]

Initially the anti-Tokolor policy went satisfactorily. Moving
through Mandinka into Bambara territory, Gallieni made a
series of treaties with chiefs (or *soi-disant* chiefs), who put their
marks to papers acknowledging some loose form of French

[1] *MMC*, Sénégal IV/73/a, de l'Isle to Comdt., Bafoulabé, 8 Nov.
1879.
[2] Galliéni, *Voyage* . . . , p. 6.
[3] *MMC*, Sénégal III/10 bis, Gallieni to de l'Isle, No. 5, Nango, 7 July
1880.

protectorate in the hope of securing French support — possibly against the Tokolors, possibly against their local rivals. The series culminated with a treaty with the chiefs of Kita, a small mountainous state strategically sited on the route to the Niger.[1] But some Bambaras noted that Gallieni was reluctant to commit himself fully against Amadu, and that he held back his most desirable presents (including four blunderbusses which they euphemistically described as cannons); hopes of booty were thus reinforced by apprehension lest the mission might after all be planning to negotiate at Ségou.[2] On 11 May, while marching towards Bamako through the notoriously disorderly Bambara country of Beledugu, the mission was ambushed at Dio; they lost twenty men killed, twenty wounded, and most of their baggage. The survivors succeeded in reaching Bamako, but they found the town much smaller and weaker than they had expected, clearly no adequate basis for opposing the Tokolors on the Niger. On the other hand, when they crossed the Niger into territory under Amadu's direct control, they felt much more secure; in the words of one member,

> 'this semblance of social organisation, in contrast to the disordered barbarism through which they had just passed, inspired in them a certain confidence in the good faith of their hosts, even leading them to hope to establish serious and durable relations with them on behalf of our country.'[3]

So far as this part of the Niger valley was concerned, Amadu's power was clearly still paramount; in face of the apparently urgent danger of British penetration, Gallieni came round to support a policy of alliance and collaboration with him in the region — at least as a temporary measure. On the other hand, his experience of Mandinka and Bambara disaffection still pulled him in the opposite direction; and he seems to have hoped to combine a policy of courting Amadu on the Niger with

[1] Text in Gallieni, *Voyage* . . . , pp. 150–3.

[2] Gallieni's report from Nango, No. 5, emphasizes the motive of loot (which would not imply any political error on his part). But cf. his *Voyage* . . . , pp. 209, 246; Pietri, *op. cit.*, pp. 176, 183–6; J. Bayol, *Voyage en Sénégambie* (Paris, 1888) pp. 47–8.

[3] Pietri, *op. cit.*, p. 208.

one of building forts with the co-operation of his discontented subjects on the upper Senegal.[1]

In these conditions it is hardly surprising that Amadu, who since Mage's visit had been given serious reasons to mistrust the French, should hesitate to negotiate with Gallieni. Instead of receiving the mission at Ségou he had it detained in the village of Nango, twenty miles away. For four months Gallieni remained there, impatient but inactive; his anxieties were fruitfully stimulated by reports from Ségou of intense British activity near the upper Niger.[2] Then, at the end of October, Amadu sent a shrewd and able emissary to negotiate a treaty: his kinsman, Seydou Djeylia.

Gallieni's published record of these negotiations conveys a clear impression of Seydou's considerable diplomatic skill. But the texts he prints differ in important particulars from the minutes recorded at the time; they conceal the full extent of the

[1] *MMC*, Sénégal III/10 bis, Gallieni to de l'Isle, No. 5, 7 July 1880.

[2] Whether deliberately or not, these reports were much exaggerated. Before leaving Medina, Gallieni heard only vague rumours of a British mission to Ségou. These were reinforced by various rumours reaching Nango, and also by a positive statement from Seydou Djeylia that three British missions were in the interior. One was said to have spent several months in Futa Jalon; another, to be at the Niger source. These reports appear to refer to the journeys of Olivier (pp. 267–8 below) and of Zweiffel and Moustier (p. 246). That these were Frenchmen might genuinely not be understood in Ségou, especially since Zweiffel and Moustier set out from Sierra Leone.

Thirdly, a 'white man' from Sierra Leone was said to have been at Dinguiray, and to have sent on an African called Wakka to Ségou. This was in fact not a white man, but the Sierra Leone government messenger Sanoko Madi, who was sent by Rowe in April 1879 to Samori and to Aguibou of Dinguiray; he returned to Freetown in September 1880. Another Sierra Leone Government Messenger, Momodu Wakka, remained at Dinguiray in the hope of being able to go on to Ségou; I have seen no record that he succeeded, and he was back in Freetown in time to leave for Timbo on 6 Jan. 1881. (C.O. 267/341, Streeten to Kimberley, 231, 3 Oct.; 240, 16 Oct. 1880, with enclosures. cf. above, pp. 244–6.) Back in Senegal, Gallieni learned of Gouldsbury's mission of 1881 (pp. 265–7) which was then reported only to have reached Timbo; and wrongly identified Gouldsbury as the 'white man' of Dinguiray. (Sénégal III/10 bis, Gallieni to de l'Isle, Tel., Bakel, 25 April 1881.) Hence the puzzling anachronisms in *Voyage* ... where he cites Gouldsbury's mission of 1881 in explanation of his own actions in 1880 (*op. cit.*, pp. 77, 171, 352, 462 n.).

concessions which Gallieni accepted, and of the duplicity of his attitude.[1] Seydou began by urging that Mage's treaty should be honoured, justly pointing out that the promised mountain guns had never been delivered, and complaining very forcefully of France's recent encroachments on Amadu's Mandinka territories. Gallieni replied by proposing a new treaty (modelled upon that which he had originally intended to sign with Bamako). By this, Amadu was to acknowledge the protectorate of France, and to accept a Resident at Ségou; to grant French subjects exclusive facilities for trading in his states and for navigating the Niger; and to permit the Senegal government to build forts and a railway in his territory.

In principle, Amadu was not unwilling to accept a close relationship with France; indeed, it could greatly ease his very real problem of re-establishing and extending his authority. But Seydou steadily refused to accept Gallieni's terms. 'We like the French, but do not trust them,' he declared, 'they on the other hand trust us, but do not like us.'[2] The essential points for the Tokolors were to obtain artillery, and to secure French recognition of their territorial claims as far down the Niger as Timbuktu. Seydou argued that it was in France's interest to support Tokolor expansion in this direction, and subsequently southwards towards the mountains of Kong; 'we shall open the road for you everywhere; you may follow us and profit from our efforts.' And the British (whose desire for close relations with Ségou the Tokolors emphasized with much skill) would thus be excluded from the Niger. But — no tangible manifestations of French presence were to be admitted to the empire of Ségou. Any Residents appointed were to be African Muslims; steamboats were to be excluded from the Niger navigation; there was to be no railway. Most important of all: Bafoulabé was to be evacuated, and no more forts built on Amadu's territory.

[1] The record published in *Voyage* . . . , pp. 398–407 should be compared with the original text in Sénégal III/10 bis; also with Galliéni to de l'Isle, No. 17, 14 Nov.; No. 18, 16 Nov.; No. 19, 18 Nov. 1880.

[2] *MMC*, Sénégal III/10 bis, minutes, 3rd session. cf. the version in *Voyage* . . . , p. 404. 'Nous aimons les Français, mais nous les craignons. Eux au contraire ne nous aiment pas, mais ne nous craignent pas non plus.'

Gallieni's position was physically weak and isolated, and he was evidently worried by the British danger; he therefore lacked the bargaining strength to move Seydou far from these conditions. He was able to avoid mentioning in the text of the treaty the restrictions concerning the nationality of the French Residents and the nature of navigation on the Niger; but this did not mean that the Tokolors waived the restrictions themselves. Gallieni did his best to bargain over the supplies of French armaments, but Seydou insisted on a firm promise of four mountain guns, and also stipulated for an initial delivery of one thousand flintlocks. Another two hundred of these were to be included annually in Amadu's stipend, whose total value was fixed at 25,000 francs. Although France in return received the exclusive right to establish *comptoirs*, improve roads, and open *voies commerciales* between the Senegal and the Niger, she had to promise 'to construct no post or military establishment in Tokolor territory'. Essentially this was a treaty of peace and friendship, drawn up as between equals. True, by Article VI of the French text, Amadu placed the river Niger, as far as it flowed through his territory, 'sous le protectorat exclusif de la France'; but no such phrase appeared in the Arabic text which eventually reached Gallieni in March 1881, bearing Amadu's seal and signature.[1]

This treaty represented a reversal of Gallieni's original policy. In his prolonged oscillation between the attractive role of liberator of the oppressed pagan peoples and the alternative of co-operating with an extensive and relatively well-organized African state, he now swung to the latter side. His sincerity has been questioned, and certainly his reports remained charged with internal inconsistency. Some of this may be explained by drawing distinctions between different parts of the Tokolor empire. On the Niger, where Amadu's rule was most effective and where Britain seemed a threat, Gallieni was prepared to try collaboration with him, and to recognize his territorial claims as far as Timbuktu. He did intend to deliver the artillery, though on the rather contemptuous assumption that it would deteriorate so rapidly in African hands that France need never

[1] French text is in Sénégal III/10 bis/c; cf. *Voyage . . .* , pp. 459–62.

K

fear it. But over the Senegal valley Gallieni continued to equivocate; he avoided promising to evacuate Bafoulabé on the plea that this was the Governor's decision, and secretly hoped to continue military encroachment upon those Mandinka and Bambara districts where the Tokolor state seemed to be 'in full decomposition'.[1] Even as a temporary expedient this ambiguous policy was certain to raise difficulties in execution.

The military advance

While Gallieni was still detained at Nango the French government, doubtless influenced by his earlier reports, decided to resume its invasion of Amadu's empire. On 6 September 1880 a Ministerial Decree placed the new military district of the Upper Senegal under the command of Colonel Borgnis-Desbordes. With a fighting strength of nearly 500, he was to advance, initially, as far as Kita, studying the country in preparation for the construction of the railway. This marked a new stage in the attempt to push a military frontier ahead of the unenterprising Senegalese traders. In this first phase, Desbordes was to play the role of liberator of subject peoples; beyond Kita, Brière de l'Isle suggested that he should claim to be a friend of Amadu — though he was also to try to make a treaty with Amadu's subjects at Bamako to exclude British influence from the Niger.[2]

Desbordes, a forthright and stubborn artilleryman, whose professional instinct was to strike directly for the objective, did not find this dual role congenial.[3] He was furious when, shortly before he reached Kita in February 1881, amended instructions arrived from Paris and St. Louis, enjoining especial efforts to conciliate the Tokolors and avoid conflicts. Fearing that lack of respect for his column might jeopardize its safety, Desbordes

[1] MMC, Sénégal III/10 bis, Galliéni to de l'Isle, 17, 14 Nov.; 18, 16 Nov. 1880; Report by Michaux, 19 May 1881; cf. Galliéni, Voyage . . . , p. 461 n.

[2] MMC, Sénégal IV/73/a, Cloué to Desbordes, 4 Oct. 1880; de l'Isle to Desbordes, 23 Nov. 1880.

[3] The primary source for Desbordes' campaign of 1880–1 is his very long MS. report in Sénégal IV/73 bis, which quotes freely from his correspondence. See especially the introduction, and Chs. 7 and 27.

decided it was time to fight. Goubanko, near Kita, was the stronghold of a lawless band of Fulas who had migrated from Birgo a dozen years earlier; partly at the instigation of a Senegalese deserter, they were interfering with the column's supply of provisions.[1] On 11 February Desbordes successfully shelled and attacked this town, though he suffered serious losses. But the political implications still remained ambiguous. Goubanko had been in rebellion against Amadu, but its reduction was nevertheless an unauthorized use of force within his empire; so too was Desbordes' construction of a fort at Kita. Such acts risked inciting reprisals against Galliéni's party at Nango. But Amadu, too prudent to welcome a conflict with France, confined himself to a dignified protest; indeed, he may have been stimulated to get rid of these potentially embarrassing visitors.[2] On 5 April Gallieni reached Desbordes' headquarters at Kita.

In the company of his senior officer, Gallieni's opinions were again transformed. At this time, indeed, his judgment seems to have been so unstable that it reflected the views of the lastcomer. 'It is curious,' Desbordes noted, 'how the over-vivid imagination of this young officer drags him now to one side, now to the other.'[3] Gallieni now embraced Desbordes' own opinion, based on experience in the Senegal valley, that Amadu's empire was doomed, and that France's policy should be, not to support it, but to promote its dissolution. For Desbordes, the only problem concerned the method. His own preference was to parley with Amadu only until the end of the rainy season of 1881; thereafter a strong French force should march on the Tokolor fortress of Mourgoula, install itself on the Niger at Bamako, and incite the subject peoples to revolt. But he scornfully admitted that a country like France — 'which has grown timid as a result of wishing to be prudent' — might prefer to postpone the conflict a little longer, moving pacifically on Bamako, and avoiding any attack on Mourgoula. The idea of taking the

[1] cf. Pietri, *op. cit.*, pp. 140–7, 263–70.
[2] *MMC*, Sénégal IV/73/c, Amadu to Governor (rec'd. 12 May 1881); Galliéni, *Voyage . . .*, pp. 455–7; Pietri, *op. cit.*, p. 238.
[3] *MMC*, Sénégal IV/73 bis, Desbordes to Governor, 1 April 1881.

Tokolor alliance seriously, even temporarily, seemed unacceptable to Desbordes.[1]

Brière de l'Isle, however, who handed over the government of
Senegal before receiving this report, returned to France a firm
advocate of trusting Amadu and carrying out the treaty of
Nango.[2] This view prevailed in Paris only until the text of that
treaty arrived. The Colonial Department — where a new
bureau had recently been formed to deal with the affairs of the
Upper Senegal and Niger — took a more literal and legalistic
view of the terms than Gallieni, and demurred at those articles
which seemed to preclude aid to the Mandinkas and Bambaras
and to require the demolition of the forts of Bafoulabé and
Kita.[3] So another French treaty with the Tokolors remained
unimplemented.

Nevertheless, the apparently inevitable conflict was averted
for nearly ten years, for the French advance was diverted
southwards towards Bouré, Sankaran and Wassulu, territories
on the upper Niger beyond Amadu's control. Although these
were believed to be populous and prosperous countries — their
caravan trade in gold and produce was well-known — the
immediate reason for going there was to meet the supposed
British menace. The rumours which Gallieni had heard at
Nango soon grew louder and more insistent, speaking even of
2,000 troops with forty British officers marching on Futa Jalon.[4]
But once headed southwards of Bamako the French came
quickly into collision with Samori, whose power was expanding
in these countries and was already being felt north of the Niger.
The first conflict occurred in February 1882; and though the
French made several attempts to co-operate with Samori, relations were more frequently hostile. But Amadu and Samori were
also rivals, politically and as religious leaders; about 1882 their
antagonism became open.[5] Rather than ally himself with

---

[1] *MMC*, Sénégal IV/73/b, Desbordes to Governor, 9 April 1881.

[2] *MMC*, Sénégal IV/73/b, de l'Isle to M.M.C., 4 May 1881.

[3] *MMC*, Sénégal III/10 bis/b, Notes for the Minister, 19 May, 15 June,
30 Nov. 1881.

[4] *MMC*, Sénégal IV/73 bis, Desbordes report, pp. 484–5; cf. *Voyage* . . . ,
pp. 526–9.

[5] Pietri, *op. cit.*, p. 397.

Samori, Amadu preferred to ignore French encroachments on his frontiers and maintain a somewhat uneasy truce with them. When Gallieni returned to the Sudan in 1886 he was again attracted by the possibilities of a Tokolor alliance.[1]

The Gouldsbury expedition

What reality was there in this supposed British menace on the upper Niger? So far as the authorities in London were concerned, very little. Colonial Office officials, reading of the new French policies in the *Journal Officiel*, regarded them with amused curiosity, mingled with some envy of a government that could obtain parliamentary credits for such extravagant schemes. When a French review spoke of reaching the markets of Hausaland through Senegal, Kimberley commented complacently, 'We shall get to the Hausa country via Lagos long before the French.'[2] But Rowe, on leave in London, saw the danger that French control of less remote areas might interrupt Sierra Leone's caravan trade with the Niger, and restrict its future development. He could not hope to obtain money to compete with the French, nor even to follow up the general professions of amity which he had received from Aguibou and Samori.[3] But the Gambia's Treasury contained a surplus of over £19,000, and on 20 August 1880 Rowe proposed to finance a geographical and political expedition up the Gambia river, to return to Freetown by way of Futa Jalon and Falaba. This was a somewhat questionable attempt to make one colony serve the interests of another; as Hemming at once perceived, Sierra Leone's trade might gain by this mission, but the Gambia itself could expect little commercial development until order and security had been forcibly restored in territories much nearer to Bathurst. But the proposal appealed to Kimberley; and Rowe spent his leave planning details of an expedition to be undertaken by V. S. Gouldsbury, Administrator of the Gambia, during the coming dry season. Rowe arranged for messengers from the Freetown Aborigines Department to be

[1] J. S. Galliéni, *Deux Campagnes au Soudan Français* (Paris, 1891) pp. 618 ff.
[2] C.O. 87/116, minute by Kimberley on F.O. to C.O., 4 Aug. 1880.
[3] See above pp. 244–6 and p. 259 n.

sent ahead to prepare the Alimami of Futa Jalon for Gouldsbury's arrival; and took much care in selecting unusual presents
for distribution at Labé, Timbo and Falaba, hoping to stimulate
new consumer demands which could later be gratified at
Freetown. Gouldsbury's instructions, as finalized in December
1880, were largely Rowe's work; they envisaged the conclusion
of treaties of peace, friendship and commerce over a wide area,
but the most important would be with Futa Jalon.[1]

Rowe's hope of raising permanent barriers against French
expansion were disappointed. Friendship and commerce were
to be the aims of Gouldsbury's diplomacy, but exclusive control
was being more purposefully sought by France. Perhaps the
outcome was pre-determined. A zealous emissary might have
raised more effective obstacles in the French path, but Gouldsbury, though an old comrade of Rowe's in the Ashanti war, was
displeased with the instructions his superior had imposed upon
him; having hoped to be allowed much more freedom of action,
he began his journey in a despondent frame of mind, in which
he was fully confirmed by subsequent experiences.[2] His report
of his journey, which lasted from 22 January until 21 April 1881,
was full of difficulties with carriers and guides, of endless
frustrating palavers with petty chiefs, of losses from smallpox;
he himself was even attacked by a swarm of bees. The upper
Gambia he epitomized as 'an abomination of desolation',
showing little sign of life or hope of trade; he failed to reach
Falaba; and his report on Futa Jalon seems deliberately designed to refute Rowe's expectations. The whole region,
Gouldsbury reported, had far smaller economic potentialities
than it had become usual to suggest. Its population was sparse,
stationary, and technically backward; it was indeed fortunate
that British manufacturers and merchants were not dependent
upon 'the El Dorado of West African commerce'.[3] His report
confirmed Hemming's old opinion that 'the trade of the Gambia

---

[1] C.O. 87/116, Rowe to C.O., 20 Aug. 1880 and minutes; Rowe to C.O.,
23 Dec. 1880; P.P., 1881, LXV, Correspondence Relating to the Recent
Expedition to the Upper Gambia under Administrator V. S. Gouldsbury.
C. 3065, No. 5, C.O. to Gouldsbury, 17 Dec. 1880.

[2] C.O. 87/117, Gouldsbury to Herbert, 21 Jan. 1881 and minutes.

[3] C. 3065, No. 17, Gouldsbury to Kimberley, 22 June 1881.

is never likely to be of much value, and that to expend money in trying to foster and increase it would only be throwing it away'.[1] And although Gouldsbury did sign a general treaty of trade and friendship with Alimami Ibrahima Suri of Futa Jalon on 30 March 1881, Sierra Leone proved unable to draw much advantage from it.

The French and Futa Jalon, 1881–2

Gouldsbury's journey, prompted by Rowe's desire for a counter-demonstration against French policy, had the effect of accelerating French penetration of Futa Jalon. Since Faidherbe had sent Lieutenant Lambert to visit the Alimamies in 1860,[2] many Frenchmen had regarded this Islamic upland state, with its relatively temperate climate and its reputed mineral resources, as part of Senegal's legitimate sphere of influence. Faidherbe himself had seen that its position in relation to the various caravan routes from the upper Niger to the coast made it an essential link between the main axis of Senegalese development and the auxiliary route which he wished to develop in the southern rivers. Rowe's message to the Alimami in 1879, the first sign of active British interest since 1873, worried many Frenchmen on the coast. In 1880, while d'Elteil was unsuccessfully proposing an expedition to Timbo,[3] a pretentious Marseillais adventurer in a tartan *boubou* was already in Timbo. This man, Aimé Olivier, in the highly romanticized account of his journey which he published in 1882,[4] made great profession of French patriotism; but this was not readily credited by the Colonial Department. Olivier, who had capital invested in a factory at Bulama, was believed to be acting solely in the interest of his own trade; it seemed curious that he went to Timbo by way of the Rio Grande, with the co-operation of the Portuguese government, and that on his return he received the Portuguese

[1] C.O. 87/117, minutes on above, 26 July, 1881.
[2] Colonel Lambert, 'Voyage dans le Fouta Djallon', *Bulletin de la Société Languedocienne de Géographie*, 1889, pp. 1–28.
[3] Above, pp. 246–7.
[4] Olivier de Sanderval, *De l'Atlantique au Niger par le Foutah-Djallon* (Paris, 1882); p. 33 of the 2nd edition (1883) for the tartan *boubou*.

title of Comte de Sanderval (a district in the Grande valley).[1] Olivier claimed that during his stay at Timbo (which he was constrained to prolong for nearly three months) Alimami Ibrahima Suri granted him a concession to build a railway from the coast, and that this might usefully be prolonged to Dinguiray; but next year the Alimami denied having signed any such treaty.[2] Certainly, Olivier's escapade had no immediate political significance.

But in 1881 the French government moved towards the Futa Jalon; news of the Gouldsbury mission, misinterpreted as the beginning of a British forward policy, led them to seek the credits that had seemed unnecessary in 1880. Dr. Bayol, an army surgeon who had accompanied Gallieni as far as Bamako, and an ardent supporter of French expansion, received instructions in France on 12 March 1881; on 17 May he left Boké, accompanied initially by Verminck's agent Moustier.[3] In July Bayol secured the signatures of Ibrahima Suri, of Hamadu (the Alimami now exercising power) and of other leading men, to two documents which, he claimed, established France's position to the exclusion of Britain. The first, in the form of a letter, granted France possession of their territories on the seaboard, including the Pongos and Mellacourie; the second was a treaty of twelve articles, placing Futa Jalon itself under French protection, and authorizing Frenchmen to trade there to the exclusion of all other nations.[4]

These documents can hardly be accepted at Bayol's own

---

[1] *MMC*, Sénégal III/15/a, Note pour le Directeur, 28 Jan. 1882. But by 1889 the Colonial department accepted Olivier as a patriotic Frenchman, and agreed that he might use his Portuguese title. (M.M.C. to M.A.E., 4 Oct. 1889.)

[2] *MAE*, Afrique 50, M.M.C. to M.A.E., 25 July 1881, encl. Olivier, 1, 4 July; C. 3065, pp. 12, 31.

[3] *MMC*, Sénégal III/11/c, Bayol to Governor, 16 May 1881; cf. J. Bayol, 'La France au Fouta-Djalon', *Revue des Deux Mondes*, 15 Dec. 1882. On p. 907 of this article Bayol suggests that the Portuguese as well as the British were planning a mission to Futa Jalon. See also E. Noirot, *A travers le Fouta-Diallon et le Bambouc* (Paris, n.d. [1885]).

[4] *MAE*, Afrique 50, Bareste to M.A.E., 6 Aug. 1881. The letter is reproduced in A. Terrier and C. Mourey, *op. cit.*, pp. 130–1; the treaty in E. Rouard de Card, *Les Traités de protectorat . . .* (Paris, 1897) pp. 205–7.

valuation. Firstly, the theocratic suzerainty which the Alimamies claimed on the seaboard had not previously impeded
France from dealing with the local chiefs as if they were independent. The letter thus represents primarily an acknowledg-
ment by Bayol of the Alimamies' claims, intended to placate
their pride, and only secondarily to secure an additional title to
the coast which might impress the legalistic British. Secondly,
the grant of exclusive trading rights appears a clear violation of
Ibrahima Suri's treaty with Gouldsbury a few weeks earlier.
Bayol tried to justify it on two apparently inconsistent grounds.[1]
He claimed that, since power in Futa Jalon alternated between
two Alimamies, treaties required the signature of both, whereas
Gouldsbury had obtained only that of Ibrahima Suri. On
European principles of jurisprudence at least, this seems a
dubious argument; since Ibrahima Suri actually wielded power
during 1881 his signature was the effective one,[2] though Bayol
was doubtless prudent to obtain the signature of the 'king to
come'. This weak argument was reinforced by the claim that
Ibrahima Suri had sent a letter to Freetown denouncing his
treaty with Britain, on the grounds that Gouldsbury had
liberated two slaves on his way to the coast. But Bayol cites only
hearsay evidence for the despatch of this letter, and it does not
seem to have reached Freetown; the Alimamies continued to
draw their British stipends until 1895.

The third and most important objection to Bayol's claims is
that the Alimamies clearly had no intention of accepting a
genuine French protectorate. When the Arabic texts were
scrutinized in Paris it emerged that, while the text of the letter
corresponded fairly well with the French version, the treaty
contained no reference to the exclusion of other nations, and
spoke, not of a French protectorate, but rather of an intimate
alliance uniting the two states.[3] This ambiguity was doubtless

[1] *MAE*, Afrique 50, Rouvier to Gambetta, 26 Jan. 1882; Afrique 84, Note
by Bayol, 9 Nov. 1883.

[2] Sanderval, *op. cit.*, p. 179 takes this view, though this is not a particularly
authoritative opinion.

[3] *MAE*, Afrique 50 ff., 368, 411–14, translator's notes. The Arabic word
used was *amenet*.

K*

accepted by Bayol out of ignorance of Arabic rather than duplicity; but the treaty, though it might have served to bar a British protectorate, had one been planned, certainly gave France no effective authority in Futa Jalon. This Bayol quickly discovered when he prepared to leave.

Bayol's original intention was to proceed from Timbo to Falaba, in the hope of closing the last caravan route from Freetown to the Niger; but Ibrahima Suri would not agree to let him pass through territory held by his revolted subjects, the Houbous.[1] Bayol then proposed instead to return to the Senegal through Dinguiray, visiting Aguibou (the brother of Amadu of Ségou); but this too was forbidden. Futa Jalon had not welcomed the rise of the Tokolor empire, which had weakened its own religious and political authority, and the Alimamies were on hostile terms with Aguibou. They feared that if France adopted a pro-Tokolor policy she might ally with Aguibou and attack Futa Jalon from the rear. So Bayol eventually took the direct route to the Senegal through Bambouk, accompanied by four ambassadors from Timbo, who were doubtless detailed to prevent any change of route. On his way he signed seven more identical treaties of protection, thus completing a chain of paper claims as far as the Senegal valley.[2]

Bayol reached Medina on 17 November, full of enthusiasm for his achievements. Desbordes, more realistically, commented that he seemed to have brought back just another treaty, and that more like an alliance than a protectorate.[3] Nevertheless, the treaty of Timbo was warmly welcomed in Paris, and the Fula ambassadors were received by Gambetta, the new Prime Minister.[4] Treaties with African states were not normally submitted to the Chambers, or given any more formal ratification

---

[1] On the Houbous, see Bayol, *loc. cit.*, pp. 923–8.

[2] *MAE*, Afrique 50, Bayol to Cloué, 24 Sept. 1881; Treaties with Beledugu, 26 Oct.; Sirimani, 1 Nov.; Killa, 3 Nov.; Kamana, 5 Nov.; Makhana and Kofé, 8 Nov.; Tambaoura, 8 Nov., Niagala and Sirimania, 13 Nov. 1881.

[3] *MMC*, Sénégal, III/11/c, Bayol to Desbordes, etc., 19 Nov. 1881, with minutes by Desbordes; Desbordes to Governor, 19 Nov. 1881.

[4] *MAE*, Afrique 84, Note by Bayol, 9 Nov. 1883; cf. Noirot, *op. cit.*, pp. 1–10.

than a simple Ministerial decision; but since this one opposed a decisive check to British designs, it was judged appropriate to publicize it by a Presidential Decree. But the Ministry for Foreign Affairs, observing the reference to exclusive commercial rights, then had second thoughts, and pointed out that such an affront to British interests might be judged a violation of the *status quo* which it had been agreed to observe during the Sierra Leone negotiations.[1]

The reply was marked by a new note of impatient anglophobia. During the Gambetta ministry, the colonial directorate had been transferred from the Ministry of the Marine to the Ministry of Commerce, which was headed by Maurice Rouvier. His reply denied that the treaty gave Britain any grounds for protest, and roundly asserted that its exclusive claims were fully consistent with the principles of French African policy. Britain's attachment to the principles of free trade was hypocritical, and bore no relation to her colonial practice; the treaty should therefore be ratified without regard to her reactions. This outburst was probably influenced by Rouvier's Marseillais friends with interests in the area; but it coincided with other signs that those responsible for French colonial policy were becoming impatient with the conventions and courtesies which the diplomatists sought to observe in their defence of French African interests.[2]

[2]

The National African Company and the development of Anglo-French rivalry in the lower Niger

The French advances in the Senegambian region were almost entirely the work of servants of the French state, even when they did not remain under the complete control of Paris. Meanwhile British influence was continuing to develop on the lower Niger,

[1] *MAE*, Afrique 50, M.M.C. to M.A.E., 10 Nov.; M.A.E. to Ministry of Commerce and Colonies, 23 Nov., 12 Dec. 1881.

[2] *MAE*, Afrique 50, Ministry of Commerce and Colonies to M.A.E., 26 Jan. 1882.

largely through the exertions of private traders. This region seemed to offer a good example of trade advancing as the reformers of 1865 had hoped, without the encumbering protection of colonial settlements — though not without government protection altogether. Through the great palm-oil trading areas around the delta, traders from Liverpool, Glasgow, and London were handling produce worth something like one million pounds annually.[1] But by the early 1880's two new developments suggested that traditional government attitudes towards this informal empire of commerce might be growing obsolete. The British up-river trade had been more strongly organized and now represented a graver challenge to the delta merchants; and, even more serious, foreign traders and governments were interesting themselves in this region, where the British had so far faced little competition.

*   *   *   *   *

During the 1870's the attempt to develop British trade up the Niger under the protection of Nupe, which W. H. Simpson had inaugurated in 1871, had some limited success. Collaboration with British traders was in many ways attractive to Emir Masaba. During most of the century his country had been troubled by a series of civil wars, fought originally to transfer power to Fulani rulers recognizing the suzerainty of Gwandu, but degenerating into faction fights among the descendants of the original leader, Mallam Dendo. By 1860 Masaba, the Mallam's son by a Nupe woman, had secured his position as ruler of an organized state; on his death in 1873 he was succeeded fairly peacefully by his nephew Umaru. But both rulers still had internal enemies to deal with, and both desired to extend their frontiers; this gave them a strong interest in securing a supply of European fire-arms for themselves, and in denying these to their rivals.[2] Masaba's terms for admitting and protecting British traders were therefore that they should centralize their business at Egga, under his control, and should not seek to trade with

---

[1] Estimate by C. Livingstone, 1871, cit. Diké, *op. cit.*, p. 198; cf. above, pp. 34-8.

[2] S. F. Nadel, *A Black Byzantium* (Oxford, 1942) pp. 76-83.

districts further inland except through Nupe middlemen. On this basis he and his successors had every interest in encouraging British commerce, for it would contribute powerfully to their military strength.[1]

Yet the commerce which Nupe itself could offer was strictly limited. Apart from ivory, exports of which increased in value from £13,500 in 1871 to £52,000 in 1878, its only product of immediate commercial value was shea-butter, a vegetable fat. In 1878 British traders bought 1,500 tons of this, valued at £58,500. Since Nupe's trade alone would hardly justify the investment of much capital in the steamships and factories needed for a competitive Niger trade, and since they were precluded from going further up-river, traders therefore turned to buy palm-oil at markets like Abo and Onitsha, where prices were much cheaper than in the delta. Laird and Baikie began this practice in 1857; their successors continued it. By 1879 exports of palm-oil from the Niger (as distinct from the delta) were valued at £195,000. Much of this represented a corresponding loss of trade to the African middlemen of the delta and their Liverpool customers. The chiefs of Brass complained with particular fluency, and resumed their practice of attacking steamers engaged in the river trade. The owners of these demanded protection from the Royal Navy, which sent warships into the river each year between 1871 and 1879, and bombarded some of the offending towns with considerable ferocity. This protection was given to a trade which even in 1878 was worth only half as much again as that of the Gambia.[2]

This limited trade was shared among four British firms, three of which were committed to all the expense of maintaining steamers on the river and an independent chain of trading posts running from Akassa on the estuary to Egga on the Niger and Loko on the Benué. (James Pinnock, the only Liverpool house to depart from that city's practice of relying on the delta

---

[1] J. E. Flint, *Sir George Goldie* . . . , pp. 23–5; cf. Diké, *op. cit.*, pp. 206–7.

[2] Flint, *op. cit.*, pp. 25–8 (esp. letter from chiefs of Brass, 7 July 1876); Diké, *op. cit.*, pp. 207–8.

Niger exports 1878, £309,200; Gambia exports, according to 1878 Blue Book, £204,300.

middlemen, had an appreciably smaller interest.) The big three were the old West Africa Company of Manchester, which had close links with the C.M.S. through the Crowther family;[1] Alexander Miller and Brothers of Glasgow (who were also among Ja Ja's earliest supporters); and Holland Jacques of London. In 1875 the latter firm ran into financial difficulties, and turned for help to the well-to-do Manx family of Taubman. Its affairs were taken in hand by a former Engineer officer, George Goldie Taubman, better known by his later name of George Goldie. After flouting all the Victorian conventions during a tempestuous youth, Goldie had found his imagination captured by the African continent, and the possibilities which it offered to his active nature. In 1876, after reconstituting Holland Jacques as the Central African Trading Company, Goldie left for the Niger in company with his brother, with some plan for travelling overland to the Nile. They did not achieve this; but the reorganization of British commerce on the Niger which resulted from their journey was in some ways an even more spectacular stroke. By November 1879 Goldie had succeeded in merging the interests of all four companies into the United African Company, with a nominal capital of £250,000 and obviously monopolistic designs.[2]

This amalgamation was a brilliant piece of business; how Goldie brought it off may never be known. His immediate aim was clearly financial; by eliminating the need for three or four separate trading posts at every market, each attempting to undercut its rivals, profits could be greatly increased. Thus the new Company might hope eventually to raise the capital needed to open regular trading relations with Hausaland. Although such reasoning is basically economic, it does not exclude the patriotic motive, such as Goldie later claimed, 'of adding the region of the Niger to the British Empire';[3] on this psychological question there seems too little evidence for a confident evaluation. But in any case, before either economic or political ends

[1] In 1877 it was reconstituted as the West African Company (Flint, *op. cit.*, pp. 26, 30).

[2] Flint, *op. cit.*, pp. 29–33.

[3] A. F. Mockler-Ferryman, *British Nigeria* (London, 1902) p. 69.

could be achieved, there were other competitors to deal with. There was the old problem of the delta traders; and there was the new factor of French competition.

*　*　*　*　*

Although Faidherbe and some of his successors had appreciated the potential importance of the lower Niger, French traders made no really serious attempt to enter the river until 1878. Capital for commerce in the Bights was not easy to raise in France; those who commanded a little, like Régis and Fabre, followed the Liverpool pattern by seeking secure situations on the coast where good profits might be obtained with a minimum of difficulty and risk. The first Frenchman to establish trade in the Niger was the Comte de Semellé, who had apparently first gone to the coast in 1867;[1] he visited Nupe in 1878, and secured an offer of factory-sites from Umaru, who could doubtless see advantages in commercial competition. Returning to France, Semellé persuaded the established Paris firm of Desprez and Huchet to float a subsidiary company — *Compagnie Française de l'Afrique Equatoriale* — with a capital of half a million francs.[2] This was a modest sum, equivalent to £20,000; nevertheless, when Semellé took the steamer *Adamawa* to the Niger in 1880 he had a most successful season. He not only covered the cost of establishing a chain of factories from Abo into Nupe, with two in the Benué, but claimed to have made sufficient profit to buy two more river steamers. But he encountered opposition from servants of the United African Company, naturally displeased by the early reappearance of competition. One of their steamers threatened to ram the *Adamawa* near Onitsha,[3] and their agents put strong pressure on Umaru to preserve their commercial monopoly in Nupe.[4]

Semellé died on his voyage home; but his success induced Desprez and Huchet to double the capital of C.F.A.E., and to buy a second steamer. As their new Agent-General they pro-

---

[1] E. R. Flegel, *Vom Niger-Benüe* (Leipzig, 1890) p. 53.
[2] Comdt. Mattei, *Bas-Niger, Bénoué, Dahomey* (Grenoble, 1890) pp. 50–1.
[3] *MAE*, Afrique 77, Semellé to Mottez, 20 Sept. 1880.
[4] Flint, *op. cit.*, pp. 36–8.

cured the secondment from the colonial infantry of an energetic Corsican officer, Captain Mattei, who was called off
parade in January 1881 to be offered this mission, 'plus
patriotique que commerciale'. Shortly afterwards the Ministry
for Foreign Affairs appointed him, along with other West
African traders, as an unpaid Consular Agent.[1] The United
African Company now reluctantly and provisionally accepted
the presence of the French; McIntosh, their Agent-General,
made an agreement with Mattei to offer common buying-
prices, not to lure away one another's African employees, and
to give mutual support in conflicts with Africans.[2] Mattei was
not personally anglophobic, and for a time there was some
co-operation. In 1881–2 the civil war was renewed in Nupe, and
the Kede, who controlled all the Niger ferries, seem to have
been willing and anxious to enter into exclusive relations with
France. Nevertheless, Mattei sent his steamer to join with the
U.A.C. in suppressing the rebellion, and in return secured
confirmation of his hitherto rather uncertain status in the Nupe
trade.[3]

But a good deal of friction was inevitable. At Onitsha the
French benefited from the bitterness still caused by the destructive British bombardment of 1879; in Nupe they man-
oeuvred to secure permission to open trade up-stream from the
British factories. Mattei visited Paris in 1882 and sought a
government subsidy which might enable the Company to
purchase this privilege. But the government gave nothing; and
though the Company's capital was raised again to 1,500,000
francs, this was not enough to let them compete with the U.A.C.

[1] Mattei, op. cit., p. 1. It is commonly said that Gambetta was personally
responsible for giving governmental support to C.F.A.E. But Gambetta was
not in office at the time of Mattei's secondment and consular appointment,
and was dead by the time the question of further official support for the
Company was discussed in 1883. Goldie told Reuter in 1899 that Gambetta
'pushed' the Senegal Company into the Niger trade in 1882 in order to
prevent the N.A.C. from acquiring a monopoly; (D. Wellesley and S.
Gwynn, *Sir George Goldie* (London, 1934) pp. 19–20); even this sounds unconvincing, though Rouvier may have provided a link with Verminck. But
I have found no evidence connecting Gambetta with C.F.A.E.

[2] Mattei, op. cit., p. 51.

[3] ibid., pp. 87–8; Flint, op. cit., pp. 38–9.

in delivering presents in Nupe.[1] Mattei's chief success was a treaty of 1882 with Amadu of Loko, which held out good hopes for developing trade on the Benué.[2]

Nevertheless, C.F.A.E. had succeeded well enough to attract a second French company into the Niger. During the 1870's Verminck's trade on the coast between Senegal and Sierra Leone had prospered so greatly that he was able to acquire five oil-mills in Marseille; he also began the conversion of his sailing-ships to steam, with the object of establishing a scheduled service to West Africa in competition with the two established British shipping lines.[3] In 1881 Verminck transferred his African interests to the new *Compagnie du Sénégal et de la Côte Occidentale de l'Afrique*, with his son-in-law, F. Bohn, as Managing Director; the aim was not only to expand its own trade but to provide shipping and credit facilities which would encourage the development of small African business-men as clients of the new Company.[4] The Senegal Company began to trade in the Niger in 1882 (employing mostly non-Frenchmen, as Verminck usually preferred to do); by 1883 they had founded about twenty factories and were employing two steamers in the river.[5]

It was probably the appearance of this second French company and its African clients which determined Goldie to try to eliminate French competition; Verminck, if he chose to concentrate on the Niger, would be able to mobilize far more capital than the C.F.A.E. From the start, Goldie had believed that monopoly was essential to the profitable development of the Niger trade (which in 1883 still barely exceeded £300,000 in value). Any breach in the company's *de facto* monopoly would greatly weaken its commercial position; but a *French* stake in the Niger could eventually bring in the French government, with even worse results.

So Goldie now began to plan to assume political control of

[1] Mattei, *op. cit.*, pp. 71 ff., 51–6; *MAE*, Afrique 77, Ministère de la Guerre to M.A.E., 25 March 1882, encl. précis of Mattei's reports.

[2] *MAE*, Angleterre (Freetown) 53, Mattei to Bareste, 29 Sept. 1882.

[3] P. Masson (ed.) *Les Bouches-du-Rhône* . . . , Tome 8, p. 184, Tome 9, pp. 386, 398–9.

[4] *MAE*, Afrique 57, Report by Capt. Penfentany, 28 Feb. 1882.

[5] *MAE*, Afrique 86, Report by Cavalié, 29 Aug. 1883.

the lower Niger in the name of the British government. The task which he claimed to have set himself, the penetration of Hausaland, would require enormous overhead expenditures that could not be immediately remunerative: communications would need to be developed, trade-routes protected, and almost certainly battles would have to be fought. The administrative framework necessary for such expansion would not be willingly provided by the British government beyond the area accessible to naval coercion; the Company would therefore have to provide it from its own trading profits. This would need a Royal Charter — similar to that granted to the British North Borneo Company in November 1881 — sanctioning its commercial monopoly and conferring quasi-governmental powers. With this end in view the United African Company was reorganized in June 1882 as the National African Company, with power to apply for Chartered privileges. Its nominal capital was increased (mainly by the book-keeping device of 'watering') to £1,000,000; Lord Aberdare, a former Liberal Minister, was recruited as Chairman; Joseph Chamberlain, President of the Board of Trade, invested £950. Late in 1882 one of its directors, J. F. Hutton (the Manchester merchant whose contacts with Marseille had helped to stop the Gambia exchange of 1876)[1] went to Paris for a first attempt to buy out the rival French companies' interest on the Niger. If amicable business negotiation failed, Goldie was preparing to apply stronger pressure.[2]

[3]

French Politics and African Problems, 1881–3

Despite the advance of the military frontier in Senegal, and the entry of French commerce into the lower Niger, the political climate in Paris was still essentially unfavourable for African expansion. Even the first ministry of Jules Ferry, which lasted from September 1880 until November 1881, marked no striking change in this respect. It is true that his government undertook the invasion of Tunis, and on 12 May 1881 imposed a treaty of

---

[1] cf. above, pp. 190–5.   [2] Flint, *op. cit.*, pp. 40–6.

protection upon the Bey. But this expansion was determined partly by the belief that a political advance in the Mediterranean would raise French prestige in Europe, partly by pressure from Algerian interests. Ferry himself was not a prime mover in this question; his main interests were still in educational problems, and many critics resented the way he dissembled his government's aims in Tunis for the sake of Parliamentary tactics. Only after leaving office did Ferry begin to reflect on the advantages which imperial expansion might have for the long-term interests of France. The debates on the Tunisian protectorate largely reflected partisan alignments and revealed no new enthusiasm for empire as such; indeed, the familiar reluctance to accept its responsibilities and its set-backs was strengthened, for many radicals, by suspicions that private business interests had exerted unjustifiable influence upon French policy.[1]

Still, the Tunisian protectorate was accepted; and many of those who voted against it did so for reasons of domestic politics rather than anti-imperialist principle.[2] And Gambetta, who succeeded Ferry in November 1881, emerged as a significantly strong supporter of the Tunisian protectorate. His earlier reservations were apparently overcome by Courcel, Political Director at the Ministry for Foreign Affairs, who argued that the expedition would strengthen France's prestige and power in Europe. As Prime Minister, Gambetta soon began to talk in unfamiliar terms about conserving, strengthening and extending France's colonial patrimony, and to foreshadow a more active French policy outside Europe — most notably in Egypt.[3]

---

[1] Two recent views of Ferry's attitude are T. F. Power, Jr., *Jules Ferry and the Renaissance of French Imperialism* (N.Y., 1944); C. A. Julien, 'Jules Ferry' in P. Renouvin, *Les Politiques d'Expansion Impérialiste* (Paris, 1949); cf. E. M. Carroll, *French Public Opinion and Foreign Affairs* (N.Y., 1931) pp. 88–90. The important work of J. Ganiage, *Les Origines du Protectorat français en Tunisie* (Paris, 1959) was received only when this book was in proof.

[2] Power, *op. cit.*, pp. 56–71.

[3] Julien, *loc. cit.*, p. 40; cf. G. Hanotaux, *Histoire de la France Contemporaine*, Vol. IV (Paris, 1908) pp. 650–1, 665, 778–9; D. Halévy and E. Pillias, *Lettres de Gambetta* (Paris, 1938) Nos. 472, 496; Gambetta to Naquet, 19 April 1881; Gambetta to Léonie Léon, 9 Nov. 1881.

Gambetta's sincere intention was to pursue this policy, as far as possible, in harmony with Britain; indeed, in Tunis British acquiescence had been a necessary condition of French expansion. But in many parts of the world defence of French colonial and commercial interests was more likely to imply conflict with Britain. Envisaging the possibility of a Gambetta ministry two years earlier, the British Ambassador had written:

> 'He is changeable and impulsive — not unlikely to aim at producing striking effects by separate action on the part of France abroad — nor incapable of taking strong and sudden measures at the instigation of French holders of Egyptian bonds or any other set of people who might get round him. In short, he would most likely keep foreign nations on the *qui vive*.'[1]

This prophecy was to be most strikingly vindicated by Gambetta's policy in Egypt; but on a smaller scale it applied in West Africa also.

Among several alterations which Gambetta introduced into the ministerial structure was the elevation of the colonial directorate into an under-secretaryship of State, and its attachment to the Ministry of Commerce (which simultaneously shed its responsibility for agriculture to a new and separate ministry). Gambetta's friend and mouthpiece, Joseph Reinach, saw three purposes behind this change: it reflected an intention to restore France's national confidence by a spirited and purposeful national policy, it removed the colonies from naval control so that they might be administered on principles more similar to those accepted in France itself, and it allowed the Ministry of Commerce scope to develop 'the most natural outlets of the nation's industry'.[2] The first Under-Secretary was Félix Faure, a shipper, formerly President of the Chamber of Commerce in Le Havre, later to be President of the Republic. The Minister of Commerce was Maurice Rouvier. Reinach attributed to both men the intentions of persuading France of the economic potentialities of her existing colonies, and of

---

[1] *S.P.*, A. 8, No. 15, Lyons to Salisbury, 4 March 1879.
[2] J. Reinach, *Le Ministère Gambetta* (Paris, 1884) pp. 190–6.

expanding those colonies further in the still open field of Africa.[1]

Certainly a new spirit seemed to enter the West African correspondence during the brief reign of Rouvier and Faure: a more exacting insistence on French rights, a greater sympathy with the claims of provincial business-men, sometimes a positively aggressive note. They alarmed their officials by advocating open and uninhibited exploitation of France's treaty rights at Porto Novo and in Futa Jalon; they even seemed anxious to re-open the question of the Scarcies as part of an actively anti-British policy.[2] In January 1882 Rouvier, alarmed by signs that Portugal was co-operating with Britain to resist France in the Congo, seemed ready to offer her concessions on the borders of Portuguese Guinea in hopes of breaking up this threatened combination and producing 'a common entente to contain the ambitions of our common rival'.[3]

The fall of the Gambetta ministry at the end of January 1882 temporarily checked this tendency towards what Rouvier had called an 'accentuation' of African policy. Under a new Frey-cinet ministry the Colonial Department was restored to the control of the Ministry of the Marine, and on 9 August 1882 it temporarily reverted from the status of an Under-Secretaryship of State to that of a *direction*.[4] For the time being there was no overture to Portugal; the Sierra Leone boundary agreement, which Rouvier had wished to renounce, was signed on 28 June 1882.[5] The Futa Jalon treaties were not published until 1885 (though it became publicly known that Bayol had signed treaties of some sort there).[6] All this seemed to reflect a return to the conciliatory attitude traditionally favoured by the Foreign

---

[1] *ibid.*, pp. 196–9; M. Blanchard, 'Correspondance de Félix Faure touchant les Affaires Coloniales', *Revue d'Histoire des Colonies françaises*, XLII, 1955.

[2] cf. above, p. 271; below, pp. 289, 295–6.

[3] *MAE*, Afrique 50, Rouvier to Gambetta, 24 Jan. 1882.

[4] A. Duchêne, *La Politique Coloniale de la France* (Paris, 1928) pp. 240 ff.

[5] *MAE*, Afrique 77, M.M.C. to M.A.E., 25 March 1882; Afrique 57, M.A.E. to M.M.C., 3 April 1882.

[6] *MMC*, Sénégal IV/71/a, M.A.E. to M.M.C., 13 Oct. 1885; Bayol, *loc. cit.*, p. 906.

Ministry. But before the end of 1882 the Egyptian question was making it increasingly difficult for French politicians to be conciliatory towards Great Britain.

The impact of the Egyptian question

Since 1876 the French and British governments had imposed, by a series of expedients, a Dual Control over Egyptian public finances — and so, indirectly, over the Khedive's administration. Their immediate aim was to secure the financial claims of Egypt's foreign creditors, who were largely French or British; but each government was aware of possessing important strategic or political interests in Egypt, which were always more likely to produce conflict than co-operation between the two controlling governments. Yet when Egyptian reactions against foreign control, led by nationalist army officers, seemed likely to establish a less compliant government in Cairo under the influence of Colonel Arabi, Britain and France had still a common interest in opposition. Gambetta seemed prepared to envisage the re-establishment of Anglo-French influence by a combined occupation; but Gladstone's government and Gambetta's own successors hesitated to go so far. In May 1882 they sent British and French warships to Alexandria, hoping that their mere presence might strengthen the authority of the Khedive (and his Controllers) against the army and the nationalists. The result was the opposite; Arabi continued to gain support, and on 11 June about fifty foreigners were killed in riots in Alexandria. British representatives on the spot now feared that, failing some more decisive foreign intervention, a xenophobic government might emerge, which would prove either impotent or disinclined to protect foreign investments and the Suez Canal. Gladstone was thus forced to reverse his policy. On 11 July Admiral Seymour's warships bombarded Alexandria, and a military expedition was somewhat tardily prepared. In September 1882 this force occupied the Suez Canal, defeated Arabi at Tel-el-Kebir, and entered Cairo on the 15th.

The Freycinet ministry had been held back by its apprehension of strong public hostility to intervention in Egypt, but became worried by the growing possibility of a solely British occupation. In late July Freycinet moved tentatively towards the idea of an Anglo-French expedition with the limited objective of occupying the Canal,[1] but on 29 July his government was refused credits in the Chamber by 416 votes to 75. This huge majority included some who felt that Freycinet's Egyptian policy had been too timorous, but more who were reacting against the diversion of resources from Europe which any expedition would have involved. This reaction, not initially anti-British, quickly became so, as it emerged that the 'temporary' British occupation was likely to last for an indefinitely extended period, and to imply sole British control of Egyptian administration. On 28 October Lyons presented proposals for the abolition of the Dual Control; Duclerc, head of the French caretaker government, commented justly that these amounted simply to the abolition of the French Controller.[2] Nevertheless, on 3 January 1883, the British government announced its intention of carrying through these and other changes in administration; Duclerc replied by reserving full 'freedom of action'. This freedom was in practice to be used to obstruct British rule in Egypt by diplomatic and administrative means. And in this obstruction, French governments were increasingly sustained by influential currents of public opinion. Charges of deliberate perfidy were publicly levelled against Gladstone's government, and very widely credited; a sense that France had been duped released a new tide of anglophobia, which for more than twenty years placed formidable obstacles in the way of any public collaboration between the two governments.

As Anglo-French relations entered this period of sharp decline, Jules Ferry formed his second government, which was to prove the most durable since 1870, on 21 February 1883. Ferry had become more interested in colonial problems since 1880–1; faced with the need to justify his Tunisian policy he had, as a good positivist, made some attempt to do so by reference to general principles.[3] Yet his 'colonial doctrine' still consisted of

---

[1] D.D.F., IV, 478, Lyons to Freycinet, 26 July 1882.

[2] D.D.F., IV, 551, Duclerc to Tissot, Pte., 28 Oct. 1882.

[3] See his preface to the re-publication of his Tunisian speeches, *Affaires de Tunisie*, ed. A. Rambaud, Paris, 1882.

ex post facto rationalizations of decisions taken pragmatically, in response to the reports from the frontiers — or to the Deputies in the ante-room. Ferry's most comprehensive attempt to develop a general justification of colonial expansion was not made until 28 July 1885, in an attempt to justify policies which had by then caused his catastrophic fall from office.[1] His government's policy in Asia and Africa evolved slowly and gradually; no other type of problem, he declared, had such need 'de réflexion et de mesure'.[2]

Ferry's policies were open to influence by his political supporters, including former followers of Gambetta who moved closer to Ferry after their own leader's death on 31 December 1882. In September 1883 Faure returned to his former post as Under-Secretary for the Colonies; though constitutionally he could act only on behalf of the Minister of the Marine, he soon acquired the right of signing departmental correspondence, and began to exercise a growing influence on colonial policy. And in October 1884 Rouvier again became Minister of Commerce, though now without direct colonial responsibilities. Often, as in Indo-China, Ferry deemed it necessary to take indirect approaches to colonial expansion, in order to circumvent those prejudices which — as Freycinet's difficulties over Egypt had shown — still possessed many Deputies. But gradually government and public alike found themselves more readily accepting arguments in favour of overseas initiatives.

The origin of the Congo question

One of the first African questions to catch the attention of the French public was that of the Congo. The international importance of this river had been transformed when H. M. Stanley arrived at its mouth in August 1877 after his great transcontinental journey. Hitherto the coast of this part of Africa had seemed to offer narrowly limited possibilities of commerce; Stanley showed that the Congo could provide many thousand miles of navigable waterway through the unexplored heart of

---

[1] *Discours et Opinions de Jules Ferry*, ed. P. Robiquet, Tome V (Paris, 1897) pp. 172–220.

[2] *ibid.*, p. 154. Speech of 27 March 1884.

Africa. All that seemed necessary to develop them was to find some usable route from the west coast to the area of Stanley Pool which would by-pass the unnavigable sections near the mouth of the river.

Two active claimants came forward to seek an option on the Congo basin. One was Leopold II of Belgium, a controversial figure whose aspirations and ambitions, already directed towards central Africa, were by 1878 concentrated upon securing control of the Congo through Stanley's agency.[1] His chief rival was French. While Stanley was still making his original journey an Italian-born officer in the French Navy, Savorgnan de Brazza, travelled further up the Ogoué than any previous traveller, crossed the watershed to the Alima, and descended that river to a point which subsequently proved to be only five days' journey from its confluence with the Congo. In 1879 de Brazza learned that Stanley was planning to return to the Congo in the service of Leopold's International Association; realizing that he had himself had a solution to the problem of access to the navigable river almost in his grasp, he retraced his steps along the Ogoué. On 10 September 1880 he obtained the signature of the ruler of the Bateke to a single-clause treaty ceding his hereditary territorial rights to France, together with a site for a military post on the northern shore of Stanley Pool. Here, at the future Brazzaville, de Brazza hoisted the French flag, posting a guard under the Senegalese serjeant Malamine. Stanley, arriving in July 1881, could only reply by asserting equivalent claims at Leopoldville, on the opposite shore.[2]

These manoeuvres, initially carried out by both Leopold and the French in the name of geographical science, gradually made other states concerned for their national interests. Britain had earlier declined opportunities of securing claims in the Congo,

[1] There is a useful essay on Leopold, with bibliography, by J. Bruhat, in P. Renouvin et al., Les Politiques d'Expansion Impérialiste (Paris, 1949). His policy has been warmly defended by Father A. Roeykens in Léopold II et l'Afrique, 1855-80 (Académie Royale des Sciences Coloniales, Bruxelles, 1958) and in other volumes of the same series; cf. J. S. Keltie, The Partition of Africa, London, 1895, Chs. 9 and 10.

[2] On de Brazza's rather complicated status, cf. Brunschwig, op. cit., pp. 42-6.

refusing to recognize treaties made by Cameron in the upper basin in 1875, or to accept an offer of Stanley's services in 1877. Disraeli's government wanted no new colonial responsibilities; and established traders, seeing no foreign menace, preferred to remain unprotected and untaxed. But just as this foreign activity began to intensify, British trade in the Congo developed rapidly; by 1884 it was valued at two million pounds, and was said to have quadrupled since 1879.[1] In these conditions a few Britons, including Sir Robert Morier, Minister in Lisbon, began to reconsider an old but hitherto unacceptable expedient: that of recognizing Portuguese claims to the Congo mouth in return for her guarantees of freedom of trade.

Portugal's claims in the Congo went back to the fifteenth century; they had some historical basis, but were never effectively enforced in the nineteenth century, largely because of British fears that her rule might encourage the slave trade. By 1880 this was no longer likely. The two countries might thus find a common interest in resisting French claims, Britain for the sake of her growing commercial and missionary interests, Portugal chiefly out of national pride. When in 1880 and 1881 the Portuguese sought British recognition of their claim, Morier was disposed to concede it. But the British government demanded in return concessions concerning Delagoa Bay in Portuguese East Africa, which Lisbon was reluctant to make. No serious progress was made until the end of 1882.[2]

Portugal's desire for an African agreement with Britain was no secret, but neither was her lack of success.[3] As early as August 1881 the French Ministry of the Marine considered, but rejected, the idea of trying to benefit from her resentment of

---

[1] R. T. Anstey, 'British Trade and Policy in West Central Africa...', *Transactions*, Historical Society of Ghana, III (Achimota, 1957) pp. 50–3.

[2] S. E. Crowe, *The Berlin West African Conference* (London, 1942) pp. 16–17; cf. S. Gwynn and G. M. Tuckwell, *Life of Sir Charles Dilke* (London, 1917) I, p. 418.

[3] A. Roeykens, *La Période Initiale de l'Œuvre Africaine de Léopold II* (Bruxelles, 1957) prints reports from Belgian Ministers in Lisbon on this subject, 9 Oct. 1880 (pp. 158–60); 12 April 1881 (pp. 166–8); 25 May 1881 (p. 170); 25 Jan. 1882 (p. 175).

British demands by proposing a Franco-Portuguese agreement instead.[1] Then, in January 1882, Rouvier formulated his idea of a wider Franco-Portuguese *entente*, whose object would be not only to check Britain but to secure to the French government some of the fruits of de Brazza's heroic journeys in the Congo.[2]

By this time de Brazza was becoming a popular figure in France; when he returned there in June 1882 he got a hero's welcome. He had an attractive public personality, and his proudly patriotic speeches were enthusiastically applauded in French newspapers. These reports were studied with some apprehension in Belgium, Portugal, and Britain.[3] In November 1882 the Bateke treaty was submitted to the Chamber — a procedure intended by the government to distinguish it from the ordinary run of African treaties. It was unanimously approved, amidst applause. The *rapporteur* was Rouvier; though he was careful to suggest that France was extending her markets and her civilizing influence rather than her empire as such, the general tone of much public comment was that of popular imperialism.[4] By March 1883, when de Brazza again left for the Congo, this time as leader of an official expedition with funds for the year of over one and a quarter million francs, there seemed every reason to doubt whether he would confine himself to those scientific enquiries which officially constituted his purpose. Already Frenchmen who felt they had been cheated in Egypt were becoming disposed to seek vicarious compensation overseas, even in tropical Africa.

The Ivory Coast Boundary Commission

The growing interest in colonial problems among French politicians, and the progressive deterioration of Anglo-French relations, meant that ground was lost rather than gained in these

[1] *MMC*, Afrique VI/28/a, M.M.C. to M.A.E., 25 Aug. 1881.

[2] cf. above p. 281, *MAE*, Afrique 58, 30 Dec. 1881; Afrique 59, Précis of report by Penfentany, made Jan. 1882.

[3] D.D.F. IV, 540, Brin to Duclerc, 7 Oct.; 543, Meneval to Duclerc, 15 Oct. 1882.

[4] *Journal Officiel; Débats (Chambre)* 22 Nov. 1882; *Débats (Sénat)* 29 Nov. 1882.

years in the attempts to solve local disputes on the West African coast. At Porto Novo this was to have serious consequences; but similar effects were experienced at Sierra Leone and even over the relatively minor question of the Ivory Coast boundary. In October 1882 the British government announced that they were at last ready to constitute the Boundary Commission which had been agreed upon two years earlier; at the same time it repeated its request, first made in 1877 but omitted in 1880, that the French should accept the principle that the line be moved three miles westward from the Anglo-Dutch line of 1869. The French refused somewhat sharply, insisting that the Commissioners should confine themselves to locating the line as fixed by existing agreements. The British dropped their request with only slight resentment;[1] but the episode showed a new readiness on the part of the French to conserve jealously their rights on the Ivory Coast. 'Whether we keep these establishments', wrote the Minister of the Marine, 'or whether we wish, later, to exchange them, we have the greatest interest in maintaining their importance and ensuring their prosperity.'[2] Dislère, the new Colonial Director, suggested sending officials and troops to symbolize 'a resumption of official possession'.[3] Verdier's complaints about hostile British activities were now listened to much more seriously; and his employee Bretignère was appointed as one of the French members when the Boundary Commission finally assembled at Assinie in December 1883.[4] All its members took unshakably national points of view, and no agreement could be reached. Nor did either government suggest overriding its Commissioners in order to clear the question out of the way.[5]

[1] C.O. 806/194, No. 36, Lyons to Duclerc, 28 Oct. 1882; No. 43, Challemel-Lacour to Lyons, 28 March 1883; C.O. 96/154, minute by Meade, 25 April 1883; cf. above, pp. 237–9.

[2] *MAE*, Afrique 77, M.M.C. to M.A.E., 12 April, 19 Sept. 1882 and minutes. Afrique 78, M.M.C. to M.A.E., 9 Jan. 1883.

[3] *ibid.*, Report by Dislère, 30 May 1883.

[4] *ibid.*, M.M.C. to M.A.E., 19 May 1883, encl. Verdier, 16 May; Bretignère, *op. cit.*, p. 51.

[5] The lengthy proceedings are recorded in *MAE*, Afrique 79, and C.O. 806/194.

Opposition to the Sierra Leone Boundary Agreement

The agreement reached in 1881 by the Commissioners on the Sierra Leone boundary also had a rough passage. Verminck and other Marseille merchants continued to resist the proposal to leave Britain in control of the Great Scarcies — not merely because of the direct injury to their trade, but also on the grounds that Britain might use the caravan route from that river to forestall France in the region of the Niger source. Their opposition almost succeeded when their ally Rouvier became Minister of Commerce. At this point the British were demurring — on formal and somewhat pedantic grounds — to a clause in the draft agreement binding them to recognize French rights to both banks of the river Nunez;[1] in this trivial point Rouvier saw a possible pretext for reopening the whole Scarcies question. At his personal direction the colonial directorate drafted a letter to Gambetta suggesting that France ought to withdraw her concession of the Scarcies; but though this alone could have wrecked the whole agreement it did not satisfy Rouvier. An even stronger version was drafted in his private office, proposing to the astonished Ministry for Foreign Affairs,

'to base ourselves on the new difficulty in order to resume our full freedom of action, and . . . profit from this by a further accentuation of our policy on the West coast of Africa.'[2]

For the first time, the 'tail' of West African commerce was aspiring to wag the diplomatic dog. The objection was dropped as soon as Rouvier left office, and the agreement was signed on 28 June 1882. But its opponents had not finished yet.

The signature of this agreement did not solve France's problems in the rivers. Although a Decree of 12 October 1882 created

[1] France wished Britain to declare that the agreement would not prejudice the rights 'que la France possède au cours du Rio Nunez et au nord de cette rivière'. The British version referred only to 'any rights which may be possessed by France. . . .' Reasons for this difference are explained in a minute by Hemming in C.O. 267/347.

[2] *MMC*, Afrique VI/30/b, Ministry of Commerce to M.A.E., 2 Jan. 1882, drafted in Cabinet du Ministre. Note by Director of Colonies, 25 Feb. 1882; Afrique VI/27/a, cancelled draft.

a non-resident post of Lieutenant-Governor of the *rivières du sud*, France's hold on the whole area remained precarious, effectively confined to the three military posts of Boké, Boffa, and Binty. Attempts to consolidate their influence by interventions in local politics at first only made things worse; within two years fighting was taking place in all three rivers — Nunez, Pongos and Mellacourie — to the great detriment of trade. In the intervening districts, between the Pongos and the Mellacourie, the French tried to fortify their position by treaties, but even where these were obtained they proved of dubious value. Balla Demba of the Kaloum Bagas, who was supposed to have signed a treaty of protection in 1880, disclaimed all knowledge of it in 1884. Bayol, appointed as Lieutenant-Governor tried to invoke the influence of Futa Jalon in France's favour, in accordance with his own treaty of 1881, but with little success.[1] After nearly twenty years in the southern rivers French authority remained tenuous and disorganized.

For this situation, British intrigues provided a convenient excuse. Indeed, after so many years of commercial connections with the rivers, and so much careful and well-informed diplomacy by Lawson, it would be surprising if Sierra Leone had not retained great influence there — and if the local rulers, when faced by inconvenient demands from the insurgent French, had not looked to Freetown in hope of playing off the barbarians one against another. To the harassed French, British designs assumed huge and sinister proportions. In January 1884 the Governor of Senegal (a former official in the colonial directorate) suggested that Britain, having been frustrated in efforts to reach the western Sudan through the Nile valley, was instead scheming to work through Samori in order to forestall French designs on the Niger.[2] But such ingenious hypotheses apart, there was some evidence of continued British influence north of the demarcation line of June 1882.

[1] *MAE*, Afrique 84, esp. M.M.C. to M.A.E., 8 April 1884, encl. Bayol to M.M.C., 6 March 1884; cf. Angleterre (Freetown) 70, Bareste to *MAE*, 14 June 1883.
[2] *MAE*, Afrique 84, M.M.C. to M.A.E., 4 Feb. 1884, encl. Bourdiaux, Jan. 1884.

There was first the case of the Kaloum Bagas; the 1882 agreement did not appease the fears which France conceived in 1880 that the British aimed at control of Konakry. During 1882 French observers were worried by visits which Balla Demba paid to the Isles de Los; and in November 1883 Governor Havelock's secretary spoke of an intention to claim the Timbo peninsula, on which Konakry stands, on the ground that it was surrounded by water at high tide and therefore formed part of the Isles de Los.[1] Nothing came of this ingenious attempt to circumvent the boundary agreement, but it did not increase French confidence in Britain's good faith.

In the Mellacourie the French complained of surreptitious British support for Bokkari. Successive commandants at Binty had tried to reduce the influence of this stubbornly independent man by encouraging claims to independent status on the part of some of his subordinate chiefs and headmen. This, in the opinion of other French observers, was a mistaken policy, based on an underestimate of Bokkari's prestige and influence.[2] Early in 1882 Bokkari took up arms against those whom he considered as revolted vassals; this began a period of wars which ended only with his death in 1885.

Operations could not possibly be contained within the proposed Anglo-French frontier — a line with no valid basis in African politics, which had not even been surveyed upon the ground. As in his earlier campaigns, Bokkari looked for aid to the Temnes of the Scarcies, notably to Alimami Sattan Lahai; the commandants at Binty were convinced that Temne intervention was being encouraged by Creole traders at Kambia (who stood to gain if trade was diverted southwards from the Mellacourie) and also by the Freetown government. By fostering trouble in the Mellacourie, it was argued, the British might hope to persuade France to get rid of that district cheaply in any

[1] *MAE*, Angleterre (Freetown) 53, M.A.E. to Bareste, 10 Aug. 1882; Bareste to M.A.E., 7 Sept. 1882; Angleterre (Freetown) 70, Bareste to M.A.E., 24 Nov. 1883.

[2] *MAE*, Afrique 57, Penfentany to M.M.C., 28 Feb. 1882; Afrique 84, M.M.C. to M.A.E., 10 July 1883; Angleterre (Freetown) 70, Bareste to M.A.E., 27 Aug. 1883.

future exchange negotiation.[1] But Havelock consistently denied all responsibility for the Temne intervention, and, in a long and acrimonious correspondence with the Consul, called upon the French to protect British traders.[2] Several British houses had recently joined Randall and Fisher in the Mellacourie, where they did more business than the French, now represented only by Verminck's new Senegal Company. Thus, by a bitter irony, France was called upon to undertake military operations in her newly-recognized possession for the immediate advantage of British trade.[3]

In these depressing conditions the French began to reconsider their position in the Mellacourie. Admiral Grivel reflected the naval view by advocating withdrawal, and reversion to the British practice of protecting trade by treaties.[4] The Governor of Senegal proposed rather to reaffirm French authority by a military expedition in force; but even he agreed that withdrawal would be better than trying to maintain 'an attenuated situation, without trade and without dignity'.[5] The colonial directorate agreed that control ought to be restored, but chiefly with a view to improving the exchange value of the Mellacourie in case there should be an opportunity to secure the Gambia.[6] They kept this object in view even though their own changing attitudes made its achievement increasingly unlikely. After Michaux retired as Director of the Colonies in 1882, both responsible ministries agreed that the security of French commerce on the Slave Coast was 'closely bound up with the maintenance of our political status there', and agreed that France's contribution to any exchange should be restricted to their possessions in the

[1] *MAE*, Angleterre (Freetown) 53, Bareste to M.A.E., 6 Nov. 1882; *MMC* Afrique VI/30/b, M.M.C. to M.A.E., 14 Sept. 1882.

[2] This correspondence may be followed in C.O. 806/196, or in *MAE*, Angleterre (Freetown) 53 and 70.

[3] *MAE*, Afrique 57, Grivel to M.M.C., 10 May 1882. For list of British firms claiming for losses in Mellacourie, Angleterre (Freetown) 53, Bareste to M.A.E., 3 Feb. 1882; cf. *MMC*, Afrique VI/30/b. Bohn (Senegal Coy.) to M.M.C., 28, 30 Dec. 1882.

[4] *MAE*, Afrique 57, M.M.C. to M.A.E., 23 May 1882, encl. Grivel, 10 May.

[5] *ibid.*, M.M.C. to M.A.E., 27 Sept. 1882, encl. Vallon, 31 Aug.

[6] *MAE*, Afrique 50, M.M.C. to M.A.E., 6 Dec. 1882; Afrique 84, M.M.C. to M.A.E., 9 May 1884.

Ivory Coast and the Mellacourie.[1] Neither place was likely to tempt the British.

Any significant exchange agreement seemed increasingly remote; the question was rather whether Marseille merchants with interests in the Scarcies might not after all succeed in upsetting the modest boundary delimitation. In August 1882 the French government ruled that they could not ratify this document until it had been approved by the Chambers. To the British, this procedure seemed tiresome and unnecessary (since no actual French territory was being surrendered); 'the fact is,' Kimberley commented, 'the Chamber is now the Government.'[2] On 15 February 1883 the Senate approved the agreement without debate, though the Committee report which recommended it to do so was strongly critical of British African policy; but the Chamber of Deputies seemed likely to raise more objections. As its Committee slowly deliberated, the Political Director of the Foreign Ministry confidentially warned Lyons that the interested merchants were fomenting opposition.[3] The report eventually presented to the Chamber in February 1884 proved to be strongly hostile, and factually inaccurate as well. The main ground for rejection was that the Scarcies, a major route to the Niger which had always been considered as French, was being surrendered without real compensation.[4]

The Committee's members were mostly undistinguished backbenchers; with one exception, they cannot be identified as African expansionists (in December 1883 they divided equally over the question of supplementary credits for the upper Senegal railway).[5]

[1] *MMC*, Afrique VI/30/a, minute by Michaux, Nov. 1882; *MAE*, Afrique 84, Note for Challemel-Lacour, Aug. 1883; Afrique 50, Marseille C. of C. to Duclerc, 12, 14 Oct.; M.M.C. to M.A.E., 8 Dec. 1882; Afrique 84, M.A.E. to M.M.C., 20 Jan. 1883.

[2] C.O. 267/350, minute by Kimberley on F.O. to C.O., 30 Aug. 1882.

[3] C.O. 806/177, No. 56, F.O. to C.O., Conf., 17 Aug. 1883.

[4] *J.O. Documents Parlementaires: Chambre*, 7 Feb. 1884, Report by Dureau de Vaulcomté (Deputy for Réunion).

[5] Members of the Committee supporting the Senegal credits: Sarlat, Ordinaire, Gasconi, Duchasseint. Members opposing: Ducroz, Edmond Robert, Blancsubé, Bouguès. Absent from the division of 17 Dec. 1883: Cadet, Dureau de Vaulcomté, Guillot. The three absentees supported credits for the railway on 3 July 1883.

L

The exception was Gasconi, deputy for Senegal, who strongly urged the need to secure at least the Great Scarcies for France, and for good measure suggested that the government should seek to bring Liberia under French control by discreet offers of financial aid.[1] In the general atmosphere of anglo-phobia, Gasconi was evidently able to impose this point of view upon the Committee. French officials — though sharing in part the apprehension about the use which Britain might make of the Scarcies route[2] — regretted the rejection, both because of the tendentious reasons on which it was based and because it might leave the way open for Britain also to adopt a more aggressive policy.[3] In 1885–6 the two ministries concerned agreed on the desirability of attempting ratification, but neither was prepared to accept responsibility for sponsoring the agreement before potentially hostile Chambers.[4] Nevertheless the British govern-ment in practice respected the terms of the agreement it had signed, and these were eventually incorporated, and extended, in a new treaty of 1889. But, immediately, it was clear that the prospects for any wider African agreement were poor.

The second French Protectorate at Porto Novo

The greatest threat to French West African trade was still on the Slave Coast; with the British at Ketenou, duty-free com-munication with Porto Novo depended on a forbearance which Lagos was clearly reluctant to continue. Bareste (d'Elteil's successor as salaried Consul, formerly an agent for Verminck) visited Lagos in May 1881, and his worst suspicions were strengthened. Alfred Moloney, the energetic acting Adminis-trator, spoke frankly and indiscreetly of his hopes to collect £25,000 a year in duties at Ketenou. With one hundred gallons of French rum exchanging for one hundred gallons of palm-oil, Bareste calculated that the imposition of the Lagos duty of 6d a

[1] *MMC*, Afrique VI/34/a, Gasconi to M.M.C. and M.A.E., 26 Oct. 1883.

[2] *MAE*, Afrique 86, Note for Challemel-Lacour, 1883.

[3] *MMC*, Afrique VI/38/c, Reply to Report of Dureau de Vaulcomté.

[4] *MAE*, Afrique 86, M.A.E. to M.M.C., 11 Feb. 1885; M.M.C. to M.A.E., 21 March; M.A.E. to M.M.C., 27 March; Note pour le Ministre, 4 July 1885; comment by Freycinet [?], 7 Aug. 1885; M.M.C. to M.A.E., 31 Oct. 1885, 16 April 1886; note by M.A.E., 1 July 1886.

gallon would raise the cost of buying oil at Porto Novo by one-third.

To check this plan Bareste recommended, first the acceptance of that protectorate which Tofa had offered to d'Elteil two years before, and secondly the military occupation of Cotonou. The physical problem of landing goods at that port remained unsolved, the ropeway system having apparently proved unsatisfactory. Underwater nets were being used in an attempt to protect canoes against sharks; but sawfish, evidently in alliance with the sharks, were destroying these. The Gold Coast canoemen showed natural reluctance to continue work while their comrades were being eaten; when French traders tried to compel them they simply deserted, leaving the canoes unmanned. Bareste believed a solution might be found by cutting a navigation channel from the coast into the lagoon, so that motor-launches could ply directly to Porto Novo; but this would involve a military occupation of Cotonou, which in turn might provoke reprisals from Dahomey.[1] In short, the effective protection of French trade seemed to demand simultaneous action on three or even four fronts: the removal of the British threat from Ketenou, the military occupation of Cotonou, the establishment of a clear title to Porto Novo, and possibly a military conflict with Dahomey.

Nevertheless, by November 1881 the Foreign Ministry was disposed to consider a more assertive line. Since the chances of a comprehensive West African agreement with Britain were, at least temporarily, diminished, they invited the colonial directorate to suggest how France might affirm her rights before they were attenuated by further British encroachments. In reply Rouvier suggested immediate acceptance of the protectorate of Porto Novo and the appointment of a Resident.[2] To this suggestion the Ministry for Foreign Affairs demurred on grounds of

[1] *MAE*, Afrique 77, Bareste to M.A.E., 20 May 1881; Angleterre (Freetown) 53, Bareste to M.A.E., 1 Sept. 1881, 11 March 1882; *MMC*, Afrique VI/30/d, Report by Penfentany, 25 Jan. 1882.

[2] *MAE*, Afrique 77, M.A.E. to M.M.C., 10 Nov. 1881; to Ministry of Commerce and Colonies, 28 Nov., Ministry of Commerce and Colonies to M.A.E., 9 Jan. 1882.

timing, suggesting that it would be diplomatically expedient to conclude the Sierra Leone agreement before flouting Britain elsewhere on the coast.[1] But in February 1882 Tofa, fearing new British advances, renewed his offer to accept a French protectorate, this time without insisting on assurances of French military support; the Ministry of the Marine urged acceptance before it was too late. The Foreign Ministry again counselled caution, but a little less insistently; on 12 April they authorized Bareste to accept Tofa's offer in case of extreme necessity only.[2]

After the Sierra Leone agreement was signed, new reasons for hesitation developed. Naval officers, ever since the experience of 1864, tended to doubt the value of Porto Novo, emphasizing the difficulties of supplying an official establishment there, and showing little sympathy with the motives of the merchants. Captain Penfentenyo of *La Bourdonnais* openly expressed his doubts in Porto Novo.[3] In September 1882 the Ministry of the Marine received a damning report from its naval commander on the coast. Admiral Grivel emphasized the sheer administrative problems of a protectorate, and belittled the possibilities of using the Cotonou route. If the isthmus were pierced, Dahomey might well make this a pretext for war; in any case, sooner or later Porto Novo would become involved in the inevitable clash between Gelele and the British at Lagos. Neither Tofa nor any other chief at Porto Novo — 'great children' as they all were — could be relied on to help France resist British power. The only way to protect French trade was to recognize British political hegemony in return for fiscal guarantees — and then, perhaps, to resume negotiations for a territorial exchange.[4]

Despite this discouraging advice, the two interested departments in Paris still inclined towards accepting the proffered protectorate: but only as a provisional measure. They did not

[1] *ibid.*, Note pour le ministre, Feb. 1882.

[2] *MAE*, Angleterre (Freetown) 53, Bareste to M.A.E., 11 March 1882, encl. Tofa to Bareste, 17 Feb. (forwarded by J. A. Colonna di Lecca); Afrique 77, M.A.E. to M.M.C., 8 April 1882; M.M.C. to M.A.E., 12 April; M.A.E. to M.M.C., 9 May; M.M.C. to M.A.E., 19 May, encl. draft to Comdt., Gabon; Angleterre (Freetown) 53, M.A.E. to Bareste, 12 April 1882.

[3] *MAE*, Angleterre (Freetown) 53, Bareste to M.A.E., 10 April 1882.

[4] *MAE*, Afrique 77, Grivel to Jauréguibery, 16 July 1882.

yet contemplate any real challenge to British paramountcy in the Bights, or doubt that it would eventually be Britain which undertook the inevitable operation against Dahomey. The protectorate should be accepted as a guarantee for the fiscal interests of French traders, not with the aim of establishing 'a genuine *mainmise* upon a country where we do not intend to establish any permanent establishment'.[1] But even after this conclusion was reached, the French hesitated. The immediate repercussions of the Egyptian affair made Ministers very wary of new commitments abroad, and official instructions about Porto Novo still contained reservations which inhibited action and created uncertainty and confusion on the coast.[2]

Although a Presidential Decree accepting the Protectorate was drafted and signed by Grévy in April 1882, it was 19 January 1883 before the Ministry of the Marine finally called for action. The weak Duclerc ministry was still in office; the change in tone was probably due to the influence of Dislère, a new and zealous Director of Colonies.[3] The Foreign Ministry, as the department responsible for protectorates, instructed Bareste accordingly, though still not too clearly; and Bonaventura Colonna di Lecca, an independent Corsican trader formerly in Régis' service, reluctantly accepted the appointment of Resident by delegation from Bareste. On 2 April 1883, with the assistance of French naval officers, di Lecca hoisted the French flag as instructed, not only at Porto Novo town, but at several points in the Agégé channel, a water-route which led to Cotonou without passing the British post at Ketenou.[4]

Di Lecca well appreciated that his position as Resident was precarious. Well-known at Porto Novo as a trader, his official authority was deficient in local eyes; and, although an able and

[1] *ibid.*, M.M.C. to M.A.E., 14 Sept. 1882; cf. M.A.E. to M.M.C., 8 Nov. 1882.

[2] *ibid.*, M.M.C. to M.A.E., 28 Sept. 1882; Angleterre (Freetown) 53, Duclerc to Bareste, 23 Nov. 1882.

[3] *MAE*, Afrique 78, M.M.C. to M.A.E., 19 Jan. 1883; Duchêne, *op. cit.*

[4] *MAE*, Angleterre (Freetown) 70, Duclerc to Bareste, 25 Jan. 1883; Bareste to M.A.E., 19 March 1883; Afrique 78, B. C. di Lecca to M.A.E., 7 April 1883.

intelligent man, he was often perplexed by the absence of clear instructions from Paris. Beneath these personal difficulties, there lay three major unsolved problems.

There was first the problem of enforcing French authority within Porto Novo, which so far depended wholly on their success in working with Tofa. The King's concerns, as in 1879, were purely practical; he wanted French support in securing Porto Novan territories against pressure from powerful neighbours, and in strengthening the dynastic position of his family. As soon as the French flag was hoisted he asked for re-endorsement of his son's right of succession, and for action against the British at Ketenou.[1] But it soon seemed that, far from strengthening Tofa's position, French protection might weaken it, by encouraging his dynastic enemies to work, with British support, for the independence of outlying provinces, and by inviting hostile pressure from Lagos and Dahomey.[2] As it became clear that the protectorate would initially mean little more than dignifying a merchant with an official title, Tofa became furious with frustration. In June he suddenly proposed changes in his own local customs tariff, on lines which were most keenly resented by the recently-arrived German trading-houses. After a bitter dispute Tofa ordered the Hamburg factories to be closed altogether; before the French Resident could appease the quarrel the German Vice-Consul at Lagos had threatened to summon naval support.[3] Next month the French did succeed in getting Tofa to sign a new treaty regulating the organization of their protectorate; he agreed not to exercise authority over foreigners without the Resident's consent, and to accept the Resident's advice in all matters affecting his foreign relations.[4] But he still seemed dangerously prone to take impetuous action over Ketenou, which was said to be his natal district; he was 'like a lion in a cage', the Resident reported early in 1884, and could be restrained only with difficulty from launching an attack on the

[1] *ibid.*, Masseron to Grivel, 10 April 1883; cf. above pp. 209–10.

[2] *Études Dahoméennes*, IX, p. 37, Dorat to Bories, 26 July 1884.

[3] *MAE*, Angleterre (Freetown) 70, Guilmin to Bories, 5 June 1883; Bareste to M.A.E., 2 Dec. 1883; Schramm, *op. cit.*, pp. 265 ff.

[4] *MAE*, Afrique 78, Bories to M.M.C., 12 Aug. 1883, encl. Treaty of 25 July.

British post, which would inevitably have implicated the French authorities.[1]

Secondly, the French position at Cotonou was still precarious. Colonel Dorat, appointed as first salaried Resident in May 1884, was appalled by its weakness. Not only was the physical problem of landing cargoes still unsolved, but the political sovereignty claimed by France was hardly in evidence.

> 'Although Cotonou is a French possession, the traders continue to pay duties to the King of Dahomey; and the village chiefs work their will on all inhabitants, judging cases between Frenchmen and their Negro employees, in a word, exercising authority in this territory of ours.'

Dorat urged that France should obtain a more explicit recognition of her sovereignty from the King of Dahomey. But the high-handed treatment which French traders still received from Dahomean officials elsewhere suggested that Gelele was unlikely to abate his claims, and that he might even reply with force if France were to attempt a military occupation of Cotonou.[2]

Even more troublesome were the British. The Governor of Lagos and the Gold Coast between 1881 and 1884 was none other than Rowe, the French *bête noire*. Motivated, as in earlier clashes, by sincerely patriotic indignation, Rowe applied himself to demonstrate that the French position at Porto Novo was as untenable as it had been in the days of Glover. Pursuing the policy begun by Ussher at Ketenou, Rowe played on dissatisfaction among Tofa's subjects, with the aim of dismembering the state of Porto Novo and reducing the French protectorate to an isolated inland town. Receiving the news of the re-establishment of the French claim with ominously frigid politeness, he warned the French that he regarded their claims on the Agégé channel as falling within the British protectorate of Ketenou; also that a request for British protection from Appa was under consideration in London. The French also feared,

---

[1] *MAE*, Angleterre (Freetown) 71, Bareste to M.A.E., 11 Feb. 1884.

[2] Many of Dorat's reports are printed in *Études Dahoméennes*, IX, esp. pp. 38–9 (26 July 1884); 41 (undated, *sc.* 23 Aug. 1884); 50 (8 Nov. 1884). Also pp. 51–2, Dorat to Gelele, 13 Aug. 1884; cf. *MAE*, Afrique 78, Bories to M.M.C., 12 Aug. 1883.

with some reason, that Rowe might be planning to extend British control on the Whemi side of Porto Novo, as part of his long-term designs against Dahomey.[1]

In fact, the French protectorate appears to have been the last straw which broke the sorely-burdened back of Britain's 'non-extension' policy at Lagos. Anderson of the Foreign Office used it as clinching proof of France's unfriendly intentions; he proposed that Britain should make one final protest with the aim of preparing public opinion for counter-action, not only in the Lagos lagoon but in the more important Oil Rivers.[2] This protest, delivered on 9 August, contained a strong hint of British retaliation; and in November 1883 a Cabinet Committee decided, among other things, to accept the renewed offer of the protectorate of Appa — thus cutting France off from a beach which might, though with difficulty, have provided an alternative to Cotonou. In February Rowe was authorized by telegram to take this step, which he did on 15 March 1884.[3]

But already serious conflicts over communications with the coast had broken the uneasy lull at Porto Novo. Early in 1884 a French naval officer, travelling with a few marines from Cotonou to Porto Novo, was stopped by British Hausa troops in the Agégé channel and compelled to turn back; the British flag was hoisted on this waterway, and the French flag hauled down (ostensibly by local people, but possibly at the instigation of a British captain).[4] French colonial officials were furious, and favoured drastic action to secure Porto Novo's access to the sea, and its routes to Dahomey and Abeokuta. Faure, back at the colonial department, wanted to insist that the British officer should be punished, and to assert France's claims strongly in both Ketenou and Appa.[5] The Foreign Ministry counselled

[1] *MAE*, Afrique 78, B. C. di Lecca to M.A.E., 21 April 1883; M.M.C. to M.A.E., 13 Aug.

[2] F.O. 84/1654, memo. by Anderson, 11 June 1883; cf. within, p. 309.

[3] Scotter, *op. cit.*, pp. 216–22; *MAE*, Angleterre (Freetown) 71, Bareste to M.A.E., 9 April 1884.

[4] *MAE*, Angleterre (Freetown) 71, Bareste to M.A.E., 11 Feb. 1884; Afrique 79, M.M.C. to M.A.E., 25 Feb., 23 March 1884.

[5] *MAE*, Afrique 79, Faure to Ferry, 26 April 1884; cf. Faure's minutes and amendments in *MMC*, Afrique VI/38/d.

restraint, insisting that France would only damage her case by seeking territory outside the limits which Glover had recognized in 1863;[1] they remained anxious for a negotiated solution to what still seemed a trivial business. But although their desire was reciprocated by most people in London, such a solution could not be reached until 1889, after more fierce local conflicts in the Lagos lagoon. And more immediately, the French initiative at Porto Novo played an important role in stimulating the British government to take action to protect its wider African interests.

[4]
The British Reaction

The Anglo-Portuguese Congo negotiation

During 1883 the British government, in the face of growing evidence of French ambitions in both Congo and Niger regions, moved slowly and reluctantly towards a more active African policy. De Brazza's triumphal reception in France sharpened their fears that the growing Congo trade might pass under French control and French tariffs. Nor were their fears confined to the districts actually traversed by de Brazza; there were rumours, which were not without foundation, that France was trying to cultivate close relations with Leopold in the hope of securing reversionary rights over the great inland territories being opened up by the International Association, a body whose status in international law was still uncertain.[2] The Cabinet would not consider entering the race for direct territorial power in the Congo themselves;[3] but the expedient of recognizing Portuguese claims as a barrier to those of others now came to seem more urgently attractive. On 18 November 1882, the day de Brazza's Treaty went to the French Chamber,

---

[1] *MAE*, Afrique 80, M.A.E. to M.M.C., 9 May 1884; cf. above pp. 60–1.

[2] D.D.F. IV, 591, Montebello to Duclerc, 3 Jan. 1883; Hanotaux and Martineau, *op. cit.*, IV, pp. 419 ff.

[3] Gwynn and Tuckwell, *Dilke*, II, pp. 84–5 n.

L*

the Portuguese renewed their request that Britain would recognize their claims to the littoral as far north as 5° 12'; on 15 December the British expressed willingness to do so provided that satisfactory guarantees were given to trade.[1]

Though the Portuguese had long desired such a change in British policy, it took them more than a year to agree to Britain's conditions for support. The Foreign Office still wished to limit the area over which Portuguese sovereignty would be recognized, and to define very rigorously her right to levy duties on Congolese trade. They also wished to set up an International Commission to supervise navigation in the Congo; but they eventually agreed to accept an Anglo-Portuguese one.[2] Besides imposing these restrictions in the Congo itself, the British also expected Portugal to compensate them elsewhere, and sat down 'to think of all the things we can ever want from Portugal in Africa'.[3] Although this time they did not press for concessions over Delagoa Bay, they decided to try to obtain the cession of the Portuguese fort at Whydah — an imperial relic which had been precariously reoccupied by a tiny garrison since 1865.[4] The British had no immediate intention of occupying Whydah, but hoped to clear the way for eventual control along the whole Slave Coast. Portugal, however, was reluctant to abandon this 'monument of her former glory', which legally remained part of her metropolitan territory until 1961; but eventually she agreed to grant Britain a right of pre-emption.[5]

Faced with Britain's hard bargaining, the Portuguese thought again of the alternative policy of co-operation with France. They quickly let it be known that Britain was willing to recognize their control of the Congo mouth, and there was even a reference to the negotiations in the Speech from the Throne in the Cortès on 2 January 1883.[6] The French wished to be con-

[1] Crowe, op. cit., pp. 17–19.

[2] ibid., p. 20.

[3] C.O. 147/52, F.O. to C.O., 25 Nov. 1882 and minutes.

[4] MAE, Afrique 53, Béraud to M.M.C., 3 April 1865.

[5] C.O. 147/53, F.O. to C.O., 15 Jan., 20 Jan. 1883 and minutes; C.O. 96/154, F.O. to C.O., 30 May 1883; cf. Scotter, op. cit., pp. 325–9.

[6] D.D.F. IV, 583, Laboulaye to Duclerc, Tel., 22 Dec. 1882; A. Roeykens, La Période Initiale . . . , p. 178.

ciliatory, and there was some attempt to implement Rouvier's idea of Franco-Portuguese partnership; but since their own aspirations precluded them from offering Portugal the essential point, control of the coast up to 5° 12', nothing came of this.[1] Although Britain's interests in the Congo fundamentally had little in common with those of Portugal, immediately only she could offer Lisbon hope of this coveted prize. On 26 February 1884, the Anglo-Portuguese Treaty was signed; it was immediately recognizable as

> 'a guarantee taken by Britain to prevent either France, or an international syndicate directed by France, from occupying the mouth of the Congo.'[2]

The questions of an Oil Rivers Protectorate and an exchange negotiation, 1882–3

Meanwhile de Brazza's exploits on the Congo, and the increasing support which he seemed to command in Paris, generated alarm in Britain about the danger of similar intervention in the Oil Rivers or the Niger. Since France's new Niger trade was developing so rapidly, there seemed to be some danger that the government, pressed by public hostility towards British policies in Africa, might be induced to give political protection to their two companies. Thus, very reluctantly and gradually, a British government whose leading members were almost all strongly hostile to any form of African expansion was drawn to consider methods of raising exclusive claims in the region as a barrier against France.

The question of new protectorates first arose in the Cameroons. Kings Bell and Akwa, two important and commercially successful rulers of the littoral near Duala, had several times already offered to place their territories under British protection. Their letters having remained unanswered, they sent new ones in November 1881. The reasons for their new request are not clear; the fact that they had been on good terms with British traders and naval officers over many decades does not alone

[1] D.D.F. V, 15, Laboulaye to Lacour, Pte., 1 April 1883; 79, Laboulaye to Lacour, 16 Aug. 1883; Crowe, *op. cit.*, pp. 18–19.

[2] D.D.F. V, 214, Waddington to Ferry, 4 March 1884.

explain this new departure. Perhaps they wanted British support against some neighbour, or a trader may have put them up to it; certainly they hoped to use British protection to fortify the monopolistic position which they enjoyed in relation to trade with the interior.

The officials responsible for Africa in the Foreign Office were already sufficiently worried about French expansion to consider Bell and Akwa's offers seriously; and Dilke, the Liberal Under-Secretary, tended to favour acceptance.[1] T. V. Lister, Assistant Under-Secretary in charge of African affairs, discussed the question with Consul Hewett, who was on leave in London from the Bights, in relation to a wider area than the Cameroons; the two men envisaged nothing less than,

> 'the possibility of altering the whole system of British policy as regards the native chiefs on the West Coast of Africa, and the abolition of the monopolies which are destructive to trade and productive of endless squabbles and wars.'[2]

Proposals resulting from these discussions were submitted to the Foreign Secretary, Granville, in Hewett's name, on 14 January 1882. First it was argued that if the Cameroons offers were declined, there might be danger of French intervention, not only there but in the Oil Rivers. If protectorates were established, as Hewett recommended, they need not be administered by the government directly; it might be possible to persuade the forty-five firms trading in the region to amalgamate into a single Company, which could then be granted a Royal Charter. Hewett, like Goldie, was evidently taking a cue from the recent revival of this old instrument of British overseas expansion in North Borneo; but at this stage it required much optimism to hope that the Liverpool firms trading in the delta could willingly be brought into amalgamation with recently-developed German competitors, with the United African Company, and with the C.F.A.E. But Hewett argued that the rewards of union could be great. Under British control it might

---

[1] Minute by Dilke, 13 Jan. 1882, *cit.*, W. O. Aydelotte, *Bismarck and British Colonial Policy* (Philadelphia, 1937) p. 9; cf. Gwynn and Tuckwell, *op. cit.*, I, p. 431.

[2] P.R.O. 30/29/135, memo. by Lister, 4 Jan. 1882.

be possible to develop trade in Iboland and the Cameroons in groundnuts, ivory, and palm kernels, possibly to the value of an additional million pounds annually. To effect this, of course, coercive measures might be needed to break the monopoly of coastal middlemen in the established oil trade, and to compel the rulers to allow European commercial penetration of the interior.[1]

These arguments were not really convincing at this time. The danger of French intrusion in the Oil Rivers was not in fact imminent, and was further reduced by the fall of Gambetta's ministry at the end of January. And there were objections on grounds both of expediency and of principle to the idea of forcing the coastal rulers who sought British protection to ruin themselves by opening the inland trade. When Hewett's memorandum was sent, without comment, to the Colonial Office, only Hemming supported its proposals, on the grounds of 'the advantages to British trade, the maintenance of peace and order, and the spread of civilization'. Meade feared that any such protectorate would prove difficult to administer; Leonard Courtney, the Parliamentary Under-Secretary, appealed to the principles of 1865.[2] Kimberley, though no 'Little Englander', had already come down against accepting the offers from the Cameroons; he feared that in Hewett's proposal the Foreign Office was trying 'to hand over to us the troublesome duty of managing our relations with the Oil Rivers'. Hemming, seeing there was no hope of a protectorate, proposed instead that there should be a new offer of the Gambia to France, on condition that she would promise not to interfere on the coast 'between Bathurst and the Gaboon'; but Kimberley was not ready to revive that idea either.[3] Still unworried by the danger of France harming Britain's essential interests in West Africa, he was happy to continue the policy of 'drifting' which seemed to serve Britain's colonial interests adequately elsewhere.[4] So on 15

[1] F.O. 27/2614, Hewett to Granville, 14 Jan. 1882.
[2] C.O. 806/203, minutes by Hemming, 19 March; Meade, 11 April; Courtney, 5, 12 April 1882.
[3] P.R.O. 30/29/135, Kimberley to Gladstone, 2 Jan. 1882; Note by Kimberley, 14 Jan. 1882; C.O. 806/203, minutes by Kimberley, 6, 13 April 1882.
[4] P.R.O. 30/29/135, Kimberley to Granville, 3 Dec. 1881 (on Raiatea and Newfoundland).

April 1882 the Colonial Office declined to accept any such plan as Hewett had proposed.

To Lister in particular, this was a grave disappointment; but there seemed no hope of removing Kimberley's veto without new evidence to prove necessity. So Hewett returned to the coast in May 1882 with instructions to report more fully on the situation in the Cameroons. Other duties, and an attack of fever, distracted him from this task; even so, it is strange that he did not submit this report until June 1883. When it arrived it provided much detailed information, and elaborated on the advantages of breaking the coastal monopolies by inland penetration; but it contained no new argument of major importance.[1]

Before Hewett's report arrived, official views on African expansion were beginning to change. This was due to the growing concern about French aims in the Congo, the sharper French attitude noted at many points in West Africa, and above all to the deepening Anglo-French estrangement produced by the occupation of Egypt. It looked as though a 'policy of pin-pricks' was developing;[2] and in the Niger region a well-directed French pin could do real damage. At the end of 1882 Hutton returned, much alarmed, from his unsuccessful negotiations in Paris with the French competitors of the National African Company; de Brazza, he claimed, had told him that his original instructions had been to go to the Niger, and that he had been diverted to the Congo only to forestall Stanley.[3] This news led Aberdare to request an interview with his former colleague Granville. The

[1] Scotter, op. cit., pp. 277–9; H. R. Rudin, Germans in the Cameroons (New Haven, 1938) pp. 21–2; C.P. 4869, Hewett reports, 7, 11 June 1883.

[2] R. Robinson and J. Gallagher with Alice Denny, Africa and the Victorians, p. 166. For comments on these pin-pricks, see, e.g., F.O. 27/2614, C.O. to F.O., 14 April 1882 (Porto Novo); C.O. 267/350, minute by Hemming on F.O. to C.O., 14 Dec. 1882 (Little Popo).

[3] This odd story, if true, must refer to de Brazza's instructions from the French committee of the Association, for whom he was acting in 1880. At the time of the journey referred to Semellé was still seeking capital to enter the lower Niger trade, and the French government was still anxious to conciliate Britain. Conceivably there may have been some suggestion of his going to join Galliéni on the upper Niger; but this was not what Hutton believed.

French government, he claimed, seemed to be planning a system of monopolistic treaties along the middle Niger, as far as the head of maritime navigation at Boussa. This would cripple Goldie's hopes of inland penetration; it would also (though Aberdare did not say so in his letter) prevent the Company from recovering its monopoly of the lower Niger trade, and so qualifying for a grant of Chartered privileges.[1] On 18 January 1883 Granville received the Company's deputation, and heard them explain the perils to which their trade would be subjected under French rule. The Company did not propose a British protectorate or raise the question of a Charter (though soon afterwards they sought Consular powers for their Agent-General, to match those of Mattei); instead they suggested dividing the Niger into French and British spheres of influence, with a dividing-line near Timbuktu. Their delegation claimed that France might be induced to accept such terms if they were linked with an offer to exchange the Gambia for her rights on the Slave Coast; they also asserted, on the high authority of Hutton, that British merchants' opposition to this scheme had 'considerably subsided' since 1876.[2]

Meanwhile the Colonial Office were already considering how to avoid the development of what Meade called 'a very unpleasant state of things, each power grabbing what it can'. Considering the danger of French intrusion on the Niger, and perhaps reflecting a little guiltily on their own plan for thwarting her in the Congo, they suggested that the Foreign Office might attempt to negotiate with France a general demarcation of West African territories.[3] But Lyons, keenly aware of the deterioration in Anglo-French relations, advised that it would be imprudent to begin such a negotiation until the Chamber showed itself willing to ratify the modest Sierra Leone agree-

[1] C.O. 147/52, C.O. to F.O., 6 Jan. 1883, encl. memo. by Meade of conversation with Hutton; F.O. 84/1654, Aberdare to Granville, 1 Jan. 1883.

[2] F.O. 84/1654, Aberdare to Granville, 28 Feb. 1883; N.A.C. to Granville, 28 Feb. 1883.

[3] C.O. 147/52, F.O. to C.O., 11 Dec. 1882, encl. letter from John Holt, 11 Dec., minutes by Hemming, 28 Dec., Meade, 30 Dec., Derby, 1 Jan.; C.O. to F.O., 6 Jan. 1883.

ment. This seemed to leave two possible courses of action. One would be to set up a protectorate in the Oil Rivers, as proposed the previous year: a course favoured by Hemming, resisted by Meade, but now provisionally endorsed by Herbert. The other would be to offer the Gambia, in hope of inducing generous French concessions. Although Herbert was still apprehensive of Parliamentary difficulties, Hutton's statement about the change in mercantile opinion suggested that these might be superable.[1] And in January 1883 this course unexpectedly received endorsement from a former opponent; Kimberley, now translated to the India Office, wrote to Granville that he had become convinced that it would be worth sacrificing the Gambia in order to secure the Niger and the Slave Coast. Along with such an agreement might go the dropping of the Portuguese negotiations in favour of an attempt to co-operate with France in the Congo also.[2] But Kimberley's successor at the Colonial Office was Derby, whose capacity for taking policy decisions had not been improved by his move from the Conservatives to the Liberals. Derby declined to adopt either of the courses proposed on the grounds that such decisions were subjects for the Cabinet; and he declined to bring them before the Cabinet on the grounds that it was a Foreign Office responsibility to do so.[3]

In fact the Foreign Office was academically considering the possibility of new Protectorates — the librarian wrote a background paper on the subject on 24 April — but with little urgency. News of the French reoccupation of Porto Novo, officially confirmed on 21 April, at first caused less concern there than at the Colonial Office, where Hemming wanted to retaliate by imposing duties at Ketenou. But in May reports of a French attempt to sign a treaty with Bonny produced a stronger reaction.[4] There was now a new force working in the Foreign Office; the old Slave Trade department, in suspended animation since Wylde's retirement in 1880, was in 1883 re-

[1] C.O. 806/203, minutes on F.O. to C.O., 5 March 1883, by Hemming, Meade, Herbert.

[2] P.R.O. 30/29/135, Kimberley to Granville, 12 Jan. 1883.

[3] C.O. 806/203, minute by Derby.

[4] C.P. 4825, Tissot to Granville, 21 April 1883; F.O. to C.O., 30 April, Conf., 23 May 1883; C.O. 96/154, minute by Hemming on above.

constituted as the Consular and African department, under the energetic care of H. Percy Anderson. In a forthright memorandum of 11 June Anderson rejected the idea of merely protesting about Porto Novo; if no action followed, France would be emboldened to intervene in the Oil Rivers.

'The French', Anderson argued, 'have a settled policy in Africa, both on the East and West Coast, and that policy is antagonistic to us. The progress of that policy is sometimes sluggish, sometimes feverish, but it never ceases.'

Doubtless there would be trouble if Britain established her protectorate in the Oil Rivers, but French policy was making trouble in any case. With the mouth of the Niger in British hands, France would know where she stood; a comprehensive negotiation — which it was still generally assumed must precede any final partition of West Africa — could then be begun from strength. By offering the Gambia, Britain might secure French withdrawal from the Slave Coast, and the union of the two portions of the Gold Coast colony:

'the African commercial policy of the two countries would ... have separate fields, ample for both, in which there would be no collision and no petty rivalries.'

But the first necessity, in Anderson's view, was to secure the Oil Rivers; he saw this, not as an alternative to an offer of the Gambia, but as an essential preliminary.[1]

But Liberal ministers, though coming round to the idea of using the Gambia in negotiation, would still have preferred a negotiation without the possible embarrassment of new protectorates. Lord Edmond Fitzmaurice, Dilke's successor as Parliamentary Under-Secretary, had also noted the need for 'a re-arrangement and exchange of territories from Sierra Leone to Gabon', and hinted unofficially to the French chargé d'affaires late in June, that a new attempt to secure the Gambia might meet a more favourable response. But the French Foreign Ministry did not accept this hint, nor even consult the Ministry

[1] F.O. 84/1654, memo. by Anderson, 11 June 1883; cf. J. P. Schwitzer, *The British Attitude towards French Colonization, 1875–87* (Ph.D. thesis, London, 1954) pp. 309 ff.

of the Marine;[1] hence throughout the summer the British government remained without a settled policy.

The French on the Niger and Benué, 1883

The National African Company's fear that the French government might be backing the French companies on the Niger was exaggerated but not groundless. On 25 January 1883, within a week of authorizing the Porto Novo protectorate, the Ministry of the Marine proposed a stronger policy on the Niger also. They saw little hope of resisting British influence to the west of the lower river, where the influence of the N.A.C. and the Colony of Lagos was reinforced by that of the missionary societies; but they hoped to guarantee French traders permanent access to the river by treaties with chiefs in the eastern delta. And on the Benué, where Mattei had opened trade and signed an agreement with Amadu of Loko, the Ministry hoped to develop permanent connections with Adamawa, Bornu, Lake Chad — even, if the theories of the German explorer Flegel were confirmed, with the river Shari, and the other area of French expansion in the Congo basin.[2] When Mattei returned to Paris shortly afterwards, he was duly authorized to make discreet efforts, as opportunities offered, along these lines.[3] But too much should not be made of these instructions. Against the mounting zeal of the Ministry of the Marine, the Ministry for Foreign Affairs called for prudence and restraint; and they soon showed their reluctance to support any expensive forward policy.

Mattei's chief concern in Paris was to obtain sufficient funds to compete with the N.A.C. in the distribution of presents to African rulers — especially in Nupe, where the Emir had again deferred the coveted permission to open new trading-posts. He produced a collection of sixteen treaties and letters from chiefs (mostly simple leases of factory-sites, but some containing

[1] F.O. 84/1634, loose minute by Fitzmaurice, with Rowe, 16 June 1883 (on Grand Popo); *MAE*, Angleterre 800, d'Aunay to Challemel-Lacour, 99, 1 July 1883

[2] *MAE*, Afrique, 86, M.M.C. to M.A.E., 25 Jan. 1883; Mattei, *op. cit.*, pp. 105–6. For C.F.A.E. and the Benué cf. E. Viard, *Au Bas-Niger* (Paris, 3rd ed., 1886).

[3] *MAE*, Afrique 86, M.A.E. to Mattei, Conf., 6 March 1883.

political clauses) and strongly urged the government to make a treaty with Brass that would neutralize the mouth of the Niger. Three Deputies, including the former Premier, Duclerc, were recruited to support these claims of the C.F.A.E., and to urge more frequent naval visits to the Niger.[1] Yet to buy presents for the rulers of Loko, Nupe and Brass, the Foreign Ministry could raise only the paltry sum of 2,993 francs. Although C.F.A.E. again doubled its capital, its financial resources were still inferior to those of its British rival.[2]

Naval visits, however, could be made without additional charges on the estimates; and in March 1883 the *Voltigeur* cruised along the delta to the Cameroons. It drew too much water to enter the Niger, but it visited Bonny and invited the head of the Manilla Pepple 'house' to renew a long-forgotten commercial treaty signed by his predecessor in 1841. In view of the hardship caused to Bonny by Ja Ja's secession ten years earlier, this offer must have been tempting; Pepple nevertheless prudently returned a polite refusal. In the Cameroons the *Voltigeur* did succeed in signing a treaty of protection with King Pass-all of Malimba; this was immediately challenged by Bell, who claimed to be Pass-all's superior, and who warned the French that his country was already on offer to Britain.[3] These inept proceedings did much to heighten the growing alarm of the British Foreign Office.

Late in July the *Oriflamme*, a vessel of shallow draught, entered the delta by the Brass river. On 4 August Mattei, on his way back from Paris, arrived on the scene with a draft treaty. The chiefs of Brass, so long hostile to British penetration up-river, were evidently willing to explore the possibilities of co-operation with France; but they refused to sign a treaty which, as originally drafted, would have placed them under French suzerainty.[4] Mattei then made for Ibi on the Benué, a

[1] *ibid.*, Mattei to M.A.E., 11 May 1883; Ascaréguy to Duclerc, 11 May, forwarded by Duclerc.

[2] *ibid.*, M.M.C. to M.A.E., 18 June; M.A.E. to M.M.C., 25 June 1883; receipt by Mattei; Mattei, *op. cit.*, pp. 55-6.

[3] *MAE*, Afrique 86, Bories to M.M.C., May 1883.

[4] *ibid.*, Report by Cavalié, 29 Aug. 1883; Angleterre (Freetown) 70, Bareste to M.A.E., 8 Sept. 1883; Flint, *op. cit.*, p. 52.

crossing-place for caravans some two hundred miles above the confluence; he signed some sort of treaty and hoisted a French flag. Then, in early September, he returned to Nupe and made one last effort to get permission from the new Emir, Maliki, to pass through his territory and open trade at Boussa. (With wild optimism, Mattei even talked of advancing up the river to meet Desbordes.) But British influence was still in the ascendent in Nupe, and Mattei lacked the resources to combat it; his highest trading-post remained at Chonga, near Rabah.[1]

Despite these failures in Brass and Nupe, the two French companies together now claimed fifty-five stations in the Niger, roughly as many as the N.A.C.; they had four in the Benué, extending further upstream than their rivals. But the commercial position of both companies was vulnerable; the latest increase raised the nominal capital of C.F.A.E. only to three million francs, and it is doubtful whether the Senegal Company committed so much to what remained, for Verminck, a subsidiary enterprise in the Niger. Much of their capital, too, was tied up in factories and vessels which were vulnerable to climatic and political hazards; 1883 brought losses to both companies, in part because of hostility from the N.A.C.[2] That Company, better able to carry temporary losses, raised buying prices by 25%, and brought political pressure against the French at other places than Nupe. The full story of their campaign may never be written; but certainly a series of calamities befell their rivals. Two C.F.A.E. steamers ran aground, another sank in a collision; their factory in Loko was burned, with a loss of 70,000 francs; the Senegal Company was prevented from opening a factory at Onitsha; British warships shelled Abo and Idah, which had seemed too friendly to the French. Britain's gunboats made Africans regard her as master of the world, Mattei wrote despairingly in November 1883; France's future on the Niger seemed increasingly insecure.[3]

[1] *MAE*, Afrique 86, Mattei to M.A.E., 5 Nov. 1883; Mattei, *op. cit.*, pp. 58-9.

[2] *MAE*, Afrique 86, Report by Cavalié, 29 Aug. 1883.

[3] *MAE*, Afrique 86, Mattei to M.A.E., 5 Nov. 1883; Angleterre (Freetown) 70, Mattei to Bareste, 11 Nov. 1883; Mattei, *op. cit.*, pp. 60-1.

The Ministry of the Marine, therefore, began to think in terms of salvage work. On 12 February 1884 Faure suggested that, since France could not compete with Britain's violent methods, she should try to use her presence in the Niger to bargain for political neutrality of the river and equal rights for trade. In fact, this new application of an old idea might have attracted the British government at this time; but the Ministry for Foreign Affairs believed that neutralization could only be bought at the price of sacrificing substantial French interests elsewhere in Africa. The National African Company seemed too confident of its strength to permit commercial competition in any case; hence, the French government would have to regard their new Niger interests as expendable.[1]

The decision to act

The British could not know of the French government's reluctance to commit itself politically in the Niger; and Goldie, even though he was winning the battle against French commerce, still pressed the government to provide a more secure political framework for his company's operations. The Colonial Office again wished to avoid new commitments by linking the Niger question with a general West African agreement. Meade, interpreting French encroachments in Porto Novo and the Popos as attempts to force the cession of the Gambia, concluded that the price would be worth paying for peace and quiet, and the chance of avoiding official responsibility for the Oil Rivers. Overestimating the Gambia's current market value, he suggested demanding in return, not only French withdrawal from the coast between Sierra Leone and Gabon, but concessions over the Newfoundland fisheries, and the proposed French convict settlements in the Pacific. (He was prepared to throw in Raiatea as a make-weight.)[2] Even Derby was converted to lukewarm support of such an agreement, though he characteristically added,

[1] *MAE*, Afrique 86, Faure to M.A.E., 12 Feb. 1884; M.A.E. to M.M.C., 11 June 1884.

[2] F.O. 84/1655, Goldie-Taubman to F.O., 26 Sept. 1883; C.O. 96/154, F.O. to C.O., 28 Sept., minute by Hemming 29 Sept., by Derby 3 Oct.; C.O. 806/214, memo. by Meade, 29 Sept. 1883.

'Of course, nothing can be done until the whole matter has been discussed in Cabinet. Perhaps nothing can be done then.'[1]

At last it seemed agreed that *some* governmental initiative was needed to protect Britain's future commerce in the Niger and the other Oil Rivers — including the Cameroons, where the case for British control was argued in Hewett's delayed report of June 1883. The outstanding question was whether an offer of the Gambia would, as Meade hoped, suffice to make the French accept satisfactory terms, or whether negotiations should be proceeded by extensive proclamations of British protectorates, even though these might remain nominal. The Foreign Office, more urgently worried about the French in the Niger, supported the latter view. In two memoranda intended for Ministers, Lister argued that, if protectorates were first safely secured, Britain might hope to obtain in exchange for the Gambia, not merely Porto Novo and the Popos (which the British public would equate with 'a gross of green spectacles') but the abolition of all differential duties in French West African colonies.[2]

Late in October the problem was at last taken to the Cabinet, who promptly referred it to a Committee. By the end of November this body had come down in favour of the Foreign Office view, and its findings were endorsed by the Cabinet. Hewett was to seek treaties of protection, not only in the Niger region but also in the Cameroons, which would provide the new protectorate with sites for a coaling-station and a sanatorium. (Here, full sovereignty would need to be acquired over a half-mile strip of coast.) Members of the Committee appear to have been influenced by arguments tending to minimize the increase in responsibility involved in these plans, and to have parted convinced that they had solved a troublesome minor problem by expedients at once economical and safe.[3]

Unfortunately their solution was incomplete. The Committee had not discussed the methods by which authority was to be

[1] P.R.O. 30/29/120, Derby to Granville, 8 Oct. 1883.

[2] C.O. 96/154, F.O. to C.O., Conf., 5 Oct. 1883 ; F.O. 84/1655, memos by Lister, 24 Oct., 16 Nov. 1883.

[3] F.O. 84/1655, Note by Lister, 21 Nov. 1883, endorsed, 'Approved by Cabinet. G.' Lister to Pauncefote, 29 Nov. 1883.

exercised in the new protectorate, except to forbid additional Imperial expenditure. Despite the assumed imminence of the French menace, nearly six months of bureaucratic discussion were needed before detailed arrangements were complete. The chief problems were the definition of the jurisdiction to be exercised in the protectorate by the British Consul; the consequent increase in his staff, and how to pay for it without approaching the Treasury for more money; the propriety of employing the Agent-General of the N.A.C. as an unpaid Consular official; and the objections of the Company and other merchants to contributing through taxation to the cost of the new establishment.[1] Only on 16 May 1884 were Hewett's instructions signed, and printed treaty-forms provided for his use. These stipulated, not only for British protection and control of foreign relations, but for free trade for citizens of all countries throughout the territory of the signatory chiefs; somewhat unwisely, Hewett's old desire to break the monopoly of coastal middlemen was to be combined with the main object, the exclusion of France.[2] The British had at last been forced to take a limited and half-hearted step towards increased government responsibility for their 'informal empire' of trade. But their plans did not work out so simply as expected.

[1] Scotter, *op. cit.*, pp. 286–95; Flint, *op. cit.*, pp. 55–9.
[2] C.P. 5004, No. 88, Lister to Hewett, 16 May 1884.

CHAPTER SEVEN

The Pattern of the Partition

[1]

The German Entry into West Africa

Problems of motivation

DURING THE spring and summer of 1884 the African situation
was transformed by the initiative of the German government.
Bismarck, hitherto conspicuously reluctant to defend Germany's
overseas trading interests by acquiring colonies, or by other
methods likely to create conflicts with other powers, now proclaimed sovereignty over substantial sectors of the African coast.
This change of policy has puzzled many commentators.

One superficially attractive explanation attributes the change
to the growth of imperialist sentiment among the German public
and intellectuals and to the development of German foreign
trade.[1] And it is true that since the 1830's traders from Hanseatic ports had been operating in West Africa with increasing
success. The most important firm was that founded by Carl
Woermann of Hamburg; entering the Liberian trade in 1849, by
1884 his house had achieved a dominant position in that state,
spread successfully to Gabon and the Cameroons, and opened
regular steamship services to the coast. Adolph Woermann, who
succeeded his father as head of the firm in 1880, was a man of
influence in German politics, a National Liberal Deputy to the
Reichstag after 1884, a friend and reputedly a confidant of
Bismarck himself. In a manner reminiscent of the history of
Régis, Woermann's business spawned others, as former agents
struck out independently in the African trade, using capital and
experience acquired in the service of the parent firm. Jantzen &
Thormählen, who made great progress in the Cameroons after

---

[1] For this view, see M. E. Townsend, *Origins of Modern German Colonization*
(N.Y., 1921); *The Rise and Fall of Germany's Colonial Empire* (N.Y., 1930).

1874; Wölber & Brohm, the leading firm in Togoland; C. Godelt — all originated their business in this way.[1] Another source of capital for West African trade was the Hamburg firm of Wilhelm O'Swald & Co.; their main interests were in Zanzibar, but by the profitable expedient of shipping cowrie shells from East African beaches to the area of Lagos and Dahomey, where they were used as currency, they developed a trade eventually taken over by other Hamburg merchants, G. L. Gaiser and Messrs. Witt & Busch.[2] Bremen's African trade was smaller. It originated in the 1850's in the desire of F. M. Vietor to support the work of local missionaries east of the Volta; but by the 1880's the Vietor family business had acquired a strong commercial position in Great and Little Popo.[3]

In the 1870's German trade began to grow more rapidly, especially in the areas of the Popos, the Cameroons, and Lagos; one reason was the early development of the palm-kernel business. Moreover, since cowries were becoming harder to obtain, spirits and other goods manufactured in Germany itself were playing larger roles in trade. Between 1871 and 1883 Hamburg's imports from West Africa are estimated to have increased by 183%, but her exports there, by 560%.[4] During 1882 96 vessels, including 27 steamers, left Hamburg for West Africa; the city's West African imports were valued at 8,588,000 marks. Although this figure still represented less than 0·3% of all German imports, such a growing commerce might legitimately expect some government encouragement. Early in 1883 the traders asked for occasional visits by German warships.[5] Bismarck never denied his general responsibility to assist German subjects overseas; and he had an especial interest in conciliating the Hanseatic

[1] P. E. Schramm, *Deutschland und Übersee* (Braunschweig, 1950) pp. 237–242, 265, 298–302. H. R. Rudin, *Germans in the Cameroons, 1884–1914* (New Haven, 1938) pp. 157–8.

[2] Schramm, *op. cit.*, pp. 264–6, 273–82.

[3] Schramm, *op. cit.*, pp. 253–60.

[4] *ibid.*, pp. 370–1 and *passim*.

[5] W(eiss) B(uch) *Deutsche Kolonien. 1. Togogebiet und Biafra-Bai.* Printed in *Das Staatsarchiv*, XLIII (Leipzig, 1884) pp. 242–3. Figures submitted by Hamburg Chamber of Commerce, 6 July 1883. C. W. Newbury, *The Western Slave Coast . . .*, pp. 110–11.

ports, which were only now, with some reluctance, in process of entering the *Zollverein*.[1] On 14 April 1883 he invited their Senates to consider the cavalier manner in which Britain and France had disposed of African territory in the Sierra Leone demarcation, and to make proposals for the future protection of their African trade.[2]

The Senate of Bremen replied very briefly, asking only for a warship to visit and support German traders at Great and Little Popo; but the Hamburg Chamber of Commerce, on 6 July 1883, submitted a lengthy analysis of the problems of German traders on the whole West African coast.[3] It is an interesting document, not only because of the specific information which it contains. For much of its length it follows the traditional mercantile argument in favour of open commerce supervised loosely and informally by the home government; it suggests more consular appointments, more naval visits, more agreements, both with chiefs and with other European governments, to protect the interests of German traders. But in the Bight of Biafra the activities of French, Portuguese and British officials seemed to present dangers to the considerable trade which Hamburg merchants had developed during the previous ten years. Here, and here alone, the Chamber of Commerce advocated, in rather tentative terms, the establishment of a 'trade-colony', to be supported if possible by a German naval station on the Spanish island of Fernando Po.

Bismarck, it seems clear, had always intended his original enquiry to be followed by some action in support of the merchants. In June 1883, even before receiving their replies, he warned the French Ambassador to expect to see German-African trade receive more active government support.[4] In December 1883 he informed the Senates of his first measures. The warship *Sophie* would visit the Popos; an Imperial Commissioner (Gustav Nachtigal, Consul-General in Tunis, and a

[1] W. H. Dawson, *The German Empire, 1867–1914* (London, 1919) Vol. II, pp. 27–9.
[2] W.B. No. 8269, Hatzfeldt to Wentzel, 14 April 1883.
[3] W. B. No. 8270, Wentzel to Hatzfeldt, 11 July; 8271, memo. by Hamburg Chamber of Commerce, 6 July 1883.
[4] *MMC*, Afrique VI/40/c, Courcel to Challemel-Lacour, 3 June 1883.

notable African explorer) would later report on the possibility
of treaties with chiefs; funds for a resident Consul would be provided in the Estimates for 1885–6.[1] But it does not appear that
Bismarck was yet envisaging formal colonial expansion; the
suggested 'trade-colony' is not excluded, but it does not appear
on Bismarck's immediate agenda before May 1884. The growth
of German trade in Africa, though meriting increased attention, would hardly have overcome Bismarck's former reluctance
to acquire colonial commitments unless considerations of higher
policy had also pointed in that direction.

Yet during 1884 Bismarck deliberately sought a series of
colonial quarrels with Great Britain, beginning with a dispute
over the singularly unproductive coastline of South-West
Africa. Though the Gladstone ministry's handling of these
questions was certainly provocatively incompetent, historians
now agree that the basic reasons for this new policy must be
sought in Europe. Some believe that Bismarck was deliberately
creating tensions with Britain in order to further reconciliation
with France; taking advantage of French resentment over the
Anglo-Portuguese Congo treaty, over Porto Novo and the Niger
question, he tried to demonstrate that, since Germany too had
trouble with the British empire, France an l Germany might
usefully co-operate in reviving some form of 'Armed Neutrality'.[2]
Other writers argue that this diplomatic purpose was secondary; that Bismarck's dominating concern was to preserve his
personal dominance over German political life. A colonial
policy executed with patriotic *élan* could rally support in an
insubordinate Reichstag, and at the autumn elections of 1884;
more specifically, it could be used to discredit the radical
Deutsch-Freisinnige Partei, with its pro-British leanings and its
dangerous connection with Crown Prince Frederick and his
English wife.[3] These interpretations are not mutually exclusive,

[1] W. B. No. 8272, Hatzfeldt to Wentzel, 22 Dec. 1883.
[2] A. J. P. Taylor, *Germany's First Bid for Colonies* (London, 1938).
[3] E. Eyck, *Bismarck* (Zurich, 1944) Vol. III, pp. 394–424; *Bismarck and the
German Empire* (London, 1950) pp. 272–81; W. O. Aydelotte, *Bismarck and
British Colonial Policy* (Philadelphia, 1937) p. 18; 'Wollte Bismarck Kolonien?', in W. Conze (ed.) *Deutschland und Europa* (Dusseldorf, 1951); cf.
N. Rich and M. H. Fisher (eds), *The Holstein Papers*, II, pp. 155, 161–2.

and the area of disagreement seems to be narrowing.[1] Most writers now agree that Bismarck's system of government, though not totally unresponsive to domestic pressures, was too authoritarian for the pressure of African traders, or the theoretical arguments of the *Kolonialverein*, to be able to dictate policy.

Still, once Bismarck had for his own reasons set the course of colonial policy, the merchants were quite capable of influencing its detailed execution; their influence on events in West Africa might still repay closer study. When Bismarck first invited Nachtigal to visit the African coast, he apparently charged him with a mission of information only, on the lines discussed with Hamburg in 1883. But on 19 May 1884, after Bismarck had broached the question of colonial co-operation to Ferry, Nachtigal was given formal instructions authorizing him to extend German protection to territories where German traders seemed threatened by foreign encroachments. Besides Angra Peqena in South-West Africa, the area between the Niger delta and Gabon was specifically mentioned; in assuming sovereignty here, Nachtigal was to be guided by the wishes of the traders, as defined in a letter drawn up in their name by Adolph Woermann.[2] Since it was expedient to become active in African affairs, Bismarck was very happy to have an opportunity of pleasing Hamburg; but he probably failed to realize that to do so would ultimately involve his government in direct colonial administration. *Schutzgebieten*, informally ⁻managed by the merchants, were all he envisaged, not *Kolonien*. 'What is colonial policy?' he asked in June, apparently in innocence. 'We must protect our fellow-countrymen.'[3]

But although Nachtigal was allowed much freedom in interpreting his instructions, Bismarck intended that he should be strictly controlled by certain governing principles of his inter-

[1] A. J. P. Taylor, *The Struggle for Mastery in Europe* (Oxford, 1954) pp. 292–8; *Bismarck* (London, 1955) pp. 215–21; cf. Schramm, *op. cit.*, pp. 430–5. For a recent analysis of German imperialism in East Africa, cf. F. F. Müller, *Deutschland-Zanzibar-Ostafrika* (E. Berlin, 1959).

[2] W.B. No. 8274, Bismarck to Nachtigal, 19 May 1884; memo. by Woermann, 30 April.

[3] *Die Grosse Politik*, IV, p. 64, minute by Bismarck, on Münster, 7 June 1884.

national policy. First, there was to be no conflict with France. Nachtigal did not attempt to visit Porto Novo, where German traders would have welcomed his support against France's protégé Tofa; his instructions to assist German traders at Little Popo did not envisage a protectorate; and in general the French government was assured that he would not encroach upon their interests.[1] But secondly, any dispute with Britain was to involve interests of a secondary order; it was not to produce any breach between the two powers incapable of speedy healing when the international situation might demand it. This cardinal principle explains why Bismarck should choose to quarrel with Britain over tropical Africa, an area of marginal importance to her interests, rather than over the vital question of Egypt. And within West Africa, it explains why he made no efforts to thwart her on the Niger.

The Cameroons Protectorate

But Nachtigal's actions in support of German traders did not always conform quite so neatly to this diplomatic pattern as Bismarck had hoped. In the Cameroons (as well as in South-West Africa) conditions did prove quite suitable for a mild Anglo-German quarrel. Even before Nachtigal arrived the Hamburg agents were active, spending money freely in the hope of obtaining treaties in the Duala region. They were probably both stimulated and assisted in this task by reports of Hewett's activities in the Niger region, where during June and early July he was pressing the chiefs to sign treaties containing the objectionable Article VI, authorizing Europeans to trade personally in the interior. On 12 July the German consular agent received a curious document expressing the desire of 'the Cameroon people' that Europeans should confine their commerce to the seaboard; two days later Nachtigal was able to sign treaties of protection with Kings Bell and Akwa (though these were not published) and to hoist the German flag.[2]

[1] *MAE*, Angleterre (Freetown) 71, Ferry to Bareste, de Brazza, Conf., 20 April 1884.

[2] W.B. No. 8280, Nachtigal to Bismarck, 16 Aug. 1884; Rudin, *op. cit.*, pp. 423–5, 39–75.

The British traders were duly shocked by this unexpected development; they insisted that Germany should maintain the Courts of Equity, and when Hewett arrived at last on 19 July they encouraged him to countermarch by concluding a series of treaties with neighbouring rulers. Cabinet Ministers too were shocked and irritated by German intervention in a district they had planned to control themselves, coming on top of the Angra Peqena affair.[1] Yet, after all, the Cameroons had been regarded as a convenient annex to the Niger protectorate, not as an area intrinsically vital. British trade was not negligible, but it could hope to be treated more favourably under German than under French rule; to many it seemed somehow less humiliating, as well as less commercially dangerous, to be thwarted by Germany than by France. As Gladstone had recently told a German visitor, 'we could have no better neighbours'.[2] The idea of resisting Germany within the Cameroons did not make sense. By the spring of 1885 the two powers had agreed on a demarcation of influence; Britain withdrew a series of treaty claims which Hewett and others had belatedly established, even giving up the site of the long-established Baptist mission at Victoria.

The counterpart of these British concessions was that Bismarck abstained from supporting the desire of Germans trading in Lagos to challenge British supremacy on the Niger itself. The house of G. L. Gaiser was trading profitably in palm produce beyond the eastern boundary of the Lagos customs; in 1882 its agent Bey, who held the consular appointment, had reconnoitred a trading site at Mahin, on the Benin coast. In January 1885 another Gaiser agent secured the cession here of a coastal strip thirty-five miles long; later Nachtigal came and assumed sovereignty in the name of the Empire. At the same time, German colonial enthusiasts were encouraging the intensely patriotic young explorer Flegel to resume his political reconnaissance of the Benué region. Serious claims in the Niger basin would have provoked Britain far more seriously than in the Cameroons; but Bismarck had no intention of pressing them.

[1] J. L. Garvin, *Life of Joseph Chamberlain*, Vol. I (London, 1932) p. 495; Gwynn and Tuckwell, *op. cit.*, II, pp. 80–3.
[2] Eyck, *Bismarck*, III, p. 407; cf. Aydelotte, *op. cit.*, p. 9.

The Mahin claims were abandoned during the boundary negotiation of 1885, and the desire of German traders to navigate the Niger and Benué was not allowed to cause serious friction in Bismarck's time.[1]

Nachtigal in Guinea

Elsewhere, however, Nachtigal's instructions to protect the interests of German traders were as likely to make trouble with France as with Britain. His very first visit, to Dembia in the rivières du sud, provided a small demonstration of this. In 1883 F. Colin, a Würtemburger who had served Verminck for twelve years, raised capital in Stuttgart and began to trade here on his own account. His patriotism had apparently been affronted by the way France and Britain had portioned out this area in their agreement of 1882, and he seems to have played an important, though indirect, role in the creation of the Kolonialverein, the expansionist pressure group.[2] Early in 1884 Colin forwarded to Berlin a request for protection by Balla Demba, who may well have been worried by the danger of French control; and when Nachtigal arrived in June he apparently considered extending German protection, until he heard that France had claims to the country.[3] Colin continued to search for chiefs without direct commitments to France who might open their territories to the German flag. He was unsuccessful in the Bramaya; but he secured a treaty from the Koba Bagas, and in January 1885 persuaded Nachtigal to hoist the German colours at his factory in their territory. These incidents naturally perturbed the French, even though Bismarck never intended to press such claims, and formally renounced them by a Convention of December 1885.[4]

---

[1] Schramm, op. cit., pp. 280–7; Rudin, op. cit., pp. 50, 60, 64–5; Scotter, op. cit., pp. 312–16. For Flegel, see K. Flegel (ed.) Vom Niger-Benüe, Leipzig, 1890, pp. 1–6, 100–1.

[2] Townsend, Origins . . . , pp. 138–9, 149.

[3] MAE, Angleterre (Freetown) 71, Guichard to M.A.E., 28 June, 27 July 1884. According to the latter report Nachtigal also attempted to secure one of the Isles de Los until informed of the established British title.

[4] MMC, Afrique VI/40/c, M.A.E. to M.M.C., 8 Nov. 1884; MAE, Afrique 84, Verminck to Ferry, 29 Dec. 1884; Arcin, op. cit., pp. 408 ff.; A. Chéradame, La Colonisation et les Colonies allemandes (Paris, 1905) pp. 104–5.

The Powers in the Popos, and the origin of Togoland

French and German claims in the Popos area proved rather less simple to disentangle. The four small states which have hitherto been referred to under this general title were, reading from west to east, Porto Seguro, Little Popo, Aghwey, and Great Popo. Each of these appears to have been under the control of local notables with commercial interests; their independent status, if not established beyond question, had been recognized by France and Britain during the Dahomey blockade of 1876.[1] The ports of Lomé and Bagida, lying between the Gold Coast boundary and Porto Seguro, were under the sovereignty of the King of Togo, who resided at Grigi, on the north side of the coastal lagoon. After 1883, some Europeans argued that this ruler was also sovereign of the Popos; but there seems to have been few outward signs of this sovereignty, and the validity of the claim remains debatable.[2]

Although missionaries and traders from Bremen had been active in this region since the 1850's, and German trade began to increase in the early 1880's, it long seemed likely that the fate of the Popos would be decided in discreetly muted conflict between French and British representatives. Fabre and Régis were prominent in the trade of all four states; between 1874 and 1879 they valued their exports of palm produce at more than four million francs a year, or one-seventh of their total African trade.[3] Control of the Popos was an essential part of British plans to close the fiscal gap between Lagos and the Gold Coast; conversely, a French protectorate would foil this scheme, and assure the French merchants of continued access to their markets. In March 1881 Bareste, when urging the renewal of the Porto Novo protectorate, had also drawn attention to the

[1] cf. above, pp. 203–4.

[2] R. Cornevin, *Histoire du Togo* (Paris, 1959) p. 130, quoting R. P. Desribes, *L'Evangile au Dahomey*.

[3] *MAE*, Afrique 77, d'Elteil to Freycinet, Oct. 1880. Bareste in a note of Sept. 1881 (Ang. (Freetown) 53) estimated the value of the trade in 1880 at only one million but his figures show a similar proportion of one-seventh. cf. Afrique 79, Note on Porto Seguro and Little Popo, 1884; Schramm, *op. cit.*, pp. 251–61; Newbury, *op. cit.*, pp. 101 ff.

Popos; next August he forwarded identical letters in which chiefs of all four states requested French protection. These letters had been secured by Fabre's agent Bocamy, with some discreet encouragement from French officials and missionaries; the exact status of some of the signatories is not clear.[1]

For various reasons, the French government delayed action on these treaties. There was some fear of provoking Dahomey into reviving her claim to sovereignty over the Popos; until January 1883 there seemed a danger of provoking British reprisals at Porto Novo; finally, the letters of invitation were mislaid and new ones had to be requested. On 19 July 1883 President Grévy signed a Decree proclaiming the French protectorate, but still this was not published.[2] Not surprisingly, rumours of French intentions leaked out to Accra, where Rowe was pressing for authority to extend British sovereignty over the Slave Coast. In 1882 an offer to cede Little Popo to Britain had been made by T. G. Lawson, Government Interpreter at Freetown, who for more than twenty years had claimed to be legitimate chief of that place. Derby, though still averse to 'any unnecessary extension of British authority', could see the advantage of preventing a French protectorate; he reluctantly authorized Rowe, first 'to consent to supervise and protect the district . . . without acquiring sovereignty', then to negotiate an agreement precluding the cession of Little Popo to any other power.[3]

Rowe, his francophobia redoubled after the Porto Novo protectorate, regarded this as sufficient authority to justify open

[1] *MAE*, Afrique 77, Bareste to M.A.E., 20 May 1881; letters from Aghwey, 6 Aug. 1884; Little Popo, 18 Aug.; Porto Seguro, 20 Aug.; Great Popo, 24 Aug.; Angleterre (Freetown) 53, Bareste to M.A.E., 12 Sept., 13 Dec. 1881; Afrique 57, Report by Penfentany, 28 Feb. 1882.

[2] *MAE*, Afrique 77, M.M.C. to M.A.E., 4 March, 25 March 1882; Afrique 78, M.M.C. to M.A.E., 19 Jan. 1883; M.A.E. to M.M.C., 28 Feb.; Angleterre (Freetown) 70, Bareste to M.A.E., 11 June, 27 June 1883 and enclosures; Afrique 78, M.M.C. to M.A.E., 10 Aug. 1883; M.A.E. to M.M.C., 17 Aug.; Fabre to M.M.C., 9 Nov. 1883.

[3] C.O. 267/350, F.O. to C.O., 14 Dec. 1882, minute by Hemming; C.O. to F.O., 23 Jan. 1883; C.O. 806/209, Derby to Rowe, 31 Jan. 1883; Rowe to Derby, Conf., 8 March, 12 April 1883; Derby to Rowe, Conf., 12 June 1883; Scotter, *op. cit.*, pp. 210–14.

M

encouragement of the pro-British Lawsons during a succession dispute which developed in Little Popo early in 1883. In April a British warship visited the town; in August Rowe himself was there.[1] And in August also William T. G. Lawson, son of the Government Interpreter and himself a former civil servant in the British settlements, arrived at Little Popo and proclaimed himself regent chief. Fabre's agent Cantaloup had hitherto based his policy on support of a rival 'cabooceer' named Pedro Cudjo; he now tardily and reluctantly admitted that his candidate's claims were weaker than those of the Lawsons. William, with much public support, proclaimed his cousin George A. Lawson the rightful king, and installed himself as chief Minister. At the end of 1883 Cantaloup was prepared to write off French policy at Little Popo.[2]

The victorious Lawsons decided to improve their financial position by annulling the agreements with the previous rulers, under which both French and German merchants had advantageously regulated the tenure of their property and their liability to taxation. This proved a fatal mistake; the French and Germans, hitherto far from friendly, now found a common interest in resistance.[3] On 30 January 1884 the German warship *Sophie*, which Bismarck had sent on an African cruise as a first response to the merchants, anchored off Little Popo.[4] Its commander Stubenrauch, on the advice of the German traders, tried to settle the dispute by enforcing recognition of the sovereign rights of the King of Togo. He naturally failed to command the assent of the Lawsons, and as soon as he had left their agents clashed with employees of Messrs. Wölber & Brohm in a dispute over the landing of imports. Stubenrauch, summoned back from Great Popo by overland messenger, sent a strong landing-party ashore, and abducted William and George Lawson, with two followers, as 'hostages' for the safety of European property. At

[1] *MAE*, Angleterre (Freetown) 70, Bareste to M.A.E., 8 May, 30 Aug. 1883.
[2] *MAE*, Angleterre (Freetown) 70, Bareste to M.A.E., 10 Oct., 13 Oct. 1883; Afrique 78, Fabre to M.M.C., 9 Nov.; M.M.C. to M.A.E., 6 Dec. 1883; Cornevin, *op. cit.*, pp. 132 ff.
[3] W.B., No. 8270, Wentzel to Hatzfeldt, 11 July 1883.
[4] W.B., No. 8272, Hatzfeldt to Wentzel, 22 Dec. 1883.

the same time he proclaimed his recognition of the King of Togo as sovereign of the whole coast; and he took away a request for German protection against British designs, written in the name of the King and of Pedro Cudjo's party.[1]

This unexpected intervention shook the standing of the Lawsons, and offered the French new hopes of escaping British control by supporting the claims of the King of Togo. Stubenrauch's *coup* could be regarded as the impetuous act of a choleric German officer; as yet there seemed no reason to regard Germany as a competitor for sovereign rights in Africa. On 14 May the German Ambassador assured Ferry that Germany, 'as a new proof of her desire to walk in agreement with France in the settlement of all colonial questions on the West coast of Africa', would not accept the offer of a protectorate which Stubenrauch had received. Accordingly, Nachtigal was instructed to visit Little Popo to arrange terms for the release of the hostages; but he was precluded from accepting its protectorate, and urged to avoid any collision with French interests.[2]

When Nachtigal reached Little Popo on 2 July, however, he found the Lawson party still insisting on its rights; the German traders feared they would invoke British protection at the first opportunity. The position was ironical; Bismarck's assurance to France seemed to preclude direct action by Nachtigal at Little Popo to avert that British protectorate which both French and Germans feared. But his instructions did not forbid him to act further to the west, where German traders at Lomé and Bagida seemed threatened by a new eastward extension of the Gold Coast frontier on the pattern of 1879.[3] Here there were no French traders; the Germans' only competitors were Sierra Leoneans, and one small Swanzy agency. Moreover, Nachtigal believed, Lomé might provide a good starting-point for developing the Volta route to Salaga and thence to the Sudan. On 5 July he therefore signed a treaty by which Mlapa, King of

[1] W.B., No. 8274, anlagen 2, 3. Stubenrauch to Admiralty, 22 Feb. 1884; *MAE*, Angleterre (Freetown) 71, Bareste to M.A.E., 18, 23, 27 Feb. 1884.

[2] *MAE*, Afrique 80, Declaration by Hohenlohe, 14 May 1884; W.B., No. 8274, Bismarck to Nachtigal, 19 May 1884.

[3] Scotter, *op. cit.*, pp. 240 ff.

Togo, accepted a German protectorate over his territory from Lomé to Porto Seguro.[1]

Even though Little Popo was deliberately excluded from this protectorate, its repercussions were inevitably felt there. George Lawson himself bowed to the new fact of German power on 7 July by accepting release on Nachtigal's conditions; the British, their hopes of a 'continuous coastline' finally ruined, no longer pressed isolated claims at Little Popo, but confined themselves to desultory representations in the personal interests of the Lawson family. France, who had opposed Britain by arguing that Little Popo was subject to the King of Togo, now found that ruler under German protection. Bismarck's African policy, originally conceived in the hope of improving relations with France, was acquiring an impetus of its own; the Popos question now lay between France and Germany. After a moment of *Schadenfreude* at Britain's discomfiture, the French discovered that German traders were talking euphorically of controlling the whole Slave Coast;[2] on 5 September a German naval officer signed a treaty at Porto Seguro. In the spring of 1885, as Franco-German relations cooled in Europe, the French moved tardily to secure their own interests. After a period of confused 'scrambling', a delimitation agreement of December 1885 left Germany in possession of a 'Togoland' which included Little Popo and Porto Seguro, while France held Aghwey and Great Popo.[3] It was a reasonable enough compromise, from the European point of view; but it hardly promoted Franco-German amity.

[2]
The Berlin Conference, 1884–5

British treaties on the Niger

Although German policy thus administered two unexpected and irritating setbacks to Britain, it did not prevent her from

[1] W.B., No. 8278, Nachtigal to Bismarck, 9 July 1884. The text is printed by Newbury, *op. cit.*, pp. 209–10.

[2] *MAE*, Afrique 80, Fabre to M.A.E., 20 Aug., 13 Sept. 1884.

[3] For these negotiations, and the attempt to arrange a common Franco-German tariff, see Newbury, *op. cit.*, pp. 114 ff.

securing her essential interests in the Niger region. The friction deliberately produced by Bismarck over the Cameroons has led many writers to place disproportionate emphasis on Britain's failure there — a distortion partly traceable to the British Blue Book of 1885.[1] Hewett was forestalled in the Cameroons; but between July and October he was able to conclude an important series of treaties in the Oil Rivers, the lower Niger, and the Benué. Although some of the African signatories refused to accept the controversial Article VI, binding them to open their territories to traders of all nations, all agreed to accept British protection, and to have no dealings with foreign powers without British consent.[2] The essential core of British commercial interests was thus safeguarded against foreign intrusion — so far, that is, as treaties with African rulers could offer effective safeguards.

Nor was this all. The National African Company, whose Agent-General McIntosh had been made an honorary Vice-Consul, was also making treaties conferring political jurisdiction upon itself — sometimes combined with monopolistic trading privileges, which Hewett was unable to approve.[3] By 1886 the number of the Company's treaties had risen to 237 (though not all of these purported to confer sovereign rights, and even fewer represented a conscious acceptance by the Africans of foreign control).[4] The most spectacular of the treaties was made by Joseph Thomson, the young Scottish naturalist who had recently distinguished himself in East Africa. The Company had become alarmed by signs of German interest in the Benué; hearing that the German Consul in Lagos was sponsoring a new journey by Flegel into Adamawa, they hastily and secretly despatched Thomson to secure treaties with the Sultans of Sokoto and Gwandu, as supreme overlords of the Fulani Emirates. In June 1885 both Sultans signed documents purporting to transfer to the Company their entire rights on

[1] Crowe, *op. cit.*, pp. 221–3.
[2] C.P. 5023, Hewett to Granville, 24 Sept. 1884; C.P. 5064, Hewett to Granville, 15 Nov. 1884, enclosing treaties.
[3] C.P. 5064, Hewett to Granville, 15 Nov. 1884.
[4] Flint, *op. cit.*, pp. 60–1, 88–91, 137–40; Diké, *op. cit.*, p. 212.

both banks of the Niger, Benué, and tributary rivers.[1] These documents did not bring any immediate increment in the influence actually enjoyed by the British in Hausaland, but they did preclude foreign claims based upon similar scraps of paper.

Meanwhile Goldie's price-war had succeeded in eliminating French commercial rivalry from the Niger. The Senegal Company sold its Niger interests to the National African Company in June 1884; the C.F.A.E. did likewise in October, receiving in return six thousand shares in the N.A.C., with two seats on the Board. The patriotic Mattei expressed anguished disappointment; but the French government had always been chary of accepting direct commitments in the river, and lacked funds with which to support their companies.[2] On 1 November Goldie could report that the National African Company was again unchallenged up the Niger.[3]

The limits of Franco-German co-operation

Even in the Congo, Bismarck's readiness to co-operate with France against the Anglo-Portuguese treaty did no irreparable damage to British policy. Between March and June 1884 there was strong international pressure against the Treaty, and particularly against the proposal to place navigation under the control of a joint Anglo-Portuguese Commission; this opposition was led by France, supported by the Netherlands, Belgium and the United States, and finally made effective by German support.[4] But for Britain recognition of Portuguese claims had never been more than an unsatisfactory expedient for keeping the Congo trade open and free, and important sections of the public opposed this policy. Humanitarians brought up in the anti-slavery tradition lacked confidence in Portugal's political and commercial principles; Protestant missions in the Congo feared Catholic control; an important group of capitalists, including

---

[1] E. Hertslet, *Map of Africa by Treaty* (2nd ed., 1896), III, pp. 972–5; J. B. Thomson, *Joseph Thomson* (London, 1896) Ch. VII.
[2] Flint, *op. cit.*, pp. 67–8; *MAE*, Afrique 86, Mattei to Ferry, 13 Oct. 1884.
[3] C.P. 5033, Goldie-Taubman to Anderson, 1 Nov. 1884.
[4] Crowe, *op. cit.*, Pt. I, Ch. II.

Sir William MacKinnon, had plans for co-operating with Leopold's International Association.[1] Gradually during 1884 Leopold's artful diplomacy secured wider international recognition for the Association. His object was to prove that its territories were not, as commonly assumed, destined ultimately to fall under French control; but that, erected into an independent state under international guarantee, they could provide the institutional structure needed for the protection of international trade. This professed aim coincided completely with the desires of the British government; and slowly they came to admit the feasibility of the means by which Leopold proposed to secure it.[2]

There was in fact very limited scope for Bismarck's scheme of working with France against Britain in those parts of Africa which seemed of secondary international importance. In such places Britain's essential concern was to do business in security without fear of restrictive tariffs; Germany, as a rapidly growing commercial power, had in principle identical interests. In so far as France was coming to seek African colonies for the sake of national self-gratification (as in the Congo) or to use them (as in Senegal) to protect home industry, she was as liable to rouse opposition in Germany as in Britain. Certainly, British colonial policy too might be objectionable to German traders, as on the Niger; but since Bismarck excluded areas of major interest to Britain from his field of manoeuvre, no basis for Franco-German entente could be found there either.

* * * * *

Bismarck, having prepared the way by some general gestures of goodwill in Ferry's direction during 1883, first developed the idea of colonial co-operation to the French ambassador on 24 April 1884, a move exactly synchronized with his first challenge to Britain over South-West Africa.[3] He opened the conversation, which ranged widely over European politics, by abusing Glad-

[1] I have drawn here on the unpublished paper submitted by Dr. R. T. Anstey to the second African History Conference at the School of Oriental and African Studies, London, July 1957.

[2] Crowe, *op. cit.*, Pt. I, Ch. VIII; cf. Gwynn and Tuckwell, *Dilke*, II, pp. 84–6.

[3] A. J. P. Taylor, *Germany's First Bid for Colonies* (London, 1938) pp. 19–31.

stone's handling of British policy; he referred to difficulties created for foreign traders by British proceedings in Africa and in the Pacific, citing as examples the Congo treaty and a dispute affecting European titles to land in Fiji. Suggesting, sensibly enough,

> 'that all the commercial nations would stand to gain by reaching agreement on general rules to be observed in those countries where no civilized nation has yet entered into possession',

Bismarck implied, by a cryptic reference to the Armed Neutrality of 1780, that such an agreement should be directed against Britain.[1]

The French treated this idea warily. Their ambassador, Courcel (who had experienced difficulties in dealing with Britain overseas while working in the Quai d'Orsay) realized that Bismarck was playing a double game, hoping to increase his own international bargaining power by embroiling France with Britain.[2] And Ferry, while not so prejudiced by the matter of Alsace-Lorraine as to exclude any idea of collaboration with Germany, could not see in Bismarck's suggestions any prospective advantages sufficiently concrete to justify such a politically perilous move. Bismarck enlarged somewhat on his idea of an anti-British League of Neutrals on 12 May, and hinted at the possibility of supporting France in Morocco; but still he won no response.[3] He therefore tried to prove his good faith by deliberately causing friction with the British. During the summer he sent Nachtigal on his African cruise, joined in the successful opposition to the Anglo-Portuguese treaty, and by progressive stages inflamed the dispute over South-West Africa. Finally, Bismarck gave some limited support to the French case in the abortive conference over Egypt, held in London in July, although he avoided compromising himself with Britain by supporting the French demand for guarantees as to British evacuation.[4]

By early August Bismarck judged it opportune to revive his

[1] D.D.F., V, No. 249, Courcel to Ferry, 25 April 1884.
[2] ibid., No. 247, Courcel to Ferry, Pte., 25 April 1884.
[3] ibid., No. 270, Courcel to Ferry, 14 May 1884.
[4] Taylor, op. cit., Chs. II, III; Crowe, op. cit., Pt. I, Chs. IV, V.

idea of an 'Armed Neutrality' — or, as he now defined it, an international agreement to guarantee commercial freedom on those African coasts not yet under European jurisdiction.[1] Courcel, in a series of interviews with the Secretary of State, pressed for more details (and also showed notable eagerness to discuss the ticklish Egyptian question). On 17 August the Germans proposed that the two powers should guarantee liberty of commerce (meaning, apparently, that they should impose no tariffs at all)[2] in any territories which they might occupy on the West coast of Africa; and that they should refuse to recognize new territorial acquisitions by powers which refused to do like-wise. Since the main purposes of such an agreement would be to limit arbitrary expansion by Cape Colony and to prevent the establishment of an exclusive régime in the Congo, Bismarck suggested it might be confined to territories south of the Equator; his avowed reason was to spare France embarrassment in the Senegal region, but another effect would have been to exclude the Niger.[3]

These proposals, though not unlike those formerly favoured by French officials, might commit France to resist Britain in the interests of German trade, and would prejudice the changes she was contemplating in her own colonial fiscal policy; Courcel and Ferry wanted something more concrete. Instead of working against Britain, Ferry preferred to try to tie her down to accept-ance of the proposed international agreement; in place of general declarations of free trade principles he preferred to work out detailed guarantees for free trade and navigation in the specific area of the Congo, and to try to extend them (at least those affecting navigation) to the Niger. And if a conference called for this purpose should evolve some general principles applicable to future cases, these might well command sufficient respect to ensure their adoption.[4] On 27 August Bismarck agreed that France and Germany should convene a conference to deal with

[1] G.P. III, No. 680, Bismarck to Hatzfeldt, 7 Aug. 1884.
[2] ibid., No. 681, Hatzfeldt to Bismarck, 11 Aug. 1884, p. 415.
[3] D.D.F. V, No. 372, Courcel to Ferry, Tel., 17 Aug. 1884.
[4] D.D.F. V, No. 376, Note by Ferry; No. 377, Courcel to Ferry, Tel., 25–6 Aug. 1884.

M*

these specific points. At the same time, answering French apprehensions about Nachtigal's proceedings in Togoland, he repeated his promise not to approve any action which might
infringe France's legitimate rights.[1]

Bismarck's readiness to accept Ferry's counter-proposals is
largely explained by his hope that such practical co-operation
might prepare for a closer Franco-German entente later. In fact
Ferry's guarded distrust was never fully overcome. The idea of
Franco-German co-operation at the head of some sort of
Armed Neutrality was discussed several more times before
Ferry's fall in March 1885; even the prudent Courcel began to
wonder whether developing economic and maritime rivalries
between Britain and Germany might not prepare the way for
real Franco-German co-operation, embracing the Egyptian
question.[2] But such expectations proved ephemeral; it became
clear that Bismarck was varying the warmth of his attitude
according to the tactical needs of his complex European policy.
By the end of 1884 a diplomatic revolution was most unlikely;
Lyons summarized the position when he wrote:

> 'Bismarck and Ferry are *jouant au plus fin* with each other at our
> expense. Each seems to think that he can use the other to help in
> thwarting us, without risk to himself.'[3]

Only the possibility of collaboration over specifically limited
issues remained; but this, if successful, might still have made an
eventual diplomatic revolution more feasible. Of such issues, the
proposed West African Conference had taken the most concrete
form.

The work of the Conference

Early in October France and Germany joined in inviting
twelve other states to a conference in Berlin to discuss three
problems. The first was liberty of commerce in the basin and
mouth of the Congo ('liberty of commerce' having been re-

---

[1] *ibid.*, No. 385, Courcel to Ferry, 30 Aug. 1884; G.P. III, No. 688,
Bismarck to Busch, 30 Aug. 1884.

[2] D.D.F. V, Nos. 407, 410, Courcel to Ferry, 23 Sept.; Pte., 28 Sept. 1884.

[3] Lyons to Granville, Pte., 20 Jan. 1885, *cit.*, Taylor, *op. cit.*, p. 65. On this
subject generally, see Taylor, Chs. IV–VI.

defined, at French initiative, so as to permit the imposition of duties to cover administrative costs). The second was the application to the Congo and the Niger of the principles adopted by the Congress of Vienna in 1815 to safeguard liberty of navigation on international rivers; the third, definition of formalities to be observed before new occupations of territory on the coasts of Africa should be internationally recognized.[1] The British government at once accepted the invitation in principle, while adding their own glosses to that ambiguous term, 'liberty of commerce'.[2] Their main concern was to establish a clear distinction between the position on the Congo, where internationalization would be both justifiable and advantageous, and that on the Niger, where Britain herself, thanks to the efforts of Hewett and Goldie, was now 'the Niger power'. Until quite recently the government might well have been content with international guarantees for its commercial interests on the Niger; but many Ministers were now determined to stand by the previous year's decision to assert British national claims, partly because of Goldie's insistence, but also in reaction to French and German policy elsewhere. Right-wing Whigs and Radicals had alike been greatly irritated by the set-backs recently suffered by Britain in Africa; Kimberley and Chamberlain, among others, now insisted on excluding both Germany and France from political control in the Niger. Gladstone and other pacifically-minded Ministers, already threatened with resignations from both wings of the disunited Cabinet over a wide range of Irish and domestic issues, had to agree to resist any real internationalization of the Niger. Derby, still loyal to his principles, saw no reason why the Niger should not be treated in the same way as the Congo, but his officials too advised against accepting any effective international Commission.[3]

---

[1] D.D.F. V, No. 419, Ferry circular, 5–6 Oct. 1884.

[2] C.P. 5023, No. 15, Granville to Plessen, 8 Oct. 1884.

[3] P.R.O. 30/29/120, memo. by Kimberley, 26 Sept., by Chamberlain, 28 Sept. 1884; Derby to Granville, Pte., 16 Oct. 1884; C.P. 5023, minutes by Lister, Anderson, 14 Oct.; No. 72, minute by Hemming, 16 Oct. 1884; cf. Robinson, Gallagher and Denny, *op. cit.*, pp. 177–80.

In fact, Britain had little real difficulty in avoiding the internationalization of the Niger. The question of enforcing commercial liberty there, it will have been noted, was not even on the Conference agenda; the French Ministry for Foreign Affairs had not thought it worth making the attempt. (The Ministry of the Marine, however, regretted this, and even seemed willing to pay the price of including its own sphere of influence on the *upper* Niger within the scope of such an international arrangement.)[1] As for navigation, the British could claim that, since they now held treaty rights and a *de facto* trade monopoly over that whole portion of the river which was navigable from the sea, there was no justification for an International Commission; the Niger, for purposes of navigation, was not an 'international river'. But Britain was *herself* willing to guarantee free navigation on the same basis as in the Congo. Two days before the Conference opened Bismarck, whose relations with France were passing through a strained period and who may have anticipated a need for British support over the Congo, agreed to accept this case; and on 16 November the French delegation too accepted the distinction between the two rivers.[2] (In making this concession they may have been influenced by fears that, if they pressed for a Commission on the Niger, Britain might demand one on other African rivers than those mentioned in the Conference programme, such as the Senegal.) In the final Berlin Act, therefore, Britain and France simply bound themselves to apply similar conditions to those imposed on the Congo along such reaches of the Niger as they respectively controlled, but no machinery for international supervision was established.[3]

On the Congo question too the upshot of the Conference proved satisfactory to Great Britain, who gradually realized that by supporting Leopold she could secure the essential purposes pursued by the abortive treaty with Portugal. During 1884 Leopold showed great diplomatic skill in obtaining recognition

---

[1] D.D.F. V, No. 437, Note for Nisard, 23 Oct. 1884; *MAE*, Afrique 109, M.M.C. to M.A.E., 12 Dec. 1884.

[2] D.D.F. V, No. 453, Courcel to Ferry, 16 Nov. 1884.

[3] Crowe, *op. cit.*, pp. 75–7, 127–30, 140–1; Flint, *op. cit.*, pp. 68–70.

of his International Association as a sovereign power in Africa,
initially from the United States and France. Even the right of
pre-emption, which he openly conceded to France as the price
of her recognition, served the cause of Congolese independence,
for it gave those powers hostile to French expansion the strongest
possible interest in strengthening international guarantees
for the new state.[1] In this task, and in the formulation of safeguards for trade and navigation through the wider area known
as 'the conventional basin of the Congo', Germany and
Britain eventually found a high degree of common interest.

The importance of the Berlin Conference has often been mis-
represented and exaggerated. Diplomatically, though it seemed
a significant novelty that France and Germany should jointly
sponsor such a conference, their African interests proved to be
widely divergent, and the idea of a Franco-German entente soon
lapsed. Wilhelm II's belief that the continental powers had
united in an anti-British league was a myth.[2] Nor is it true that
the Conference 'partitioned Africa'. Territorial questions were
specifically excluded from the agenda, and those requiring
settlement were dealt with in a series of bilateral agreements
extending over many years (though it is true that important
questions affecting boundaries in the Congo basin were discussed by delegates in Berlin outside the Conference sessions).[3]

One aim of the Conference, as defined in the third 'basis', was
to limit the effects of future African disputes upon international
relations in Europe by prescribing some new code of conduct.
The final Act provided that any power acquiring territory or
establishing protectorates on the coasts of Africa should at once
notify all other signatory powers; and declared that possession
of territory on those coasts implied a responsibility for 'the
establishment of authority ... sufficient to protect existing
rights, and, as the case may be, freedom of trade and of transit
upon the conditions agreed upon'.[4] But both these provisions
were restricted to the coastal districts, virtually all of which were

---

[1] Crowe, *op. cit.*, Pt. I, Ch. VIII.
[2] *ibid.*, p. 192.
[3] *ibid.*, Pt. II, Ch. V.
[4] Hertslet, *op. cit.*, I, No. 17, Articles xxxiv, xxxv (p. 43).

already appropriated by 1885; and protectorates were not covered by the wording of the second. (This was a victory for the British, who, although they had formerly questioned the French claims to Cotonou and Porto Novo on the grounds that there was no effective occupation, were not ready to assume extensive administrative commitments in their new Niger protectorates.) These provisions of the Berlin Act, like its vague references to the abolition of slave dealing and to the welfare of the peoples of the Congo basin, had little practical effect on the coming partition of Africa.

[3]
Survey of the Partition of West Africa, 1885–98

The Berlin Conference caused no sudden change in the basic attitudes of the European states. After 1885 as before, pressures for expansion which originated with French or British subjects on the West African coast were counter-balanced in Paris and London by diplomatic caution, by the political instinct to avoid commitment and to economize. The extension of European control along the coasts meant that the administering powers were becoming increasingly involved in the affairs of their new hinterlands; but in practice the inland extension of govern-mental power was slow and often reluctant.

In June 1885 Great Britain constituted the territories between Lagos and the Cameroons, together with the banks of the Niger up to Lokoja and of the Benué up to Ibi, into the Niger Coast Protectorate; but in principle her governments were willing and even anxious to leave the administration of the area beyond the delta to the National African Company, as 'the cheapest and most effective way' of discharging the obligations to maintain free navigation which had been accepted at Berlin. (Had Goldie been able to come to terms with the Liverpool oil traders of the delta, the government would have been delighted to leave the entire protectorate to Company rule.) Negotiations about the terms on which this might be done began early in 1886; they did not run smoothly, and Goldie even threatened wildly to transfer his Company's treaty rights to France; but in July 1886 the Charter was finally issued. The Company was empowered to exercise in the name of the Crown all such rights as it might acquire by its treaties in the Niger; it was allowed to levy customs duties for the purpose of covering administrative costs — a provision which afforded an important loophole for oblique discrimination against the imports of competitors, and which permitted the Company to achieve in practice that commercial monopoly which was forbidden by the letter of the Charter. With the fruits of this monopoly the Royal Niger Company (as it now became) created a rudimentary governmental framework which for several years appeared impressive enough to deter France and Germany from any serious challenge on the lower Niger.[1] In practice Company rule had many grave faults and weaknesses; but the British government, as a recent study emphasizes, was still content to leave its major West African interest beneath this light administrative umbrella, while itself devoting slightly increased diplomatic vigour to defending its interests in East Africa.[2]

But it was not only the British government which gave a low priority to West African policy. The fall of Jules Ferry at the end of March 1885, in consequence of a military set-back in Indo-China, meant a pause in the French advance towards the upper Niger. All colonial enterprises were temporarily discredited by the failure of one; the Chambers became even more reluctant to vote funds for military expeditions, just when French troops on the Niger were meeting potentially more formidable opposition. In February 1883 the French occupied Bamako, which at last brought them near the main centre of Tokolor power at Ségou; but, having clashed with Samori's advanced forces near Siguiri, they were forced to recognize the existence of a second formidable African state in the upper Niger. Moreover their own operations (involving requisitioning of foodstuffs and the use of forced labour) had created resistance in the rear. During the middle 1880's substantial French forces had to be diverted into Cayor, where since 1882 Lat-Dior had again been

[1] Flint, *op. cit.*, pp. 70–87 and App. II.
[2] Robinson, Gallagher and Denny, *op. cit.*, pp. 180–98, 393.

opposing France over the construction of her railway, and into Galam, where Mamadu Lamina, a well-travelled Muslim scholar, was organizing resistance among the Sarakulé.

Fortunately for the French, their enemies failed to combine. Although Amadu had been re-organizing his dominions with a view to their eventual defence against France, he seemed equally determined to resist the challenge to his authority represented by the rise of rival African empires. Formerly, it is said, he had held Mamadu Lamina six years in prison; certainly he did not wish to encourage a militantly Muslim Sarakulé state within his own sphere of power and influence.[1] He was also on bad terms with Samori, and seems to have made no serious attempt to co-operate with him. Prudently enough, Amadu would have preferred to avoid a battle with the French and their superior technology; when they appeared willing to co-operate with him, Amadu responded loyally, signing and observing a new treaty in 1887.[2] The French were meanwhile more worried about Samori, who in 1885 turned to the British Governor at Freetown, offering to accept British protection and seeking an assured supply of fire-arms.[3] Frightened lest the Niger sources should come under British control, the French in 1886 and 1887 sent envoys to Samori, and on each occasion claimed to have obtained his signature to treaties of protection. Whatever passed on these occasions, Samori certainly did not intend to alienate his sovereign independence; but the British government accepted the treaties in this sense and did not interfere when France eventually undertook the task of bringing this over-mighty protégé to heel.

This temporary shift of French policy was not exclusively due to the difficulty of obtaining money for military operations. During the middle 1880's there was some disillusioned reaction, both in Paris and in St. Louis, against the policies of Faidherbe and Brière de l'Isle. Gallieni, back in the Sudan as military commander, but still impetuously following the swing of his

---

[1] L. L. C. Faidherbe, *Le Sénégal* (Paris, 1889) pp. 420–1.

[2] J. S. Gallieni, *Deux Campagnes au Soudan Français* (Paris, 1891) pp. 34, 185, 618–19.

[3] J. D. Hargreaves, *A Life of Sir Samuel Lewis* (London, 1958) pp. 48–50.

enthusiasms, now proposed the abandonment of the attempt to reach the Niger by way of the Senegal (and the writing-off of the ill-fated railway) in favour of developing alternative routes through Futa Jalon and the *rivières du sud*.[1] From this point of view, the prevention of any alliance between Samori and the British was clearly of prior importance. But other African rulers in the extreme western Sudan might also need to be associated with French policy. In 1887 Gallieni signed a treaty of protection with Amadu's brother and nominal vassal, Aguibou of Dinguiray, and next year sought, somewhat clumsily, to tighten French control over Futa Jalon.

Still other possible approaches to the Niger were also being examined by Frenchmen. Between 1887 and 1889 Captain Binger was carrying out the most important journey of West African exploration since Barth, travelling from the upper Niger to Grand Bassam through Mossi and Dagomba, and so exploding the geographical myth that the 'mountains of Kong' would always prevent commercial expansion from the Ivory Coast in the direction of the Sudan.[2] Verdier's once-despised holdings now began to assume considerable interest. At Porto Novo too there was some talk of redressing the failure on the lower Niger by establishing commercial contact with Boussa by way of Abeokuta; unsuccessful probes in this direction were made by Viard, a former agent of C.F.A.E.[3]

These developments redirected attention to the coastal settlements, suggesting to both sides the need for a settlement of pending Anglo-French boundary disputes. At the same time, the French operations against Lat-Dior and Mamadu Lamina in the Senegal raised difficulties concerning the limits of British jurisdiction in the Gambia valley. For a time the old idea of 'comprehensive dealing' revived. In 1887 a new incident in the Porto Novo lagoon led the Intelligence Branch of the British War Office to prepare a paper on West African problems. General Brackenbury (who had served in Ashanti under

[1] Gallieni, *Deux Campagnes . . .* , Ch. 37.

[2] L. C. Binger, *Du Niger au Golfe de Guinée* (Paris, 2 Vols.) 1892.

[3] C. W. Newbury, 'The Development of French Policy on the lower and upper Niger', *Journal of Modern History*, xxxi (1959) pp. 24–5.

Wolseley) argued that such places as Appa and Ketenou were of very minor importance, now that the chance had been lost of uniting Lagos with the Gold Coast; but that Freetown, which the Carnarvon Commission on Imperial Defence (of 1879–82) had designated for re-fortification, demanded prior attention. Samori now seemed militarily capable of capturing Sierra Leone, and reports of his treaties with the French had therefore caused great apprehension.[1] In order to ensure the exclusion of French influence from the near vicinity of Freetown, both in-land and on the coast, Brackenbury suggested concessions both at Porto Novo and in the Gambia.[2]

Nothing was done immediately, except to negotiate a *modus vivendi* to prevent further conflicts around Porto Novo; Holland, a former official who was now Colonial Secretary, suggested grouping the various pending boundary disputes into a single comprehensive agreement, but refused to consider ceding the Gambia.[3] But next summer the Gambia question was again brought forward by Hutton, now as eager to promote an ex-change as he had once been to block one.[4] His friend Harry Johnston, Vice-Consul in the Cameroons, spent a weekend at Hatfield with Lord Salisbury, and urged the exchange of the Gambia as part of a broadly visionary scheme for the planned partition of the whole African continent. Salisbury, impressed, agreed that Johnston should air his views in *The Times*, in an attempt to influence public opinion; and Holland reluctantly agreed to consider an exchange.[5] But conditions were far less favourable than in 1876. The French felt a less acute need for the Gambia route now their railway plans had been begun, and the general climate of Anglo-French relations was frigid. Even

[1] cf. C.O. 806/265, esp. No. 28, W.O. to F.O., 22 Jan. 1887.

[2] C.O. 806/281, No. 121, W.O. to C.O., 1 July 1887.

[3] C.O. 806/281, No. 165, F.O. to C.O., 12 Aug.; No. 175, C.O. to F.O., 29 Aug. 1887; C.O. 806/288, No. 88; C.O. to F.O., 13 March 1888.

[4] C.O. 806/288, Ncs. 88, 97, C.O. 806/299, Nos. 44, 47, Hutton to C.O., 19 March, 6 April, 10, 15 Oct. 1888.

[5] R. Oliver, *Sir Harry Johnston and the Scramble for Africa* (London, 1957) pp. 134–44; also pp. 99 ff. and, for Johnston's relations with Hutton, pp. 84–88; C.O. 806/299, Nos. 47–8, C.O. to F.O., 16 Oct. 1888; C.O. 806/301, memo. by Hemming, Nov. 1888.

in Britain, the abatement of mercantile opposition would not remove all difficulties; opposition was feared from Irish M.P.s and perhaps from the Queen. So in 1889 it was decided to grasp an opportunity to negotiate a comprehensive frontier settlement which would reduce friction and protect Freetown against encirclement, but without attempting an exchange. A Convention of 10 August 1889 settled boundaries, on the coast and for short distances inland, at the Gambia, Sierra Leone, Assinie, and Porto Novo (where Britain at last withdrew from Ketenou and part of Appa).[1]

★　★　★　★　★

During the 1890's the policies of the European powers in West Africa became rather more widely and consistently influenced by new political attitudes, best characterized by that overworked word 'Imperialist'. This is not the place for any serious analysis of these attitudes, nor of the changes in European society which made them so widely acceptable Their essential features were a new conviction that future economic benefits would follow from the 'possession' of colonial territories, undeveloped and unpromising though these might actually be; and a new readiness to justify the deployment of military force in order to compel recalcitrant Africans to collaborate in the 'civilizing mission' of the Europeans. This 'new imperialism' affected France's African policy earlier than Britain's; its rise is well illustrated by the career of Eugène Étienne, an Algerian-born disciple of Gambetta, who represented Oran in the Chamber after 1881.

Étienne was a friend and former business associate of Rouvier, and served as under-secretary for the Colonies in his government of 1887. He held that office again from 1889 until 1892; it was now re-attached to the Ministry of Commerce, and Étienne himself was given the right to attend Cabinet meetings. Étienne was becoming the leader of a growing colonial pressure-group, which operated inside and outside parliament; he was closely associated with the *Comité de l'Afrique française*, founded in 1890, and

[1] Hertslet, *op. cit.*, II, No. 110; cf. C.O. 806/317, No. 60; memo. by D.M.I., 21 May 1889; Cecil, *Salisbury*, IV, p. 253.

in 1892 became chairman of a group of ninety-one colonially-minded Deputies, drawn from all parts of the Chamber.[1] Under his direction the advance into *Soudan français* was resumed. Between 1890 and 1893 Amadu's armies were defeated and the Tokolor empire broken; on 16 December 1893 French troops entered Timbuktu. Thereafter they advanced rapidly down the Niger, and into the lands south of the great bend. Meanwhile in Dahomey the insistence of the new King Behanzin upon the independence of his kingdom and its right to Cotonou (which had recently superceded Whydah as the principal port) drew the French into a series of military campaigns, which led to the occupation of Abomey in November 1892 and the dismemberment of the kingdom in 1894.[2]

Now for the first time the French, advancing from two directions, were in a position physically to test that claim to Hausaland which the Niger Company had still not converted into effective control, and to revive their challenge to the Company's monopoly of the Niger navigation below Boussa. It was true that in 1890, in an unguarded moment, the Foreign Ministry had renounced French claims south of a line from Say to Barruwa (and in 1890 had offered the British an even more favourable demarcation line south of Say),[3] but now that circumstances provided the opportunity to pursue more ambitious aims, ingenious men were able to interpret their commitments rather loosely. The famous 'race to Borgu' between Captain Decoeur and Captain Lugard in 1894 opened a new struggle for position on the navigable portion of the lower Niger, a struggle in which really substantial interests seemed to be at stake.[4]

For a time, it seemed that this struggle might become a triangular one. Although Bismarck showed little interest in his African colonies after they had been marked out, and there was

[1] For an excellent analysis of these developments, H. Brunschwig, *op. cit.*, Chs. 7, 8.

[2] Newbury, *The Western Slave Coast* . . . , pp. 123–33.

[3] Flint, *op. cit.*, pp. 156–68, 217–18.

[4] M. Perham, *Lugard: the Years of Adventure* (London, 1956) Part IV; Flint, *op. cit.*, pp. 220–7.

even talk of German withdrawal,[1] both Togoland and Kamerun had nevertheless begun to expand inland, under pressure from local traders or administrators; they began to make their own demands upon German policy. Bismarck's successors, less strongly resolved to maintain the priority of continental over colonial interests, thus found themselves drawn into Anglo-French rivalries in West Africa. In November 1893 the British, by an apparently generous recognition of Germany's claims in Kamerun, tried to use her to block France's expansion from the Congo towards both Nile and Benué; in March 1894 France turned the tables.[2] On the Niger, Frenchmen and Germans rediscovered common interests in opposing the regulations made by the Niger Company; in March 1894 Dr. Kayser, who as Colonial Director in the German Foreign Office was securing a stronger voice for colonial interests in the formulation of national policy, warned the British Ambassador that the Niger navigation might become 'the next great international question'.[3] For a time there was even talk of France and Germany agreeing to give a north-easterly turn to the inland expansion of Togoland and Dahomey, so that both territories might touch the Niger below Boussa; on the other hand Goldie thought of co-operating with Germany in order to seal off French expansion from Dahomey.[4] Nothing important came of these plans for a stronger German role; but they added an extra element of uncertainty to Anglo-French relations during the troubled 1890's.

Until 1895 British governments still tried to limit their commitments in West Africa. Salisbury, who by a decision of 1888 confirmed that British interests in Southern and Eastern Africa should receive higher priority, was successful in imposing 'a

[1] e.g. C.O. 806/300, No. 6, Griffith to Holland, Conf., 21 March 1888.

[2] W. L. Langer, *The Diplomacy of Imperialism* (2nd ed. 1950) pp. 131–2; Robinson, Gallagher and Denny, *op. cit.*, pp. 391–3.

[3] Malet to Kimberley, 7 March 1894, printed in T. A. Bayer, *England und der Neue Kurs* (Tübingen, 1955) pp. 117–20.

[4] F.O. 64/1358, Malet to Salisbury, 117 Africa, 3 Oct. 1895, encl. *Kölnische Zeitung* article; F.O. 64/1373, D.M.I. to Sanderson, 4 Oct. 1895; cf. Flint, *op. cit.*, pp. 184–8, 228–31.

selective regulation of the British advance' in the west.[1] He, and his Liberal successors, were under some pressure to be less rigorously selective. During the 1890's merchants and officials on the west coast, supported by Chambers of Commerce in British cities, were increasingly anxious to expand the frontiers of British influence, either by direct action or by supporting Samori in his prolonged resistance to the French advance. But these West African interests represented 'an energetic but not a compulsive lobby in British politics',[2] and could not determine policy. Sierra Leone was finally delimited, within modest boundaries, in January 1895, the Colonial Office complaining that the diplomatists had traded its interests for the sake of gains in 'the Niger-Congo and Nile questions.'[3] To the north of the Gold Coast, some belated efforts were made after 1892 to conclude treaties with the states of the savanna belt; but though most of Gonja, Mamprussi and Dagomba was thus saved for eventual British control, the northern Mossi states could not be kept out of French hands. In Yorubaland the expansion of the Colony of Lagos, though accelerated by Governor Carter after 1892, remained gradual, and subject to restraints imposed from London.[4]

Even on the Niger, where British claims were most valuable and extensive, it was intended to dispose of the revived French challenge by negotiation. But in this as in other aspects of colonial policy there was a notable change of emphasis after Joseph Chamberlain went to the Colonial Office in 1895. This ex-radical business-man saw tropical Africa as an 'undeveloped estate', capable of profitable improvement by energetic and purposeful administration, and by increased public investment. Convinced of the benefits which the discharge of Britain's Imperial mission would bring to all affected by it, Chamberlain insisted on maintaining British territorial claims to the fullest practical extent. In December 1895 he was prepared to protect the lower Niger by a complicated, three-sided, territorial ex-

---

[1] Cecil, *Salisbury*, IV, p. 336; cf. Oliver, *op. cit.*, p. 136.
[2] Robinson, Gallagher and Denny, *op. cit.*, p. 394.
[3] C.O. 267/409, minute by Meade, 26 June 1894.
[4] cf. Aderibigbe, *op. cit.*

change, involving the cession of the Gambia and Dominica to France in return for Dahomey;[1] but when Salisbury preferred a more limited and local negotiation, Chamberlain insisted on some very tough bargaining. As a leader of the Liberal Unionists in a coalition Cabinet, he was powerful enough to veto some of Salisbury's proposed concessions to France, and eventually to initiate a risky policy of replying to French military encroachments in kind. Though increasingly at odds with Goldie over future policy, Chamberlain strongly supported the Niger Company's insistence on keeping the French off the navigable Niger below Boussa, and out of the main part of Hausaland. Salisbury would have preferred to be much more conciliatory over details; however, it seems doubtful whether even he would have conceded anything which he considered essential to the embryonic territory of Nigeria. Despite the growth of anglophobe colonial enthusiasm in France, it was doubtful whether that government would deliberately risk war against the British navy for the sake of the Niger; sure enough, on 14 June 1898, they conceded the essential points of the British demands.[2]

★   ★   ★   ★   ★

This agreement virtually completed the diplomatic partition of West Africa, though both Britain and France still had to undertake military campaigns to make their power effective in Ashanti and in Hausaland, around the middle Niger and on the borders of the desert. One problem which still seemed open concerned the future of Liberia, where there had been frequent rumours during the 1880's and 1890's of impending annexation by either France, Germany, or Britain. Nevertheless this tenacious little Republic, helped by much luck, succeeded in maintaining its national sovereignty. Elsewhere there were frequent proposals for frontier revision, and some succeeded. The most important formed part of the Anglo-French 'Entente' agreement of 1904; but even this included only a frontier

---

[1] Robinson, Gallagher and Denny, *op. cit.*, p. 402, quoting Salisbury Papers. On Chamberlain in Africa generally, pp. 395–409.

[2] Perham, *op. cit.*, Part VI; J. L. Garvin, *Life of Joseph Chamberlain*, III (London, 1934) Ch. LV; Flint, *op. cit.*, Ch. 12.

rectification in northern Nigeria, a smaller one in the Gambia, and the cession to France of the Isles de Los.

On this occasion the French made another determined effort to obtain all the Gambia; they had discovered that their railway was overtaxing the navigable capacity of the Senegal river, and wanted the Gambia as an auxiliary 'feeder'.[1] They tried again, offering compensation in Asia and the Pacific, and in 1908 Sir Edward Grey apparently agreed that the colony might be ceded without the city of Bathurst, provided the compensation was adequate. In 1911 the French made another overture, sadly mismanaged, asking for huge slices of Nigerian territory at the same time.[2] And even this was not the end of the matter. There is a file in Dakar entitled *Projets d'Échange de la Gambie, 1916–20*.[3] But, apart from the repartition of the German colonies in 1919, the frontiers which had been defined by 1898 were essentially those within which the modern African states have grown to national consciousness and independence. To a very considerable degree, their main configurations had already been foreshadowed by the relations between the European powers and the coastal peoples of Africa before 1885.

* * * * *

Nobody will claim that these frontiers, determined by distant and ill-informed negotiators, were well-adapted to African needs. It is true that their arbitrary nature is often over-emphasized; relatively few were settled by ruler and compasses alone.[4] Since European claims were often based upon treaties with African rulers, there were many cases where the new frontiers

[1] See undated memo. in *MMC*, Afrique IV/70.

[2] D.D.F. (2e série) XI, No. 510, P. Cambon to Pichon, 28 Oct. 1908; No. 593, Pichon to Milliès-Lacroix, 28 Dec. 1908. *British Documents on the Origins of the War*, ed. G. P. Gooch and H. Temperley, Vol. VII, No. 588, Note communicated Sept. 1911 and minutes. (This document was obviously drafted as a letter from the Colonial to the Foreign Ministry, and communicated to Britain by a gross diplomatic error.)

[3] J. Charpy, *Gouvernement Général de l'A.O.F.*; *Répertoire des Archives. Série F. Affaires Etrangères, 1809–1921* (Rufisque, 1955). I have not seen the file in question; its number is I/F/30.

[4] cf. J. R. Prescott, 'Nigeria's International Boundaries', *West Africa*, 4, 11, 18 June 1961.

coincided with traditional ones; other things being equal, the colonial powers preferred to follow chiefdom boundaries, where these were known. But even these boundaries might still divide Africans of the same language and culture; and once they came under effective European occupation they became harder to cross than would have been the case in the past. And in addition there were numerous cases where European political requirements, such as the desire to have frontiers convenient for the collection of customs duties, led to the deliberate partition of an African state; to take three varied examples, it was so in Samu, in Appa, and in Dagomba.

It was within these new border-lines that the technology, culture, and institutions of the several colonial powers gradually made their impact during the twentieth century. Neighbouring Africans with virtually identical cultural traditions now found themselves subject to different laws, learning different languages and different doctrines in school, using new transport routes which carried them towards different ports and capital cities. These new forces of division were of course felt more quickly and more strongly in commercially-developed areas than in the back country. Distant places without schools or roads often preserved old relationships with their neighbours across the frontier, sometimes to the confusion of colonial officials. Yet even in such places, the new colonial frontiers would in the long run shape the political future.

I shall not attempt a full bibliography of this subject, but shall list here the main sources and authorities used, in a form which I hope may prove of assistance to future workers in the field. I do not include well-known sources or works of reference not primarily of African importance, such as *Hansard*, the *Journal Officiel*, *The Dictionary of National Biography*, or Vapereau's *Dictionnaire des Contemporains*, nor well-known biographies of European statesmen of incidental relevance. Some additional references may be found in footnotes to the text of the book.

Plan of the Bibliography

UNPUBLISHED SOURCES

    I. Official British Archives
   II. Archives of the Government of Sierra Leone
  III. Official French Archives
       A. Archives of the Ministère des Affaires Etrangères
       B. Colonial Archives
  IV. Private Collections of Manuscripts in the United Kingdom
       A. Wesleyan Missionary Society
       B. Granville Papers
       C. Salisbury Papers
       D. Disraeli Papers
       E. Carnarvon Papers
   V. Unpublished Theses

PUBLISHED SOURCES

    I. Official or semi-official documentary collections
   II. Works by contemporaries containing primary material
  III. Bibliographies, works of reference, and general histories
  IV. Modern studies of special topics

UNPUBLISHED SOURCES

1. *Official British Archives*

I have used, extensively but not exhaustively, the records of the Foreign and Colonial Offices deposited in the Public Record Office,

London. These sources are well-known, and I shall not attempt to describe them in detail. The references to the most important series are F.O. 84/ (Slave Trade), and F.O. 27/ (France); C.O. 87/ (General correspondence, Gambia), C.O. 96/ (Gold Coast), C.O. 147/ (Lagos), and C.O. 267/ (Sierra Leone). It has also been convenient, and in many cases essential (because the original documents have been destroyed) to refer to the Confidential Prints.

In the footnotes I refer to the Foreign Office Confidential Prints simply by the official number. Copies of these are to be found in various places, including the archives of the Paris Embassy (P.R.O. number F.O. 146/2679 to 2685). I have normally used the copy in the Granville papers. I list the official numbers of the prints below according to the P.R.O. number of the volume of Granville papers in which they may be found.

PRO/30/29/263. Africa Misc., 1880–4. Includes:
    C.P. 5064. Treaties between Her Majesty and the Various Tribes on or near the Niger and Binué Rivers, 1883–4.
PRO/30/29/267. Portuguese Claims on the River Congo, 1877–83.
PRO/30/29/268.   do.   do.   do.   1884.
    C.P. 4960. Jan.–March 1884.
    C.P. 5000. April–June 1884.
    –   July–Oct. 1884.
PRO/30/29/269.
    C.P. 4418. Correspondence respecting the British Protectorate over Katanu, 1879–80.
    C.P. 4824. Correspondence respecting the Oil Rivers District and the Question of a British Protectorate, 7 Aug. 1879–5 Feb. 1883.
    C.P. 4825. do., Pt. II, 11 Dec. 1882–11 June 1883.
    C.P. 4869. do., Pt. III, 3 June 1883–30 Oct. 1883.
    C.P. 4955. do., Pt. IV, 12 Aug. 1883–31 Dec. 1883.
    C.P. 4962. do., Pt. V, 7 Feb. 1884–31 March 1884.
    C.P. 4994. Further Correspondence respecting Affairs on the Gold Coast, April–June 1884.
    C.P. 5020. do., July–Oct. 1884.
    C.P. 5004. Correspondence respecting Affairs in the Oil Rivers Districts of the West Coast of Africa, and the Increase of Consular Supervision and British Responsibilities, Pt. I, 20 Nov. 1883–30 June 1884.
    C.P. 5021. Further do., 4 July–30 Oct. 1884.
    C.P. 5063.   do.,   Nov–Dec. 1884.

PRO/30/29/270.

C.P. 5023. Correspondence respecting the Proposed West African Conference, 26 May–29 Oct. 1884.

C.P. 5033. Further do., Nov. 1884.

After 1873, the Colonial Office confidential prints are kept separately in the series C.O. 806/ . . . . In the following select list the number of the print is preceded by this P.R.O. call number. Short titles are used.

C.O. 806/12. African 50. Gold Coast: Enquiry of 1865. Memo. by Hemming, 1 April 1874.

C.O. 806/36. African 75. Correspondence respecting the proposed Exchange of Possessions . . . March 1875.

C.O. 806/40. African 77. Further do. . . . June 1875.

C.O. 806/57. African 92. Correspondence respecting the Affairs of the Gambia and the Proposed Exchange, July 1876.

C.O. 806/60. — Proposed Exchange. memo. by Hemming. 17 Feb. 1876.

C.O. 806/70. African 106. Memo. by Rowe . . . Sierra Leone, Sept. 1876.

C.O. 806/78. African 114. Proposed Acquisition of Territory in the Neighbourhood of Sierra Leone, Jan. 1877.

C.O. 806/79. African 115. Rowe: Proposed Embassy to Dahomey, Jan. 1877.

C.O. 806/85. African 124. British Jurisdiction in the Gambia, 1876–7.

C.O. 806/94. African 139. Affairs of Sierra Leone, Dec. 1877.

C.O. 806/107. African 152. British Jurisdiction in the Gambia, 1876–8.

C.O. 806/114. African 159. Further Correspondence . . . Sierra Leone, 1879.

C.O. 806/118. African 163. Kittam Region, 1878.

C.O. 806/129. African 175. Further Correspondence . . . Sierra Leone, 1879.

C.O. 806/130. African 178. Lagos, 1879.

C.O. 806/151. African 206. Sierra Leone, 1879.

C.O. 806/158. African 214. Sierra Leone, Oct. 1880.

C.O. 806/170. African 226. Sierra Leone, June 1881.

C.O. 806/177. African 233. Sierra Leone; Negotiations with France, 1884.

C.O. 806/194. African 250. Boundary at Assinee, 1877–1884.

C.O. 806/195. African 251. Negotiations with Liberia, 1881–3.

C.O. 806/196. African 252. Disturbances in Moriah, 1882–3.

C.O. 806/203. African 259. Trade in the Niger, May 1883.

C.O. 806/209. African 265. Gold Coast territorial, 1883–4.

C.O. 806/214. African 270. Memo. respecting French Proceedings upon the West Coast of Africa. R. Meade, Sept. 1883.

C.O. 806/265. African 318. Correspondence respecting the advance of Almamy Sahmadoo towards the coast, Nov. 1888.

C.O. 806/279. African 332. Despatch . . . regarding the different districts and tribes of Sierra Leone . . . Feb. 1886 (sc. 1887).

C.O. 806/281. African 334. Gold Coast and Lagos, Oct. 1887.

C.O. 806/288. African 345. Lagos . . . and proposed negotiations with France on various West African matters, Aug. 1888.

C.O. 806/299. African 355. Proposed negotiations with France, Jan. 1889.

C.O. 806/300. African 356. Anglo-German claims in the neighbourhood of the Gold Coast, Feb. 1890.

C.O. 806/301. African 357. Memo. by Hemming: Gambia exchange, Nov. 1888.

C.O. 806/346. African 411. Collection of Treaties with Native Chiefs, 1642–1891.

2. *Archives of the Government of Sierra Leone*

Before starting the present research, I made some study of the correspondence of the Native Affairs Department in this collection, which is kept at Fourah Bay College, Freetown. Some references from this work are incorporated in the book.

3. *Official French Archives*

A. *Archives of Ministère des Affaires Etrangères, Paris*

The most important material for African affairs is contained in the bound volumes of *Mémoires et Documents* which contain correspondence with the Colonial Department, and with merchants, deputies, and other bodies and individuals. I have used the following volumes:

Afrique 47. Sénégal et Dépendances, 1859–67.
Afrique 48. do. do. 1868–75.
Afrique 49. do. do. 1876–8.
Afrique 50. do. do. 1879–82.
Afrique 84. do. do. 1883–4.
Afrique 55. Possessions anglaises, 1819–65.
Afrique 56. do. do. 1866–80.

Afrique 57.   do.   do.   1881–2.
Afrique 86.   do.   do.   1883–8.
Afrique 51. Etablissements français du Golfe de Guinée, 1848–
                                                            1862.
Afrique 52.   do.   do.   1863.
Afrique 53.   do.   do.   1864–8.
Afrique 54.   do.   do.   1869–
                                          1876.
Afrique 76.   do.   do.   1877–9.
Afrique 77.   do.   do.   1880–2.
Afrique 78.   do.   do.   1883.
Afrique 79.   do.   do.   Jan.–April 1884.
Afrique 80.   do.   do.   May–Dec. 1884.
Afrique 58. Congo-Gabon, 1839–81.
Afrique 59.   do.   1882.
Afrique 108. Conférence de Berlin, 1884–5. (Printed protocols,
                                          etc.).
Afrique 109.   do.   do.   1884–5. (Correspondance,
                                          divers).

The political correspondence with the Vice-Consul in Freetown is of uneven value before 1881. After the appointment of V. Bareste in that year it becomes more voluminous. A number of merchants were appointed as unpaid consular agents down the coast, and their reports were copied in Bareste's own correspondence. The relevant volumes are:

Correspondance Politique des Consuls, Angleterre (Freetown), Vol. 53, 1851–82; Vol. 70, 1883; Vol. 71, 1884.

I have also consulted some of the general volumes of political correspondence in the series *Angleterre*.

B. *Colonial Archives*. (In custody of Ministère de la France d'Outre-mer.)

The documents are placed in folders which are grouped in cartons and classified first according to territory, secondarily according to subject. The bulk of the general correspondence with the Governors of Senegal is in the series *Sénégal I* (which I have consulted but not examined systematically). The somewhat elaborate scheme of classification is illustrated by the following list of the dossiers which I have consulted with most profit.

Afrique IV: Pays étrangers.
     Afrique IV/9. Dahomey indépendant, 1845–64.

Afrique IV/10. Do., 1862–78. (*a*) Renseignements généraux, 1864–9. (*b*) Renseignements généraux, 1870–5. (*c*) Renseignements généraux, 1875–8. (*d*) Agence consulaire à Ouidah, 1862–70.

Afrique IV/17. Gambie.

Afrique IV/19. Sierra Léone.

Afrique IV/70. Considérations sur l'échange de la Gambie, 1899–1913.

Afrique VI: Affaires Diplomatiques.

Afrique VI/11. Angleterre. (*a*) Echange de la Gambie, 1863–70. (*f*)Affaires de la Gambie, 1864–7. (*g*) Nunez et Mellacorée, 1868–70.

Afrique VI/15. Angleterre, 1871–4. (*a*) Projet d'échange, 1871–4.

Afrique VI/16. Angleterre, 1875. Projet d'échange.

Afrique VI/17. Angleterre, 1876. (*a*) Projet d'échange.

Afrique VI/24. Angleterre, 1879–80. (*a*) Projet d'échange.

Afrique VI/27. Angleterre, 1881. (*a*) Délimitation, Sierra Léone.

Afrique VI/28. Portugal, 1881. (*a*) Généralités.

Afrique VI/30. Angleterre, 1882. (*a*) Projet d'échange. (*b*) Délimitation, Sierra Léone. (*d*) Porto Novo et Lagos.

Afrique VI/34. Angleterre, 1883. (*a*) Délimitation au nord de Sierra Léone. (*c*) Porto Novo et Lagos.

Afrique VI/38. Angleterre, 1884. (*a*) Délimitation au nord de Sierra Léone. (*d*) Porto Novo et Lagos. (*e*) Brass River et bas-Niger.

Afrique VI/40. Allemagne, 1884.

Sénégal III: Explorations, Missions.

Sénégal III/9/b. Poisson, 1863.

Sénégal III/9/c. Mage-Quintin, 1863–6.

Sénégal III/10/c. Canard, 1876.

Sénégal III/10 bis. Galliéni, 1879–81.

Sénégal III/11/c. Bayol, 1881.

Sénégal III/15/a. Sanderval.

Sénégal IV: Expansion et politique indigène.

Sénégal IV/55. Mellacorée, 1859–67.

Sénégal IV/56. Mellacorée, 1867–79.

Sénégal IV/71/a. Fouta Djallon, 1879–85.

Sénégal IV/73. Soudan, 1880–1.

Sénégal IV/73 bis. Rapport par Colonel Desbordes sur la campagne de 1880–1.

Sénégal VI: Questions Diplomatiques.
  Sénégal VI/13/a. Angleterre, 1881–5.
Sénégal XIII: Commissions.
  Sénégal XIII/2. Commission du Commerce et des Comptoirs d'Afrique, 1850–1.
  Sénégal XIII/3. Commission du Commerce et des Comptoirs d'Afrique, 1850–1. (Minutes and report.)
Gabon-Congo I: Correspondance Générale.
  Gabon-Congo I/2/b. Didelot, despatches.
  Gabon-Congo I/3/b. Laffon de Ladebat, despatches.
Gabon-Congo IV: Expansion territoriale et politique indigène.
  Gabon-Congo IV/3. Porto-Novo et Cotonou, 1865–88. (b) Porto-Novo, 1865.
Gabon-Congo VI: Affaires Diplomatiques.
  Gabon-Congo VI/1. Angleterre. (b) Porto-Novo, 1863–5.
  Gabon-Congo VI/2. Angleterre. (a) Projet d'échange, 1875. (b) Commerce des Armes.

4. *Private Collections of Manuscripts in the United Kingdom*

A. *Archives of the Wesleyan Missionary Society.* (In the care of the Methodist Missionary Society, London.)
This important collection was useful in connection with the opposition to the exchange of the Gambia.

B. *Granville Papers.* (Public Record Office, London; call number P.R.O./30/29/. . . .)
Besides its convenient collection of confidential prints, contains some correspondence relevant to the formation of policy.

C. *Salisbury Papers.* (In the custody of Christ Church, Oxford. Used by permission of Lord Salisbury and the Governing Body of Christ Church.)

D. *Disraeli Papers.* (At Hughenden Manor. Used by permission of the National Trust.)

E. *Carnarvon Papers.* (Public Record Office, London; call number P.R.O./30/6/. . . .)
These three collections all contain some correspondence relevant to the formation of British policy.

5. *Unpublished Theses*
Many of these are pioneer works, which have been invaluable as guides, both to the sources and to their interpretation, in large parts

of my field. Without distinguishing among them, I would like to record my indebtedness to the authors of those listed below; and also to Dr. John Flint, who was kind enough to lend me his London Ph.D. thesis on *British Policy and Chartered Company Administration in Nigeria, 1879–1900*. Happily the substance of this has now been published in Dr. Flint's work on Sir George Goldie, listed elsewhere.

A. A. B. Aderibigbe, *Expansion of the Lagos Protectorate, 1863–1900*, Ph.D., University of London, 1959.

A. A. Boahen, *British Penetration of the Sahara and Western Sudan, 1788–1861*, Ph.D., University of London, 1959.

Cherry Gertzel, *Imperial policy towards the British Settlements in West Africa, 1860–1875*, B.Litt., University of Oxford, 1953.

W. H. Scotter, *International Rivalry in the Bights of Benin and Biafra*, Ph.D., University of London, 1933.

J. P. Schwitzer, *The British Attitude towards French Colonization, 1875–1887*, Ph.D., University of London, 1954.

Freda Wolfson, *British Relations with the Gold Coast, 1843–1880*, Ph.D., University of London, 1950.

PUBLISHED SOURCES

I. *Official or Semi-Official Documentary Collections*
   A. *British*
Parliamentary Papers. (Cited as P.P., or by Command Numbers.) A select list.

1865, Vol. V. Report from Select Committee on West African Settlements.

1870, Vol. L. Correspondence respecting the Proposed Cession of the Gambia to France. (C. 264)

1876, Vol. LII. Correspondence respecting the Affairs of the Gambia and the Proposed Exchange with France of Possessions on the West Coast of Africa. (C. 1409)

1876, Vol. LII. Copy of Petition from the Inhabitants of the Gambia, praying that that Settlement be not Ceded to France. (C. 1498)

1877, Vol. LX. Correspondence respecting the Limits of British Jurisdiction in the River Gambia. (C. 1827)

1881, Vol. LXV. Correspondence Relating to the Recent Expedition to the Upper Gambia under Administrator V. S. Gouldsbury. (C. 3065)

J. J. Crooks. *Records relating to the Gold Coast Settlements from 1750 to 1874.* Dublin, 1923.

E. Hertslet, *The Map of Africa by Treaty* (London, 2nd ed., 1896). Three Vols.

B. *French*

Documents Diplomatiques Français (Paris, from 1929). (Cited as D.D.F. Unless otherwise stated, the first series of this officially-sponsored publication is referred to.)

C. Schefer, *Instructions Générales . . . aux Gouverneurs . . . en Afrique Occidentale,* Tome II, 1831–70, Paris, 1927.

E. Rouard de Card, *Les Traités de Protectorat conclus par la France en Afrique, 1870–95* (Paris, 1897).

Ministère de la Marine et des Colonies, *Sénégal et Niger : la France dans l'Afrique Occidentale, 1879–83* (Paris, 1884). An official publication intended to interpret French policy on the upper Senegal to the public.

Etudes Dahoméennes, No. IX, Porto Novo, 1953. A selection of documents from the local archives, by J. Lombard.

C. *German*

Die Grosse Politik der Europäischen Kabinette, 1871–1914 (Berlin, 1922–1927).

Weiss Buch, *Deutsche Kolonien. 1. Togogebiet und Biafra-Bai,* reprinted in *Das Staatsarchiv,* XLIII (Leipzig, 1884) pp. 224–74.

II. *Works by Contemporaries Containing Primary Material*

T. J. Alldridge, *The Sherbro and its Hinterland,* London, 1901. The author was a trader who later became a District Commissioner.

W. B. Baikie, *Narrative of an Exploring Voyage up the Rivers Kwora and Binue in 1854,* London, 1856.

H. Barth, *Travels and Discoveries in North and Central Africa . . . 1849–1855,* London, five volumes, 1857–8.

J. Bayol, 'La France au Fouta-Djalon', *Revue des Deux Mondes,* Dec. 1882. By the leader of the French expedition of 1881.

J. Bayol, *Voyage en Sénégambie,* Paris, 1888. Duplicates above material, but also adds his account of the Galliéni mission of 1879.

L. C. Binger, *Du Niger au Golfe de Guinée . . . 1887–9,* Paris, two volumes, 1892.

Fr. Borghero, 'Lettre au Sujet de la Côte des Esclaves', *Bulletin de la Société de Géographie,* Paris, July 1866.

Fr. Bouche, *Sept Ans en Afrique Occidentale. La Côte des Esclaves et le*

Dahomey, Paris, 1885. Two accounts by priests sent to the Slave Coast by Missions Africaines, of Lyon. Fr. Borghero, a Genoese, was first Superior of the mission; Fr. Bouche served at Porto Novo, Whydah, Lagos and Aghwey between 1866 and 1875.

M. A. Bretignère, *Aux Temps Héroïques de la Côte d'Ivoire*, Paris, 1931. The author entered M. Verdier's service on the Ivory Coast in 1881.

R. F. Burton, *Wanderings in West Africa*, London, two volumes, 1863. Largely an account of the author's journey down the coast on a mail-boat, but contains some interesting observations.

R. F. Burton, *Abeokuta and the Cameroons Mountain*, London, two volumes, 1863.

R. F. Burton, *A Mission to Gelele, King of Dahome*, London, two volumes, 1864. The most interesting of his works on West Africa.

R. F. Burton and V. L. Cameron, *To the Gold Coast for Gold*, London, two volumes, 1883. Account of early European mining on the Gold Coast, with observations on the other settlements.

Rev. H. Caswall, *The Martyr of the Pongas*, being a Memoir of the Rev. H. J. Leacock, London, 1857. Account of the foundation of the Anglican mission in that river.

L. L. C. Faidherbe, *Le Sénégal; la France dans l'Afrique Occidentale*, Paris, 1889. Largely based on his official reports while Governor.

C. Fitzgerald, *The Gambia and its Proposed Cession to France*, London, 1875. A pamphlet opposing the exchange. Fitzgerald may also be the author of the anonymous pamphlet: *Has the Crown the right to cede the Gambia to France?* London, 1870.

K. Flegel (ed.), *Vom Niger-Benüe, Briefe aus Afrika von Eduard R. Flegel*, Leipzig, 1890. Letters written between 1876 and 1885, edited by the explorer's brother.

J. S. Galliéni, *Voyage au Soudan Français (Haut-Niger et Pays du Ségou) 1879–81*, Paris, 1885.

J. S. Galliéni, *Deux Campagnes au Soudan Français, 1886–88*, Paris, 1891.

W. N. M. Geary, *Nigeria under British Rule*, London, 1927. By a lawyer who knew Lagos in the early twentieth century.

Lady Glover, *Life of Sir J. H. Glover, R.N., C.M.G.*, London, 1897.

J. M. Harris, *Annexations to Sierra Leone and their Influence on British Trade with West Africa*, London, 1883. Complaints by the merchant whose factories in the Gallinas area had recently been brought under British rule. Harris had been in the area since 1860.

A. C. G. Hastings (ed.), *The Voyage of the* Dayspring, London, 1926. Glover's journal during his voyage on the Niger, 1857–Jan. 1858.

J. C. D. Hay, M.P., *Ashanti and the Gold Coast; and what we know of it*, London, 1874.

James Africanus B. Horton, M.D., *West African Countries and Peoples, British and Native, with the Requirements Necessary for Establishing that Self Government recommended by the Committee of the House of Commons, 1865, and a Vindication of the African Race*, London, 1868. An interesting work by a Sierra Leonean doctor.

J. F. Hutton, *The Proposed Cession of the British Colony of the Gambia to France*, Manchester, 1876. A pamphlet opposing the exchange; prints report of deputation from Manchester Chamber of Commerce to Carnarvon, 31 January 1876.

Amadou Kouroubabi, 'Histoire de l'Imam Samori', *Bulletin de l'I.F.A.N.*, xxi, Dakar, July–Oct. 1959. An account first recorded by M. Delafosse about 1901.

Colonel Lambert, 'Voyage dans le Fouta Djallon', *Bulletin de la Société Languedocienne de Géographie*, 1889. Lambert's report of his journey of 1860.

O. Lenz, *Timbouctou*, Paris, two volumes, 1886.

Liverpool Chamber of Commerce. Memorial to Lord Salisbury, 18 November 1891. Affairs of the West African Colonies. Report of the Committee of the African Trade Section . . . , Liverpool, 1892.

E. Mage, *Voyage dans le Soudan Occidental (Sénégambie-Niger) 1863–1866*, Paris, 1868. An important source of information about the Tokolor empire.

A. Marche, *Trois Voyages dans l'Afrique Occidentale*, Paris, 1879. The first voyage, of 1872, was to the Senegambian region; the others, in 1873 and 1875, to Gabon.

Comdt. Mattei, *Bas-Niger, Bénoué, Dahomey*, Grenoble, 1890. Essential for the origins of French Niger trade.

E. Noirot, *A travers le Fouta-Diallon et le Bambouc*, Paris [1885]. A superficial account by a member of Bayol's mission of 1881.

Capt. Pietri, *Les Français au Niger*, Paris, 1885. Pietri accompanied Galliéni's mission to the Tokolor empire in 1879–81.

W. Winwood Reade, *Savage Africa*, London, 1864.

W. W. Reade, *The African Sketch-Book*, London, two volumes, 1873. A literary curiosity, but contains some interesting material.

W. W. Reade, *The Story of the Ashanti Campaign*, London, 1874.

W. W. Reade, 'La Côte d'Or', *Bulletin de la Société de Géographie*, Paris,

May, 1869. Some sidelights on the French possessions on the Ivory Coast.

Dr. F. Ricard, *Le Sénégal: Etude Intime*, Paris, 1865.

Royal Colonial Institute, Report on the Gambia Question, Jan. 1876. Memorial on the Cession of the Gambia, 16 Feb. 1876. These two documents may be found in the *Proceedings* of the Institute, 1875–6.

Sanderval, Comte de (Aimé Olivier). *De l'Atlantique au Niger par le Foutah-Djallon*. Paris, 2nd ed. 1883.

Sanderval, Comte de (Aimé Olivier). *Conquête du Fouta Djallon*, Paris, 1899.

J. A. Skertchly, *Dahomey as it is*, London, 1874. The author went to Dahomey under the patronage of Swanzy in 1871. His primary purpose, he claims, was to collect insects. Detained eight months in Abomey; gives an interesting account of the court and the 'customs'.

J. B. Thomson, *Joseph Thomson, African Explorer*, London, 1896. Biography by his brother, with some documents.

A. Verdier, *Trente-cinq Ans de Lutte aux Colonies*, Paris, 1896. Important account of the growth of French interests on the Ivory Coast.

A. Verdier, *Echange de Territoire Coloniale*, La Rochelle, 1876. A pamphlet opposing the exchange.

E. Viard, *Au Bas-Niger*, Paris, 3rd ed., 1886.

J. Whitford, *Trading Life in Western and Central Africa*, Liverpool, 1877.

J. Zweiffel and M. Moustier, *Expédition C. A. Verminck: Voyage aux Sources du Niger*, Marseille, 1880.

III. *Bibliographies, Works of Reference, and General Histories*

C. Faure, *Les Archives du Gouvernement Général de l'A.O.F.*, Paris, 1922. A descriptive guide by the archivist, to be used in conjunction with:

Gouvernement Général de l'A.O.F., Répertoire des Archives, Rufisque. A fuller and more recent account of the individual series. Volumes include: Série B, *Correspondance Générale, 1779–1895*, by C. Faure and J. Charpy, 1955. Série F, *Affaires Etrangères, 1809–1921*, by J. Charpy, 1955. Série G, *Politique et Administration Générale, 1782–1920*, by J. Charpy, 1955.

E. Joucla, *Bibliographie de l'A.O.F.*, Paris, 1912. Unclassified.

J. L. G. Tuaillon, *Bibliographie Critique de l'A.O.F.*, Paris, 1936.

E. Lewin, *Subject Catalogue of the Library of the Royal Empire Society*, Vol. I, *The British Empire Generally, and Africa*, London, 1930.

H. C. Luke, *A Bibliography of Sierra Leone*, London, 1925. A new bibliography by P. E. Hair began to appear in *Sierra Leone Studies* in 1958.

E. A. Benians and others (ed.), *The Cambridge History of the British Empire*; Vol. II, *The Growth of the New Empire, 1783–1870*, Cambridge, 1940; Vol. III, *The Empire-Commonwealth, 1870–1919*, Cambridge, 1959. Though the treatment of West Africa in the text of these volumes is on the whole disappointing, both contain good bibliographies.

School of Oriental and African Studies, University of London, *History and Archaeology in Africa*, Report of a Conference held in July 1953 (1955). Second Conference held in July 1957 (1959). I have also used some of the typescript papers submitted to the second and third Conferences.

J. D. Fage, *An Atlas of African History*, London, 1958.

J. D. Fage, *An Introduction to the History of West Africa*, 2nd ed., Cambridge, 1959.

J. Suret-Canale, *Afrique Noire*, Paris, 1958. An interesting attempt at interpretation by a Marxist geographer; but restricted to the areas which became French.

J. Richard-Molard, *Afrique Occidentale Français*, Paris, 1952. The best geographical survey; admirably wide in scope.

R. J. H. Church, *West Africa*, London, 1957. Useful for geographical reference; historical information less reliable.

A. McPhee, *The Economic Revolution in British West Africa*, London, 1926. An important pioneer work.

G. Hanotaux and A. Martineau, *Histoire des Colonies françaises et de l'Expansion de la France dans le Monde*, Tome IV (Paris, 1931). A valuable reference work, with an old-fashioned narrative approach. The relevant chapters on West Africa are by M. Delafosse.

IV. *Modern Studies of Special Topics*

J. F. Ade Ajayi, 'The British Occupation of Lagos, 1851–61', *Nigeria*, No. 69, Aug. 1961.

A. Akindélé and C. Aguessy, *Contribution à l'Etude de l'Histoire de l'Ancien Royaume de Porto Novo*, Dakar, 1953. A useful revision of a traditional history first published in Yoruba in 1914.

A. Akindélé and C. Aguessy, *Dahomey*, Paris, 1955.

F. J. Amon d'Aby, *La Côte d'Ivoire dans la Cité Africaine*, Paris, 1951.

R. T. Anstey, 'British Trade and Policy in West Central Africa between 1816 and the Early 1880's', *Transactions*, Historical Society of Ghana, Vol. III, Part 1, Achimota, 1957.

A. Arcin, *Histoire de la Guinée française*, Paris, 1911. An early study by an administrator, using colonial archives.

W. O. Aydelotte, *Bismarck and British Colonial Policy*, Philadelphia, 1937.

W. O. Aydelotte, 'Wollte Bismarck Kolonien?' in W. Conze (ed.), *Deutschland und Europa* (Festschrift für H. Rothfels) Dusseldorf, 1951.

Tamsir Dusmane Ba, 'Essai Historique sur le Rip', *Bulletin de l'I.F.A.N.*, xix, Dakar, 1957. An account of Badibu and the rise of Maba, by a grandson of the latter's brother.

T. A. Bayer, *England und der Neue Kurs*, Tübingen, 1955.

S. O. Biobaku, *The Egba and their Neighbours, 1842–72*, Oxford, 1957.

M. Blanchard, 'Correspondance de Felix Faure touchant les Affaires Coloniales', *Revue d'Histoire des Colonies françaises*, xlii, 1955.

H. Blet, *Histoire de la Colonisation française*, Tomes II, III, Grenoble and Paris, 1946, 1950.

C. Bloch, *Les Relations entre la France et la Grande Bretagne, 1871–78*, Paris, 1955.

C. A. Bodelsen, *Studies in Mid-Victorian Imperialism*, New York, 1925.

H. Brunschwig, *Mythes et Réalités de l'Impérialisme colonial français, 1871–1914*, Paris, 1960.

R. L. Buell, *Liberia: a Century of Survival, 1847–1947*, Philadelphia, 1947.

F. Bullock, *La Fondation de la Colonie française de la Côte d'Ivoire*, London, 1912. Largely an account of the work of Treich-Laplène after 1883.

A. C. Burns, *History of Nigeria*, 4th ed., London, 1948.

F. Carrère and P. Holle, *De la Sénégambie française*, Paris, 1855. An interesting account of the problems of the French colony, by a French official and a Eurafrican *habitant*.

E. M. Carroll, *French Public Opinion and Foreign Affairs, 1871–1914*, New York, 1931.

R. Catala, 'La Question de l'échange de la Gambie Britannique contre les Comptoirs français du Golfe de Guinée', *Revue d'Histoire des Colonies françaises*, xxxv, 1948.

le comte Chailley, *Les Grandes Missions françaises en Afrique Occidentale*, Dakar, 1953. The photographs are more interesting than the text.

J. Chaput, 'Treich-Lapleine et la naissance de la Côte d'Ivoire française', *Revue d'Histoire des Colonies françaises*, xxxvi, 1949.

J. de Chambrun, *Brazza*, Paris, 1930.

J. Charpy, *La Fondation de Dakar* (1845–1857–1869), Paris, 1958.

A. Chéradame, *La Colonisation et les Colonies Allemandes*, Paris, 1905.

A. N. Cook, *British Enterprise in Nigeria*, Philadelphia, 1943.

R. Cornevin, *Histoire du Togo*, Paris, 1959.

J. J. Crooks, *A History of Sierra Leone*, Dublin, 1903. Annals rather than history, but usually reliable.

S. E. Crowe, *The Berlin West Africa Conference, 1884–5*, London, 1942.

P. Cultru, *Histoire du Sénégal du xve siècle à 1870*, Paris, 1910.

J. Darcy, *France et Angleterre. Cent Années de Rivalité Coloniale, L'Afrique*, Paris, 1904.

N. F. da Souza, 'Contribution Historique à la Famille de Souza', *Etudes Dahoméennes*, XIII, Porto Novo, 1955. The *chachas* of Whydah.

A. Demaison, *Faidherbe*, Paris, 1932.

M. Delafosse, *Haut-Sénégal-Niger (Soudan Français)*. T. i, *Les Pays, Les Peuples, Les Langues*; T. ii, *L'Histoire*; T. iii, *Les Civilisations*, Paris, 1912. A pioneer study by a scholarly administrator.

A. Demeugeot, 'Histoire du Nunez', *Bulletin du Comité d'Etudes Historiques et Scientifiques de l'A.O.F.*, Vol. XXX, Dakar, 1938. An administrator's study of the nineteenth century; uses the archives.

K. O. Diké, *Trade and Politics in the Niger Delta, 1830–1885*, Oxford, 1956. A pioneer work.

K. O. Diké and others, *Eminent Nigerians of the Nineteenth Century*, Cambridge, 1960. A series of simple biographical sketches, originally broadcast in Nigeria.

A. Duchêne, *La Politique Coloniale de la France*, Paris, 1928.

A. Duchêne, *Un Ministre Trop Oublié: Chasseloup-Laubat*, Paris, 1932.

E. Dunglas, 'Contribution à l'Histoire du Moyen-Dahomey'. *Etudes Dahoméennes*, XIX, Porto Novo, 1957.

E. Eyck, *Bismarck*, Vol. III, Zurich, 1944.

J. E. Flint, *Sir George Goldie and the Making of Nigeria*, London, 1960.

E. Foà, *Le Dahomey*, Paris, 1895.

C. H. Fyfe, *A History of Sierra Leone*, London, 1962.

C. H. Fyfe, 'European and Creole Influence in the Hinterland of Sierra Leone before 1896', *Sierra Leone Studies*, new series, VI, Freetown, 1956.

J. Gaillard, 'Un Français, Roi du Fouta-Djallon', *Bulletin du Comité d'Etudes Historiques et Scientifiques de l'A.O.F.*, VII, Dakar, 1924. Of small value.

R. J. Gavin, 'Nigeria and Lord Palmerston', *Ibadan*, June 1961.

A. Girault, *The Colonial Tariff Policy of France*, Oxford, 1916.

A. Gouilly, *L'Islam dans l'Afrique Occidentale Française*, Paris, 1952.

J. M. Gray, *A History of the Gambia*, Cambridge, 1940. A good history of the colony, based on research in the local archives; but sometimes reflects rather uncritically the viewpoint of the reigning Governor.

H. L. Hall, *The Colonial Office*, London, 1937.

G. Hardy, *La Mise en Valeur du Sénégal de 1817 à 1854*, Paris, 1921.

G. Hardy, *Faidherbe*, Paris, 1947.

W. K. Hancock, *Survey of British Commonwealth Affairs*, Vol. II, Part II, London, 1942.

J. D. Hargreaves, *A Life of Sir Samuel Lewis*, London, 1958.

J. D. Hargreaves, 'The Evolution of the Native Affairs Department', *Sierra Leone Studies*, n.s. III, Freetown, 1954.

J. D. Hargreaves, 'The French Occupation of the Mellacourie, 1865–67', *ibid.*, V, 1955.

J. D. Hargreaves, 'Winwood Reade and the Discovery of Africa', *African Affairs*, LVI, London, 1957.

J. D. Hargreaves, 'Towards a History of the Partition of Africa', *Journal of African History*, I, London, 1960.

P. Hazoumé, *Le Pacte de Sang au Dahomey* (Université de Paris: Travaux et Mémoires de l'Institut d'Ethnologie, xxv, 1937).

M. J. Herskovits, *Dahomey: an Ancient West African Kingdom*, New York, two volumes, 1938.

T. L. Hodgkin, *Nigerian Perspectives*, London, 1960. A very good documentary anthology.

Samuel Johnson, *The History of the Yorubas*, 2nd ed., Lagos, 1937.

Sir H. H. Johnston, *A History of the Colonization of Africa by Alien Races*, Cambridge, 1899.

Sir H. H. Johnston, *Liberia*, two volumes, London, 1906.

J. S. Keltie, *The Partition of Africa*, 2nd ed., London, 1895.

A. H. M. Kirk-Greene, *Adamawa, Past and Present*, London, 1958.

A. le Herissé, *L'ancien Royaume du Dahomey*, Paris, 1911. Chap. XII records a version of recent events according to the brother of Behanzin.

C. P. Lucas, *A Historical Geography of the British Colonies*, Vol. III, *West Africa*, Oxford; 2nd ed., 1900, revised by H. E. Egerton.

C. P. Lucas, *The Partition and Colonization of Africa*, Oxford, 1922. Lucas was a Colonial Office official.

J. H. T. Macpherson, *History of Liberia*, Baltimore, 1891.

G. E. Marindin (ed.), *Letters of Frederic, Lord Blachford*, London, 1896.

P. Marty, *Etudes sur l'Islam au Sénégal*, Vol. I, Paris, 1917.

P. Marty, *L'Islam en Guinée*, Paris, 1921.

P. Masson, *Marseille et la Colonisation française*, Marseille, 1906. A valuable study, using papers of the Régis family.

P. Masson (directeur), *Les Bouches-du-Rhône: Encyclopédie Départementale*; Tome VIII, *Le Mouvement Economique: Industrie*, 1926; Tome IX, *Le Commerce*, 1922.

A. Mévil, *Samory*, Paris, 1899.

C. Monheim, *L'Affaire du Rio Nunez, 1848-1858*, Louvain, 1931.

E. D. Morel, *Nigeria*, London, 1912.

H. Moüezy, *Assinie et le Royaume de Krinjabo*, Paris, 1953. By a missionary priest, twenty-five years in the Ivory Coast.

A. Murphy, *The Ideology of French Imperialism*, Washington, D.C., 1948.

S. F. Nadel, *A Black Byzantium*, London, 1942. A fine ethnographical study of Nupe.

C. W. Newbury, 'The Development of French Policy on the Lower and Upper Niger, 1880-98', *Journal of Modern History*, xxxi, Chicago, 1959.

C. W. Newbury, *The Western Slave Coast and its Rulers*, Oxford, 1961.

R. Oliver, *Sir Harry Johnston and the Scramble for Africa*, London, 1957.

F. V. Parsons, 'The North-West African Company and the British Government', *Historical Journal*, I, Cambridge, 1958.

H. J. Pedraza, *Borioboola-Gha: The Story of Lokoja*, London, 1960.

W. S. C. Pemberton, *Life of Lord Norton*, London, 1909.

M. Perham, *Lugard: The years of Adventure, 1858-1898*, London, 1956.

T. F. Power, Jr., *Jules Ferry and the Renaissance of French Imperialism*, New York, 1944.

P. Renouvin and others, *Les Politiques d'Expansion Impérialiste*, Paris, 1949.

J. Gallagher and R. E. Robinson, 'The Imperialism of Free Trade', *Economic History Review*, 2nd series VI, 1953.

R. Robinson and J. Gallagher with Alice Denny, *Africa and the Victorians*, London, 1961. This important study appeared in time for me to insert references to its thesis, which is largely complementary to my own, during the revision of my manuscript.

Fr. A. Roeykens, *Léopold II et l'Afrique, 1855–80* (Essai de Synthèse et de mise en point). *Académie Royale des Sciences Coloniales*, Mémoires, N.S. 14. Bruxelles, 1958. A recapitulation of Fr. Roeykens' extensive writings on Leopold II.

H. R. Rudin, *Germans in the Cameroons, 1884–1914*, New Haven, 1938.

P. E. Schramm, *Deutschland und Übersee*, Braunschweig, 1950. Important study of the growth of German interests in Africa and elsewhere.

M. G. Smith, *Government in Zazzau, 1800–1950*, London, 1960. An important study; but see also the review by T. L. Hodgkin in *West Africa*, 26 Aug., 2 Sept. 1961.

J. Suret-Canale, 'La Guinée dans le Système Colonial', *Présence Africaine*, XXIX, 1959–60.

C. Tardits, *Porto Novo, Les Nouvelles Générations Africaines entre leurs Traditions et l'Occident*, Paris and La Haye, 1958. A sociological study with useful historical background.

A. J. P. Taylor, *Germany's First Bid for Colonies*, London, 1938.

A. Terrier and C. Mourey, *L'Expansion française et la Formation Territoriale*, Paris, 1910. A popular work of 'drum and trumpet' history, written at the request of Governor-General Ponty of A.O.F.

M. E. Townsend, *Origins of Modern German Colonisation*, New York, 1921.

M. E. Townsend, *The Rise and Fall of Germany's Colonial Empire*, New York, 1930.

J. S. Trimingham, *Islam in West Africa*, Oxford, 1959.

J. S. Trimingham and C. H. Fyfe, 'The Early Expansion of Islam in Sierra Leone', *Sierra Leone Bulletin of Religion*, ii, Freetown, 1960.

A. Villard, *Histoire du Sénégal*, Dakar, 1943. Useful bibliography.

W. E. F. Ward, *A History of Ghana*, London, 1958.

Freda Wolfson, 'The Krobo Oil Boycott, 1858–66', *Economic History Review*, 2nd series, VI, 1953.

Freda Wolfson, *Pageant of Ghana*, London, 1958. A documentary anthology.

E. J. Yancy, *The Republic of Liberia*, London, 1959. An elementary text by a Liberian.

ADDENDA

Two of the many important works received after galley-proofs had been passed contain new material of direct relevance to this study.

B. Schnapper, *La Politique et le Commerce français dans le Golfe de Guinée de 1838 à 1871* (Paris & La Haye, 1961) is very informative on affairs in the Ivory Coast, and on general aspects of French policy. H. Stoecker (ed.), *Kamerun unter Deutscher Kolonialherrschaft* (E. Berlin, 1960), though presented as an anti-colonialist polemic, contains a chapter by H. P. Jaeck on 'Die Deutsche Annexion' which presents new evidence from the colonial archives, notably on the role of Woermann.

J. D. H.

December 1962

ADDENDA, 1966

Francis Agbodeka, 'The Fanti Confederacy, 1865–69', *Transactions, Historical Society of Ghana*, VII, 1964.

J. F. Ade Ajayi, *Christian Missions in Nigeria 1841–1891*, London, 1965.

Roger Anstey, *Britain and the Congo in the Nineteenth Century*, Oxford, 1962.

Paul Atger, *La France en Côte d'Ivoire de 1843 à 1893*, Dakar, 1962.

François Berge, *Le Sous-Secrétariat et les Sous-Secrétaires d'Etat aux Colonies*, Paris, 1962.

Adu Boahen, *Britain, the Sahara and the Western Sudan 1788–1861*, Oxford, 1964 (cf. p. 357).

George E. Brooks, 'A Note on French Influence in the Oil Rivers in the 1840s and 1860s', *Journal, Historical Society of Nigeria*, III, 1965.

Henri Brunschwig, *L'Avènement de l'Afrique Noire*, Paris, 1963.

Henri Brunschwig, Les Origines du Partage de l'Afrique Occidentale', *J[ournal] [of] A[frican] H[istory]*, V, 1965.

Catherine Coquery 'Le Blocus de Whydah (1876–1877) et la rivalité franco-anglaise au Dahomey' *Cahiers d'Etudes Africaines*, VII, 1962.

Catherine Coquery-Vidrovitch, 'La Fete des Coutoumes au Dahomey', *Annales*, XIX, 1964.

Christopher Fyfe, *Sierra Leone Inheritance*, London, 1964.

Ronald Hyam, 'The Partition of Africa', *Historical Journal*, VII, 1964.

A. S. Kanya-Forstner, 'The French in West Africa: A Study in Military Imperialism'. Unpublished Ph.D. thesis, University of Cambridge, 1965.

Martin Legrassick, 'Firearms, Horses and Samorian Army Organisation, 1870–1898', *J.A.H.*, VII, 1966.

W. Roger Louis, 'Sir Percy Anderson's Grand African Strategy, 1883–1893', *English Historical Review*, LXXXI, 1966.

W. D. McIntyre, 'Commander Glover and the Colony of Lagos, 1861–73', *J.A.H.*, IV, 1963.

W. D. McIntyre, 'British Policy in West Africa: The Ashanti Expedition of 1873–4', *Historical Journal*, V, 1962.

Vincent Monteil, *L'Islam Noir*, Paris, 1964.

Colin W. Newbury, *British Policy Towards West Africa: Select Documents 1786–1874*, Oxford, 1965.

Colin W. Newbury, 'Victorians, Republicans, and the Partition of West Africa', *J.A.H.*, III, 1962.

Yves Person, 'Les Ancetres de Samori', *Cahiers d'Etudes Africaines*, XIII, 1963.

Yves Person, 'Le jeunesse de Samori', *Revue française d'histoire d'Outremer*, 1962.

David A. Ross, 'The Career of Domingo Martinez in the Bight of Benin', *J.A.H.*, VI, 1965.

Yves Saint-Martin, 'Les Relations Diplomatiques entre la France et l'Empire Toucouleur de 1860 a 1887'; 'L'Artillerie d'El Hadj Omar et d'Ahmadou', *Bulletin de l'IFAN*, XXVII, series B, 1965.

Jean Stengers, 'L'Impérialisme Colonial de la fin du xixe Siècle: Mythe ou Réalité? *J.A.H.*, III, 1962.

INDEX

FIJI, 170, 177, 332

FINDEN, HARRY, Liberated African trader and shopkeeper in Bathurst, 161–2

FITZGERALD, C., ex-officer, West India Regiment; joint Secretary, Gambia Committee, 1875–6: 188n, 359

FITZGERALD, (Sir) W. R. SEYMOUR V. (1818–85), Conservative M.P., 1852–1865, 1874–5; Under-Secretary at F.O. 1858–9; Governor of Bombay, 1867–72: 74

FITZJAMES, ALEXANDER, Trinidad barrister; Queen's Advocate, Sierra Leone, and acting Governor, 1859–1860: 104

FITZMAURICE, Lord EDMOND GEORGE PETTY (1846–1935), Liberal M.P., 1868–85; 1898–1905; Under-Secretary at Foreign Office, 1883–5, 1905–1908: 309

FLATTERS, Colonel, commanded French expedition destroyed in Sahara, 1881: 254

FLEGEL, EDUARD R. (1832–86), went to Africa, 1875, in employment of Gaiser; explored Benué, 1879–83: 310, 322, 329

FODAY KABBA, Muslim leader in Combo, Gambia, 1855–1901: 233

FODAY SILLA, Muslim leader in Combo, Gambia, c. 1873–94: 233

FODAY WISE, Alimami, of Moriah, 132

FOOTE, HENRY GRANT, British Consul at Lagos, 1860–1: 59

FORSTER, WILLIAM EDWARD (1818–86), Liberal M.P. 1861–86; Under Secretary for the Colonies, 1865–6; Vice-President of the Council, 1868–74; Chief Secretary for Ireland, 1880–2; first Chairman, Imperial Federation League, 75–6, 82–3, 145, 158

FORSTER & SMITH, London merchants trading in the Gambia, c. 1830–70: 153, 157, 176

FORTESCUE, CHICHESTER SAMUEL (1823–1898); (Lord CARLINGFORD, 1874), Liberal M.P. 1847–74; Under-Secretary for the Colonies, 1857–8, 1859–1865; in Cabinet 1865–6, 1868–74, 1881–5: 61, 73–5, 83

FOURICARIA, 129, 135, 151, 221–2

FREEMAN, HENRY STANHOPE, Consul, and later Governor, Lagos, 1862–5: 56–61, 114, 118

FREETOWN, 28–30, 42, 72, 80, 87, 131,

146–8, 245–6, 342–3; see also SIERRA LEONE; CREOLES

de FREYCINET, CHARLES L. de SAULCES (1828–1923), French politician, President of the Council and Foreign Minister, 1879–80, 1882, 1886: 235–236, 281–4

FULA people (or FULANI), 5–9, 12–14, 19–20, 78, 122–3, 245, 263, 272

FULADUGU (Map No. 2), 10

FUTA JALON, 5, 10, 13–14, 94, 126, 129, 131, 147–8, 244–6, 259n, 264–71, 281, 290, 341

FUTA TORO, 5, 9–13, 99–102, 121–3, 165, 253

GABON, 1, 25, 95, 110, 126–8, 136, 138–140, 153, 178, 185–6, 316

GAILLARD frères, French traders in Northern Rivers during 1870's, 230

GAISER, GOTTLIEB LEONHARD (1817–1892), b. Wurtemburg; founded Hamburg trading house and oil-mills, 317, 322

GALLIENI, JOSEPH SIMON (1849–1916), Captain Marine Infantry; Political Director, Senegal 1879–81; Commandant, French Sudan, 1886–8; governed Madagascar, 1896–1905: 256–65, 268, 340–1

GALLINAS (Chiefdom), 45–6, 73, 85–8, 145–6, 240–3

GALLINAS, River (or MOA), 45–6, 241

GAMBETTA, LÉON M. (1838–82), French politician: President of the Council and Foreign Minister, 1881–2: 229, 270–1, 276n, 279–84, 305, 343

GAMBIA (British settlements), 23–4, 27, 49–53, 107–9, 137, 139, 149, 164, 232–4, 265–7, 273n; proposed exchange of, 126–9, 134–44, Ch. IV passim, 197–8, 208, 212, 219–20, 224–227, 234–7, 248–50, 292, 305–9, 313–314, 341–3, 346–8

GAMBIA (river), 13, 33, 93, 106, 126–8, 139, 216, 341

GARDNER, A. W., President of Liberia, 1878–83: 243

GASCONI, A. (1842–1927), Representative of Senegal in Chamber of Deputies, 1879–89: Catholic supporter of Gambetta, 293n, 294

GAVARD, CHARLES, Counsellor to French Embassy in London, 1871–7: 166, 174–6, 181, 191, 204

GEISLINGER, EMMANUEL, French trader in Sherbro, 43

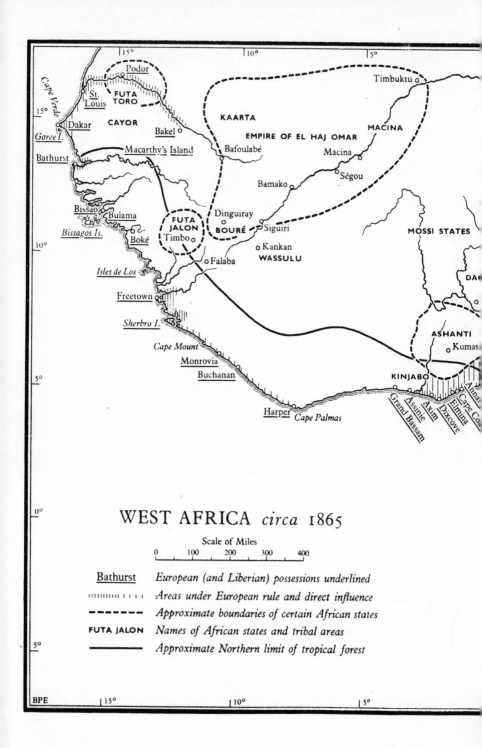

WEST AFRICA *circa* 1865

Scale of Miles

0   100   200   300   400

Bathurst — European (and Liberian) possessions underlined

⊔⊔⊔⊔⊔⊔ — Areas under European rule and direct influence

- - - - - — Approximate boundaries of certain African states

FUTA JALON — Names of African states and tribal areas

——— — Approximate Northern limit of tropical forest

Map labels:

Cape Verde, Podor, St. Louis, FUTA TORO, Dakar, CAYOR, Goree I., Bakel, Bathurst, Macarthy's Island, KAARTA, EMPIRE OF EL HAJ OMAR, Bafoulabé, MACINA, Timbuktu, Macina, Bamako, Ségou, Bissao, Bulama, Bissagos Is., Boké, FUTA JALON, Timbo, Dinguiray, BOURÉ, Siguiri, MOSSI STATES, Falaba, Kankan, WASSULU, Isles de Los, Freetown, Sherbro I., ASHANTI, Kumasi, Cape Mount, Monrovia, Buchanan, KINJABO, Grand Bassam, Assinie, Axim, Dixcove, Elmina, Cape Coast, Anna, Harper, Cape Palmas, DA

BPE

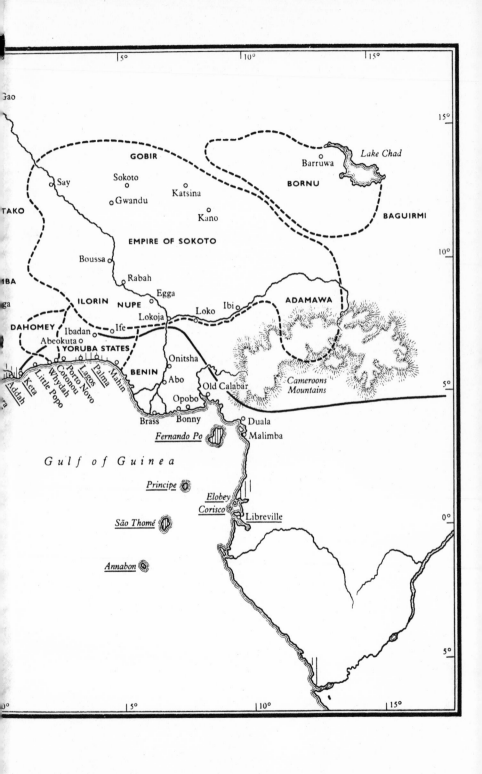

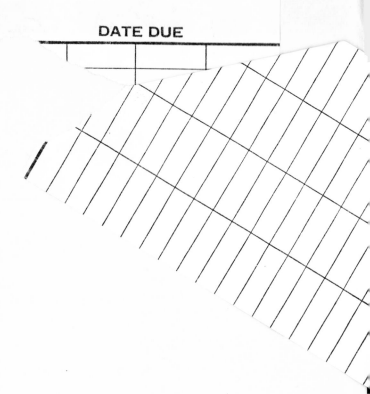
DT
471
H27

Hargreaves, John D
    Prelude to the partition of West Africa.
London, Macmillan; New York, St. Martin's
Press, 1963.
    385p. maps (1 fold.) 22cm. index.

    Bibliography: p.[350]-368.

1.Africa, West-Colonization. 2.Africa, West-Comm.-Hist.
3.Europeans in West Africa. I.Title.